DILEMMAS OF PRESIDENTIAL LEADERSHIP

DILEMMAS OF
PRESIDENTIAL LEADERSHIP
FROM WASHINGTON
THROUGH LINCOLN

Richard Ellis

Aaron Wildavsky

Transaction Publishers
New Brunswick (U.S.A.) and Oxford (U.K.)

Copyright © 1989 by Transaction Publishers
New Brunswick, New Jersey 08903

Library of Congress Catalog Number: 88-19043
ISBN: 0-88738-221-5
Printed in the United States of America

Library of Congress Cataloging–in–Publication Data

Wildavsky, Aaron B.
  Dilemmas of presidential leadership from Washington through Lincoln: a cultural theory/Aaron Wildavsky and Richard J. Ellis.
    p.   cm.
  Bibliography: p.
  Includes index.
ISBN 0-88738-221-5
  1. Presidents—United States—History. 2. United States—Politics and government—1789–1815. 3. United States—Politics and government—1815–1861. I. Ellis, Richard J. II. Title.
JK511.W55 1988   88-19043
353.03′23′09—dc19   CIP

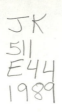

Contents

Preface

What was wrong with Jimmy Carter? He paid too much attention to detail. Presidents, the pundits informed us, need to focus on the big picture, delegating the rest to subordinates. But what, by contrast, was wrong with Ronald Reagan? He paid too little attention to detail. In the wake of the Iran-Contra affair, we are now told that presidents must not become detached from the details of policy-making. Gerald Ford's troubles were attributed to the fact that he was too much a government insider, and Carter's difficulties were chalked up to his being an outsider lacking experience with the ways of Washington. Each presidency appears to teach a different lesson and different presidencies opposing lessons.

Discussions of the presidency are extraordinarily sensitive to the tides of current events. Models of the presidency are created in the image of the most recent incumbent. The perception that Eisenhower was an amateur in politics brought forth an academic literature oriented around ways in which a president could increase his influence. Disillusionment with presidential action in Vietnam and Watergate generated the view of an "imperial presidency" unaccountable to other actors in the political system. Jimmy Carter's difficulties ushered in models of a "tethered" or "imperiled" presidency, confronted with a cynical public, a fragmented Congress, and an intractable bureaucracy.[1] Not so long ago the office of the presidency was deemed to have an ennobling effect—Harry Truman being the classic example of the man who, as Clinton Rossiter put it, "grows in office."[2] But during the administrations of Lyndon Johnson and Richard Nixon, the White House seemed to be an "unhealthy environment," bringing out the worst features of the president and transforming those around him into sycophants.[3]

Why do scholarly opinions, and research agendas, react with so much volatility to the day's headlines? The tendency to interpret the presidency in light of the most-immediate past chief executive reflects a lack of historical memory. But why this institutional forgetting?[4] Why are we unable to relate the performance of the current administration to that of previous presidencies or of other executives? The answer, we contend, along with many of those who study the presidency, is the lack of a framework to compare presidents.

James MacGregor Burns was right when, in 1965, he offered this paradoxical assessment of the state of presidential studies: "We know everything about the Presidents and nothing about the Presidency."[5] Memoirs, biographies, and insider accounts have accumulated without adding up to a coherent body of knowledge about the institution of the presidency. Historians, journalists, and political scientists have produced a number of fine studies of individual presidents, yet we seem no closer to a framework that would allow us to make comparisons of patterns of behavior across administrations. This inability constitutes the major stumbling block to producing studies of the presidency as an institution that persists over time. An episodic, rather than systematic, approach makes it difficult either to cumulate similar instances of behavior or to formulate propositions that explain discovered patterns. "Adhocracy" reigns supreme.

We hope to make presidencies comparable by focusing on the interactions between leaders and followers. For us, moreover, these relationships are not just free-floating. Presidents and citizens exist within political cultures (or ways of life) that guide and constrain how they behave. Presidents, we argue, face constraints of two kinds: conflicts within the culture (or cultures) to which they adhere, and conflicts between opposing cultures. Such conflicts—being torn between opposing forces—create the dilemmas with which presidents grapple. Our main purpose is, first, to formulate a cultural theory of presidential dilemmas, which we do in the first chapter, and, second, to try out these hypotheses on U.S. presidents from Washington through Lincoln.

Why, some may wonder, have we not looked at all the presidents? The very thought makes us pale. By following the hints dropped here and there, however, others, we hope, will try to extend this cultural analysis not only by bringing in additional presidents but also by applying it to other executives—mayors, governors, prime ministers, school principals.

Why Washington through Lincoln? The passions of yesteryear have cooled sufficiently so that these presidencies are more likely to be treated dispassionately. The objectivity that time gives is, we think, an advantage. Were we concerned largely with recent presidents, we fear that disagreement with the policies of these presidents would interfere with the objective of comparing and evaluating presidencies. Most readers will have fewer preconceptions about many of these presidents—Millard Fillmore, anyone?—and therefore will have made fewer prejudgments. Taking these presidents one by one—those whose behavior might fit our theory along with those whose actions might be inconvenient—gives us a series of sufficient length to allow for considerable variety.

There is another reason for selecting these early presidents. For us and, we suspect, for others, early U.S. history has become a blur, not merely from inattention to history but also because of confusion concerning what these presidencies were about. If our claim to a "theory" seems too grand, then we would be pleased to have our culturally induced dilemmas serve as mnemonic devices summarizing what these presidencies were about: we can then know what we have remembered, and why we have remembered it.

We wish to remember and thank the Spencer Foundation, which supported Aaron Wildavsky's foray into political culture, and the Bradley Foundation, whose program for supporting graduate students took care of Richard Ellis. The space, facilities, and encouragement of the Survey Research Center joined our two efforts, the product of which is, we think, better than either of us could have done alone.

We have been fortunate in having readers whose critical comments have challenged us. Our gratitude goes to Hugh Heclo, Paul Peterson, Michael Rogin, Barry Schwartz, Stephen Skowronek, Brian Weiner, and Major Wilson.

Notes

1. See Erwin C. Hargrove and Michael Nelson, *Presidents, Politics, and Policy* (New York: Knopf, 1984), pp. 3-11.
2. Clinton Rossiter, *The American Presidency* (New York: Harcourt, Brace & World, 1960), p. 157.
3. George E. Reedy, *The Twilight of the Presidency* (New York: New American Library, 1970), quotation on p. xi.
4. On ''institutional forgetting,'' see Mary Douglas, *How Institutions Think* (Syracuse: Syracuse University Press, 1986), pp. 69-90.
5. James MacGregor Burns, *Presidential Government: The Crucible of Leadership* (New York: Avon, 1965), p. xi.

1

A Cultural Theory of Presidential Dilemmas

Types of leadership (and followership), we hypothesize, vary by political culture.[1] By *political culture* we do not mean national customs. Nor are cultures countries. All those residing in the United States are not adherents of the same political culture, as we use the term. Rather, we analyze politics from a perspective of cultural dissensus, i.e. the conflict within a country between rival cultures or ways of life. We posit the existence of three competing political cultures: hierarchical, individualist, and egalitarian.[2]

Leadership as a Function of Political Culture

The individualist regime maximizes the scope of individual autonomy and thus minimizes the need for authority. Expertise, for instance, is not, as in egalitarian collectives, condemned for producing inequality but, rather, is lauded for limiting the scope of authority (if they don't know how you're doing it, they can't tell you what to do), thereby extending the sphere of self-regulation. Individualists fear both anarchy—leadership too weak to provide the minimal order necessary to insure enforcement of contracts and protection of property—and autocratic leadership that refuses to make way when its task is done. Individualist regimes therefore perform a delicate balancing act between accepting leaders when they are needed and getting rid of them when they are not. Ideally, only as much autonomy is given up as the immediate engagement requires. Adherents of individualist regimes know that from the leader flows the hierarchy, and that within its multitudinous ranks are found police officers and tax collectors. Not wanting the one, they choose not to keep the other any longer than absolutely necessary. Following Groucho Marx's maxim about clubs, they believe that any leader strong enough to help them is too strong to be trusted. Although the meteoric leaders of such regimes will be rewarded handsomely, they are expected to step down as soon as their task, e.g. winning a war, is completed. Individualists dread most the leaders who overstay their welcome.

Egalitarians are dedicated to diminishing differences among people.

1

Would-be egalitarian leaders are thus in trouble before they start, for authority makes a prima-facie instance of inequality. Followership, for egalitarians, implies subordination of one person to another. Job rotation and task sharing are methods commonly used in egalitarian organizations to "demystify" authority, and to redistribute power and knowledge on a more equal basis.[3] Leaders who push themselves forward, attempting to lead rather than merely to convene or facilitate discussion, will be attacked for attempting to lord it over others. Aspiring leaders must therefore dissemble, looking and sounding at once persuasive about the right course to follow and self-effacing, as if they were not leading at all. Leadership may, however, be justified in the name of redressing inequalities. To invest the leader with the aura of higher purposes—charisma—allows egalitarians to legitimize the exercise of power deemed necessary to achieve their goal of increasing equality.

In a hierarchical regime it is much easier to exercise leadership. Prospective leaders are expected to lead; authority inheres in the position. Here, the regime that guides and constrains people gives consistent advice: leadership is necessary and should be supported. Fearing disorder, hierarchies shore up authority in every way they can. While sharing the credit, leaders generally are absolved from blame. The different levels of prestige or privilege that accompany positions of authority in a hierarchy are legitimized by the greater sacrifices required of the superior in the name of the whole. Errors are attributed to the deviance of subordinates. Secrecy and mutual protection are techniques for protecting those in positions of authority. Because they give leaders so much backing, hierarchies also fear the charismatic leader who, instead of working through the hierarchy and obeying its notions of reciprocal restraints, substitutes himself for the law, intervening autocratically at every level and thereby breaking down all gradations of rank and status.

The reader is not being offered cultural determinism. Situating a leader within a political culture allows us to identify the types of leadership behavior that will be rejected by followers, and thereby anticipate the options foreclosed to that leader. Culture alone, however, does not allow us to predict which of the possible options or strategies a leader will pursue or whether he will be successful. Cultural analysis instructs us that a leader faced with egalitarian followers, for instance, if he is to succeed, must either practice dissembling leadership, leading while appearing not to, or justify his leadership in the name of limiting authority and furthering equality. The theory does not tell us which of these two options the leader will adopt. Nor does it say the leader will necessarily pursue either of these strategies—he might, for instance, opt for complete passivity—but, rather, that if he is to be successful, he must. Moreover, although they are necessary preconditions for successful leadership, these strategies are not a guarantee of success.

Why Political Culture?

Why use this new vocabulary of individualism, egalitarianism, and hierarchy rather than the more familiar categories of liberalism and conservativism? We offer two reasons. First, the liberal/conservative continuum does not travel well across space and time. Efforts to read the left/right distinction back into early U.S. history succeed only in making a hash of it. Second, the concepts of liberalism and conservatism suffer from an extraordinary lack of precision. Do these concepts refer to the social basis of support, dispositions toward change, attitudes toward government action, equality, or individual rights? The political culture categories, we believe, have more precise referents than do the conventional left/right categories and more readily lend themselves to historical and cross-national comparisons.

The designation *liberal* or *left* lumps together individualism's emphasis on individual rights and opportunity and egalitarianism's emphasis on redistribution and reduction of differences. The meaning of the term, moreover, shifts from country to country. In the contemporary United States, *liberal* often means a preference for greater use of central government to carry out redistributive welfare measures. In Europe, however, *liberal* does not carry the same egalitarian connotation. Instead, the term retains its original individualist connotation, stemming from the nineteenth century, when liberalism was opposed to both hierarchical aristocracies and egalitarian working-class movements. The liberal in the United States is more akin to the European Social Democrat than to the European liberal.

The referent of *conservative* or *right* is equally confused and contradictory. The concept of conservatism indiscriminately joins together two fundamentally different political cultures: competitive individualism, and hierarchical collectivism. Who is more conservative or further to the right: Margaret Thatcher or the old Tories? This question cannot be answered within the confines of the liberal/conservative continuum. Employing the categories of individualism and hierarchy, however, allows us to see that Thatcher is an individualist, and that her "Tory" critics belong to the hierarchical wing of the Conservative party.

The liberal-conservative distinction fails also to sort out differences on contemporary social issues, such as abortion or women's rights. In a recent study of Republican party delegates, Byron Shafer found that "those delegates who were clearly 'conservative' on economic issues were not reliably 'conservative' on cultural [i.e. social] issues, while, conversely, those who were clearly 'conservative' on cultural issues were not reliably 'conservative' on economics."[4] Again the label of conservativism misleads because it does not distinguish between hierarchy and individualism. Individualists—economic conservatives—prefer minimal regulation in the economic *and* social spheres. Thus, they are in conflict with hierarchical proponents—social conservatives—who favor governmental intervention in private life to support community norms.

A further layer of confusion and ambiguity is added by using the terms *conservative* and *liberal* to designate attitudes toward change. The conservative, writes Clinton Rossiter, is distinguished by a "discriminating defense of the social order against change and reform." Liberals, Rossiter continues, "are reasonably satisfied with their way of life yet believe they can improve upon it substantially without betraying its ideals or wrecking its institutions." The liberal chooses "change over stability, experiment over continuity, the future over the past."[5] This definition of liberalism and conservatism is bound to be misleading because the historical context alters which wants to preserve, which to repudiate, existing circumstances. We prefer here to classify people not by a psychological commitment to change or the lack of it but, rather, by their preference for a particular form of social relations. The greater the gap between real and ideal, we hypothesize, the greater the desire for change. Antifederalists, for instance, resisted change, believing that this would only promote hierarchy; Federalists, universally regarded as the party of the right, on the other hand, tried to make radical alterations in institutional arrangements in order to strengthen authority. Similarly, social conservatives of today, believing that important values have been trampled upon, seek radical change on such matters as abortion and school prayer.

A glance backward at U.S. history reveals further shortcomings of the left/right distinction. Were the Jacksonians liberal or conservative, left or right? If the definition of liberal and conservative is based on attitudes toward government intervention in the economy, then Jackson's Democratic party must be considered conservative—ideological forerunners not of a Rooseveltian New Deal but of Reagan Republicanism.[6] If, however, one focuses on the social class from which the parties drew their support, or on their attitudes toward equality, then the Jacksonian party must be counted as the left-wing party.[7] Finally, if dispositions toward social change distinguish liberalism from conservatism, then the Jacksonians, who were trying to preserve a disappearing agrarian world, would be the conservatives.[8]

The confusion engendered by using the terms *liberal* and *conservative* can also be witnessed in the dispute over whether Lincoln was, as J. G. Randall tags him, a "liberal statesman" or, as Norman Graebner contends, a "conservative statesman." Historiographical disputes, particularly about character as complex as Lincoln's, are not uncommon; what is unusual about this debate is that Randall's and Graebner's characterizations of Lincoln, other than the labels they attach to him, are much the same. Lincoln's conservatism, argues Graebner, "ruled out a war for righteousness . . . Lincoln would mitigate man's inhumanity, not through moral crusades, but through tolerance and magnanimity.'' The defining quality of Lincoln's liberalism, according to Randall, was ''the supreme quality of tolerance,'' ''innocent of the holier-than-thou attitude which [characterized] extremists of his day.''[9] The portrait of Lincoln that emerges from the two essays is essentially the same—tolerant, moderate, pragmatic, opposed to fanaticism and self-righteousness—only the labels differ. We have so hard a time reaching agreement in the social sciences that it seems advisable to jettison terms laden with meanings that foster spurious controversies.

Cultural Dilemmas of Presidential Leadership

Why focus on dilemmas, that is, choice-situations characterized by undesirable alternatives? If, as we assert, there is not a single political culture, and if people in different political cultures expect different modes of leadership and policy outcomes, then a president continually faces the need to reconcile contradictory demands. Each presidency, we hypothesize, derives its basic character from culturally induced dilemmas. At the most elementary level, this means that presidents must choose between competing ways of life. Satisfying the individualist demand for economic opportunity, for instance, may entail forsaking the egalitarian demand for equal results.

Even within his own political party, the president will be subject to the conflicting demands of competing political cultures. National political parties, like other complex social organizations, encompass more than one political culture. The Democratic party under Andrew Jackson, for example, constituted an alliance of individualism and egalitarianism. This cultural hybrid, we think, is the historical source of ''American exceptionalism.'' United by its opposition to hierarchy, the coalition is virulently antiauthority. The Jacksonian alliance was held together by a belief that minimal government intervention in individual lives would increase equality of condition. Despite their shared distrust of hierarchy, however, the viability of the individualist-egalitarian alliance is problematic. Individualists, for instance, may find that the egalitarian opposition to inequality constrains their preference for risk-taking. Martin Van Buren's cultural dilemma as president consisted in managing the strained relations between egalitarian Democrats who wished to extend Jackson's war on the national bank to include all banks, and individualist Democrats who worried that egalitarian policies would stifle economic expansion and opportunity.

Joint rule by individualism and hierarchy, a cultural combination known in current parlance as ''the establishment,'' is an option open to those individualists who find the alliance with egalitarianism undesirable. Individualists get sufficient order to carry on bidding and bargaining, while hierarchy gains the growth and flexibility it might otherwise lack. Despite these mutual benefits, the establishment alliance, too, suffers from disagreements. If individualists find the egalitarian benchmark of equality of conditions constricting, they may also be frustrated by hierarchy's penchant for rules and regulations. Millard Fillmore's presidency was torn apart by dissension within the Whig party as the marriage of economic growth and social order, individualism and hierarchy, unraveled.

Presidential leadership is, in large part, the art of building or sustaining cultural coalitions. When presidents are unable to hold together competing political cultures their presidencies will fail. The string of failed presidencies that preceded the Civil War supports this proposition. Franklin Pierce, for instance, tried to reestablish the Jacksonian coalition of individualism and egalitarianism but was foiled by the slavery issue, which brought to the surface the hitherto submerged tension between majority rule and the property rights of a minority. The optimistic doctrine that liberty and equality were mutually supportive had been able to soften class conflict, but in the end it could not cope with racial conflict. Witnessing the failure of both Pierce and Fillmore to reconstitute their old cultural coalitions, James Buchanan tried to create a new alliance that would unite the establishment against egalitarian abolitionists. Although individualists were willing albeit reluctant to protect slave property where it already existed, the issue of the expansion of slavery into the territories forced many northern individualists to repudiate an establishment alliance with hierarchy.

Control of the agenda—both getting some items on and keeping others off—is essential if presidents are to keep their cultural alliances together. Party unity depends on focusing the followers' attention on certain issues rather than others, say, economic growth or geographic expansion instead of slavery. By centering attention on the common cultural enemy, the president can deflect attention from disagreements between his supporters. In Andrew Jackson's time, for example, individualists and egalitarians, though they differed over much else, could agree that hierarchical institutions like the "Monster Bank" or "King Caucus" were undesirable. Similarly, by focusing on the virtues of economic growth and the vices of welfare dependency, Ronald Reagan has been able to weld together the establishment alliance of individualism and hierarchy.

A president's cultural dilemma is not limited to reconciling competing cultures. Cultural dilemmas are shaped also by *cultural propensity*, a president's identification with one or more of the cultures; *cultural context*, the strength of rival cultures; and the *historical situation*. Let us unpack these terms.

Cultural propensity refers to a preferred pattern of social relations. A belief in structured inequality is the telltale sign of a hierarchical propensity. In identifying adherents of hierarchy, we also look for themes of social order, stability, harmony, and solidarity. Those who express a concern with growing inequalities or who are impressed with the need to diminish differences we code as egalitarians. Individualists can be recognized by their celebration of competition, regard for expanding opportunities, and above all, their preference for self-regulation.

In identifying who belongs to which political culture, it is critical to keep in mind that propensities do not lead to invariable instruments of public policy. Cultural theory is not a substitute for historical analysis. Instruments of policy emerge from interaction with historical experience. Believing that government was a source of inequality, for instance, egalitarians in the early republic sought to limit the central government's ability to interfere with the natural equality generated by American conditions. After the rise of corporate capitalism and the depression of the 1930s, however, egalitarians came to believe that national government was a potential source of greater equality. Historical experience has altered their beliefs about the desirability of government action, but the objective—increased equality—remained the same. Similarly, the Federalist alliance of individualism and hierarchy desired a more active national government to counter egalitarian tendencies; in the modern era, however, their Republican successors have wished for a less interventionist government because of a belief that it would engage in redistributive policies. The means, instruments of policy, may vary, but the ends, cultural propensity, remain the same.

Identifying the cultural propensities of a president and his party is not by itself sufficient. The cultural propensities of the president and his party must be considered in the context of what others will allow. *Cultural context* denotes the relative strength of the competing cultures in the national polity at any given time. Historically, the United States has been characterized by relatively strong individualism, weak hierarchy, and waxing and waning egalitarianism. This means what Alexis de Tocqueville and Louis Hartz and Samuel Huntington have said it does: support for authority is relatively weak in the United States.[10] Because egalitarians reject authority, individualists want to escape from it, and hierarchical forces are too weak to impose it, presidents seeking to rely on formal authority alone ocuppy a precarious position. Suspicion rather than support is what normally comes with the office. The reluctance of individualists and egalitarians to support authority, combined with formal constitutional provisions—separation of powers, and checks and balances, themselves a product of antiauthority dispositions—means that support for presidential leadership must be earned instance by instance. This antiauthority cultural context justifies Richard Neustadt's emphasis on persuasion,[11] for presidents must persuade when they cannot rely on the authority inherent in their position.

In addition to knowing what culture(s) the president (and his party) identifies with and the relative strength of the rival ways of life, we need to bring in the *historical situation*. But in introducing historical situation do we make generalization impossible? If each presidency is embedded in a unique concatenation of events, our goal of comparing types of presidential dilemmas becomes hopeless.

To avoid the chaos of infinite situations, we ask two, and only two, questions of every historical situation. First, what is the president reacting against?[12] That is, is presidential power perceived to have aided or undermined one's political culture in the immediate past? Which past president does the incumbent administration identify with as supporting its preferred way of life; and which presidents are rejected as being antithetical to that preferred way? Second, are contemporary events perceived as a threat to the culture's viability? That is, are present circumstances construed as calling for temporary suspension or abridgment of normal cultural practices?

Cultural context and cultural propensity give us the major tendencies (other things being equal, to use the economists' dodge), but the mutability of history insures that other things are not equal. Thus, these historical questions act as switching rules that specify in advance the conditions under which we can expect, for instance, normally proauthority cultures to try to restrain presidents, or usually antiauthority cultures to demand increased leadership. Rather than history's being a stumbling block to comparing presidential dilemmas, it allows us to examine the conflicts between cultural propensity and historical situation to derive cultural dilemmas.

Where the presidency has repeatedly been used to attack the hierarchical way of life, adherents of hierarchy are torn between their cultural propensity, which tells them to support authority, and their historical experience, which instructs them that the presidency is dangerous. This dilemma, of course, is most likely to occur in a cultural context of weak support for hierarchy, for it is in this context that hierarchical parties are likely to spend most of their time in opposition. This was precisely the dilemma faced by Whig party leaders who, on account of their traumatic historical experience with "King Andrew," found themselves advocating a hierarchy without a hierarch. Fearing the rise of another charismatic leader who would substitute his personal will for the law, Whigs—who defended authority in every other sphere of social life—strived to restrict the executive's power to promote, or veto, legislation. How Abraham Lincoln overcame this Whig prohibition on presidential authority is a crucial part of his success story.

Historical experience may also reinforce cultural propensities. The antiauthority ethos of egalitarians is frequently reinforced by their position on the fringes of society. The abolitionists, for instance, finding no sympathy for their cause in the White House, unmercifully berated successive occupants of the presidential office. A hierarchical leader whose formative historical experience is either a strong chief executive favoring hierarchical culture, or a weak executive thwarting hierarchical ends, also finds historical experience reinforcing cultural propensities. The Federalists' predilection for "an efficient and responsible Executive," for example, was reinforced by their experience with the "anarchical confusion" prevailing under the weak Articles of Confederation.[13]

In a cultural context in which hierarchy is strong, plentiful support for leadership is likely. The leadership dilemmas here will stem from ossification, rigidity, and inefficiency. Despite the frequent jeremiads throughout U.S. history about the bloated executive bureaucracy, this is not the affliction of the presidency that concerns us. The point of departure for our analysis is not the problem of too much hierarchy but of too little.

Because the antiauthority cultures of individualism and egalitarianism tend to dominate in the United States, the president who (mistakenly) thinks he operates in a hierarchy is likely to fail. Leadership is, in part, the art of understanding the cultural context in which one operates. Behavior that works in one cultural context may fail in another. A nonhierarchical context makes success difficult for all leaders, but hierarchically inclined leaders are caught in an especially acute dilemma. Authority in a hierarchy inheres in the position, that is, leaders are obeyed by virtue of the office they hold. It is unnecessary to convince subordinates that a directive is valid, as the egalitarian would demand, nor need they be bargained with, as the individualist would require. Thus, leaders with hierarchical cultural propensities will be inclined to issue directives, expecting them to be followed. Bargaining and persuasion will be seen not only as unnecessary but indeed as undercutting one's authority. In the absence of a hierarchical context, relying on formal position will result in continued frustration, recrimination, and defeat. John Adams and John Quincy Adams provide telling examples of hierarchs without a hierarchy, i.e. hierarchically disposed leaders unable to comprehend the antileadership nature of the U.S. system.

This is not, however, simply a problem of comprehension but rather is a cultural dilemma. Successfully adjusting to the requirements of the cultural context may call for assimilation, which may mean abandoning a preferred way of life. For a hierarch to behave as if authority does not inhere in the position of president, or that leadership should not be overt, entails a retreat from one's cultural identification.

Where the antiauthority cultures of individualism and egalitarianism dominate, the hierarchical leader confronts a further dilemma. Lacking the substance of power, the hierarchical leader often will stress the appearance of power. "The right to give a performance," as Victor Thompson argues in *Modern Organization*, becomes more important than "the performance itself." Thompson's brilliant analysis of "dramaturgy" in a hierarchical modern bureaucracy (caused, he argues, by the growing gap between those in positions of formal authority who have the right to decide and those who have the specialized ability or knowledge needed to make the decision) is generalizable to all insecure hierarchies.[14] The presidency of George Washington provides an excellent illustration of the dilemma of presidential leadership in an insecure hierarchical regime. Often lacking the power to act effectively, Washington heavily emphasized the appearance of strong leadership. A firm and resolute exterior covered the president's thinly veiled weaknesses.

If the proauthority president tends to stress the appearance of leadership, the leader of antiauthority cultures, although equally engaged in impression management, is inclined to do just the opposite: leading without ever seeming to do so. Rather than impressing with displays of strength, the dissembling, "peach-pit" president displays a soft exterior to disguise inner resolve and direction. Thomas Jefferson and Dwight Eisenhower were masters of this form of dramaturgy.

This "hidden-hand" leadership style[15] resolves the cultural dilemma for an incumbent but fails to establish precedents that will aid his successors. In a historical context in which antiauthority cultures routinely control the presidency, there will be a great temptation to find some more enduring basis to justify presidential leadership. The Jacksonians, for instance, came to portray the president as mandated by the people to check political and economic power. Strengthening the presidency, rather than emboldening hierarchy, would flatten the pyramid by increasing popular control of those in positions of authority. Ronald Reagan similarly justifies activist presidential leadership in the name of decreasing the size and scope of domestic government activity. Doing more in the name of doing less, unlike the hidden-hand strategy, empowers not only the incumbent but also his cultural successors.

Antiauthority principles insure that regardless of the historical situation, an individualist or egalitarian president will face the dilemma of reconciling antipower principles with the necessary exercise of power. Variations in historical conditions, however, can exacerbate the leadership dilemma. More specifically, during periods of perceived crisis, those favoring antiauthority cultures may find the demand for leadership outrunning support.

In the absence of total war, massive economic depression, or internal rebellion, individualist and hierarchical regimes are characterized by a rough balance between demand for and support of authority. Because, through self-regulation, individualist regimes are organized to reduce the need for authority, a small amount suffices. In hierarchies, where authority inheres in position, ample support matches the strong demand for leadership. The difference, then, is that hierarchies are balanced at a high, and individualism at a low, level of reliance on authority. Egalitarian cultures share individualism's skepticism toward authority, but because egalitarians require collective decision making, they also need far more authority than they are willing to support. Beset by a permanent imbalance between the low levels of support for authority and the need to enlist the aid of authority to reduce inequalities, the egalitarian leaders—or any kind of leader who must manage egalitarian followers—faces a dilemma in trying to match the numerous demands with such sparse support.

Crises, such as the American Revolution or Civil War, can upset the delicate balance in an individualist regime between the need for and the willingness to support authority. Great emergencies create a shift in the need for leadership, which, unless matched by an increase in the willingness to support leadership, may invite destruction of the culture. The individualist regime must choose between offering support for authority, and perhaps permanently enhancing the stature of hierarchy, or refusing support and risking the inability to resist foreign aggression or quell internal rebellion. Individualists, we would predict, will seek to solve this cultural dilemma through temporary leases of extraordinary yet limited power—what Clinton Rossiter has termed "constitutional dictatorship."[16] Their hope is that the meteoric leader will flame bright and then burn out, retiring after the task is completed.

For the sake of survival, egalitarians, too, during crises, may mute their hostility to authority. Although individualists, uncomfortable with notions of group purpose, desire to limit the grant of extraordinary powers to only what is absolutely necessary to terminate the emergency, egalitarians, who emphasize equality of condition, are likely to make the justice of the cause a condition of support. To justify a surrender to authority, therefore, egalitarians will seek leaders who assert transcendent purposes. When egalitarians are influential enough to force their desires to be taken into account by those in national leadership positions, such leaders may be trapped between the conflicting conditions placed on support offered by individualists and egalitarians. During the Civil War, for example, Lincoln was faced with the dilemma of satisfying individualists by limiting war aims, or gaining egalitarian approval by extending the war aims to include emancipation of slaves.

Believing that "tyranny is oftener produced by making it necessary to assume power, than by giving large powers in the first instance,"[17] hierarchical proponents are uneasy with temporary grants of extraordinary powers. Where the antiauthority cultures of individualism and egalitarianism prevail, however, crises do provide an opportunity for hierarchical advocates to enhance the scope of authority. Coping with a crisis may establish precedents that future generations can invoke to bolster hierarchy. Witness, for instance, Franklin Roosevelt's actions during the Great Depression and World War II.

Because crises empower those in positions of authority, moreover, there is a tremendous temptation for leaders to fabricate crises, especially in a cultural context in which support for authority is low. Jimmy Carter's attempt to focus the nation's attention on "the energy crisis" provides a recent example. Similarly, Richard Neustadt's argument that the "mid-century" presidency is characterized by a permanent state of "emergency" stems from a desire to overcome a perceived weakness of presidential authority.[18] If the threat can be made credible—that is, if egalitarians and individualists can be persuaded that they are in crisis—then invoking a crisis may indeed afford an antidote to the failed presidencies endemic to an antileadership system. The Civil War, for instance, helped to terminate the string of presidential failures from Zachary Taylor through James Buchanan.

But no cultural solution is forever. The dilemmas presidents create for their successors are an important part of our subject matter. Though resolving one set of dilemmas, great presidents invariably create new ones for their successors. George Washington's substitution of the appearance of power for the reality of power helped leave his hierarchical successor, John Adams, under the erroneous impression that he operated in hierarchical system. The hidden-hand strategy served Jefferson superbly, but his refusal to openly defend presidential prerogative left James Madison, who lacked Jefferson's stature, political savvy, and/or luck, without the tools to govern. Andrew Jackson's genius lay in his energetic negativism—combining forceful presidential action with a diminution of federal governmental power—but his successor, Martin Van Buren, was unable to duplicate this feat in the midst of calls for positive action during the depression that followed the panic of 1837. The Whig dogma of hierarchy without a hierarch crippled the party's ability to exert the type of governmental authority it desired. Lincoln resolved his cultural dilemmas by keeping his war aims ambiguous, by relying on his implicit powers as commander in chief, and by spending money on his own, asking Congress to ratify his actions only after the fact. What were solutions for Lincoln, however, left his successor, Andrew Johnson, faced with a Congress eager to restore the presidency to its constitutional position, and with little guidance on how to proceed with reconstructing the Union.

To summarize and simplify, this book addresses two general categories of presidents. First is the president with some blend of egalitarian and individualist cultural propensities. Spawned by the American Revolution, this antiauthority cultural alliance dominated U.S. politics until torn asunder by what Charles Beard has called "the Second American Revolution," the Civil War.[19] The Jeffersonian and Jacksonian presidents—Jefferson, Madison, Jackson, Van Buren, Polk, and Pierce—labored, with varying degrees of success, to square the exercise of authority with their own and their followers' antiauthority principles, while also trying to reconcile the intraparty conflicts that periodically flared up between egalitarians and individualists.

The second type is the president of hierarchical cultural propensities. Although the precise contours of the dilemma varied with the historical situation and configuration of cultures, all hierarchical presidents struggled, in one form or another, to reconcile their (and their party's) hierarchical cultural preferences with the antihierarchical ethos that inhered in the society and polity. This conflict animates the presidencies of George Washington, John Adams, and John Quincy Adams. Whig leaders—Henry Clay, Daniel Webster—who aspired to the presidency also were hamstrung by this dilemma. Abraham Lincoln, a loyal adherent of the Whig party for as long as it existed, resolved the hierarch's dilemma by (a) operating in wartime where he could invoke the commander-in-chief clause, and (b) creating a new cultural combination in which hierarchy was subordinated to individualism. Herein, we shall suggest, lies a key to Lincoln's greatness.

Evaluating Presidential Performance, or "Greatness" Revisited

If all presidents face cultural dilemmas, albeit of different kinds and intensities, then the ability to resolve them is a crucial aspect of performance. In addition to whatever explanatory power it may possess, cultural theory thus creates an alternative framework for evaluating the performance of presidents. Our position is that presidencies can be evaluated in terms of cultural dilemmas confronted, evaded, created, or overcome. "Great presidents," in our usage, are those who provide solutions to cultural dilemmas.

Polling a panel of "experts" has become the accepted way of rendering history's judgment of presidential performance. The presidential greatness game began in earnest in 1948, when Arthur Schlesinger asked fifty-five prominent historians to grade our past presidents: A signified Great; B, Near Great; C, Average; D, Below Average; and E, Failure. Schlesinger repeated the exercise in 1962. Believing there to be wisdom in numbers, subsequent surveys have expanded the panel of "experts" from 571 in Gary Maranell's 1970 survey to 953 in the 1983 poll conducted by Robert Murray and Tim Blessing.[20]

The practice of evaluating presidential performance by polling historians is a curious one. Characteristically, surveys are conducted to obtain information about the respondent, either in the form of preferences (Which candidate or party do you prefer?) or beliefs about the empirical world (How many members are in the House of Representatives?) We do not as a rule conduct surveys to gauge the validity of an assertion. Why, then, do we do so with respect to presidential performance? The answer is that we lack agreed-upon criteria for making these judgments. If we had accepted criteria, surveys would be superfluous (and subject to corroboration); we would need only to check presidential performance against the established yardsticks.

Although these surveys have yielded interesting information about the respondents—Murray and Blessing's poll, for instance, finds that U.S. historians specializing in women's history hold George Washington in much lower esteem than the sample as a whole—they are not a good tool to evaluate presidential performance. There is no reason to think the mean judgment of 1,000 historians more valid than the estimate of a single scholar specializing in past presidents. Insofar as our aim is to compare the performances of presidents rather than gather information about the pollees, energies should be directed to devising appropriate criteria for evaluating performance.

The original Schlesinger survey completely sidestepped the issue of establishing the criteria to be used in appraising presidential performance. In the first poll, the only instructions were that "the test in each case is *performance in office*, omitting anything done before or after."[21] How one was to gauge that performance was left unspecified; thus, the finding that president X ranked higher than president Y was impossible to interpret.

In *Presidential Greatness*, Thomas Bailey tried to remedy this deficiency by identifying specific criteria through which presidents could be measured. He came up with forty-three yardsticks for measuring presidential greatness: achievement, administrative capacity, appointees, blunders, eloquence, industriousness, scandals, sensitivity, and many more.[22] If the Schlesinger survey suffered from a lack of guidelines (as to the unit of comparability), the surfeit of tests devised by Bailey left the reader with a commendably broader view of the many facets of the presidency but equally helpless. By including everything and excluding nothing, we were no better than before at evaluating presidential performance.

Suggestive, but unsatisfactory, is Schlesinger's recommendation accompanying his second questionnaire, that presidents be judged by whether they "exhibit a creative approach to the problems of statecraft,"[23] for this begs the question of what is counted as a creative act. Similarly, in asking respondents to evaluate the significance of each president's accomplishments,[24] Maranell's 1970 survey dodges the critical issue of what should be considered significant. What is offered as criteria for gauging greatness is merely greatness relabeled. In this book, we have defined a creative act of statecraft or significant accomplishment as one that resolves a cultural dilemma.

Often the standard of presidential greatness employs measures such as amount of legislation passed, activity in office, or number of objectives pursued. But these criteria create a pronounced bias toward activist presidents. That such criteria sneak in ideological judgments about the ends of government is indicated by Schlesinger's conclusion that the 1962 survey showed that average or mediocre presidents "believed in negative government, in self-subordination to the legislative power."[25] Why should a contemporary activist view—the presidency is best that adds functions to government and/or the presidency—be a standard for scholars?

Though acutely aware of the limitations of presidential ratings as currently conducted, we do not accept the assertions that "comparing eminent figures is only a game," or that "each [president] operated within a unique political environment."[26] By so doing, attention is deflected from what is a more significant defect: the tendency to wrap each president and his times in a unique cocoon, thereby reducing the study of the presidency to a series of political biographies. It would be both ironic and unfortunate to use the best known effort to compare presidencies as a way to discredit the laudable, indeed essential, goal of making comparisons among administrations. The presidential greatness game remains popular precisely because it holds up the tantalizing prospect of comparing presidencies. Our aim is to do just that.

Notes

1. See Aaron Wildavsky, "Political Leaders Are Part of Political Systems: A Cultural Theory of Leadership," in *Political Leadership from Political Science Perspectives*, ed. Byron D. Jones. (Lawrence: Univ. Press of Kansas, 1989).
2. These categories are derived form the work of anthropologist Mary Douglas; see especially *Natural Symbols: Explorations in Cosmology* (London: Barrie & Rockliff, 1970); and "Cultural Bias," in *In the Active Voice*, ed. Douglas (London: Routledge & Kegan Paul, 1982). The theory is further elaborated in Mary Douglas and Aaron Wildavsky, *Risk and Culture* (Berkeley: University of California Press, 1982).

   Douglas posits the existence of four basic political cultures: hierarchical, individualist, egalitarian (or sectarian), and fatalist. This fourfold typology is derived from the cross-tabulation of "group" and "grid." The grid dimension measures how far an individual's behavior is socially prescribed: in a low-grid environment, roles are ill-defined; in a high-grid environment, all know their station. The group dimension gauges the extent to which an individual is bound by decisions of the collectivity. In a high-group context, strong boundaries identify and separate members from nonmembers. In the absence of strong group-boundaries, the individual is free to transact with all comers.

   Strong group-boundaries combined with numerous prescriptions form a hierarchical culture. Strong group-boundaries coupled with minimal prescriptions make for an egalitarian culture based on voluntary consent. Competitive individualism joins weak boundaries with few prescriptions. When group boundaries are weak and prescriptions are strong—so that most decisions are made by people outside the group—the controlled culture is fatalistic.
3. See Joyce Rothschild-Whitt, "The Collectivist Organization: An Alternative to Rational-Bureaucratic Models," *American Sociological Review* (August 1979): 509-27.
4. Byron E. Shafer, "The New Cultural Politics," *P.S.* (Spring 1985): 221-31; quotation on p. 224. This anomaly has prompted a number of social scientists to posit two liberal/conservative dimensions: one economic and one social.
5. Clinton Rossiter, *Conservatism in America: The Thankless Persuasion*, 2d ed. (New York: Vintage Books, 1962), p. 12. In a survey conducted by Herbert McCloskey the following agree/disagree statements were used as measures of conservatism: "It's better to stick by what you have than to be trying new things

you don't really know about'' and ''If you start trying to change things very much, you usually make them worse'' (Herbert McCloskey, ''Conservatism and Personality,'' *American Political Science Review* [1958]: 27-45).

6. Lee Benson, *The Concept of Jacksonian Democracy: New York as a Test Case* (Princeton: Princeton University Press, 1961).
7. Arthur M. Schlesinger, Jr., *The Age of Jackson* (Boston: Little, Brown, 1945).
8. Marvin Meyers, *The Jacksonian Persuasion: Politics and Belief* (Stanford: Stanford University Press, 1957).
9. J. G. Randall, *Lincoln: The Liberal Statesman* (New York: Dodd, Mead, 1947), pp. 175-206, quotation on p. 182; Norman A. Graebner, ''Abraham Lincoln: Conservative Statesman,'' in *The Enduring Lincoln*, ed. Graebner (Urbana: University of Illinois Press, 1959), pp. 67-94, quotation on p. 83.
10. Alexis de Tocqueville, *Democracy in America* (New York: Harper & Row, 1966); Louis Hartz, *The Liberal Tradition in America* (New York: Harcourt Brace Jovanovich, 1955); Samuel P. Huntington, *American Politics: The Promise of Disharmony* (Cambridge: Harvard University Press, 1981).
11. Richard E. Nuestadt, *Presidential Power: The Politics of Leadership* (New York: Wiley, 1980).
12. Apart from William E. Leuchtenburg's *In the Shadow of FDR: From Harry Truman to Ronald Reagan* (Ithaca: Cornell University Press, 1983), this remains a relatively unexplored topic.
13. George Washington, cited in Leonard D. White, *The Federalists: A Study in Administrative History* (New York: Macmillan, 1948), p. 13; James Iredell, cited in Gordon S. Wood, *The Creation of the American Republic, 1776-1787* (Chapel Hill: University of North Carolina Press, 1969), p. 474.
14. Victor A. Thompson, *Modern Organization* (New York: Knopf, 1961), quotation on p. 146.
15. The term is borrowed from Fred I. Greenstein, *The Hidden-Hand Presidency: Eisenhower as Leader* (New York: Basic Books, 1982).
16. Clinton Rossiter, *Constitutional Dictatorship* (Princeton: Princeton University Press, 1948).
17. George Nicholas, quoted in Richard E. Ellis, *The Jeffersonian Crisis: Courts and Politics in the Young Republic* (New York: Oxford University Press, 1971), p. 128.
18. Neustadt, *Presidential Leadership*, esp. pp. xi, 5.
19. Charles A. Beard and Mary R. Beard, *The Rise of American Civilization*, 2 vols. (New York: Macmillan, 1927), ch. 18.
20. Arthur Schlesinger, ''A Yardstick for Presidents,'' in *Paths to the Present* (New York: Macmillan, 1949), pp. 93-111; Arthur Schlesinger, ''Rating the Presidents,'' in *Paths to the Present* (Boston: Houghton Mifflin, 1964), pp. 104-14; Gary M. Maranell, ''The Evaluation of Presidents: An Extension of the Schlesinger Polls,'' *Journal of American History* (June 1970): 104-13; Robert K. Murray and Tim H. Blessing, ''The Presidential Performance Study: A Progress Report,'' *Journal of American History* (December 1983): 535-55. Other greatness polls conducted in the past decade include the U.S. Historical Society's 1977 survey of the heads of one hundred history departments (reported in Robert E. DiClerico, *The American President* [Englewood Cliffs, N.J.: Prentice-Hall, 1979], p. 332); David L. Potter's 1981 unpublished survey of forty one historians (see Murray and Blessing, ''The Presidential Performance Study,'' p. 536); and the *Chicago Tribune*'s 1982 survey of forty nine presidential scholars.

21. Thomas A. Bailey, *Presidential Greatness: The Image and the Man from George Washington to the Present* (New York: Appleton-Century, 1966), p. 24; emphasis in original.
22. Ibid., pp. 262-66.
23. Schlesinger, ''Rating the Presidents,'' p. 104.
24. Maranell, ''Evaluation of Presidents,'' p. 106.
25. Schlesinger, ''Rating the Presidents,'' p. 107.
26. Bailey, *Presidential Greatness*, pp. 33-34; Curtis Arthur Amlund, ''President-Ranking: A Criticism,'' *Midwest Journal of Political Science* (August 1964): 309-15, quotation on p. 309.

2

The Cultural Formation
of the American Presidency

Revolutions are hard on authority. A nation schooled to defy symbols of power finds it difficult to reestablish respect for those in positions of leadership. The American War of Independence was no exception to this rule. Having undermined obedience to, and then waged war against, a distant British monarchy, the hierarchical relations of colonial American society began to unravel. Out of this rebellion was forged an alliance of antiauthority political cultures that would dominate the first century of the nation's existence.

Prior to the American Revolution—the wilderness environment and absence of feudal institutions notwithstanding—hierarchical role expectations were an integral part of colonial social relations. "Americans of 1760," attests Bernard Bailyn, "continued to assume, as had their predecessors for generations before, that a healthy society was a hierarchical society, in which it was natural for some to be rich and some poor, some honored and some obscure, some powerful and some weak . . . that authority would continue to exist without challenge, and that those in superior positions would be responsible and wise, and those beneath them respectful and content."[1] The criticism of authority fostered by the Revolution challenged the deferential social relations upon which colonial America was based.

The rebellion against Britain had made resistance to authority "a doctrine according to godliness."[2] "For a decade or more," observes Bailyn, "defiance to the highest constituted powers poured from the colonial presses and was hurled from half the pulpits of the land. The right, the need, the absolute obligation to disobey legally constituted authority had become the universal cry."[3] Instructions sent by the freeholders of Augusta, Virginia, to their delegates to the state's Provincial Congress in 1776 are indicative of the way in which Americans had begun to apply to domestic politics the distrust of authority learned in the struggle with Parliament. They reminded their representatives that

> your constituents are neither guided nor will ever be guided by the slavish maxim in politics, "that whatever is enacted by that body of men in whom the

19

supreme power of the state is vested must in all cases be obeyed,'' and that they firmly believe attempts to repeal an unjust law can be vindicated beyond a simple remonstrance addressed to the legislators.[4]

By 1776 the fight for ''home rule'' not only had broadened into an internal struggle over who would rule at home after independence but also had created a formidable set of antipower attitudes that made it an open question whether anyone would be allowed to rule.

In the service of the struggle with British authority, egalitarian and individualistic arguments were unsheathed that could not be put back. Gordon Wood has drawn attention to ''the egalitarian atmosphere spread by the Revolution,'' and Bailyn emphasizes ''the contagion of liberty'' sparked by the conflict with Britain.[5] Some Americans might stress individual freedom, and others equality, but few perceived any contradiction between the two values. Individualism and egalitarianism were united by what they were against: hierarchical authority. The fusion of the two values can be seen in the republican conception of equality, which, as Wood perceptively observes, ''possessed an inherent ambivalence: on the one hand it stressed equality of opportunity which implied social differences and distinctions; on the other hand it emphasized equality of condition which denied these same social differences and distinctions.'' The fusion was accomplished, suggests Wood, through the widely held belief that ''equality of opportunity would necessarily result in a rough equality of station, that as long as the channels of ascent and descent were kept open it would be impossible for any artificial aristocrats or overgrown rich men to maintain themselves for long.''[6] Here we have the origins of American exceptionalism, for if liberty and equality are compatible, at least under American conditions, class conflict might be contained.

Three Types of Governors during the American Revolution

The emerging alliance of egalitarianism and individualism found constitutional and institutional expression in the state constitutions written in 1776 and 1777. Its antiauthority thrust manifested itself most visibly in the weakening of executive power. According to Wood, ''The Americans' emasculation of their governors lay at the heart of their constitutional reforms of 1776.''[7] Selected in most states by the legislature, governors were also commonly subject to annual elections and/or rotation in office.[8] More important than the limits set on their tenure were the severe restrictions imposed on the power of the executive while in office. The governor was denied the power to veto legislation, and his powers of appointment were drastically curtailed.[9] In sum, Wood concludes, the state constitutions of 1776 "destroyed the substance of an independent magistracy."[10]

But not all state constitutions were of a piece. Some states granted significantly greater power to the executive. The variation among states— from the egalitarianism of Pennsylvania to the individualism of Virginia to the hierarchy of New York—presents us with an opportunity to gauge the validity of some of the hypothesized relationships between political culture and leadership.

Historians agree that the Pennsylvania constitution of 1776 was written by radical egalitarians.[11] Property qualifications for officeholding were eliminated, and the suffrage was extended to virtually every white male over the age of twenty-one. Echoing Thomas Paine, the Pennsylvania radicals repudiated the notion of mixed government, preferring instead a simple structure of government in the form of a unicameral legislature.[12] Elections to the legislature were to be held annually, and rotation in office meant that no representative could serve more than four years in seven. Most indicative of the egalitarian character of the constitution was the requirement that a bill could not become law until after it had been publicized throughout the state for consideration by the people, and then repassed by the legislature at the following session. This mechanism constituted an ingenious way to approximate the egalitarian ideal of direct democracy, to achieve not simply popular control of elites but popular participation in the decision-making process.[13]

Given the egalitarian propensities of the framers of the Pennsylvania constitution, cultural theory leads us to predict an extraordinarily weak executive expected to do little beyond executing the will of the people. Comparison of the Pennsylvania constitution with other state constitutions shows the Pennsylvania executive to be by far the weakest. The governor under the colonial charter was replaced by a twelve-person executive council, looked to do little more than carry out the will of the assembly. To insure strict popular accountability, the council was to be elected directly by the people; also, each year, one-third of the council would leave office. The legislature selected annually a president of the council, who did exactly what the title suggested: he presided.

Virginia, according to historian Robert Kelley, manifested a more "libertarian" version of republican political culture. Most Virginians, like most southerners, believed that "government should be small and inactive, limiting itself to the simplest social functions." Government intervention "in the lives of individuals to regulate their behavior," continues Kelley, "was anathema."[14] The leading framers of the Virginia constitution—George Mason, Patrick Henry, James Madison, and Edmund Randolph, among others— voiced an individualistic suspicion of authority rather than the positive commitment to egalitarianism that characterized the Pennsylvania framers.

The Virginia constitution's provisions regarding the executive were typical of the first wave of state constitutions. The governor was to be elected annually (by a joint vote of the two legislative bodies) and was limited to three consecutive terms. The few, limited powers granted to the governor—such as granting reprieves and pardons, making interim administrative and judicial appointments when the legislature was not in session, and calling out and directing the militia—depended on the consent of an eight-member council of state (also selected by the legislature, with two members replaced every three years). This tightly tethered executive, perhaps adequate in peacetime, was notably deficient for conducting a war.[15]

Virginia faced the dilemma of reconciling the need to repel a foreign invasion with the individualistic desire to limit the scope and duration of executive leadership. Crisis situations endanger individual autonomy, for leaders may attempt to extend their power beyond a narrowly defined sphere and/or make themselves permanent. The individualist solution to this dilemma is either to issue the leader short-term grants of power confined to specific purposes and hope those powers are sufficient to meet the crisis, or if that fails, to vest the leader with sweeping powers and hope that when the crisis passes the leader will, like Cincinnatus, return to the plow.

Under Virginia's first two wartime governors, Patrick Henry (1776-79) and Thomas Jefferson (1779-81), the legislature pursued the strategy of temporary grants of power in precisely defined spheres, limited primarily to military operations and supply. Because authority was never granted for longer than until the next meeting of the assembly, the contract with the governor could be repeatedly renegotiated in light of changing circumstances. Denied the power to keep a permanent military force on active duty, Henry and Jefferson were involved in a perpetual struggle to get out the militia and to keep it in service. Vital military fortifications along the rivers often went unbuilt because, as Jefferson explained, the governor had no "power to call a freeman to labor even for the Public without his consent."[16]

Although the legislature's strategy of temporary and limited extensions of authority worked tolerably well for a time, the British invasion of Virginia at the end of 1780 revealed the shortcomings of such a strategy in the face of a full-scale crisis. With the British army moving around the state virtually at will, it was evident that self-preservation required drastic action.[17] Faced with imminent disaster, the legislature opted for a "union of the civil and military powers" and selected Brigadier General Thomas Nelson, Jr., as governor.[18] The legislature granted Nelson what one student of the period has described as "almost dictatorial powers," including the power to impress food, supplies, and slaves for labor on defense fortifications; seize loyalists and banish them without jury trial; redistribute the property of persons who opposed laws for calling up militia; call out the state militia in such numbers as he saw fit, and send it where he deemed its services necessary; and declare martial law within a twenty-mile radius of the enemy or American camps.[19] With the crisis passed, cries of usurpation were quickly raised. Nelson retired from office in November 1791, only eight months after taking office. Having served his function, the meteoric leader dutifully returned to private life.[20]

If Virginia was the bastion of individualism, New York traditionally had been home to strong hierarchical forces. New York City, with its strong Anglican establishment, was the hub of Loyalism.[21] Other, more adaptable New York hierarchs had learned to swim with the revolutionary tide. It was these accommodating Patriot hierarchs—among them Gouverneur Morris, John Jay, and Robert Livingston—who were most influential in framing the New York constitution of 1777.[22] Given the cultural propensities of these framers, we would expect to find a greater willingness to invest the executive with power.

And so we do. Legislative control over the governor was loosened by making him directly electable by the people—or more accurately, men with £100 freeholds. Elected for a three-year term, and with no limit set on reeligibility, the governor retained the power of his royal predecessors to convene and prorogue the assembly. Moreover, the governor was granted a veto power, to be exercised jointly with a council of revision composed of several high judges, and the power of appointment, to be utilized in conjunction with a council of appointment made up of four senators. That these powers were shared with councils reflected the concessions made by supporters of hierarchy to egalitarians and individualists who feared anything resembling royal prerogative.[23] Despite these and other concessions, the constitution represented a significant victory for the hierarchical advocates of "energy and order."[24] Although the New York constitution was to provide an influential model for delegates to the Constitutional Convention in 1787,[25] for the present it stood out as an aberration from the antiauthority current of the Revolution.

The antihierarchical ethos generated by the Revolution found constitutional expression at the national level in the Articles of Confederation. Congress was tightly tethered: members faced annual election, could be recalled at any time, and could serve no more than three years in six. No provision was made for an executive, government operations being left to ad hoc or standing committees of Congress.[26] Fearing the exchange of one distant hierarchical authority for another, the framers of the Articles refused to grant the new national government the power to levy taxes or coerce states. Beginning with the premise that each state was sovereign and equal, the Articles made unanimous consent a prerequisite for any alteration of the Constitution. The Articles had thus institutionalized a form of organization that was not merely suspicious of authority but radically egalitarian. Two plans to reform the financial structure of the confederation by augmenting congressional powers failed for lack of unanimous consent.[27] Finding it impossible to modify the Articles and believing the national government as constituted woefully weak, many dissatisfied Americans looked around for a remedy to what they perceived as the egalitarian excesses of the Revolutionary period.

The Federal Constitution: Bringing Hierarchy Back In

The debate over the executive at the Constitutional Convention has long puzzled scholars seeking significant patterns. Most seem resigned to Max Farrand's conclusion that ''in all these debates over the executive, while there was the greatest diversity of opinion, lines of division do not seem to have been clearly drawn. Members expressed simply their individual and personal points of view.''[28] We shall try to show that these apparently idiosyncratic views of executive power were in fact grounded in cultural preference.

Attitudes to executive authority at the convention were a function not only of cultural propensity but of historical experience. Older members, whose formative experiences had been with royal governors and George III, tended be, ceteris paribus, more suspicious of executive power. The two oldest, Benjamin Franklin (eighty one) and Roger Sherman (sixty seven), were leading advocates of a weak, plural, and dependent executive, as was the sixty-two-year-old George Mason. Indeed, of the seven delegates to the Convention sixty years or older, none could be counted as a friend of a strong executive.[29]

The more recent historical experience had tended to push younger individualists in a less adamant antiexecutive direction. The formative years of such convention delegates as James Madison, Abraham Baldwin, Nicholas Gilman, William Houston, Charles Pinckney, and Richard Spaight (all of whom were between the ages of eighteen and twenty six in 1777, and would become staunch Jeffersonians later in life) had been with the weak executives of their state constitutions and the Articles of Confederation. Believing the Articles unable to provide the minimal level of government authority necessary to fend off foreign invasions and insure that debts were paid and contracts honored—the two essential conditions for a life based on self-regulation—individualists became sympathetic to arguments that favored strengthening central authority.

If historical experience interacted with cultural preference to generate attitudes toward the executive, we would expect to find that, holding experience constant, the more hierarchical the cultural preference, the more likely was the individual to prefer a strong executive. To test this proposition, we have measured cultural preference by future party identification. Those delegates who became Jeffersonian Republicans we have identified as individualists;

those who became adherents of the Federalist party we have designated as hierarchical. Of the forty nine convention delegates who supported the Constitution, twenty three would later align themselves with the Federalist party, and fifteen would become Jeffersonian Republicans.[30]

We found that delegates who became Federalists did tend to be more supportive of a powerful executive than were future Republicans. Support for an executive veto requiring a three-fourths legislative override, for instance, came disproportionately from those who would later manifest some commitment to the Federalist party. In contrast, support for only a two-thirds legislative override came primarily from future Republicans.[31] Future Federalists alone supported an absolute executive veto. The only state delegation to favor the absolute veto was that of Delaware, which was to become the most solidly Federalist state in the nation. (Delaware also was the only state that favored Gouverneur Morris's proposal to strike out the existing provision for selecting presidential electors "in order that some other provision might be substituted which would restrain the right of suffrage to freeholders.[32]) Of the future Federalists who did support a two-thirds override, moreover, all were essentially moderates. Of those who supported the absolute veto, Alexander Hamilton, Gouverneur Morris, and Rufus King qualify as "high" Federalists.

Hamilton and Gouverneur Morris, the convention's two most vocal defenders of a hierarchical way of life, clearly and consistently articulated a vision of a powerful chief executive. Their hierarchical proclivities were evident even in the heat of the Revolutionary struggle with Britain. In 1775, Hamilton expressed his concern that "the same state of the passions which fits the multitude . . . for opposition to tyranny and oppression, very naturally leads them to a contempt and disregard for all authority."[33] Morris, too, worried about the effect that mass participation in resisting Great Britain would have on the existing, hierarchical social order. "The mob begin to think and reason," wrote Morris in the spring of 1774. "Poor reptiles! it is with them a vernal morning; they are struggling to cast off their winter's slough, they bask in the sunshine, and ere noon they will bite, depend on it."[34] To make the United States a second Britain was the aim of both Morris and Hamilton.

Hamilton's famous five-hour speech to the convention on June 18 laid out the hierarchical blueprint for an American executive. Hamilton proposed a "Governour" to be selected by electors and to serve during "good behavior." This elective monarch was to be vested with an absolute veto over legislation, and would appoint the "chief officers" of the departments of finance, war, and foreign affairs without congressional approval. All other nominations were subject to approval by the Senate, the members of which were also to serve for life. Under Hamilton's plan, only the judiciary could impeach the president.[35]

Morris judged Hamilton's speech "the most able and impressive he had ever heard.''[36] His approval reflected substantive agreement: Morris supported life tenure, believed the executive should have an absolute veto, and opposed empowering the legislature to impeach the president.[37] Morris's speeches on the convention floor in defense of executive power betray the hierarchical assumption that the people are embodied in the executive. ''The Executive Magistrate,'' he contended, ''should be the guardian of the people, even of the lower classes.''[38] Morris was quick to second any motion to increase executive power, for he fervently believed that ''in the strength of the Executive would be found the strength of America.''[39]

In Number 69 of *The Federalist*, Hamilton expressed the same conviction a bit differently: ''The true test of a good government is its aptitude and tendency to produce a good administration.''[40] Hamilton, as Gerald Stourzh has pointed out, was relatively uninterested in theories of checks and balances. Good government, in Hamilton's mind, was a function not of checks and balances but rather an ''energetic'' executive.[41]

A relative lack of interest in checks and balances was characteristic of hierarchical political thinkers in the United States; for them the primary political question was not how to check government but rather, as Fisher Ames asked, ''how our government is to be supported,''[42] In his lengthy address to the convention, Hamilton argued that ''support of Government'' depended on ''influence,'' i.e. on ''a dispensation of those regular honors and emoluments which produce an attachment to the Government.''[43] A few days later Hamilton elaborated on this point, warning that ''we have been taught to reprobate the danger of influence in the British government, without duly reflecting how far it was necessary to support a good government.''[44] If executive patronage (known to republicans as ''corruption'') were required to insure elite support necessary for effective government, how could popular support be obtained? Hamilton's answer was that effective government would secure popular support. Rejecting the egalitarian view that ''a numerous representation was necessary to obtain the confidence of the people,'' Hamilton argued that ''the confidence of the people will easily be gained by a good administration.''[45]

Two points need to be emphasized concerning the hierarchical presidency advocated by Gouverneur Morris and Alexander Hamilton. First, as Douglass Adair has correctly observed, Hamilton's proposal for what amounted to an elective monarch was neither ''original nor unrepresentative of the thought of important segments of American opinion in 1787.''[46] Second, although a stronger executive did emerge from the Constitutional Convention (in large part due to the parliamentary skills of Morris), it fell far short of the hierarchical ideal. Upon signing the Constitution, Hamilton declared that ''no man's ideas were more remote from the plan than his.'' Fifteen years later, in a letter to Gouverneur Morris, Hamilton would refer to the document as a ''frail and worthless fabric."[47] Hamilton recognized that the result was the best the advocates of authority could do, but he was also painfully aware that the Constitution—having institutionalized suspicion of national authority in its complex division of powers, and checks and balances—would make presidential leadership an arduous task.

The distinction we have drawn between the hierarchical propensities of a Hamilton or Morris and the moderate individualism of a James Madison is often missed by those who indiscriminately lump them together under the label of "nationalist." Differentiating between these two strands of nationalism allows one to understand not only why Morris, Hamilton, and those like them moved into the Federalist party—while Madison and those like him gravitated toward the Republican party—but also why the two sides adopted different stands at the Constitutional Convention over the scope of executive power.

A comparison of Madison's and Morris's refutations of the "maxim in political science" that republicanism can survive only in small territories reveals fundamental differences between individualism and hierarchy. Beginning from the premise that "Republican government is not adapted to a large extent of Country, because the Executive Magistracy can not reach the extreme parts of it," Morris concludes that the solution is to "provide an Executive with sufficient vigor to pervade every part of it."[48] Morris's solution, however, was unlikely to convince many republicans because it assumed the very compatibility between republicanism and executive power that was in question.

In contrast, Madison's solution to the republican dilemma shared the individualistic assumption about the incompatibility of power and liberty but made the brilliant argument that it is in the extended national territory that power is most completely fragmented and atomized. Competition among diverse groups and power centers, reasoned Madison, makes the extended territory not only compatible with but the ideal setting for republican liberty to flourish.[49]

Madison's reasoning shows him to be a nationalist but not a hierarch. Though in favor of giving the national legislature an absolute veto over state legislatures, Madison opposed granting the national executive an absolute veto over the national legislature.[50] The Senate rather than the president was Madison's choice as the proper body in which to vest the power to appoint judges; eventually he did change his mind, but only after the Senate was reconstituted to represent the states.[51] The Virginia plan, of which Madison was the primary author, was strongly nationalist but provided for a rather weak national executive: unspecified in number, elected by the legislature, and ineligible for reelection. Madison repeatedly defended the Virginia plan's provision for having the president share veto power with a "council of revision."[52] In the closing days of the convention, we see Madison supporting

George Mason's proposal for a six-member executive council to be appointed by the Senate.[53] Even within the executive branch, as Richard Pious has suggested, Madison wanted to establish a system of checks and balances.[54]

If the Virginia plan was a rough approximation of the preferences of the individualist culture, and Hamilton's plan represented the hierarchical ideal, then the executive that finally emerged from the convention was compromise between these two cultures. The coalition of hierarchy and individualism that produced Article II (and the entire Constitution for the matter) constitutes what in today's parlance would be labeled "the establishment."

Ambiguity was instrumental in securing this tentative alliance of individualism and hierarchy. Article II was the most ambiguous section of a document that left a tremendous amount unsaid. Take the opening words of Article II, "The Executive power shall be vested in a President": was this a grant of power, or merely a gratuitous prologue indicating the unitary nature of the executive and his title? Agreement on the proposition that the executive had "the executive power" thinly masked sharp disagreement about what that power included. Was a declaration of neutrality, for example, an executive power? Within a few short years precisely this question would dredge up the submerged differences between Hamilton and Madison about what was "the executive power."

Perhaps Madison should have heeded more closely his own warning at the convention that the powers of the executive "should be confined and defined" so as "to fix the extent of the Executive authority."[55] Ambiguity may have facilitated agreement by leaving the definition of executive powers to future presidents, but it also advantaged those who, like Hamilton, favored an expansive construction of executive power. Much of the indefiniteness of Article II is attributable to the five-member Committee of Style, which was chaired by Gouverneur Morris, and included as members Hamilton and King.[56]

But it was not ambiguity alone that made agreement between individualists and hierarchs possible. Adherents of both cultures agreed, although for different reasons, on the need to make the executive independent from the legislature. For hierarchs, an independent executive was an essential prerequisite to a powerful chief executive. Individualists like Madison, on the other hand, came to feel that a system of competing powers required the executive to have an independent power base. Selection by the legislature would result in the executive's being swallowed up by the legislature, and thus reduce competition. In the one case, independence was a prerequisite to the exercise of executive prerogatives; in the other, independence was necessary to maintain competition within the government.

Creating an independent executive had the further advantage of making the presidency easier to sell to the egalitarians. Supporters of the Constitution could steal the egalitarians' thunder by parading the president, in the words of James Wilson, as "the man of the people."[57] The consequence, as Hamilton observed during the debate in New York over ratification, was that the mode of presidential election was "almost the only part of the system, of any consequence, which has escaped without severe censure or which has received the slightest mark of approbation from its opponents."[58]

In defending the Constitution at the ratifying conventions it was natural for "nationalists" to downplay the divisions that separated them. Hence in *The Federalist*, Madison often could appear almost indistinguishable from Hamilton. Yet, it is revealing of their underlying disagreements that it was Hamilton rather than Madison who penned the defense of presidential power in the *Federalist* papers. Failing to perceive the cultural differences between Hamilton and Madison, historians like Charles Beard have been unable to make sense of what they perceive to be Madison's "radical change" subsequent to the convention.[59] Jettisoning the assumption of bipolarity in favor of a trichotomous designation of political beliefs allows us to see the consistency in Madison's actions. Having gained the modicum of increased authority to insure "security against external and internal danger," Madison and other moderate individualists moved back toward the cultural alliance with egalitarianism.[60]

Although Madison desired a "checked, limited and precisely defined" executive that differed fundamentally from the kind of president preferred by Hamilton, Gouverneur Morris, Rufus King, and George Washington,[61] it is nevertheless true that Madison, more than many other individualists, was sympathetic to presidential power. The Virginia plan had left the number of the executive unspecified in order to avoid conflict with the three Virginians, Edmund Randolph, George Mason, and John Blair, who preferred a plural executive.[62] Randolph, according to Hamilton's notes, argued that because "great exertions [were] only requisite on particular occasions," it was better to have the legislature "appoint a dictator when necessary" than to live with a strong, permanent executive.[63] At the Virginia ratifying convention, arch-individualist Patrick Henry expressed the same sentiment. Rather than vesting permanent power in a president, Henry preferred that these great powers be granted only in times of "great danger," as they had been during the Revolution, when "we gave dictatorial powers to hands that used it gloriously; and which were rendered more glorious by surrendering it up."[64] Henry spoke for those ardent individualists, unwilling to sanction any increase in authority, who refused outside of war to abandon the antiauthority alliance with egalitarianism.

Thomas Paine was one of the few egalitarians prepared to support the Constitution. But his support came despite, rather than because of, the provisions relating to executive power. Paine's nationalism led him to the view that "any kind of hooping the barrel, however defectively executed, would be better than none," but his egalitarianism led him to object vehemently to Article II. For Paine, as for most egalitarians, the function of the executive was to execute the popular will. "The executive," wrote Paine, "can be considered in no other light than as inferior to the legislative. The sovereign authority in any country is the power of making laws, and everything else is an official department." In a letter to George Washington, Paine explained that he had "always been opposed to a single executive." "A plurality is far better," he reasoned, " for "it is necessary to the manly mind of a republic that it loses the debasing idea of obeying an individual.'"[65]

The personal embodiment and political leader of the alliance of egalitarianism and individualism, Thomas Jefferson, was similarly ambivalent about the Constitution. Despite "a disposition to subscribe to it," Jefferson initially confessed that he found himself "nearly a neutral," for while there was "a great mass of good in it" there was also "a bitter pill or two." Perhaps the bitterest was the presidency. The president, complained Jefferson, because he not only commanded the armed forces but could be reelected indefinitely, "seems a bad edition of a Polish King." In a letter to Madison, Jefferson revealed the two features of the Constitution that he "greatly disliked." The first was the omission of a bill of rights; the second was "abandonment of the necessity of rotation in office, and most particularly in the case of the President." Jefferson worried that "the first magistrate will always be reelected" and become "an officer for life," thereby effectively creating an American monarchy.[66]

Opponents of the Constitution echoed and amplified these criticisms of the executive office. The ideological core of Antifederalism was a coalition of egalitarians and extreme individualists.[67] What separated Jefferson from the Antifederalists was that they believed the Constitution contained not merely a few bitter pills but a lethal dose of hierarchical "remedies." Concentration of power in the president presented compelling evidence of the Constitution's hierarchical character. Some believed that the new document created "a military King, with a standing army devoted to its will."[68] The fact that the Constitution did not limit the president's reeligibility convinced many that Patrick Henry was correct in believing the Constitution "squints towards monarchy."[69] To Antifederalists, the proposed government seemed calculated to resuscitate hierarchy by enthroning an elective monarch and supporting him with a haughty aristocracy in the Senate.[70] Dazzled by visions of "stately palaces, . . . glory, wealth and power," the framers of the Constitution, Antifederalists believed, had repudiated the very principles for which the Revolution had been waged.[71]

The Antifederalists were correct in interpreting the Constitution as a blow against local egalitarianism but erred in their portrayal of the Constitution as an unambiguous victory for hierarchy. The view is in error because it ignores the coalitional nature of support for the document, and the consequent impediments put in the way of presidential authority. This is not to deny that the new Constitution, compared to the Articles of Confederation, greatly strengthened the central government and the executive. Nor is it to deny that the hierarchical culture was an important element in the coalition that created and ratified the new government. What the Antifederalists failed to appreciate, however, was the vital role of individualism in crafting, and gaining support for, the Constitution.

In accounting for the success of the Federalist proponents of the Constitution, we have also laid the grounds for an explanation of the subsequent collapse of the Federalist party. The Federalists of 1787 were a coalition of hierarchy and individualism. Almost immediately after the Constitution was ratified, however, individualists began to defect, giving the Federalist party of the 1790s an increasingly hierarchical makeup. In the first Congress, Madison's championing (at Jefferson's urging) of the Antifederalist demand for a Bill of Rights presaged the reemergence of the antiauthority alliance of the Revolution. The Washington administration's preference for a standing army, direct taxation, and assumption of the debt drove many other individualists out of the Federalist coalition.[72] Under the banner of the Republican party, Madisonian individualists joined with egalitarian Antifederalists to recreate the antiauthority alliance that had been dominant during the Revolution.

Notes

1. Bernard Bailyn, *The Ideological Origins of the American Revolution* (Cambridge: Harvard University Press, 1967), pp. 302-3. See also J. R. Pole, "Representation and Authority in Virginia from the Revolution to Reform," in *Paths to the American Past* (New York: Oxford University Press, 1979), pp. 3-40; John M. Murrin, "The Myths of Colonial Democracy and Royal Decline in Eighteenth-Century America: A Review Essay," *Cithara* (1965): 53-69.
2. Quoted in Bailyn, *Ideological Origins*, p. 304.
3. Ibid.
4. Quoted ibid., p. 307. Elbridge Gerry wrote, "The people . . . now feel rather too much their own importance, and it requires great skill to produce such subordination as is necessary" (Merrill Jensen, "The American People and the American Revolution," *Journal of American History* [June 1970]: 31). See also Gordon S. Wood, "The Democratization of Mind in the American Revolution," in *The Moral Foundations of the American Republic*, ed. Robert H. Horwitz (Charlottesville: University Press of Virginia, 1977), pp. 102-28.
5. Gordon S. Wood, *The Creation of the American Republic, 1776-1787* (Chapel Hill: University of North Carolina Press, 1969). Bailyn, *Ideological Origins*, ch. 6.
6. Wood, *Creation of American Republic*, pp. 70, 72.
7. Ibid., p. 149.

8. Ibid., pp. 139-40. New York was the only state not to adopt one or the other limitation. Maryland, Virginia, North Carolina, and Georgia had both annual election and rotation of office.
9. Ibid., pp. 132-50; Jackson Turner Main, *The Antifederalists: Critics of the Constitution, 1781-1788* (Chicago: Quadrangle Books, 1964), p. 18.
10. Wood, *Creation of American Republic*, p. 138.
11. The following analysis of Pennsylvania draws from Wood, *Creation of American Republic*, pp. 83-90, 137-38, 226-37; Elisha P. Douglas, *Rebels and Democrats: The Struggle for Equal Political Rights and Majority Rule during the American Revolution* (Chicago: Quadrangle Books, 1965), pp. 263-86; Donald S. Lutz, *Popular Consent and Popular Control: Whig Political Theory in the Early State Constitutions* (Baton Rouge: Louisiana State University Press, 1980), pp. 129-42; Jackson Turner Main, *The Sovereign States, 1775-1783* (New York: New Viewpoints, 1973), pp. 151-56, 218-20; Richard Alan Ryerson, "Republican Theory and Partisan Reality in Revolutionary Pennsylvania: Toward a New View of the Constitutionalist Party," in *Sovereign States in an Age of Uncertainty*, ed. Ronald Hoffman and Peter J. Albert, (Charlottesville: University Press of Virginia, 1981), pp. 95-133.
12. Wood, *Creation of American Republic*, p. 230. Also see Alfred F. Young, "Conservatives, the Constitution, and the 'Spirit of Accommodation,' " in *How Democratic Is the Constitution?* ed. Robert A. Goldwin and William A Schambra (Washington, D.C.: American Enterprise Institute, 1980), pp. 120-21. On the Antifederalists' preference for simple government, see Herbert J. Storing, *What the Anti-Federalists Were For* (Chicago: University of Chicago Press, 1981), pp. 53-63.
13. See especially Main, *Sovereign States*, p. 153; Young, "Spirit of Accommodation," p. 121.
14. Robert Kelley, *The Cultural Pattern in American Politics: The First Century* (New York: Knopf, 1979), p. 84; Robert Kelley, "Ideology and Political Culture from Jefferson to Nixon," *American Historical Review* (June 1977): 531-62, quotation on p. 537.
15. See Emory G. Evans, "Executive Leadership in Virginia, 1776-1781: Henry, Jefferson, and Nelson," in *Sovereign States in an Age of Uncertainty*, ed. Ronald Hoffman and Peter J. Albert (Charlottesville: University Press of Virginia, 1981), pp. 185-86; Main, *Sovereign States*, pp. 156-59; Wood, *Creation of American Republic*, pp. 136-37. On the two waves of constitution writing, see Lutz, *Popular Consent*, pp. 44-45.
16. Evans, "Leadership in Virginia," pp. 199, 206-7, 217; Jefferson quoted on p. 206.
17. Ibid., p. 220.
18. Jefferson, quoted ibid., p. 218.
19. The list is taken essentially verbatim from ibid., pp. 219, 207.
20. Ibid., pp. 222-25.
21. Kelley, *Cultural Pattern*, pp. 63-70.
22. Young, "Spirit of Accommodation," pp. 125-26. On the New York constitution also see Douglas, *Rebels and Democrats*, pp. 55-66; Wood, *Creation of American Republic*, p. 433; Main, *Sovereign States*, pp. 172-76; and Alfred F. Young, *The Democratic Republicans of New York: The Origins, 1763-1797* (Chapel Hill: University of North Carolina Press, 1967), pp. 17-21.
23. Douglas, *Rebels and Democrats*, pp. 64-65; Young, "Spirit of Accommodation," p. 126; Young, *Democratic Republicans*, p. 120.

24. Wood, *Creation of American Republic*, p.433.
25. The influence of the New York constitution on the framers of the federal Constitution is emphasized in Charles C. Thach, Jr., *The Creation of the Presidency, 1775-1789: A Study in Constitutional History* (Baltimore: John Hopkins University Press, 1923), pp. 34-43.
26. Richard M. Pious, *The American Presidency* (New York: Basic Books, 1979), p. 21; Main, *Antifederalists*, p. 16.
27. J. R. Pole, *Political Representation in England and the Origins of the American Republic* (Berkeley: University of California Press, 1971), pp. 351-52.
28. Max Farrand, *The Framing of the Constitution of the United States*, (New Haven: Yale University Press, 1913), p. 118.
29. The others were Daniel Jenifer (sixty four), William Livingston (sixty four), George Wythe (sixty three), and William Samuel Johnson (sixty). See Stanley Elkins and Eric McKitrick, "the Founding Fathers: Young Men of the Revolution," *Political Science Quarterly* (June 1961): 181-216.
30. The fifteen Federalists of 1787 who became Republicans were Abraham Baldwin, William Blount, Pierce Butler, John Dickinson, William Few, Nicholas Gilman, William Houstoun, John Langdon, James Madison, Alexander Martin, Charles Pinckney, Edmund Randolph, John Rutledge, Rich Spaight, and George Wythe. Those who supported the Constitution and aligned with the Federalists were Richard Bassett, John Blair, Jacob Broom, Gunning Bedford, George Clymer, William Davie, Jonathan Dayton, Oliver Ellsworth, Thomas Fitzsimmons, Nathaniel Gorham, Alexander Hamilton, Jared Ingersoll, William Samuel Johnson, Rufus King, James McHenry, Thomas Mifflin, Gouverneur Morris, William Paterson, Charles Cotesworth Pinckney, George Read, Caleb Strong, George Washington, and James Wilson. This list is drawn from David Hackett Fischer, *The Revolution of American Conservatism: The Federalist Party in the Era of Jeffersonian Democracy* (New York: Harper & Row, 1965), p. 222. The only difference is that Fischer considers Gorham unclassifiable. Though Gorham died in 1796, his Federalist credentials are strong enough—stronger probably than those of Blair, Mifflin, Wilson, and Broom—for him to be included in the category of "future Federalist."
31. Because individual votes were not recorded, it is impossible to obtain precise figures. We do know, however, that Pennsylvania, Virginia, Delaware, and Massachussetts voted in favor of the three-fourths veto, and that Maryland, Connecticut, New Jersey, North Carolina, South Carolina, and Georgia opted for a two-thirds veto. If the vote in each state was unanimous (not counting Strong, Wythe, Ellsworth, Martin, Houston and Davie, all of whom were absent), support for the three-fourths veto would have come from twelve future Federalists and four future Republicans. Making the same assumption for the two-thirds veto would mean that the lesser veto was supported by five future Federalists and seven future Republicans. The convention record allows us to refine this estimation. We know that McHenry from Maryland supported the three-fourths veto, and that Randolph of Virginia and Gerry of Massachusetts were opposed to it. We also know that New Hampshire's two delegates—both would become Jeffersonians—split on the question. Finally, though Hamilton could not vote because New York did not have a quorum, Hamilton was present and spoke in favor of the three-fourths proposal. By factoring in this information, we conclude that approximately fourteen future Federalists—including Washington, Blair, King, Gorham, Read, G. Morris, Wilson, and McHenry—voted in favor of the three-fourths veto; only three Republicans, including Madison did the same; and four future

Federalists supported the two-thirds veto compared to ten Republicans. These figures remain crude approximations, but they are sufficient, we think, to sustain our basic contention that those who identified with hierarchy, operationalized by future party affiliation, were more supportive of increasing executive power.

32. Max Farrand, ed., *The Records of the Federal Convention of 1787* (New Haven: Yale University Press, 1937), 2: 201-6.
33. Gerald Stourzh, *Alexander Hamilton and the Idea of Republican Government* (Stanford: Stanford University Press, 1970), pp. 7. 24.
34. Young, "Spirit of Accommodation," p. 119.
35. Farrand, *Federal Convention*, 1: 292.
36. Ibid., 293.
37. Ibid., 2: 33, 54, 200, 53. "Sooner or later," Morris believed, "we must have a monarch" (Young, "Spirit of Accommodation," p. 131).
38. Farrand, *Federal Convention*, 2: 52.
39. Ibid., 407.
40. Stourzh, *Alexander Hamilton*, p. 83. Also see ibid., p. 39; Farrand, *Federal Convention*, 1: 289.
41. Stourzh, *Alexander Hamilton*, p. 82.
42. Ames, quoted in David H. Fischer, "The Myth of the Essex Junto," *William and Mary Quarterly* (April 1964): 211. Jonathan Jackson agreed that "the restoration of . . . confidence in rulers" was the central objective (quoted, ibid., p. 209).
43. Farrand, *Federal Convention*, 1: 284-85, 302.
44. Ibid., 381. Also see Stourzh, *Alexander Hamilton*, p. 83.
45. Stourzh, *Alexander Hamilton*, p. 82.
46. Douglass Adair, "Experience Must Be Our Only Guide: History, Democratic Theory, and the United States Constitution," in *Fame and the Founding Fathers: Essays by Douglass Adair*, ed. Trevor Colbourn, (New York: Norton, 1974), p. 117.
47. Forrest McDonald, *The Formation of the American Republic, 1776-1790* (Baltimore: Penguin Books, 1967), pp. 187-88. Stourzh, *Alexander Hamilton*, p. 39. Also see Farrand, *Federal Convention*, 1: 524. On the parliamentary skill of Morris, see William H. Riker, "Gouverneur Morris in the Philadelphia Convention," in *The Art of Political Manipulation* (New Haven: Yale University Press, 1986), pp. 34-51.
48. Farrand, *Federal Convention*, 2: 52.
49. *The Federalist*, No. 10.
50. Farrand, *Federal Convention*, 1: 107, 99-100.
51. Ibid., 120.
52. Pious, *American Presidency*, p. 31.
53. Farrand, *Federal Convention*, 2: 542.
54. Pious, *American Presidency*, p. 31.
55. Farrand, *Federal Convention*, 1: 66, 70.
56. Pious, *American Presidency*, p. 38; Thach, *Creation of Presidency*, pp. 138-39.
57. Wilson, quoted in Pious, *American Presidency*, p. 39. Tench Coxe could, for instance, defend the convention's design for the presidency on the grounds that it "is created by their [the people's] breath" (Michael P. Riccards, "The Presidency and the Ratification Controversy," *Presidential Studies Quarterly* [Winter 1977]: 41). See also Gouverneur Morris's observation at the convention that making the executive independent of the legislature "would render it [the plan] extremely palatable to the people" (Farrand, *Federal Convention*, 2: 54). On the

Federalists' attempt "to cover their aristocratic document with a democratic mantle," see Gordon S. Wood, "Democracy and the Constitution," in *How Democratic Is the Constitution?* ed. Robert A. Goldwin and William A. Schambra (Washington, D.C.: American Enterprise Institute, 1980), pp. 1-17, quotation on p. 16.

58. Hamilton, quoted in Riccards, "Ratification Controversy," p. 41.

59. Charles A. Beard, *The Economic Origins of Jeffersonian Democracy* (New York: Macmillan, 1915), p. 51.

60. Madison, quoted in John R. Howe, *From the Revolution through the Age of Jackson: Innocence and Empire in the Young Republic* (Englewood Cliffs, N.J.: Prentice-Hall, 1973), p. 67.

61. Pious, *American Presidency*, p. 38.

62. Ruth Weissbound Grant and Stephen Grant, "The Madisonian Presidency," in *The Presidency in the Constitutional Order*, ed. Joseph M. Bessette and Jeffrey Tullis (Baton Rouge: Louisiana State University Press, 1981), p. 60; Farrand, *Federal Convention*, 1: 97.

63. Farrand, *Federal Convention*, 1:72-73.

64. Herbert J. Storing, ed., *The Complete Anti-Federalist* (Chicago: University of Chicago Press, 1981), 5.16.11.

65. Paine, cited in Young, "Spirit of Accommodation," p. 144, and Thach, *Creation of the Presidency*, p. 30. Paine's egalitarian credentials are evident in his support of the Pennsylvania constitution as "good for a poor man" (cited in Young, "Spirit of Accommodation," p. 144).

66. Jefferson, cited in Young, "Spirit of Accommodation," p. 142, and Pious, *American Presidency*, p. 39.

67. There is a lively debate in the historical literature as to whether Antifederalism reflected an extreme egalitarianism or extreme individualism. In part this dispute is due to the considerable variety of views housed under the label Antifederalist. More important in producing the confusion, however, is that the Revolution produced a fusion of egalitarianism and individualism that makes separating out the two cultures exceedingly difficult. Forced to choose, we think the weight of evidence indicates that the Antifederalists tended to lean toward the egalitarian side of the antiauthority alliance.
The Antifederalists' preoccupation with the importance of the small-scale community defies the characterization of them as pure individualists. Antifederalist criticisms of the proposed constitution operated from the premise that only a small republic, where face-to-face relationships among people relatively equal in condition prevailed, could secure the voluntary allegiance of its people. Therefore, they concluded, the new national government must rely on coercion to obtain consent (Storing, *What the Anti-Federalists Were For*, pp. 16-17, 41). Their concern was not the individual's becoming dependent on government—the individualist's concern—but rather an insufficient identification with the government. A distant central government, by making participation impossible, would create apathetic fatalists—an argument echoed in modern-day egalitarian thought. For the Antifederalists, explains Herbert Storing, politics depended on "the alert public-spiritedness of the small, homogeneous, self-governing community" (p. 40). The centrality of the small, egalitarian community to the Antifederalist vision justifies, in our estimation, Gordon Wood's conclusion that the Antifederalists "were true champions of the most extreme kind of democratic and egalitarian politics expressed in the Revolutionary era" (Wood, *Creation of American Republic*, p.

516). The most influential statement of the view of the Antifederalists as extreme individualists is Cecilia M. Kenyon, "Men of Little Faith: The AntiFederalists on the Nature of Representative Government," *William and Mary Quarterly* (January 1955): 3-43. The communitarian and egalitarian side of the Antifederalists is stressed in Joshua Miller, "Democracy and the Politics of Experience in Antifederalist Thought" (Paper delivered at the 1984 Annual Meeting of the Western Political Science Association, Sacramento, April 12-14, 1984); and Wilson Carey McWilliams, "Democracy and the Citizen: Community, Dignity, and the Crisis of Contemporary Politics in America," in *How Democratic Is the Constitution?* ed. Robert A. Goldwin and William A. Schambra (Washington, D.C.: American Enterprise Institute, 1980), pp. 79-101.

68. Alarm over the president's control over the military is most strikingly expressed by "Philadelphiensis," quoted in Cecelia M. Kenyon, ed., *The Antifederalists* (Indianapolis: Bobbs-Merrill, 1966), p. 72. See also Storing, *Complete Anti-Federalist*, Cato IV 2.6.31; An Old Whig V 3.3.31; Officer of the Late Continental Army 3.8.3; Maryland Ratifying Convention 5.4.7; A Georgian 5.9.10-11; Tamony 5.11.6-7; A Countryman 6.7.1; Patrick Henry in Kenyon, *Antifederalists*, pp. 257-58; Main, *Antifederalists*, p. 142.

69. Henry, cited in Kenyon, *Antifederalists*, p. 257. See also Storing, *Complete Anti-Federalist*, Edmund Randolph 2.5.41; Officer of the Late Continental Army 3.8.3; Samuel Chase 5.3.17; Cato (S.C.) 5.10.2; James Lincoln and George Clinton in Kenyon, *Antifederalists*, pp. 185, 303; Elbridge Gerry and George Mason, cited in Riccards, "Presidency and the Ratification Controversy," pp. 41, 43; Main, *Antifederalists*, pp. 140-41. The Virginia and North Carolina conventions proposed constitutional amendments limiting tenure in office to eight years in sixteen (Pious, *American Presidency*, p. 39).

70. Main, *Antifederalists*, p. 142. See, for instance, "Philadelphiensis," in Kenyon, *Antifederalists*, p. 72; and Storing, *Complete Anti-Federalist*, Centinel II 2.7.49,51; Officer of the Late Continental Army 3.8.3; Minority of Convention of Pennsylvania 3.11.45; The Impartial Examiner 5.14.40; A Countryman 6.7.1; and George Clinton 6.13.32. On the Antifederalist obsession with aristocracy, see Wood, *Creation of American Republic*, esp. pp. 488-92, 513-15.

71. Quoted in Storing, *What the Anti-Federalists Were For*, p. 31. On the Antifederalist view of the Constitution as a repudiation of the principles of the Revolution, see ibid., p. 8, and Wood, *Creation of American Republic*, pp. 499, 523.

72. This explains Gordon Wood's observation that "the Federalists of 1787-1788 were not the Federalists of the 1790s" (Wood, "Democracy and the Constitution," p. 16). Irving Brant contends that by fighting Hamilton's assumption scheme, Madison "split the original Federalists asunder, fused one part of them with the radical wing of the vanishing Anti-federalists and gave direction to the political cleavage which swiftly divided the American public into Federalists and Republicans" (Irving Brant, *James Madison: Father of the Constitution, 1787-1800* [Indianapolis: Bobbs-Merrill, 1950], p. 305).

3

The Dilemma of Weak Hierarchy: George Washington and John Adams

President-raters agree that George Washington was a great, perhaps even our greatest, president.[1] But wherein lies Washington's greatness? Scholars such as J. G. Randall, William Hesseltine, and David Donald have succeeded in giving Lincoln a believable stature,[2] but the substance of Washington's greatness remains elusive. Stripping away the myths surrounding "the godlike Washington" has left the basis of his preeminence unclear. If, as Marcus Cunliffe concludes, he was "a good man, not a saint; a competent soldier, not a great one; an honest administrator, not a statesman of genius," then what made him "an exceptional figure?"[3] How can good, competent, and honest—a characterization that also well describes Jimmy Carter—add up to a great president?

Gaining Power by Giving It Up

We begin to address our question by asking why his contemporaries revered Washington. Recent work by Barry Schwartz provides refreshing illumination: How and why, Schwartz queries, was "a cult of veneration formed around one man in a culture . . . in which complete deference to higher authority was ridiculed and every form of power deliberately and systematically scrutinized?" Schwartz shifts the focus away from Washington's personal characteristics and achievements, and toward the dispositions of his followers. "Statements about Washington," argues Schwartz, "must be matched by statements about the central needs and concerns of his society."[4] Thus, his analysis fits well with our cultural conception of leadership, in which followers and leaders are analyzed together.

The deepest fear in an individualist political culture, we have suggested, is of the leader who overstays his welcome. The central dilemma is to balance having leaders when they are needed and getting rid of them when they are not. The War for Independence raised the specter of a temporary leader who would refuse to depart when his services were no longer desired. Washington was admonished that "whenever this important contest shall be decided . . .

[we expect] you will cheerfully resign the important deposit committed into your hands and re-assume the character of our worthy citizen." Bondage, as William Tudor warned in 1779, "is ever to be apprehended at the close of a successful struggle for liberty, when a triumphant army, elated with victories, and headed by a popular general may become more formidable than the tyrant that has been expelled. . . . Witness the aspiring Cromwell."[5]

Acutely aware of this individualist fear, Washington took every opportunity to reassure his countrymen of his desire to step down immediately after completing his assigned task. Before assuming command of the Revolutionary armies, he told the Continental Congress that he harbored "no lust for power."[6] Upon the disbanding of the army, Washington insisted, in a letter to the governors of the states, that he had no wish to "share in public business hereafter," and longed only for "the shade of retirement."[7] Both as general and as president he repeatedly advertised his aversion to the glare of public life and his preference to quit public life for "the shadow of my own vine and my own fig tree."[8] Although Washington's public pronouncements were well suited to alleviate prevailing fears, it was his actions—twice retiring from the most powerful office in the land—that brought him the country's highest accolades.

Washington, writes Schwartz, "distinguished himself not by feats performed to acquire power but by the length he went to avoid power, and by the enthusiasm with which he relinquished the power vested in him by his countrymen."[9] Not how he exercised power but how he resisted it earned Washington his country's adoration. "He left mankind bewildered with the splendid problem," the Virginian John W. Daniel later explained, "of whether to admire him most for what he was or what he would not be." In a study of fifty five orations given on the occasion of Washington's death, Schwartz finds that the one event that was always described with "pointed emotion" was Washington's voluntary surrender of his leadership of the Revolutionary armies after the termination of the war.[10] To a population that believed that power was "restless, aspiring, insatiable," a jaw "always open to devour," an appetite "whetted, not cloyed, by possession," Washington's self-denial was nothing short of superhuman;[11] and thus he became the paragon of individualist political leadership. "Commitment to a political culture," Schwartz argues, "shows up in the form of devotion to a man." By spurning offers to make his leadership permanent, Washington became a "visible symbol" of individualist values and tendencies.[12] In being good he thus became great.

That Washington was revered for leaving office did not, however, guarantee support when he was in office. As a symbol of a political culture, he could expect adoration and praise; as president, however, he became the target of increasingly harsh criticism. When Washington toured the predominantly Republican southern states in 1791, he witnessed an adoration that equaled that shown during his earlier tour of Federalist New England. But when he acted as president to further the Federalist preferred way of life—hierarchy—Washington found himself unmercifully attacked by the Republican press.

The Hierarchical Washington

Although his self-denial led those with individualist cultural propensities to shower him with accolades, Washington himself, at bottom, was an adherent not of the individualist but of the hierarchical way of life. Somewhat submerged at the outset of his first term, the president's cultural affinities became increasingly apparent in his second. Washington's often expressed concern about his "reputation" was justified, for there was a danger that as he became increasingly identified with the hierarchical Federalists, Washington would be likened not to Cincinnatus but George III.

Of Washington's hierarchical propensities there can be little question; his attitudes and behavior reveal an "unspoken philosophy" consistent with hierarchical Federalism. Behind Washington's antipathy to "levellers" and commitment to the "cause of order" lay a coherent if unarticulated set of assumptions about society. Washington's social attitudes, as David Hackett Fischer has noted, were colored with an unmistakable "collectivist tinge." "This corporate conception of society," continues Fischer, was "combined with a consciousness of inequalities among men."[13] Washington's outlook reflected an uncritical acceptance of the Federalist persuasion. Society, in the Federalist cosmology, was a collectivity of unequal and interdependent parts; social harmony rested on acceptance of one's unequal but indispensable position in the hierarchy, with deference towards men above reciprocated by noblesse oblige on the part of "betters."[14]

Washington also embraced the Federalist belief in the need for strong government, "a controulling power" to restrain the passions of the populace.[15] All Federalists would agree with Hamilton that the Jeffersonian doctrine "which promises men, ere long, an emancipation from the burdens and restraints of government" was visionary, and subversive to a well-ordered society.[16] Governmental authority was necessary to insure that "every citizen shall sustain his just part, and keep his proper place." Without the institutions of government teaching or, failing that, imposing "the habits of just subordination," society would rapidly degenerate, as under the Articles, to a state of licentiousness and anarchy.[17]

The first president's relations with Congress and the executive branch reflected a hierarch's concern for proper spheres of action. James Thomas Flexner has stressed Washington's "restraint in exerting his great power beyond what he considered the legitimate province of the executive." "In his relations with both the Continental Congress and the federal Congress," continues Flexner, "Washington never reached, in any manner that would open him to a denial, beyond his right and power to command."[18] His refusal to interfere personally in what he considered the proper domain of Congress not only accorded with his hierarchical self-conception but also minimized the possibility that the opposition would accuse him of a lust for power.

If adherence to a hierarchical culture inhibited Washington from trying to control Congress, it also compelled him to be "master in his executive house."[19] At a period when the relationship of department heads to president was ill-defined, Washington moved decisively to subordinate them to the president.[20] Equally significant, Washington refused to circumvent department heads by reaching down into departmental operations, preferring instead to maintain clear hierarchical channels of authority. "It is not agreeable to me," explained Washington, "to go into the details of business with any except the head of the Department to which it belongs."[21]

We would expect a person who was comfortable with hierarchical relationships to be uncertain, even confused, when confronted by relations that do not fit the hierarchical pattern. Washington was personally much more at ease with the formal superordination and subordination that characterized the president's relationship with the executive branch than with the ill-defined rivalry that marked the president's relationship to Congress. Early in his administration, Washington came to Congress to get the "advice and consent" of the Senate on a treaty with the Creek Indians but became confused and enraged by the Senate's proclivity for endless debate on every point. Forrest McDonald accounts for the president's outburst as a result of the fact that he was "accustomed to dealing with advisers as subordinates."[22] Running throughout Washington's career was the consistent pattern of an inability to deal constructively with rivals whose relationship to him was not that of subordinate.[23] Washington's solution to his ambiguous relationship with Congress was to leave the latter to perform in its legislative sphere while the president exercised the functions of the executive.

Some have seen Washington's desire to avoid conflicts with Congress as evidence of a "passive-negative" character. The passive-negative president, James David Barber argues, tends "to withdraw, to escape from the conflict and uncertainty of politics." He is "someone who does little in politics and enjoys it less."[24] Because Washington often expressed his reluctance to assume the presidency, complained bitterly while in power, and expressed joy only at the prospect of leaving office, we find a cultural explanation for his behavior superior to a psychological one.

Whether reluctant to serve or not, Washington had to act that part; otherwise adherents of an antiauthority culture would have been quick to accuse him of a lust for personal power. No doubt Washington often felt miserable in office; he suffered from criticism, Jefferson wrote, "more than any person I ever yet met with."[25] As a believer in hierarchy, Washington was distressed when his (in his own view) paternalistic desire to serve the common interest was subject to ridicule, even vilification, by the opposition press. No doubt Washington felt genuine joy at escaping from a position in which he was not treated according to his station. Had he been the head of a hierarchical regime, difficult as that is to imagine in the United States, he might have been much happier with a life in politics.

As for passivity, Washington's use of the Indian wars to create a military establishment,[26] his active involvement in putting down the Whiskey Rebellion in western Pennsylvania, and his decisive role in securing the Jay Treaty suggest otherwise. There was nothing passive, moreover, about Washington's administrative style. He closely supervised the three heads of departments, demanding daily written reports on every item of business transacted, as well as requiring frequent written opinions and compilations of information.[27] An energetic administration accorded well with Washington's preference for an active central government.

The charge of passivity is particularly curious in view of the landmark, domestic financial legislation initiated by the executive branch during Washington's first term. Usually the reconciliation is accomplished by portraying Washington as an unwitting dupe of the "all-powerful" Alexander Hamilton.[28] Washington plays Othello to Hamilton's Iago. The fiction of a gullible Washington being manipulated by the evil genius of Hamilton was first created by Jeffersonians who were frustrated by the protective shield that Washington's prestige afforded Hamilton's financial schemes. The president, wrote William Maclay, "had become in the hands of Hamilton the dishcloth of every dirty speculator, as his name goes to wipe away blame and silence all murmering."[29] Subsequent admirers (and detractors) of Hamilton and his policies have propagated this version of history. If the deified Washington seems unsatisfactory, Washington the unsuspecting pawn is even more so.

The unwitting-dupe interpretation of Washington's behavior is incorrect because it ignores the agreement on cultural preferences and policy goals between Hamilton and Washington. To be sure, Washington knew little about fiscal management, taxation, commerce, and other subjects that fell under the jurisdiction of the Treasury Department (in marked contrast to his experience and knowledge in areas that concerned the Department of State and Department of War).[30] In view of Hamilton's expertise in matters of national finance, it is not surprising that Washington relied on his secretary of Treasury to formulate a plan for the nation's economy. Those who would argue the unsuspecting-dupe thesis must show not that Washington relied on Hamilton but that (a) Hamilton's policy preferences were not known to Washington when he selected Hamilton to head the Treasury Department, and (b) Washington did not understand the implications of those things Hamilton was doing in the president's name.

Hamilton's preference for a strong central government was no secret. In the Constitutional Convention, at which Washington presided, Hamilton—by recommending the delegates model their new goverment on the British monarchy—had distinguished himself as the most extreme exponent of centralized authority. His First Report as secretary of the Treasury, recommending that central government assume the financial responsibility for states' revolutionary war debts, and the Second Report, proposing a national bank, were both consistent with Hamilton's previously stated positions. Hamilton's financial program accorded with the British model he so much admired: the public debt and public sector revenues were centralized, and the Bank of the United States, as James Savage comments, "was created in the mirror image of the Bank of England."[31]

Though President Washington had no part in preparing these famous reports, and probably did not understand the technical details of the methods Hamilton had designed for financing the debt, nor for that matter did members of Congress, the evidence suggests that Washington fully endorsed the aims of the financial system Hamilton was attempting to erect. High finance was not the president's metier, certainly—though he knew enough about finance to engage (very successfully) in land speculation and manage his own estates—but he did understand that effective government demanded stable revenues and sound credit, the absence of which had so badly hurt his revolutionary armies and disgraced the government under the Articles of Confederation. Indeed, precisely because Washington was so confident that Hamilton's aims were in agreement with his own (increasing support for central authority), "he felt it unnecessary . . . to do more than watch benevolently while Hamilton prepared the reports and plans he had been asked for by the House."[32]

The president shared his Treasury secretary's belief that establishing the nation's credit took precedence over retiring the debt or balancing the budget. "An accession of strength to the national government, and an assurance of order and vigor in the national finances by doing away with the necessity of thirteen complicated and different systems of finance," Washington and Hamilton both believed, were "the leading objects" of assumption.[33] And both agreed that it was desirable to centralize public revenues, expenditures, and debts. In fact, only a year before Washington had drawn up the (admittedly unsophisticated) "Plan of American Finance" that envisioned the national government's collecting all taxes.[34] Even Forrest McDonald, an ardent admirer of Hamilton who continually downplays Washington's role, concedes that the president "knew—or at least sensed—what he [Hamilton] was doing.''[35] What could have fit Washington's desires better than tying people to central authority through self-interest by giving them a stake in its viability?

That Washington's prestige afforded a protective cover for Hamilton's policies is undeniable. ''An Aegis [shield] very essential to me'' is the way Hamilton expressed his relationship with the president.''[36] Less often appreciated is that Hamilton served also as a convenient lightning rod for the president on highly controversial issues. According to Jefferson, the funding-assumption bill, defeated in the House on five separate occasions before it was finally passed, ''produced the most bitter and angry contest ever known in Congress before or since the Union of the States.''[37] The Treasury secretary, therefore, rather than the president—who visibly kept a proper distance from Hamilton's schemes—became the villain among opponents of centralized government. Yet, all the while the hierarchical agenda of centralization that Washington preferred was being enacted. We are thus led to conclude that Washington was not ''a sick, tired old man who went grimly through the ceremonies laid out for him'' but ''an actual leader of his people, whose own deepest convictions and ultimate aims were expressed in the policies he was shaping.''[38]

The Dilemma of an Insecure Hierarchy

Well aware of the Revolutionary distaste for central rule, Washington viewed his primary task as president of the United States as one of building support for the authority of the federal government,[39] particularly for the office of chief executive established by the new Constitution. In an influential book, *The First New Nation*, Seymour Martin Lipset drew proper attention to Washington's indispensable role in establishing the legitimacy of the new government; Lipset's characterization of Washington as a charismatic leader, however, is misconceived. The charismatic's credo, ''It has been written . . . , but I say unto you,'' would have been anathema to Washington, who, as a supporter of hierarchy, was concerned first and foremost with getting people to support the government established by the newly drawn up Constitution. The substitution of personal will for written law (the essence of charisma as we conceive it) would, as Washington understood, undermine the hierarchical regime he was attempting to establish.[40]

Hierarchical regimes characteristically place a premium on overt leadership. Because vigorous and public leadership is believed to inspire admiration and respect, disguising the exercise of power makes no sense. Concealed leadership might be taken for infirmity or indecisiveness. All hierarchies are inclined to the overt display of authority, but in a cultural context in which authority is actively questioned, there is a tendency for the hierarchy to adopt an exaggerated concern with the appearance of strength. Limits on the substance of authority make the appearance of authority that much more important.

An exaggerated concern with the semblance of power can have adverse, unintended consequences. First, it can produce a form of goal displacement, with the image of effectiveness driving out its substance. Second, and more important for our purposes, those who do not share the cultural assumptions of hierarchy may find the display of power anywhere from alarming to ridiculous. The insecure hierarchy is trapped by a dilemma in which a mode of behavior designed to compensate for its weakness may actually undermine already limited authority. A vicious circle is created: the weaker the hierarchical culture, the more insecure it is; the more insecure, the greater is its emphasis on compensatory display; and the greater its appearance of strength, the more ridiculous and/or oppressive the regime will appear to adherents of egalitarian and individualist cultures.

An emphasis on power and privilege is to be expected in hierarchies. The glory of the head is presumed to reflect on—rather than divert from—the resources of the collectivity. Thus did Washington travel around the capital in highly decorated carriage drawn by six cream-colored horses, attended by four servants in livery. Like the other Federalists, Washington believed that pomp and ceremony would, as Ralph Ketcham writes, "nourish public respect for the head of the nation and therefore for the nation as a whole."[41] When people question the assumption that what is good for the hierarch is good for the lowerarchs, however, insecurity sets in.

This insecurity manifested itself during the early days of the new nation in an often comical preoccupation with forms and ceremony. The first weeks of Congress were absorbed with efforts to invest Washington with an exalted title that would convey the "dignity and splendor" necessary to support authority in the public mind. Vice President John Adams lectured a Senate, that on the whole needed little convincing, about "the efficacy of pageantry." "A royal or at least a princely title will be found indispensably necessary," Adams explained, "to maintain the reputation, authority, and dignity of the President . . . and support his state in the minds of our own people or foreigners."[42] Evidently the Senate agreed with Adams, proposing the title "His Highness, the President of the United States of America, and Protector of the Rights of the Same." During the Constitutional Convention Washington had expressed a preference for a similar title: "His High Mightiness, the President of the United States and Protector of their Liberties."[43] The House, however, under James Madison's leadership, refused to go along with what it perceived as pompous foolishness, and its preference for the unadorned title "President" prevailed.[44] The sum of Federalist efforts to enhance the prestige of the office of the presidency was ridicule. Congressmen from Pennsylvania, a state in which egalitarianism was particularly strong, took to addressing each other in mock ceremony as "Your Highness of the House" and "Your Highness of the Senate." Portly John Adams was granted the title "His Rotundity."[45]

Although defeated in their efforts to grant the president a ceremonious title, the Federalists under both Washington and Adams attempted, according to Richard Buel, "to surround the President with royal pomp and circumstance whenever he appeared in public."[46] Intended to bolster authority, these acts frequently provoked intense criticism. "Naked he [Washington] would have been sanctimoniously reverenced," Jefferson explained to Madison, "but enveloped in the rags of royalty, they can hardly be torn off without laceration."[47]

An acute theoretical analysis of the insecure hierarchy is presented by Victor Thompson in his *Modern Organization*. Thompson suggests that when those in superordinate positions in the hierarchy feel insecure, they try to maintain their authority through "dramaturgy" or impression management.[48] Washington's obsession with putting distance between himself and others is a perfect example of the "exaggerated aloofness" that Thompson describes as resulting from an insecurity about maintaining hierarchical relationships.[49] Washington defended the aloofness with which he presented himself in public as necessary "to preserve the dignity and respect that was due to the first Magistrate." "Too free an intercourse and too much familiarity," reasoned Washington, would lead to a "reduction of respectability."[50] Not personality but cultural organization explains this often-noted feature of Washington's presidential behavior.

Here as elsewehere, however, a mode of behavior designed to bolster authority provoked criticism from Republicans. Representative Theodorick Bland, for instance, criticized Washington's bows, which he found "more distant and stiff" than those of a king.[51] What was dignity to proponents of hierarchy bespoke arrogance to egalitarians and individualists.

An insecure hierarchy, continues Victor Thompson, is also characterized by an exaggerated "insistence on the rights of office." "Since his [the superior's] behavior stems from insecurity," argues Thompson, "he may be expected to insist on petty rights and prerogatives, on protocol, on procedure.[52] A good example of this was Washington's insistence that on a presidential visit to Boston, John Hancock, the governor of Massachusetts, visit Washington rather than vice versa. To demonstrate that governors were subordinate to presidents, the bedridden Hancock was carried to where Washington was staying.[53]

Disrespect toward the hierarch is likely to be perceived as a fundamental challenge. As the insecurity mounted, even trivial vulgarity could be seen as a threat to presidential authority. Luther Baldwin, for instance, was prosecuted under the Federalist Sedition Law because, as James Morton Smith so delicately expresses it, "he expressed a wish that a cannon shot had lodged in the president's posterior.'' Tried before a circuit court presided over by Robert Morris and George Washington's nephew, Bushrod Washington, Baldwin and a drinking buddy were imprisoned for speaking ''sedicious words tending to defame the President and Government of the United States.'' The incident stands as a ''comic footnote'' to the menacing Alien and Sedition Acts, but it also symbolizes that quandary of a hierarchical regime in a predominantly antiauthority cultural context.[54] Designed to set an example, to teach respect for those in positions of authority, the prosecution of Baldwin further discredited the Federalist party as Republicans mixed derisive scorn with their sincere alarm at the rise of a new monarchy.

That reactions were so contrary to the intentions of Washington and the Federalists shows how profound was the cultural divide between the Republican and Federalist parties. Viewing the politics of the 1790s through very different cultural lenses, Federalists expressed concern over executive impotence, while Jeffersonians were fretting that ''the Executive had swallowed up the legislative branch.'' Washington's belief that liberty depended on ''an efficient and responsable Executive'' differed radically from Jeffersonian ideology, which posited a perpetual, antagonistic struggle between liberty and executive power.[55] Tyranny was best avoided, in the Jeffersonian view, by granting power only when absolutely necessary. But Washington believed that by denying leaders the power necessary to govern in everyday circumstances, Republicans only increased the likelihood of tyranny, for leaders might then feel impelled to seize power. Unfortunately for Washington, it was the Jeffersonian premise that dominated the early republic.

The Whiskey Rebellion

The intractability of the Federalists' dilemma is indicated by the Washington administration's failure to profit from the Whiskey Rebellion. A violent insurrection, with which few national elites sympathized, including Jefferson and Madison, threatened—in a historical rerun of Shay's Rebellion—to cast the national government in the valiant role of defender of law and order. It was expected that the rebellion would therefore favor hierarchical proponents of a strong central government. ''The insurrection,'' predicted Hamilton, ''will do us a great deal of good and add to the solidity of every thing in this country.''[56] That Hamilton's expectations proved illusory is explainable in terms of the dilemma of a hierarchy operating in an antihierarchical context.

A concern with building support for authority animated the Washington administration's response to the ''Whiskey Rebels.'' Rather than regard resistance to the excise tax as useful information about the efficacy of that policy, members of the administration attributed the resistance to deviants intent on subverting the government.[57] The issue, as Hamilton posed it, was ''whether the Government can maintain itself.''[58] Washington agreed with his secretary of the Treasury that "the very existence of Government and the fundamental principles of social order" were at stake. If the rebels were not subdued, declared Washington, "we may bid adieu to all government in this Country.''[59]

Why did the Washington administration choose to behave in this confrontational manner? Playing down the events and working behind the scenes to defuse the issue would have been as likely to resolve the conflict. Instead, with the president's blessing, Hamilton actually went to the newspapers with a lengthy and provocative report on the uprising that he had written for Washington. This deliberate upping of the ante was not due, as Forrest McDonald claims, to Hamilton's "policy of keeping the public informed," but rather to a fear that silence on the subject would be construed as weakness.[60] Washington's correspondence reveals little interest in covert bargaining to mollify the aggrieved; rather, the correspondence is geared to canvassing elite opinion with the aim of finding out whether support existed for "the most spirited and firm measures.''[61] The long-standing historiographical dispute over whether or not the administration, particularly Hamilton, desired to *use* force against the rebels misses the point. Only the *display* of force was necessary to achieve the administration's overriding goal, which was neither to smite the rebels nor to avoid the shedding of blood but, rather, to bolster the authority of national leadership roles.[62]

Once the administration's aim is understood as one of impressing the nation with an overt show of power, we can begin to understand the disproportionate nature of the government's military response. So anxious were Hamilton and Washington to demonstrate federal authority that the military force they gathered to crush what was a local rebellion rivaled the total fighting force of the entire Revolutionary army.[63] Much ceremony and fanfare accompanied the army's impressive march across Pennsylvania, with Washington at its head for most of the way.[64] This ostentatious display of military might was designed, in Washington's words, to give "testimony to the world of being able or willing to support our government and laws," and was consistent with Hamilton's belief that "whenever the government appears in arms it ought to appear like a Hercules and inspire respect by the display of strength.''[65] Yet, beneath the impressive appearance of strength lurked the government's barely disguised weakness, for the massive military force, in truth, was not a well-trained, national standing army but a disorganized conglomeration of state militias.

The troops marched into four counties of western Pennsylvania, rounded up twenty or so prisoners, and the government pronounced law and order restored. The administration trumpeted its success by parading the prisoners through Philadelphia. Hamilton spoke for the administration when he concluded the government had gained in "reputation and strength" from the events.[66] Washington's conviction that the action would reflect positively on the cause of authority is evident in his decision to devote virtually his entire annual message to describing how the government had put down what he termed the "insurrection."[67] Confident that the government's deeds would be applauded, there had been no attempt to disguise the use of power.

Had the show of might enhanced the government's "reputation and strength," as Hamilton contended? The high priest of Federalism, Fisher Ames, seems to have been more accurate in gauging the effects of such government actions. "A regular government, by overcoming an unsuccessful insurrection, becomes stronger," observed Ames, but in the United States, "rulers can scarcely ever employ physical force without turning public opinion against the governent."[68] Put another way, given an antiauthority context, overt action designed to strengthen government may actually undermine support for leadership.

To many, the government's behavior appeared asinine if not downright dangerous. Observing that the troops encountered no resistance and that an extensive manhunt had netted an unimpressive ragtag of prisoners, Jefferson sardonically remarked that "an insurrection was announced and proclaimed and armed against, but could never be found." But if Jefferson thought the government's actions comical, he also found it menacing that the government would march "against people at their plows."[69] Madison was equally critical of the forces marshaled to quell the rebellion, believing that Hamilton and his friends were trying not only to "accumulate force" in the federal executive but also to "establish the principle that a standing army was necessary for enforcing the law."[70] Washington, lamented Jefferson, had been "dazzled by the glittering of crowns and coronets."[71] Far from impressing, the administration's display of might had only invoked images of oppressive monarchy.

In his message to Congress defending the government's actions, Washington blamed the uprising on the subversive "self-created" Democratic Societies that, as Washington told his brother-in-law, were "endeavoring to destroy all confidence in the administration by arraigning all its acts." These societies, spawned by popular enthusiasm for the French Revolution, attempted to influence government policy in a pro-French, anti-Hamiltonian direction by campaigning for candidates they approved of, instructing their representatives how to vote, and mobilizing voters. The president believed that these societies breathed the spirit of radical egalitarianism that was then convulsing France. Direct democracy, Washington worried, would circumvent and therefore undermine established institutions and undo the work of the Constitution. If not "discountenanced," Washington was "perfectly convinced . . . these self-created societies . . . will destroy the government of this country."[72]

Washington's attack on the Democratic Societies was an important turning point in his presidency. Hitherto he had avoided being linked in the public mind with the hierarchical Federalists, but this speech alarmed many Republicans and persuaded them that Washington was either a committed Federalist or an unwitting dupe of Hamilton.[73] The president's open attack on the societies was "the greatest error of his political life," Madison judged, for it put him "ostentatiously at the head of the other party."[74] Becoming thus linked with hierarchy, Washington lost the shield of invulnerabilty that his Cincinnatus image had given him.

Washington's vulnerability to personal criticism was heightened, ironically, by Hamilton's departure from the administration.[75] The resignation of the secretary of the Treasury deprived Washington of a valuable lightning rod that had served to deflect criticism of the administration away from the president during his first term. The harshest attacks on Washington emanated from the egalitarian elements of an emerging opposition. Benjamin Bache, editor of the radical *Philadelphia Aurora*, savaged Washington as "the scourge and misfortune of our country."[76] Perhaps the most venomous criticism came from Thomas Paine, the symbol of egalitarianism. In an open letter to Washington, Paine wrote: "Almost the whole of your administration" was "deceitful if not perfidious." "The world will be puzzled to decide," continued Paine, "whether you are an impostate or an imposter; whether you have abandoned good principles or whether you ever had any."[77]

Individualists did not, however, as they did after Shay's Rebellion, unite with proponents of hierarchy against radical egalitarianism. Rather than accept Washington's hierarchical characterization of the societies as jeopardizing national authority and social order, Madison and Jefferson defined the situation in terms of a challenge to individual liberties. In a ringing defense of free speech and free association, Madison argued before the House that "the censorial power is in the people over the Government, and not in the Government over the people."[78] Jefferson, too, was troubled "that the President should have permitted himself to be the organ of such an attack on the freedom of discussion, the freedom of writing, printing, and publishing."[79] Rather than strengthening the establishment, Washington had galvanized individualist and egalitarian opposition to hierarchy.

Yet, the weakness of hierarchy should not be exaggerated; its strength varied significantly by region. In some areas, particularly in New England, hierarchy remained the dominant political culture. As our theory would lead us to expect, in those states like Massachusetts where hierarchy was most influential, Washington's overt demonstrations of authority, as well as his attention to form and ceremony, did have their intended consequence of strengthening authority. By the same token, where hierarchy's hold was tenuous, as in Pennsylvania, the adverse effects of Washington's actions were most in evidence.

Washington's Farewell Address as a Cultural Solution

In the realm of foreign affairs, Washington was more successful in resolving the Federalist dilemma of a hierarchical regime in a nonhierarchical context. His foreign policy artfully combined a commitment to a strong central government with an appreciation for the limits of authority in the United States. The threat of foreign attack, moreover, was far superior to that of quelling internal insurrection as a justification for increasing the coercive capacities of the national government.[80] To the supporters of hierarchy, foreign affairs presented an opportunity to further their domestic agenda; to egalitarians and individualists, foreign affairs was the Trojan horse through which their preferred way of life might be subverted.

Desiring to promote hierarchical relations domestically, Federalists continually played up threats from abroad. Hamilton was the most vocal of those who were pointing out the vulnerability of the country to foreign attack and intrigue, and the consequent need to increase military defense and strengthen the authority of the national executive. The often-heard maxims that "the genius of republics is pacific" and "the spirit of commerce" extinguishes the passion for war, Hamilton regarded as a "deceitful dream of a golden age."[81] So he tried to minimize the thousands of miles that lay between the United States and Europe, arguing that "improvements in the art of navigation have . . . rendered distant nations in a great measure neighbors." He bolstered his warning against "an excess of confidence or security" by drawing attention to the fact that the new nation was surrounded on the one side by British settlements and on the other by Spanish colonies.[82] Given that "the circumstances that endanger the safety of nations are infinite," Hamilton regarded it as the height of folly "to model our political systems upon speculations of lasting tranquility."[83]

National defense had been a compelling argument for jettisoning the Articles of Confederation in favor of a stronger central government.[84] But having ceded as much authority as they believed necessary to secure the nation from attack, individualists and egalitarians were loath to extend its scope further. Hoping to minimize the need for authority, Jefferson and his followers constantly downplayed the threat posed by foreign nations. Great Britain, argued William Branch Giles on the House floor, was a dying hierarchy "tottering under the weight of a King, a Court, a nobility, a priesthood, armies, navies, debts, and all the complicated machinery of oppression."[85] Involvement in European politics repelled Jeffersonian Republicans because they believed that to give foreign policy the primacy that Hamilton advocated would endanger the Republican domestic agenda of low taxes and minimal government designed to maintain widespread equality.

Foreign policy and domestic policy were tightly coupled throughout Washington's administration. Hamilton's domestic program was financed largely by import duties, and because most trade was with Great Britain, peaceful relations with that nation were a prerequisite to the success of Hamiltonian policies.[86] The Neutrality Proclamation of 1793 was thus a vital link in the Federalist domestic agenda.[87]

When Citizen Edmond Genet arrived in the United States in the spring of 1793 as a special emissary from the newly proclaimed Republic of France, he was greeted with enthusiastic popular applause. Having declared itself at war with all European monarchies, France hoped that sending Genet to the United States would promote American support for the cause of "liberty, equality and fraternity." Although most Federalists were very doubtful that their own revolution could be discerned "in the mirror of French affairs,"[88] Jeffersonians leaped to adopt the French Revolution as akin to their own. "The liberty of the whole earth," gushed Jefferson, hinged on the success of the French armies.[89] Fearing that popular enthusiasm might sweep an unprepared nation into a holy war on behalf of liberty, Washington's response was to issue a Proclamation of Neutrality.

Much of the Republican press was outraged by what it perceived as Washington's betrayal not only of France but of the new nation's own revolutionary principles. "The cause of France is the cause of man," trumpeted the *National Gazette*, "and neutrality is desertion."[90] More moderate Republicans were committed to noninvolvement in the European war but nonetheless were dissatisfied with a policy of total impartiality as well as with the manner in which the policy was announced.[91] Jefferson and Madison were both deeply troubled by what they believed to be Washington's usurpation of the constitutional power of Congress to determine whether the nation was at war or peace.

The Republican leadership might have been placated by assurances that only the extraordinary circumstances of the time had sparked Washington's action. Rather than minimize the exercise of executive power, however, Hamilton used the proclamation as an opportunity to advance an expansive conception of executive prerogative.[92] Hamilton's Pacificus letters turned Republican concern into genuine panic. Jefferson dashed off a letter to Madison: "For God's sake, my dear Sir, take up your pen, select the most striking heresies, and cut him to pieces in the face of the public."[93] With uncharacteristic severity, Madison, under the pen name Helvidius, denounced Hamilton's doctrines as vicious and monarchical.[94] Madison's views were effectively transmitted to the local level. A meeting of citizens in Caroline County, Virginia, for instance, resolved that Washington's proclamation was "a leading step towards assimilating the American government to the form and spirit of the British monarchy."[95]

Popular anti-British sentiments were subsequently fanned by the news that Britain had seized nearly 250 unsuspecting and unarmed American ships in the West Indies. The Republican press urged retaliation; war seemed imminent. Federalists, though anxious to avoid war with Britain, were nonetheless determined that the nation be adequately prepared for that eventuality. Hamilton and his allies in Congress pressed for increased taxes and strengthened armed forces. But although Republicans in Congress were eager to adopt a hard line in terms of commercial restrictions against the British, they still refused to support efforts to strengthen national defense.[96]

These events make clear the leadership dilemma faced by Washington and Hamilton in foreign policy. The basic goal of Hamilton's and Washington's thinking was to increase the government's prestige at home and abroad. Both men supported a strong national defense that would permit the United States, in Washington's words, "to bid defiance to any power on earth."[97] Given the opposition's unwillingness to support a buildup in national defense, however, Washington correctly perceived that involvement in European affairs was far more likely to result in a humiliated national government.

Washington's Farewell Address provided a creative solution to this dilemma. It disarmed the Republican opposition by echoing the familiar warning against "entangling alliances." Republicans could see in these words an affirmation of their isolationism. European struggles were to be avoided, from the Republican point of view, because power politics was the road to corruption, executive aggrandizement, and standing armies. To be drawn into the sordid eighteenth-century game of power politics would tarnish the nation's exemplary status as a city on the hill.

Washington's motivation for warning against becoming embroiled in foreign disputes was radically different. He feared that the new nation, through misfortune or ideological fervor, might be drawn into a war that would thoroughly discredit the new national government. Once the revolutionary "infancy" had passed and the people had gotten over their hostility to standing armies, executive power, central government, taxation, and debt, then and only then, Washington believed, would the United States be able to throw itself into the global scales of power and assume a leading position in the world of nations.[98] In the absence of public support for peacetime preparations, Washington avoided committing U.S. military forces to ventures that might expose the weakness beneath the carefully cultivated appearance of strength.

Here, as elsewhere, Washington revealed a deep appreciation for the weak appeal of authority in the new nation. As president, his fundamental cultural dilemma flowed from the discrepancy between his own hierarchical dispositions and the antihierarchical tendencies of many of his followers. Shoring up national authority was his overriding aim as president; but to do so without looking like a George III proved difficult. One solution that Washington employed was to insure that government, particularly the executive branch, acted only in those areas and circumstances where its authority would not be challenged. Often, however, as during the Whiskey Rebellion, his actions—because they sprang from hierarchical assumptions that conflicted with the antiauthority beliefs of many of his countrymen—proved counterproductive. Washington's action in his second term greatly tarnished his reputation; it could be redeemed only through the route it was gained—by once again relinquishing power.

John Adams: Hierarch without a Hierarchy

If George Washington avoided dealing directly with Congress out of a desire to avoid nonhierarchical relationships, his hierarchical successor, John Adams, followed Washington's example of a hands-off approach toward Congress in the quite different belief that the executive-legislative relationship *was* hierarchical. Washington's often skillful substitution of the appearance of power for the reality seems to have left Adams with the mistaken impression that presidents operate in a hierarchical political system, in which support for presidential authority was not problematic. Where Washington, recognizing that hierarchy was weak in the United States, carefully nurtured support for authority, Adams assumed that support for authority inhered in position.

Adams as president suffered from the same difficulty that plagued him as a political theorist: he underestimated the individualistic bias of the Constitution. The framers had established a government, Adams believed, in which the chief executive was supposed to mediate between the few and the many, the rich and the poor, the gentlemen and the simplemen, the Senate and the House. The pivot of conflict was not between the legislative and executive branches of government but, rather, between the unequal social classes represented in the upper and lower houses. Solomon-like, the president, perched atop this hierarchical structure, was responsible for keeping the peace by arbitrating between the parts in the name of the whole.[99]

Although disappointed that the Constitution gave the Senate the right to consent to executive appointments and denied the president an absolute veto,[100] Adams nevertheless was much impressed with the great formal power of the president. Adams believed the Constitution to be modeled on the British example, though purged of its "corruption," i.e. executive influence in the legislature.[101] The framers, wrote Adams approvingly, had created "a monarchical republic, or if you will, a limited monarchy. . . . [The president's] power during those four years is much greater than that of an avoyer, a consul, a podestà, a doge, a stadtholder; nay, than a king of Poland; nay, than a King of Sparta. I know of no first magistrate in any republican government, excepting England and Neuchatel, who possesses a constitutional dignity, authority, and power comparable to his."[102]

Adams, in other words, believed mistakenly that the Constitution had established a hierarchical government in which power inhered in position. The framers, however, rather than placing the executive atop a hierarchical government, had (in Edward Corwin's famous phrase) issued the executive "an invitation to struggle" with the legislature.[103] To achieve objectives, the system required that the president enter the fray.

Are Adam's theories relevant to a study of his presidency? Historian Joseph Charles has commented that "Adams seems to have followed his theories instead of letting them be framed by his experience."[104] We intend to demonstrate that, as president, Adams did act on his beliefs about the nature of the political system; more specifically, he acted as if he were indeed a hierarch atop a hierarchical system.

Jean Holder contends that Adams's reliance on formal, constitutional powers provides "an ideal test case for evaluating recent arguments concerning the sources of presidential power." Where Richard Neustadt asserts that being president grants merely a ticket to the White House door, Richard Pious's thesis is that presidential power rests "on the successful assertion of constitutional authority." Holder contrasts these views, declaring that Adams's success—in spite of his neglect of what Neustadt identifies as the power to persuade and bargain—vindicates Pious's contention as to the nature of presidential power.[105]

We agree with Holder that Adams did neglect the political tools of bargaining and persuasion, but it is less clear to us that Adams's presidency was the success that she ranks it. He did achieve his objective of avoiding war with France, but the meaning of that "victory" is misleading. In both the 1948 and 1962 Schlesinger surveys, Adams received a ranking of Near Great status. But Thomas Bailey's sober reevaluation of Adams's presidential greatness comes, in our view, much closer to the mark: "If a rating is called for, no higher than Below Average."[106] After all, in the first thirty-six years of the republic, Adams was the only president to be defeated for reelection—a defeat that, according to Adams's biographer, Page Smith, "inflicted a raw wound that would never entirely heal."[107] By looking at his French policy, we shall show how even in the area that Adams considered his greatest success,[108] the assumption that he was atop a hierarchal system frustrated his efforts.

The most important political decision of Adams's presidency came on February 18, 1799, when he named William Vans Murray as minister plenipotentiary to France. The result of this appointment was an irreparable fracture in the Federalist party that, in turn, was instrumental in Adams's defeat in 1800.[109] Murray's appointment was, as Joseph Charles writes, "an act of political suicide."[110] Why and how Adams made this decision reveals much about the dilemma of a hierarch without a hierarchy.

The president's decision to reopen negotiations with the French took the entire nation, Federalist and Republican, by surprise. No one—not the cabinet, not Congress, not even personal counselors—had been informed, let alone consulted, about the decision.[111] Adams did not view his decision as a policy for which he needed to seek support among competing political actors; rather, it was the wisest policy for the nation and therefore should be carried out. If authority inheres in the position there is no need to persuade people; nor to make it in their interest to support you.

The Federalist party was thrown into disarray (France, after all, stood for social leveling and disorder) and immediately lashed out at the president. Longtime defenders of the president hurled abuse at him.[112] Cabinet members quickly ran for cover, assuring friends that they had no part in the "insane" action.[113] The Federalists are "graveled and divided," Jefferson observed, with understandable satisfaction, "some are for opposing, others know not what to do." In a letter to her husband, Abigail Adams confirmed that "nobody had their story ready; some called it a hasty measure; others condemned it as an inconsistent one; some swore, some cursed."[114]

Adams's defenders have contended that because he did not have the loyalty of his cabinet, he was forced to keep his own counsel. But why did he not have a cabinet that was personally loyal to him? The usual list of excuses—reluctance to disturb his predecessor's arrangements; fear that given the low pay and heavy duties, he could not find other competent men to serve—all avoid the unavoidable. Adams did not place a premium on personal loyalty to the president because he assumed that power inhered in the office. We are back then to the hierarch without a hierarchy.

To understand Federalist confusion and rage, one must back up a few years. Deteriorating relations with France dominated Adams's tenure as president. In an attempt to improve relations and prevent an undeclared naval war from becoming full-fledged combat, Adams, with the full support of Hamilton—both knowing full well that the United States was not militarily prepared to fight—sent a distinguished three-man commission to France. Once in Paris, the commissioners were spurned and humiliated by the Directory, which was not eager to settle a lucrative quasi-war in which the French were free to seize neutral American ships and cargo.

When the American public learned about how the French had treated their ministers (including Talleyrand's attempt to elicit a bribe as a prerequisite to negotiations), a wave of patriotic outrage swept the new nation: "Millions for defense but not one cent for tribute." The XYZ affair—so dubbed because President Adams's report to Congress designated the three Talleyrand agents who approached the U.S. plenipotentiaries as X, Y, and Z—paved the way for public acquiescence in the military buildup that Adams and the Federalists hitherto had pushed with only limited success. The French insults to American pride, writes John Miller, raised President Adams and the Federalist Party "to the pinnacle of their popularity with the American people."[115] "Formerly all but ignored by the people," comments another historian, "Adams was now wildly cheered whenever he appeared in public."[116] A fearful nation well served the Federalists, as the party of a strong national authority; Adams and the Federalists milked it for all it was worth.

Publication of the X,Y,Z dispatches in April 1798 had completely disorganized the Republican party and given a tremendous shot in the arm to the Federalist party's electoral fortunes and to its domestic agenda of defense measures, tax increases, and security acts. Several congressional Republicans were so demoralized that they quit the capital city, leaving the triumphant Federalists in control of Congress.[117] Now, less than a year later and without warning, Adams swept the ground out from under the Federalists' feet by suddenly announcing his intention to send another peace mission to France.

Adams's defenders have accepted the president's own definition of his action: a courageous and wise act of statecraft, opting for the good of the country (peace, not war) over party politics.[118] But this rationale also accepts Adams's premise that the national interest and the party interest could not be served at the same time. It ignores the fact that within the year the French and British had ceased fighting; a policy of "muddling through" might therefore have avoided war and kept the party together. This rationale, which also accepts Adams's view of the "Arch Federalists" as a faction panting for war with the French, neglects France's extreme unwillingness to engage the United States in war. Moreover, though Adams believed deeply in the necessity of a strong navy, his decision, by dividing the Federalist party, allowed the Jeffersonians to come to power and virtually dismantle the fledgling navy. The courageous Adams rising above partisan gain makes for good melodrama but poor history.

Why disorient your own party and aid the opposition? The battle between the French and the British, and between Federalists and Republicans, Adams subsumed under his view of politics as a conflict between the social orders of the national hierarchy. His task as the hierarch was to act in the name of the whole in order to keep the parts from making war on each other. In the absence of a hierarch "to appeal to for decision," Adams believed, "no contest could be decided but by the sword."[119] By early 1799 Adams was persuaded that the conflict between Federalists and Republicans over how to regard France—as the source of subversion, leveling, and irreligion or as the bastion of liberty and equality—was in danger of erupting into civil war, and therefore required the intervention of an impartial moderator.[120] Despite fully sharing the Federalist party's fear that the French Revolution had unleashed passions that, as he wrote to his son John Quincy, "would produce anarchy among us,"[121] President Adams's conception of himself as a hierarch dictated the decision to undercut his own party.

Outraged at Adams's decision to send a peace envoy to France, a committee of leading Federalist senators called upon the president and pleaded with him to withdraw the nomination. Adams rejected their appeal on the grounds (according to one of the petitioners, Theodore Sedgwick) "that to defend the executive against oligarchic influence, it was indispensable that he should insist on a decision on the nomination."[122] The president's perception that a private appeal from members of his own party constituted an "oligarchic" challenge to executive independence and integrity stemmed, in part, from his conception of the chief executive as a hierarch who sits above the battle, mediating between the intrigue of the aristocrats and the licentiousness of the democrats. It was this conception of the presidential role, we contend, that led Adams to conclude that he had to sacrifice his party in order to save his office.

Adams's hierarchical theory of governing was at odds with a constitutional design that demanded the president bargain with competing political actors. Ralph Adams Brown sums up (approvingly) Adams's view of the presidency "as a lonely and difficult search for the correct answers, the best decisions and actions."[123] A parallel with the presidency of Jimmy Carter immediately suggests itself. Carter's former speech-writer, James Fallows, complained that "he thinks he 'leads' by choosing the correct policy."[124] Because what mattered was the correct policy, Carter, like Adams, repeatedly made decisions without consulting or warning others. Carter, for instance, announced that he wanted to cut funds for various water projects around the country without prior consultation with anyone in Congress. Only a week later, he raised another political firestorm within his party by announcing, again without consulting anyone, that he was withdrawing a promised $50 tax rebate.[125] Believing that authority inhered in position, Carter, like Adams, behaved as if he were a hierarch in a hierarchical political system.

Both Adams and Carter failed to gain reelection, in large part, we contend, because their hierarchical conceptions of the nature of the presidential office were at odds with the antihierarchical character of the political system. Their Solomon-like pronouncements repeatedly surprised and disarmed their natural friends and allies. Although Adams and Carter did inherit parties with important divisions, their behavior consistently brought those divisions to the fore. For both men, the divided nature of the party—rooted in large part in the party elite's personal distrust of the incumbent—was pivotal in their electoral losses.

If Adams's narrow defeat in 1800 was by no means inevitable, the demise of the Federalist party perhaps was. Adams later explained his loss and the collapse of the Federalists in terms of the willful spite of the Arch Federalists,[126] revealing again his underestimation of the weakness of hierarchy in the United States. Adams could never see that the Federalist party ceased to exist in large part because its hierarchical propensities were out of tune with the prevailing antiauthority ethos. In proposing the peace mission to France, Adams saw himself as adjusting the balance in favor of the "simplemen" to compensate for the increased power of the gentlemen. But this was not Europe. The last thing the Federalists needed was a chief executive adjusting the scales to advantage the antihierarchical cultures. The rapid disintegration of the Federalist party after the Jeffersonians came to power in 1800 revealed just how tenuous hierarchy's grip on power had been.

Notes

1. In the 1948 and 1962 Schlesinger polls, Washington finished second to Lincoln. Thomas A. Bailey, however, places Washington ahead of Lincoln in the premier position; *Presidential Greatness: The Image and the Man from George Washington to the Present* (New York: Appleton-Century, 1966), pp. 24-25, 267-69.
2. G. S. Boritt, *Lincoln and the Economics of the American Dream* (Memphis: Memphis State University Press, 1978), pp. 301-2.
3. Marcus Cunliffe, *George Washington: Man and Monument* (Boston: Little, Brown, 1958), p. 212.
4. Barry Schwartz, "George Washington and the Whig Conception of Heroic Leadership," *American Sociological Review* (February 1983): 18-33, quotation on p. 20. Also see Barry Schwartz, *George Washington: The Making of an American Symbol* (New York: Free Press, 1987).
5. Schwartz, "Whig Conception of Heroic Leadership," pp. 23, 26-27.
6. Washington to President of Congress, December 20, 1776, in Saul K. Padover, ed., *The Washington Papers* (New York: Grosset & Dunlap, 1955), p. 100.
7. Circular Letter to the Governors of All the States on Disbanding the Army, June 8, 1783, ibid., pp. 206, 213.
8. See e.g. letters to Archibald Cary, June 15, 1782; to Robert Stewart, August 10, 1783; to Lafayette, February 1, 1784; to James Madison, May 20, 1792; to David Humphries, June 12, 1796; to Henry Knox, March 2, 1797; and to Oliver Wolcott, May 15, 1797; ibid., pp. 78, 79, 83, 88, 90, 91, 92, quotation on p. 83.
9. Schwartz, "Whig Conception of Heroic Leadership," p. 19.
10. Ibid., p. 27. Barry Schwartz, "The Character of Washington: A Study in Republican Culture," *American Quarterly* (Summer 1986): 207.
11. Schwartz, "Character of Washington," pp. 207-8. Schwartz, "Whig Conception of Heroic Leadership," passim,," passim, quotation on p. 26.
12. Schwartz, "Whig Conception of Heroic Leadership," p. 30.
13. David Hackett Fischer, *The Revolution of American Conservatism: The Federalist Party in the Era of Jeffersonian Democracy* (New York: Harper & Row, 1965), pp. 377-78.
14. On the hierarchical propensities of the Federalists, see James M. Banner, Jr., *To the Hartford Convention: The Federalists and the Origins of Party Politics in Massachusetts, 1789-1815* (New York: Knopf, 1970), esp. ch. 2; David Hackett Fischer, "The Myth of the Essex Junto," *William and Mary Quarterly* (April 1964): 191-235; David Hackett Fischer, *Revolution of American Conservatism*, ch. 1 and Appendix 2; and Linda Kerber, *Federalists in Dissent: Imagery and Ideology in Jeffersonian America* (Ithaca: Cornell University Press, 1970), esp. ch. 6.

We offer here a sampling of Federalist values and beliefs, taken from Banner's study of Massachusetts Federalism, that we have coded as expressions of a hierarchical propensity. We consider them as evidence of a hierarchical disposition because they voice a preoccupation with organic or familial metaphors of the body politic, with the sacrifice of parts for the whole, with fixed relationships among unequal and interdependent members of society, or with such themes of harmony, stability, order, and deference.

The social body is composed of various members, mutually connected and dependent. Though some may be deemed less honorable, they may not be less necessary than others. As the eye, the ear, the hand, the foot of the human body, cannot say to the other, I have no need of you, but all in their respective places have indispensable uses; so in the Commonwealth, each citizen has some gift or function, by which he may become a contributor to the support and pleasure of the whole body (p. 53).

In all societies some must be uppermost. The levellers only change and pervert the natural order of things (p. 54).

Distinctions of rank and condition in life are requisite to the perfection of the social state. There must be rulers and subjects, masters and servants, rich and poor. The human body is not perfect without all its members, some of which are more honorable than others; so it is with the body politic (p. 57).

It has pleased God "to place mankind in different stations and to distinguish them from each other by a diversity of rank, power, and talent" (p. 57).

Order is the glory of the universe. The excellence of creation results from the subordination of the parts to the whole. Revolving worlds move in obedience to fixed laws. In civil government, the people obey, the magistrates rule, and order and security follows (p. 57).

The Federalist preference for hierarchical social relations was evident in all areas of life, from politics to the family to schools. Banner writes: "The best place, thought Federalists, to initiate this training in deference was in the tightly regulated and patriarchal family circle, where age differences assumed the same significance as distinctions between social classes in the general society. Children must be taught to honor and obey their elders, control their whims, and restrain their youthful energies in the general interest of the whole household. It was within the home that the growing child must first be exposed to the necessary distinctions among men and taught that only a few possess the privilege to rule." And so in Federalist families it was common for children to bow before their parents and address them by a deferential "Honored Papa" and "Honored Mama" (pp. 55-56).

"Habits of subordination" were also to be taught in school. "It is necessary," wrote Jonathon Jackson, "to pay great attention to the education of the youth; teaching them their just rights, at the same time they are taught proper subordination." The people, echoed another writer, "must be taught to confide in and reverence their rulers." "It is not enough," reasoned another, "to teach children to read and write, and understand the first rules of arithmetic; it is also of importance to habituate them to restraint." A Federalist minister concluded that the whole purpose of education of children was "to inculcate on their expanding minds the necessity of sub-ordination and obedience to their superiors" (pp. 55-56; Fischer, "Essex Junto," p. 210).

The Massachusetts Federalists quoted above closely resemble the pure type of hierarchy. Not all of those who called themselves Federalists were this extreme (or articulate). Political parties are, after all, coalitions that inevitably house considerable ideological diversity. Other members of the party—like John Marshall—tried to blend their preference for hierarchy with a preference for the individualist values of social mobility and competition. Yet having conceded this much, we believe that an adherence to hierarchical social relations—the defense of structured inequality, the preoccupation with social order and solidarity, and so on—was the dominant tendency of the Federalist party elite (see Fischer, *Revolution of American Conservatism*, Appendix 2).

15. Fischer, *Revolution of American Conservatism*, p. 379.
16. Hamilton, cited in Dumas Malone, *Jefferson the President: First Term, 1801-1805* (Boston: Little, Brown, 1970), p. 104.
17. Jonathon Jackson, quoted in Banner, *Hartford Convention*, p. 58. See also Gordon S. Wood, *The Creation of the American Republic, 1776-1787* (Chapel Hill: University of North Carolina Press), pp. 391-564.
18. James Thomas Flexner, *George Washington and the New Nation, 1783-1793* (Boston: Little, Brown, 1969), pp. 221, 403. See also Forrest McDonald, *The Presidency of George Washington* (Lawrence: University Press of Kansas, 1974), pp. 78, 184.
19. Ibid., p. 399. Also see Leonard D. White, *The Federalists: A Study in Administrative History* (New York: Macmillan, 1948), p. 37.
20. White, *The Federalists*, p. 27.
21. Ibid., pp. 30-31, quotation on p. 30.
22. McDonald, *Presidency of Washington*, p. 28.
23. Flexner, *Washington and the New Nation*, p. 403.
24. James David Barber, *The Presidential Character: Predicting Performance in the White House* (Englewood Cliffs, N.J.: Prentice-Hall, 1972), p. 13.
25. McDonald, *Presidency of Washington*, p. 133.
26. Richard H. Kohn, *Eagle and Sword: The Federalists and the Creation of the Military Establishment in America, 1783-1802* (New York: Free Press, 1975); Francis Paul Prucha, *The Sword of the Republic* (Lincoln: University of Nebraska Press, 1986).
27. Forrest McDonald, *Alexander Hamilton: A Biography* (New York: Norton, 1979), p. 128. Also see White, *The Federalists*, pp. 27, 31-35, 106.
28. William Maclay, cited in Morton Borden, "George Washington," in *America's Ten Greatest Presidents*, ed. Morton Borden (Chicago: Rand McNally, 1961), p. 9.
29. Flexner, *Washington and the New Nation*, p. 252.
30. McDonald, *Alexander Hamilton*, p. 129.
31. James D. Savage, *Balanced Budgets and American Politics* (Ithaca: Cornell University Press, 1988), p. 95. See also McDonald, *Alexander Hamilton*, pp. 117-210, esp. p. 159.
32. Flexner, *Washington and the New Nation*, p. 238.
33. Hamilton, quoted ibid., p. 243; see also pp. 248-50.
34. Ibid., p. 249.
35. McDonald, *Presidency of Washington*, p. 65.
36. Joseph Charles, *The Origins of the American Party System* (New York: Harper & Row, 1961), p. 39.
37. *The Life and Selected Writings of Thomas Jefferson*, ed. Adrienne Koch and William Peden (New York: Modern Library, 1944), p. 123. Also see Flexner, *Washington and the New Nation*, p. 246.

38. Charles, *Origins of American Party System*, p. 38. Charles comes to the opposing conclusion.
39. In making federal appointments, for instance, Washington's criterion was to nominate those who ''would give dignity and lustre'' to the government (quoted in White, *The Federalists*, p. 259). When those he selected turned down government posts—as they frequently did—Washington's primary concern was that government prestige would suffer (Flexner, *Washington and New Nation*, p. 224). Before announcing appointments for the Supreme Court, Washington was careful to gain assurances that the nominee would accept the post so as to avoid the government's being embarrassed by a candidate's refusing to serve (James R. Perry, ''Supreme Court Appointments, 1789-1801: Criteria, Presidential Style, and the Press of Events,'' *Journal of the Early Republic* (Winter 1986): 371-410, esp. pp. 373, 397).
40. Seymour Martin Lipset, *The First New Nation: The United States in Historical and Comparative Perspective* (New York: Basic Books, 1963), pp. 16-23. The quotation is from Max Weber, *Economy and Society*, ed. Guenther Roth and Claus Wittich (Berkeley: University of California Press, 1978), p. 1115. On charisma as a substitute for authority, see Aaron Wildavsky, *The Nursing Father: Moses as a Political Leader* (University: University of Alabama Press, 1984); and Richard Ellis, ''A Theory of Charismatic Leadership in Organizations,'' IGS Studies in Public Organization, Working Paper No. 86-2.
41. Ralph Ketcham, *Presidents above Party: The First American Presidency, 1789-1829* (Chapel Hill: University of North Carolina Press, 1984), p. 91.
42. Page Smith, *John Adams, Volume II: 1784-1826* (Garden City, N.Y.: Doubleday, 1962), pp. 750-58, esp. pp. 754-55. Also see White, *The Federalists*, p. 108 f30.
43. White, *The Federalists*, p. 108; McDonald, *Presidency of Washington*, p. 29.
44. Smith, *John Adams*, p. 758; Irving Brant, *The Fourth President: A Life of James Madison* (Indianapolis: Bobbs-Merrill, 1970), p. 228; Ralph Ketcham, *James Madison: A Biography* (New York: Macmillan, 1971), p. 285.
45. Smith, *John Adams*, p. 758.
46. Richard Buel, Jr., *Securing the Revolution: Ideology in American Politics, 1789-1815* (Ithaca: Cornell University Press, 1972), p. 156.
47. Jefferson to Madison, June 9, 1793, cited in James Thomas Flexner, *George Washington: Anguish and Farewell, 1793-1799* (Boston: Little, Brown, 1969), pp. 46-47. In March of the same year, Freneau's *Gazette* referred to Washington's birthday celebration as a ''monarchical farce'' (McDonald, *Presidency of Washington*, p. 132).
48. Victor A. Thompson, *Modern Organization* (New York: Knopf, 1961), esp. ch. 7. The terminology and idea are borrowed from Erving Goffman's seminal study, *The Presentation of Self in Everyday Life* (Garden City, N.Y.: Doubleday, 1959).
49. Thompson, *Modern Organization*, pp. 161-63.
50. James Hart, *The American Presidency in Action, 1789: A Study in Constitutional History* (New York: Macmillan, 1948), p. 15; Flexner, *Washington and the New Nation*, p. 196.
51. Schwartz, *George Washington, p. 59.*
52. *Thompson, Modern Organization*, pp. 164-65.
53. Flexner, *Washington and the New Nation*, p. 230; Hart, *Presidency in Action*, pp. 18-20.

54. James Morton Smith, *Freedom's Fetters: The Alien and Sedition Laws and American Civil Liberties* (Ithaca: Cornell University Press, 1956), pp. 270-74. Buel, *Securing the Revolution*, p. 156.

55. Jefferson and Washington, quoted in White, *The Federalists*, pp. 67, 13. For an extreme example of the Federalist concern over executive impotence, see Fisher Ames's letter to Hamilton, ibid., pp. 93-94.

56. James Roger Sharp, "The Whiskey Rebellion and the Question of Representation," in *The Whiskey Rebellion: Past and Present Perspectives*, ed. Steven R. Boyd (Westport, Conn.: Greenwood Press, 1985), pp. 119-33, quotation on page 124. Zephaniah Smith agreed that "the suppression of this insurrection will give the Government of the United States a tone, an energy, and dignity, which will defy all the efforts of Anarchy and Jacobinism" (Alexander DeConde, *Entangling Alliances: Politics and Diplomacy under George Washington* [Durham: Duke University Press, 1958], p. 46).

57. For an analysis of this phenomenon in modern hierarchical organizations, see Martin Landau and Russell Stout, Jr., "To Manage Is Not to Control: Or the Folly of Type II Errors," *Public Administration Review* (March/April 1979): 148-56. For representative samples of Washington's attitude, see John C. Fitzpatrick, ed., *The Writings of George Washington, 1745-1799* (Washington, D.C., 1931-1944), 33: 463, 464, 475, 506; J. A. Carroll and M. W. Ashworth, *George Washington: First in Peace* (New York: Scribner's, 1957), p. 182.

58. Richard Kohn, "The Washington Administration's Decision to Crush the Whiskey Rebellion," *Journal of American History* (December 1972): 567-84, quotation on p. 571.

59. Washington, quoted in Carroll and Ashworth, *First in Peace*, p. 181; Fitzpatrick, *Writings*, 33: 523. See also Kohn, "Whiskey Rebellion," p. 573.

60. McDonald, *Alexander Hamilton*, p. 301. In his sixth annual address, Washington expressed the fear that the government's activity with respect to the Whiskey Rebellion would "create an opinion of impotency or irresolution in the Government" (Padover, *Washington Papers*, p. 286).

61. Washington, quoted in Kohn, "Whiskey Rebellion," p. 573. For examples of Washington's correspondence, see Fitzpatrick, *Writings*, 33: 463, 506.

62. For the argument that Hamilton's "primary goal" was "to avoid the use of force," see McDonald, *Alexander Hamilton*, p. 432. The opposite argument, that Hamilton "yearned to smite the rebels with the full force of the army," is presented in John C. Miller, *The Federalist Era, 1789-1801* (New York: Harper & Row, 1960), p. 158.

63. Miller, *Federalist Era*, p. 158; Thomas P. Slaughter, "The Friends of Liberty, the Friends of Order, and the Whiskey Rebellion: A Historiographical Essay," in *Whiskey Rebellion: Past and Present Perspectives*, ed. Steven R. Boyd (Westport, Conn.: Greenwood Press, 1985), p. 10.

64. See Carroll and Ashworth, *First in Peace*, pp. 198-213, for a description of "the impressive march of men" (p. 208).

65. Miller, *Federalist Era*, pp. 157-58; Ralph Adams Brown, *The Presidency of John Adams*, (Lawrence: University Press of Kansas, 1975), p. 127. Hamilton's comment was actually in response to Fries' Rebellion in 1799.

66. Miller, *Federalist Era*, p. 159.

67. Sixth annual address, November 19, 1794, in *Padover, Washington Papers*, pp. 285-91, quotation on p. 285.

68. Hamilton and Ames, quoted in Miller, *Federalist Era*, p. 159.

69. Dumas Malone, *Jefferson and the Ordeal of Liberty* (Boston: Little, Brown, 1962), pp. 188-89.

70. Madison, quoted in Ketcham, *Madison*, p. 354. Jefferson's and Madison's critical attitude toward the government's display of military power is pointed out in Richard E. Ellis, *The Jeffersonian Crisis: Courts and Politics in the Young Republic* (New York: Oxford University Press, 1971), p. 273; and Morton Borden, *Parties and Politics in the Early Republic, 1789-1815* (Arlington Heights, Ill., AHM, 1967), p. 28.

71. Flexner, *Washington: Anguish and Farewell*, p. 191. On the failure of the government's actions to increase support for the government, see Miller, *Federalist Era*, p. 159; and Smith, *John Adams*, p. 862.

72. Flexner, *Washington: Anguish and Farewell*, pp. 182-92; quotations on pp. 183-84, 191, 182. The actual connection between these Democratic Societies and the Whiskey Rebellion has been a subject of some debate among historians. There were three active Democratic Societies in western Pennsylvania, and some of the leaders of these societies were prominent in the rebellion. On the other hand, not only did many members of Democratic societies volunteer for service against the rebels but resistance to the excise tax predated the appearance of these societies (Miller, *Federalist Era*, p. 161). For a thorough examination of this question—which comes to the conclusion that the insurrection was not inspired by Democratic Societies—see William Miller, "Democratic Societies and the Whiskey Insurrection," *Pennsylvania Magazine of History and Biography* (July 1938): 324-49.

73. Miller, *Federalist Era*, p. 162; Flexner, *Washington: Anguish and Farewell*, p. 192.

74. Flexner, *Washington: Anguish and Farewell*, p. 191. Flexner labels Washington's decision to attack the societies "the most divisive of all the personal acts he engaged in during his entire Presidential career" (p. 181). Earlier, when he was part of the cabinet, Jefferson had warned Washington that to attack the Democratic Societies would be "calculated to make the President assume the station of the head of a party instead of the head of the nation" (p. 191).

75. Washington delivered the address on November 15, 1794. Hamilton formally announced his resignation on December 1, effective January 31, 1795.

76. Miller, *Federalist Era*, p. 233.

77. Flexner, *Washington: Anguish and Farewell*, p. 324.

78. Miller, *Federalist Era*, p. 162.

79. Flexner, *Washington: Anguish and Farewell*, p. 191.

80. Gerald Stourzh, *Alexander Hamilton and the Idea of Republican Government* (Stanford: Stanford University Press, 1970). p. 164.

81. *The Federalist*, No. 6; Stourzh, *Alexander Hamilton*, pp. 148-53. Ten years later Hamilton referred to "the phantom of perpetual peace [that] danced before the eyes of everybody" at the close of the Revolution (ibid., p. 255, f 88).

82. *The Federalist*, No. 24; Stourzh, *Alexander Hamilton*, p. 165.

83. Stourzh, *Alexander Hamilton*, pp. 161-64.

84. Frederick W. Marks III, "Foreign Affairs: A Winning Issue in the Campaign for Ratification of the United States Constitution," *Political Science Quarterly* (September 1971): 444-69.

85. Drew R. McCoy, *The Elusive Republic: Political Economy in Jeffersonian America* (Chapel Hill: University of North Carolina Press, 1980), p. 141.

86. DeConde, *Entangling Alliances*, pp. 46-47. See also Charles, *Origins of American Party System*, pp. 13, 30-31; Paul A. Varg, *Foreign Policies of the Founding Fathers* (Lansing: Michigan State University Press, 1963), pp. 77-78; McCoy, *Elusive Republic*, p. 198; Buel, *Securing the Revolution*, p. 92; McDonald, *Presidency of Washington*, p. 119; McDonald, *Alexander Hamilton*,

p. 269; Banning, *The Jeffersonian Persuasion: Evolution of a Party Ideology* (Ithaca: Cornell University Press, 1978), ch. 8, esp. pp. 212-14.

87. DeConde, *Entangling Alliances*, p. 47. "The funding system is the Declaration of Neutrality," proclaimed one Republican (Banning, *Jeffersonian Persuasion*, p. 226).

88. Hamilton wrote: "The cause of France is compared with that of America during its late revolution. Would to Heaven that the comparison were just. Would to Heaven we could discern in the mirror of French affairs the same humanity, the same decorum, the same gravity, the same order, the same dignity, the same solemnity, which distinguished the cause of the American Revolution. . . . I own I do not like the comparison" (Richard B. Morris, ed., *Alexander Hamilton and the Founding of the Nation*, [New York: Dial Press, 1957], p. 407).

89. Jefferson to William Short, January 3, 1793, cited in Gilbert Lycan, *Alexander Hamilton and American Foreign Policy: A Design for Greatness* (Norman: University of Oklahoma Press, 1970), p. 134. Also see Banning, *Jeffersonian Persuasion*, pp. 211-12; DeConde, *Entangling Alliances*, pp. 178-179.

90. Banning, *Jeffersonian Persuasion*, p. 212.

91. Ibid., p. 213; Miller, *Federalist Era*, p. 130.

92. Clinton Rossiter, *Alexander Hamilton and the Constitution* (New York: Harcourt, Brace & World, 1964), pp. 213-14; Edward S. Corwin, *The President: Office and Powers, 1787-1957* (New York: New York University Press, 1957), pp. 179-80.

93. Miller, *Federalist Era*, p. 131.

94. Banning, *Jeffersonian Persuasion*, p. 217.

95. Ibid., p. 213. Also see Carroll and Ashworth, *First in Peace*, p. 53.

96. Banning, *Jeffersonian Persuasion*, p. 222; Miller, *Federalist Era*, p. 148; Lycan, *Hamilton and Foreign Policy*, p. 213; McDonald, *Alexander Hamilton*, pp. 268-69.

97. Burton Ira Kaufman, "Washington's Farewell Address: A Statement of Empire," in *Washington's Farewell Address: The View from the 20th Century*, ed. Kaufman, (Chicago: Quadrangle Books, 1969), p. 183.

98. Washington's hope for the United States to assume a respected position in the world of nations is pointed out in DeConde, *Entangling Alliances*, p. 48; and Harold W. Bradley, "The Political Thinking of George Washington," *Journal of Southern History* (February 1945): 472. Washington apparently envisioned about a twenty-year period of "infancy" (Kaufman, "Washington's Farewell Address," p. 183), while Hamilton, in the Camillus letters, expressed the belief that the nation needed to "avoid a war for ten or twelve years" before "a higher and more imposing tone" could be adopted (Morris, *Hamilton and the Founding*, p. 385). Also see Stourzh, *Alexander Hamilton*, p. 198-99.

99. See Gordon Wood, "The Relevance and Irrelevance of John Adams," chapter 14 in *The Creation of the American Republic 1776–1787* (Chapel Hill: University of North Carolina Press, 1969), pp. 567-92; George A. Peek, Jr., "Introduction," *The Political Writings of John Adams: Representative Selections* (Indianapolis: Bobbs-Merrill, 1954), p. xix; Peter Shaw, *The Character of John Adams* (Chapel Hill: University of North Carolina Press, 1976), p. 247.

100. Peek, *Political Writings*, p. xix. Joyce Appleby, "The New Republican Synthesis and the Changing Political Ideas of John Adams," *American Quarterly* (December 1973): 586.

101. Charles, *Origins of American Party System*, p. 65.

102. Corwin, *The President: Office and Powers, 1787-1957* (New York), p. 317.

103. Ibid., p. 171.
104. Charles, *Origins of American Party System*, p. 65.
105. Jean S. Holder, "The Sources of Presidential Power: John Adams and the Challenge to Executive Primacy," *Political Science Quarterly* (1986): 601-2, 615.
106. Bailey, *Presidential Greatness*, p. 271.
107. Smith, *John Adams*, p. 1056. It will not do, as Holder wishes, to dismiss the significance of Adams's failure to gain reelection on the grounds that "popularity had never been his primary goal" ("Sources of Presidential Power" p. 616), for, as Richard Kohn demonstrates, whatever his professions, "Adams ran and ran hard for reelection" (Richard H. Kohn, *Eagle and Sword: The Federalists and the Creation of the Military Establishment in America, 1783-1802* [New York: Free Press, 1975, p. 266]).
108. Adams suggested for his epitaph: "Here lies John Adams, who took upon himself the responsibility of peace with France in the year 1800" (Bailey, *Presidential Greatness*, p. 269).
109. On the decision's divisive impact on the party see, e.g., Stephen G. Kurtz, "The French Mission of 1799-1800: Concluding Chapter in the Statecraft of John Adams," *Political Science Quarterly* (December 1965): 543. Page Smith argues that the division among the Federalists was "the basic cause of Adams' defeat" (Smith, *John Adams*, p. 1058).
110. Charles, *Origins of American Party System*, p. 62.
111. Similarly, Adams had nominated Washington as commander in chief of the New Army without consulting anyone or even obtaining the former president's prior approval (McDonald, *Alexander Hamilton*, p. 341). Lack of consultation is also evident in Adams's method of appointing justices to the Supreme Court. In marked contrast to George Washington, writes James Perry, "Adams did not consult with advisers, communicate with individuals knowledgeable about proposed candidates, or contact the candidates themselves." Because he did not consult members of Congress, Adams's nominees often ran into difficulty in the Senate (Perry, "Supreme Court Appointments, 1789-1801," esp. pp. 398, 400, 410; quotation on p. 398).
112. Smith, *John Adams*, p. 1000.
113. Stephen G. Kurtz, "John Adams," in *America's Ten Greatest Presidents*, ed. Morton Borden, (Chicago: Rand McNally, 1961), p. 49.
114. Smith, *John Adams*, p. 1000.
115. Miller, *Federalist Era*, p. 210. See also Brown, *Presidency of John Adams*, pp. 52-53.
116. Thomas M. Ray, " 'Not One Cent For Tribute': The Public Addresses and American Popular Reaction to the XYZ Affair, 1798-1799," *Journal of the Early American Republic* (Winter 1983): 389-412, quotation on p. 390.
117. Ibid., p. 391.
118. See, for example, Brown, *Presidency of John Adams*, p. 120.
119. Adams, quoted in Peek, *Political Writings*, p. xix.
120. Kurtz, "The French Mission," esp. pp. 543, 551-52.
121. On Adams's hostility to the French Revolution, see Smith, *John Adams*, pp. 797, 810, 831; Adams quoted on p. 831. On Adams's hierarchical dispositions more generally, see Peek, *Political Writings*, esp. pp. xv-xvi; Appleby, "New Republican Synthesis," esp. pp. 585-88; Clinton Rossiter, *Conservatism in America: The Thankless Persuasion* (New York: Vintage Books, 1962), pp. 110-15; and Russell Kirk, *The Conservative Mind* (Chicago: Regnery, 1953), pp. 80-129.

122. Bruce Miroff, "John Adams' Classical Conception of the Executive," *Presidential Studies Quarterly* (Spring 1987): 365-82; Sedgwick quoted on p. 376.
123. Brown, *Presidency of Adams*, p. 215.
124. James Fallows, "The Passionless Presidency: The Trouble with Jimmy Carter's Administration," *Atlantic Monthly* (May 1979): 33-58, quotation on pp. 42-43. See also Nelson W. Polsby, *Congress and the Presidency* (Englewood Cliffs, N.J.: Prentice-Hall, 1986), p. 60.
125. Haynes Johnson, *In the Absence of Power: Governing America* (New York: Viking, 1980), pp. 158, 161.
126. Years later, Adams bitterly recounted how "the [Federalist] party committed suicide; they killed themselves and the national president (not their president) at one shot" (Adams to James Lloyd, February 6, 1815, cited in Kurtz, "The French Mission," p. 552).

4

Leadership Dilemmas
in an Antiauthority Regime:
Thomas Jefferson and James Madison

The ideology of the Republican party was conceived and developed in opposition. Jeffersonians were heavily indebted to "Country" opposition
spokesmen in England who traditionally assailed the "Court" party and its
means of control: centralized government, high taxes, national debt, standing
armies, and the network of patronage by which the executive "corrupted"
Parliament. This Country ideology had a great resonance for Americans, who
for the past twelve years had been fighting domestic hierarchy in the form of
the Federalists, and who in the years preceding had waged war against the
distant hierarchy of George III. In Britain, the Country spokesmen remained
an outraged minority crying out on the fringes of politics. In the New World,
however, "the revolution of 1800," as Thomas Jefferson was fond of calling
it, meant that the Country was now coming to Court.[1] When Jefferson became
president, the Republican amalgam of egalitarianism and individualism faced
the task of reconciling their principles (that warned against the perils of executive encroachment) with the exercise of executive power. The Jeffersonian
dilemma, as Lance Banning phrases it, was "to govern in accordance with an
ideology that taught that power was a monster and governing was wrong."[2]

Consistent with their antipower principles, Jeffersonians, once in power,
moved to reduce the need for authority. By abolishing internal taxes and revenue collectors, emasculating the standing army and navy, pledging to eliminate the public debt by 1817, and repudiating the Alien and Sedition Laws,
Republicans took a giant step toward the "rigorously frugal and simple" government they desired.[3] The policies of the Jefferson administration constituted
a self-conscious war on hierarchical institutions, whether in the form of the
state, church or army. Jefferson and his followers subsumed the evils of hierarchy under the codeword *monarchy*.[4] In his inaugural address Jefferson expressed his cultural preference positively: good government was government
that left people "free to regulate their own pursuits."[5]

If the Jeffersonians had, as Forrest McDonald asserts, "reversed the flow of history'' by reducing the need for authority,[6] it was a necessary reversal in view of their unwillingness to support authority. In *The Washington Community*, James Sterling Young has skillfully sketched the antiauthority ethos of the Jeffersonian regime. Young discovers ''a community ethos hostile to leadership and followership roles per se [that] was especially hostile to any effort toward supplanting the constitutionally orthodox relationship between President and Congress with a superordinate-subordinate relationship.'' An in-depth study of Jefferson and his Congresses portrays congressional Republicans as a ''conglomerate of individuals who were more at home as an opposition than as a majority.'' And Wilfred Binkley contrasts Jefferson's party of ''strict individualists'' with the Federalists' ''well-disciplined following.'' Leonard White, too, is struck by ''the suspicious attitude of the Republican rank and file toward strong leadership'' and the ''marked individualism that characterized many of their members.''[7]

The deep suspicion of authority evinced by Jefferson's followers did not go unnoticed by contemporaries. Only a few days after the first session of the 7th Congress opened, Roger Griswold of Connecticut noted that among the Republicans were ''a great number of . . . persons who are impatient of controul and disposed to revolt at any attempts at discipline.'' The man soon to become Governor of Massachusetts, Republican James Sullivan, believed a number of Republicans ''are in opposition to all regular well established governments.''[8] Acknowledging the problem of dealing with his congressional followers, Jefferson referred to them as ''our rope of sand.''[9] In this antiauthority environment with its pervasive mistrust of leadership,[10] Jefferson opted to lead without appearing to lead; to instruct while appearing only to suggest; to guide while seeming to defer.

Jefferson's Solution: The Hidden-Hand Presidency

Aware that overt displays of presidential leadership were likely to raise the cry of executive usurpation, Jefferson opted for a covert, dissembling leadership style. Jefferson's biographer, Dumas Malone, finds his protagonist always making a ''conscious effort to avoid all appearances of dictation.'' The key to Jefferson's political leadership, continues Malone, was that ''he did not permit his followers to think of him as a boss at all.''[11]

In view of the fact that all important legislation during Jefferson's tenure originated in the administration,[12] this was no easy task. Although Jefferson's messages politely suggested only the broad outlines of a program, he swiftly followed these up with private communications to legislative leaders specifying the policy in detail. It was not unusual for Jefferson actually to draft the bill himself and then send his draft to influential and sympathetic members of Congress. Jefferson was extraordinarily careful, however, to shroud his leadership of Congress in secrecy. No bill drafted by the president was ever submitted openly to Congress. And he always impressed upon his confidants the value of keeping his leadership of Congress hidden from public view, often going so far as to ask the member to copy and then burn or return the original.[13]

Jefferson's informal influence was carefully concealed behind a public facade of deference to Congress. In a formal reply to notification of his election, Jefferson vowed to be "guided by the wisdom and patriotism of those to whom it belongs to express the legislative will of the nation [and] . . . give to that will a faithful execution."[14] His first presidential address opened by referring to Congress respectfully as "the great council" of the nation, and closed with a pledge to "carry . . . the legislative judgement . . . into faithful execution."[15] Indeed, Jefferson's decision to submit the annual message in writing rather than deliver it in person—a practice that many Republicans viewed as aping the British custom of having the monarch speak to parliament in person—was calculated to underline executive subordination to the legislative branch.[16] While preparing the third annual message, Jefferson was reminded by Treasury Secretary Albert Gallatin to discuss the happy circumstances of United States neutrality, "without expressing anything like executive self-applause but referring everything to the moderate and wise policy adopted by the last Congress." Heeding Gallatin's advice, Jefferson attributed the nation's good fortunes to the "wisdom and moderation [of] our late legislative councils."[17]

To avoid the appearance of domination, comments Robert Johnstone, Jefferson "had to conquer . . . by seduction rather than coercion." Jefferson's nightly dinners provided a regular opportunity to build sympathy for himself and his program without appearing to issue commands. The table at these small, informal gatherings was circular, in order to break down hierarchical distinctions and to foster an air of collegiality.[18] The purpose of the dinners, Jefferson explained, was to "cultivate personal intercourse with the members of the legislature that we may know one another and have opportunities of little explanations of circumstances."[19] It was the rare dinner guest, Johnstone concludes, who could "withstand entirely the seductive force of the president's personality."[20]

This hidden-hand style of leadership was not simply a clever adaptation to an antiauthority culture; it also suited Jefferson's own cultural preferences. Jefferson preferred to hide the exercise of power even from himself. After leaving the presidency, Jefferson wrote that he could not "conceive how any rational being could propose happiness to himself from the exercise of power over others." To another correspondent he confided, "I have no ambition to govern men."[21] Leadership based on conciliation and persuasion were for Jefferson, and for the culture he both led and symbolized, the only legitimate forms of power. Jefferson was an ideal leader for an antiauthority culture because, as Johnstone suggests, "his personality and character seem always to have favored conciliation rather than confrontation, the flanking movement rather than the frontal assault. He preferred to work his will by methods of persuasion rather than by force of command."[22]

Jefferson's distaste for public confrontation was expressed by one of his favorite maxims: "Take things always by their smooth handle."[23] Like Dwight Eisenhower, the hidden-hand president whose style so much resembles his own, Jefferson would not publicly challenge even the most abusive of opponents. When John Randolph recklessly vilified the administration, Jefferson responded, as did Eisenhower to McCarthy, by privately undercutting rather than publicly attacking his adversary.[24]

Jefferson's relations with his department heads displayed the same emphasis on persuasion, conciliation, and discussion that characterized his leadership of the Republican party in Congress. Cabinet members were treated as peers rather than subordinates.[25] "By conversing and reasoning," declared Jefferson, the cabinet "scarcely ever failed . . . so to modify each other's ideas, as to produce an unanimous result."[26] In fact, however, as Johnstone makes clear, Jefferson "dominated their collective proceedings and insured his final authority."[27] By leading consensually, the act of leadership—setting the agenda and making decisions—was disguised. In any event, the collegiality of Jefferson's executive relations contrasts markedly with the hierarchical subordination that had characterized Washington's and Adams's executive relations.

Jefferson strived to keep the presidential door open not only to executive officers[28] but to all comers. In addition to making himself accessible to visitors from all walks of life, the president further broke down distinctions by receiving callers, including foreign dignitaries, in "republican simplicity." The British envoy was outraged when, having appeared at the Executive Mansion in full court dress to present his credentials to the president of the United States, he was greeted by Jefferson dressed only in his "usual morning attire." Also, in contrast to the magnificent coach employed by George Washington, Jefferson opted to ride on horseback with only a lone servant in attendance. By cultivating the image of an unceremonious and accessible chief executive, Jefferson hoped to symbolize for the nation the differences between the hierarchical culture of the Federalists and European monarchies and the American republican experiment.[29]

The Louisiana Purchase: Benefits of the Hidden-Hand

The hidden-hand strategy was designed to conceal not simply executive activity but also government activity in general. For Jefferson and his followers, a quiet political climate made possible an active, industrious private realm. "More blest is that nation," Jefferson rhapsodized, "whose silent course of happiness furnishes nothing for history to say." He wrote, too, that "a noise-less course, . . . unattractive of notice, is a mark that society is going on in happiness."[30] To preserve this surface calm, Jefferson had to act as the rudder beneath the waters, steering the ship of state away from rocky shoals and keeping it on what Jefferson called its "republican tack." By concealing his vigorous leadership, he could have the nation believe it was on automatic pilot.

Impending peril presented itself in the form of Spain's cession of the Louisiana territory, including the mouth of the Mississippi River, to the expansionist France of Napoleon. While the port of New Orleans was still in the feeble hands of the Spanish, Jefferson was confident that American interests could be protected. But French possession of the river mouth of the Mississippi radically transformed the nature of the threat to American commerce.

In the early spring of 1802, when Jefferson received confirmation that Louisiana had been retroceded to France, he responded rapidly with firm, blunt warnings to the French government about the dire consequences that would result from occupation of New Orleans, but to the American public and Congress he said nothing.[31] Congress convened in December, looking to Jefferson for guidance and information on what was fast becoming recognized as a major foreign policy crisis.[32] Jefferson provided neither, at least publicly. To a friend, the president suggested that "the path we have to pursue is so quiet that we have nothing scarcely to propose to our legislature."[33] His message to the newly assembled Congress notably avoided mentioning the issue of New Orleans. Jefferson would say only that Spain's cession, if carried into effect, would "make a change in the aspect of our foreign relations which will doubtless have just weight in any deliberations of the Legislature connected with that subject."[34]

Jefferson's message greatly disappointed Alexander Hamilton, who aptly dubbed it a "lullaby message." "In an emergency like the present," wrote Hamilton, "energy is wisdom."[35] Hamilton's harsh criticism of the "feebleness and pusillanimity"[36] of Jefferson's policy revealed not simply a difference of strategy (Hamilton advocated military seizure of New Orleans followed by negotiations, while Jefferson opted for negotiations to purchase the territory with military force as a last resort) but also a disagreement over political style. While sympathetic to the need for secrecy in conducting foreign affairs, Hamilton, who always preferred to lead and direct public opinion openly, was disturbed by the appearance of inactivity and weakness that Jefferson exhibited. The aims and advantages of Jefferson's covert leadership style were never appreciated by the hierarchical Hamilton.[37]

Hamilton's criticisms soon were stilled by the news that not only New Orleans but the whole of Louisiana had been acquired by the United States negotiators in Paris. Republicans universally hailed this achievement. Removing the French from the American doorstep had averted the need for a dangerous military establishment. The likelihood of being drawn into a distant European war necessitating taxes, debt, and regulation also had been markedly reduced. Expansion across space enabled the nation to avoid the hierarchical development through time that had characterized European nations, thereby preserving the cultural combination of egalitarianism and individualism that made the nation unique.[38]

Hamilton minimized Jefferson's accomplishment, arguing that the acquisition was "solely owing to a fortuitous concurrence of unforseen and unexpected circumstance, and not to any wise or vigorous measures on the part of the American government."[39] Intended as barbed criticism, Hamilton's indictment fell flat. To most Americans it was all the more to the president's credit that an (apparently) inactive and unaggressive government could exact such concessions from a great European power.

The Louisiana Purchase brought Jefferson unprecedented acclaim, but it also landed him on the horns of an uncomfortable dilemma. Consummation of this "noble bargain"[40] had entailed trampling on cherished Republican tenets of limited government and strict construction of the Constitution. For the Constitution nowhere explicitly granted the federal government the power to expand the Union; such an act—absent a constitutional amendment—had therefore to rely on implied powers.

The notion that the federal government could do only what the Constitution explicitly permitted—strict construction—was at the heart of Republican thinking. The principle of strict construction, as Henry Adams observed, was the very "breath of Jefferson's political life." "In questions of power," Jefferson had proclaimed just a few years earlier, "let no more be heard of confidence in man, but bind him down from mischief by the chains of the Constitution."[41] As long as this idea remained dominant the size and scope of government could not greatly expand, but were the Federalist doctrine of implied powers to become widely accepted, the Republican way of life, as Jefferson recognized all too clearly, would become endangered.

In private, Jefferson expressed qualms about turning the Constitution into "a blank paper by construction." He suggested amending the Constitution in order to avoid establishing a precedent "which would make our powers boundless," but publicly he would acknowledge no contradiction between Republican theory and the purchase.[42] Private reservations about the legitimacy of the government's behavior were made behind a front of public silence. Publicly Jefferson appeared chained to the Constitution, while behind the scenes his hidden hand vigorously worked to secure ratification of the treaty "sub silentio."[43] Fearing that Federalists might exploit Republican reservations about the legitimacy of the purchase to delay and thereby jeopardize the sale, Jefferson informed his friends that "it will be desirable for Congress to do what is necessary in silence."[44] The extent of Jefferson's influence in Congress is indicated by a request (command?) to his secretary of the Treasury: "Would it not be well that you should have a bill ready drawn to be offered on the first or second day of the session? It may be well to say as little as possible on the constitutional difficulty, and that Congress should act on it without talking."[45] The Republican-dominated Senate willingly obliged, hastily ratifying the treaty with only minimal debate.[46]

The tension between Jeffersonian principles and the Louisiana Purchase did not lead Jefferson either to repudiate the purchase or accept Hamiltonian principles. In part, Jefferson and his followers resolved the contradiction by ignoring or denying it—hence the deafening public silence. But Jefferson also utilized a mode of justification characteristic of individualist leadership.

National emergencies or great public goods may, as John Locke argued, force the individualist leader to act "without the prescription of the law, and sometimes even against it," and then afterwards to throw himself on the people to sanction his act.[47] To his trusted friend and influential senator, John Breckenridge, Jefferson explained:

> The Executive in seizing the fugitive occurrence which so much advances the good of the country, have done an act beyond the Constitution. The Legislature in casting behind them metaphysical subtleties, and risking themselves like faithful servants, must ratify and pay for it, and throw themselves on their country for doing for them unauthorized what we know they would have done for themselves had they been in a situation to do it.[48]

Jefferson's sentiments were echoed by the conscience of Jeffersonian political culture, John Taylor of Caroline, who as a senator from Virginia voted in favor of the purchase and then declared his intention to "throw myself on the people for pardon" for violating the Constitution.[49] The function of the emergency executive prerogative in antiauthority cultures is to allow for leadership in extraordinary cases without establishing precedents for authority in everyday circumstances.[50] As Virginia Congressman Alexander White argued, it was better for the president "to extend his power on some extraordinary occasion, even when it is not strictly justified by the constitution, than [that] the Legislature should grant him an improper power to be exercised at all times."[51]

Rather than undermine, the Louisiana Purchase served to solidify faith in Republican doctrine. The great good obtained strengthened confidence in the wisdom of the Lockean prescription of emergency prerogative. The purchase also gave added credence to the belief that foreign affairs could be successfully conducted without a strong national defense (the purchase was financed in part by cutting an already weak navy), and without resort to war. Finally, it cemented Jefferson's confidence in the efficacy of the hidden-hand leadership style. All three of these beliefs were to be severely tried by the embargo of 1807-1808.

The Embargo: Limits of the Hidden Hand

Foreign affairs had played a relatively minor role in Jefferson's first term but, during his second, developments in Europe brought foreign policy to center stage. Great Britain and France were locked in a struggle that increasingly infringed on the young republic. Britain's impressment of American sailors; its unprovoked attack on the American frigate Chesapeake; and, finally, the new British orders-in-council prohibiting any neutral trade with the Continent except under British license led Jefferson in December 1807 to call for an embargo in order, he told Congress, "to keep our seamen and property from capture, and to starve the offending nations."[52]

Jefferson's preference for an embargo as a strategy of "peaceable coercion" stemmed from the Republican aversion to the consequences of war. War, reflected Secretary of the Treasury Albert Gallatin, will make us "poorer," and "our debt and taxes will increase." In addition, Gallatin foresaw that war would necessitate an "increase in executive power and influence . . . and the introduction of permanent military and naval establishments."[53] Trade restrictions, on the other hand, promised to keep hierarchy at bay domestically while bringing the "tottering" hierarchy of Britain to its knees.[54]

Upon reflection, however, it was not so evident that an embargo would entail less domestic centralization, coercion, or regulation than would war. Gallatin, for one, began to have second thoughts. On the morning of the day Jefferson was to send his special message to Congress calling for an embargo, Gallatin wrote to the president urging him to limit its scope and duration:

> I prefer war to a permanent embargo. Government prohibitions do always more mischief than had been calculated; and it is not without much hesitation that a statesman should hazard to regulate the concerns of individuals as if he could do it better than themselves.[55]

A more accurate exposition of market individualism would be difficult to find. Jefferson, the philosopher of liberty, had earlier voiced identical sentiments, proclaiming that the sum of good government was to leave men "free to regulate their own interests."[56] But, for now, Jefferson, the chief executive, rejected Gallatin's plea. Gallatin swallowed his misgivings and pledged himself to implement the embargo.

Having secured congressional approval, Jefferson and his administration faced the dilemma that Gallatin had anticipated. To make the embargo effective, the administration, with congressional acquiescence, dramatically enlarged the scope of executive power, imposed extensive restrictions on individual liberty, and even employed the regular armed forces to quell resistance.[57] These violations of Republican principles were infinitely more egregious than had gone on during the Louisiana Purchase.

The more illegitimate is power within a political culture, the greater is the probability that the leadership will tend to glorify the ends in order to justify the (otherwise unjustifiable) means of that power. Jefferson's private correspondence reveals an increasing tendency to transform what began as a lesser evil—a way to avoid war and protect American ships, cargoes, and seamen from British seizure—into a noble experiment carried out in the name of future generations, which would also deliver Americans from the bondage of foreign fashion and luxury.[58] Although exalting the ends of the embargo became increasingly prominent in administration thinking, on the whole Jefferson chose to rely on his familiar hidden-hand strategy rather than publicly justify the coercion of the embargo. Jefferson presented, in the words of Leonard Levy, "an imperturbable, almost sphinxlike silence to the nation."[59] Jefferson concealed from the public the reasons for and consequences of an embargo, and revealed little more to Congress, except privately to those congressional leaders who enjoyed his confidence.[60] In no message to Congress did Jefferson argue in favor of an embargo.[61] "Darkness and mystery," complained one congressman on the floor of the House, "overshadow this House and the whole nation. We know nothing, we are permitted to know nothing."[62]

Although enforcement of the embargo produced an unprecedented concentration of power in the hands of the chief executive,[63] Jefferson assiduously tried to deflect responsibility for that policy onto Congress. The president sought, according to Dumas Malone, "to give the impression that the measure was not imposed from above but represented the judgement of Congress."[64] In response to petitions from the three major port towns of New England voicing opposition to the embargo, Jefferson, in his first public defense of the policy, reminded citizens that the embargo laws had been created by the legislature, and therefore as president he was merely executing national policy.[65] This view was not contrived simply for public consumption. To Gallatin Jefferson wrote, "The great leading object of the Legislature was, and ours in execution of it ought to be, to give complete effect to the embargo laws." Equally revealing was another letter to Gallatin in which Jefferson insisted that if embargo was to be chosen over war, "Congress must legalize all means which may be necessary to obtain *its* end" (emphasis added).[66] By ignoring the undisputable fact that the embargo expressed the executive's will—even the Enforcement Act had been drafted by the administration—Jefferson evidently had convinced himself that he was merely executing the will of the legislature.[67] Only by ascribing the end to another body did Jefferson feel able to justify to himself and to others his exercise of draconian powers.

The embargo strikingly revealed the limitations of Jefferson's hidden-hand leadership. Severe economic deprivation for many segments of the public had resulted from the embargo. The effectiveness of such a policy, therefore, depended on publicly explaining to the citizenry that such sacrifice was necessary to further a collective goal.[68] But Jefferson did no such thing; rather than trying to rally the country around him, comments Malone, the president "followed the general policy of keeping as much out of sight as possible."[69] "Going public" would be to admit to himself and others that he was not only the rudder but also the only one steering. The hidden-hand style, which had hitherto served Jefferson so well, now insured that the embargo would be a disaster. Previous Jeffersonian policies, such as cutting taxes or making the Louisiana Purchase, had not called for material sacrifices from individuals nor had people needed persuading that a great public good was being furthered. Well suited to achieve popular goals, Jefferson's covert style of leadership was ill-equipped to manage unpleasant tasks that required the leader to be a public educator.

In the face of mounting popular discontent, as well as the president's mystifying abdication of leadership in his last four months,[70] Congress repealed the embargo. Jefferson's noble experiment in peaceable coercion had ended by ignobly coercing American citizens.[71] The collapse of the embargo fanned Republican suspicions of the dangers of executive energy and initiative, even as the Louisiana Purchase had strengthened confidence in that same executive. Jefferson's failure guaranteed that under Jefferson's successor, James Madison, Congress would be far less willing to follow presidential guidance or to grant presidential discretion. If Jefferson's term had been "splendid misery," Madison's would prove to be unadulterated misery.[72]

The Meager Inheritance of James Madison

Even without the collapse of the embargo, Jefferson's "hidden-hand" solution contained within it an unavoidable contradiction. Disguising the use of power had created alarm among the most doctrinal adherents of Jeffersonian political culture, for if the overt exercise of power was bad, how much more terrible was it to have power cloaked and hidden. Led by John Randolph, these "Old Republicans" became increasingly disturbed by what they decried as the Jefferson administration's "back-stairs influence."[73]

Jefferson's concealed influence was only one aspect of the Old Republicans' dissatisfaction with the abandonment of "principle" they perceived taking place within the Republican party.[74] These extreme proponents of an antiauthority political culture wanted Jefferson to support extensive constitutional revision, including limiting the president to one term, shortening senatorial terms, reducing the president's power of appointment, and curtailing the power of the government to borrow money.[75] For Jefferson's failure to enact the "pure republican" program, Old Republicans were inclined to fault James Madison, Hamilton's coauthor of *The Federalist*.[76]

But blame, or credit, for any retreat from Republican principles rested squarely on Jefferson's shoulders.[77] Jefferson made a conscious decision to mollify and attract Federalist supporters in the mass public; his policy of conciliation necessarily entailed moderating the party's out-of-power principles. To John Taylor, ideological guiding star of the Old Republicans, Jefferson's policy appeared "very like a compromise with Mr. Hamilton's."[78]

Ultimately, it was not abandonment of principle, however, that brought the nation to grief but, rather, adherence to principle.[79] As Robert Kelley points out, Hamilton had long worried that "in its egalitarian and libertarian forms, republicanism seemed to distrust governments so blindly that it would leave them too weak and the prey of foreign enemies."[80] Jefferson, however, confusing the strength of society with the strength of government, had maintained that the United States government was "the strongest government on earth."[81] Events soon were to prove Hamilton's concerns justified and Jefferson's confidence misplaced.

Despite their moderation, Jefferson's policies had been designed to curtail sharply the size and scope of government, a necessary step in view of the Jeffersonians' unwillingness to support centralized authority. A rough balance between the need and support for leadership could be maintained, however, only if events did not drive the need for authority too high. War, or even preparation for hostilities, would compel the nation to raise armies, pay taxes, and increase the coercive capacity of government.

The same cultural propensities that had led the Republican party to embrace commercial coercion left the nation pitifully unprepared for the War of 1812.[82] Under Jefferson the army had been rendered, in Forrest McDonald's estimation, "so small as to be ineffectual." Explicitly rejecting his predecessor's policy of "peace through strength," Jefferson evinced particular hostility toward the navy, believing that it not only increased the likelihood of war but also promoted an arrogant, aristocratic officer caste.[83]

Beginning in 1805 Jefferson's (and subsequently Madison's) administration did seek increased defense appropriations and preparations but met with little success in a Congress so well-versed in Jeffersonian principles.[84] As Robert Smith, secretary of the navy under Jefferson and secretary of state under Madison, complained, "We have established theories that would stare down any possible measures of offense or defense."[85] It is to these "theories" and their adherents that one must turn in order to understand the disarmed state in which the United States entered the War of 1812.

The nation's unpreparedness is commonly attributed to a lack of leadership emanating from Madison's White House. President-raters characteristically rank Madison low, typically criticizing him for not being "a dynamic leader of men." Leonard White, for instance, has argued that Madison "lacked force and driving power, and was not endowed with political insight, wisdom, or art."[86] Perhaps, as John Calhoun declared on the eve of war, Madison did lack "those commanding talents" (whatever they might be), but it is even more certain that those he was supposed to lead were doggedly resistant to the idea of being commanded. Nine months later Calhoun was willing to concede this fact. Madison's difficulties, wrote Calhoun, "lie deep; and are coeval with the existence of Mr. Jefferson's administration."[87] Madison's failures in the presidency, we contend, are better understood by focusing not on Madison himself but on the qualities of his followers.

An explanation that focuses on Madison's personality or political skill runs into the difficulty that Madison had already proven himself, in Forrest McDonald's words, "an adroit manipulator of men"—both at the Constitutional Convention and, more impressively, as leader of the House Republicans in the 1790s.[88] Why did he succeed as the leader of the congressional Republicans but then fail as president? While in opposition the party was united against the Federalists, but once in power many Republicans, whose "bias," as Wilson Cary Nicholas told Madison, "is strongly against those who rule," instinctively took to attacking the incumbent.[89] Stephen Skowronek has argued that presidents allied with a dominant party when its basic policy commitments are being called into question—e.g. John Quincy Adams, James Buchanan, Herbert Hoover, or Jimmy Carter—face "the very definition of the impossible leadership situation."[90] In our view Madison—though allied with, in Skowronek's terms, a resilient rather than a vulnerable dominant party—faced the literal definition of the impossible leadership situation: followers who refuse to follow.

The scope of Madison's followership problem is well illustrated by a letter written to James Monroe in early 1810 by John Taylor. Informing Monroe that he would do everything possible to help him beat Madison in the coming election, Taylor hastened to add that if such a victory occurred, he would be compelled immediately to resist Monroe's executive leadership. "Majority republicanism," explained Taylor, "is inevitably . . . corrupted with ministerial republicanism."[91] Republicanism, for Taylor, was defined in terms of a refusal to follow the president's lead.

Far from being the lone ravings of an eccentric, this antiauthority disposition had been institutionalized by the very structure of Congress. Congress was committed not only to its autonomy vis-à-vis the executive but also to the autonomy of every individual member within Congress. The organization and values of the institution, James Sterling Young has persuasively argued, prevented congressional leadership from filling the void created by the tearing down of presidential leadership. As Young phrases it, "The congressional party did not change masters, . . . it ceased to have them."[92]

Madison's followership problem did not evaporate with the commencement of war with Great Britain. Rather, the war fulfilled Jefferson's brooding prediction, written to Madison, that "no government . . . would be so embarassing in war as ours."[93] Garnering the necessary support for the war from the Congress and nation proved extraordinarily trying. Madison faced, according to Young, "a perverse citizenry who demanded a magician for a President, and expected a victory without sacrifice or inconvenience to themselves."[94]

Madison's ineffective leadership was due in part to his own preference for prosecuting the war in a manner consistent with Republican principles. Like his Treasury secretary, Albert Gallatin, Madison hoped to conduct the war so that the nation "may be burdened with the smallest quantity of debt, perpetual taxation, military establishment, and other corrupting or anti-Republican habits or institutions."[95] Secretary of the Navy William Jones perceptively observed that Madison had "difficulty in accommodating to the crisis some of those political axioms which he has so long endulged, . . . which from the vicious nature of the times . . . require some relaxation."[96] Madison's refusal to relax Jeffersonian axioms stemmed largely from a desire to prove his Jeffersonian credentials, for his role in the formation of the Constitution had left him suspect in the eyes of more doctrinaire Republicans. Jefferson, whose Jeffersonianism was beyond question, could afford to invoke the Lockean concept of emergency leadership without impugning his Republicanism, but Madison could not allow himself even a temporary lapse from orthodoxy.

Though rigid adherence to antiauthority cultural propensities contributed to the administration's ineffective prosecution of the war, they also sustained an admirable respect for individual autonomy under the most trying of circumstances. In marked contrast to Federalist behavior during the war scare of 1798-99, Madison adamantly refused to suppress dissent despite its hampering of the war effort. "Here the government has an anxious and difficult task," Madison commented approvingly, "while the people stand at ease."[97]

Like Jefferson, Madison confronted a party imbued with "habits of behavior more conducive to obstruction and factionalism than to constructive cooperation under a central leadership."[98] Unlike Jefferson, however, Madison was ineffective in leading this fractious fusion of individualists and egalitarians. Madison's ineffectiveness points up not only the extraordinary nature of Jefferson's accomplishment but also the severe shortcomings of Jefferson's leadership strategy. Jefferson's success was due in large part to his refusal to justify leadership in public, a strategy that left his successors in an unenviably precarious position.

By failing to reconcile Republican theory with his de facto political leadership, Jefferson bequeathed Madison a vexing dilemma. To conceal power was an admission of its illegitimacy. In the absence of a public justification for presidential power, discovery of Jefferson's actual power was bound to fuel Republican suspicions of the chief executive. The unprecedented concentration of authority in the president's hands during Jefferson's ill-fated embargo only exacerbated an inevitable Republican backlash.

Madison inherited these newly revived fears of executive power but, because of the highly personal nature of his predecessor's leadership, nothing to help manage these fears. Jefferson's mode of governing relied greatly on personal influence, which in turn derived in large part from his unique position as symbol of the Republican party.[99] No successor had this mystique to use as a bargaining tool. Jefferson's solution, in short, relied too heavily on his own personal qualities to provide a viable groundwork for future incumbents.[100] A formula capable of institutionalizing leadership in an antiauthority culture would have to await the presidency of Andrew Jackson.

Republicans had long feared that wars tended to centralize and ennoble authority. "It is in war," Madison warned in 1793, "that laurels are to be gathered; and it is the executive brow they are to encircle."[101] The War of 1812 vindicated Republican forebodings but, ironically, national authority was strengthened not by being ennobled by victory but, rather, by discrediting Jeffersonian precepts. The palpable lack of military preparedness undermined confidence in the wisdom of relying on a civic-minded militia for national defense. Federally sponsored "internal improvements"—roads, canals, and the like—and a return of the national bank seemed more desirable in light of the inadequate roads that had inhibited the movement of troops and supplies, and the localized financial system that had inhibited movement of currency from one place to another and left the Treasury bankrupt.[102]

None was more shaken in his confidence than President Madison. In a special message to Congress (delivered a week after receiving official word that peace had been signed at Ghent), he declared, "Experience has taught us that a certain degree of preparation for war is not only indispensable to avert disasters in the onset, but affords also the best security for the continuance of peace."[103] Madison not only suggested that Congress maintain an adequate regular miltary and naval force in peacetime but also proposed a system of direct internal taxation; advocated higher salaries for public officers; supported a new national bank; and urged protection for domestic manufactures. In his seventh annual message, Madison reiterated most of these proposals in addition to recommending that Congress consider federally sponsored internal improvements.[104] Federalists wondered aloud whether this was not an "exchange of Jeffersonian policy for federalism."[105]

Madison's dramatic policy reversals have made him among the most puzzling figures in the nation's history. A decade after championing national

authority during the Constitutional Convention, he penned the Virginia Reso-
lutions that asserted primacy of the states. From having been the leading opponent of the attempt to establish a national bank, he was now leading the way
to reestablish just such a bank.

Nevertheless, there was a cultural consistency to Madison's actions. When
he thought hierarchy might dictate terms to individualism, abrogating essential freedoms—as during the 1790s—Madison leaned toward an egalitarian
alliance against hierarchy. But when he thought authority was too weak to
protect the nation against invasion and to maintain political, social, and economic stability—as during the 1780s—he inclined toward shoring up authority. For Madison, the War of 1812 was akin to Shay's Rebellion: it signaled
that individualism must make peace with hierarchy. Dubbed by many "the
second war of independence," the War of 1812 was a critical turning point in
Jeffersonian political culture, for in the minds of many it removed the possibility that the republican experiment might be undone by a restoration of monarchy.[106] Confident that hierarchy could not gain the dominance to abridge the
individualist way of life, many Republicans became much more relaxed about
strengthening national authority. Madison could thus recommend a national
bank, secure in the knowledge that it would be "safely subordinated to Republican ends," or so he thought.[107]

Even more surprising than Madison's promotion of defense, tariffs, improvements, and a national bank was that Congress promptly acted on nearly
all of the president's suggestions. Some congressional Republicans did
vehemently object to Madison's agenda. Kentucky Congressman Samuel
McKee warned that these "projects, if persisted in, would change every idea
of Government established in America, to the pernicious doctrines which
have for centuries prevailed in the Old World."[108] But the threat of hierarchy
was no longer credible. At the extreme, admitted John Calhoun, a coercive
national government was dangerous to liberty, but he argued "the extreme of
weakness [is] not only the most dangerous of itself . . . but . . . [is] that extreme to which the people of this country are particularly liable."[109] In other
words, given the dominant antiauthority climate in the early United States, the
nation had little to fear from an excess of power; rather, the danger stemmed
from insufficient national authority. Calhoun's argument carried the day. The
amount of important legislation passed during the 14th Congress was sur-
passed only by the 1st Federalist Congress.

Though the true believers voiced opposition to the policies suggested by
Madison—he "out-Hamiltons Alexander Hamilton," stormed Randolph—
they did not raise their usual cry of executive usurpation.[110] Madison's self-
effacing style of leadership and his unwillingness to defy Congress before and
during the war had given him an image of weakness that ironically shielded
him from even the harshest critics of executive authority. Who would believe

that "poor Jemmy . . . a withered little applejohn" could usurp power?[111] Yet Madison's administration did exert considerable influence in Congress in the postwar years. Madison's carefully qualified proposals in his addresses to Congress were followed up by direct contact between his secretaries and key committee chairmen. Treasury Secretary A.J. Dallas, for instance, worked closely with Calhoun, chairman of the House Committee on National Currency, in formulating a plan for a national bank and currency reform.[112]

In the area of national defense, Madison praised the navy's "signal services" and expressed confidence that Congress would provide for the gradual enlargement of the naval establishment. Secretary of the Navy Benjamin Crowninshield followed by submitting a detailed plan for the step-by-step creation of a "permanent naval establishment." A few months later Crowninshield's proposal emerged from Congress as the Act for the Gradual Increase of the Navy of the United States. That act, reports a naval historian, "represented a complete reversal of the policy of two decades, authorizing as it did the construction of nine of the largest class of battleships along with twelve heavy frigates and three steam-driven batteries." Perhaps even more telling is that the law left the decision as to whether the fleet would remain in service during peacetime or be kept out of the waters as wartime "insurance" to the president's discretion![113]

That act of Congress is eloquent testimony to Madison's success at rebuilding trust in the executive branch. By conducting the war without suspending civil liberties or encroaching on congressional powers, Madison avoided the backlash against executive "usurpations" that so often follows wartime leadership in an individualistic political culture. (Witness, for instance, the fate of Andrew Johnson after the Civil War.) Bequeathed a backlash against executive power by Jefferson's high-handed actions during the embargo, Madison's restraint during the War of 1812 left his successor, James Monroe, to reap the benefits of a "frontlash effect."[114]

Notes

1. John M. Murrin, "The Great Inversion, or Court versus Country: A Comparison of the Revolution Settlements in England (1688-1721) and America (1776-1816)," in *Three British Revolutions: 1641, 1688, 1776*, ed. J. G. A. Pocock, (Princeton: Princeton University Press, 1980), pp. 368-453, esp. pp. 411, 414.
   A historiographical debate currently rages as to whether Jeffersonian Republicans were liberal capitalists or classical republicans. (Useful reviews of this debate can be found in John Ashworth, "The Jeffersonians: Classical Republicans or Liberal Capitalists," *Journal of American Studies* [1984]: 425-35; and Richard Vernier, "Interpreting the American Republic: Civic Humanism vs. Liberalism," *Humane Studies Review* [Summer 1987]: 6ff.) By looking at this dispute through the lens of cultural theory we hope not only to clarify the argu-

ment but also to sharpen our own cultural characterization of the Jeffersonian party.

Those who advance the "republican hypothesis" believe that Jeffersonian ideology was significantly shaped by the Country party tradition of eighteenth-century England, which in turn owed much to Renaissance and classical republican thought. Joyce Appleby, the leading critic of the republican hypothesis, rejects this portrayal of Jefferson and his followers in favor of a portrait of them as inventors of liberal capitalism. Observing that Montesquieu and Bolingbroke defended a hierarchical social order and that Jeffersonians wanted to liberate men from formal constraints, Appleby concludes that it was the Federalists and not the Republicans who "in all essentials . . . remained classical republicans" (Joyce Appleby, *Capitalism and a New Social Order: The Republican Vision of the 1790s* [New York: New York University Press, 1984], p. 59). But here Appleby attacks a straw man. For the republican hypothesis is not that Jeffersonians endorsed a social order with many prescriptions but, rather, that they believed in the importance of civic participation in the community.

Lance Banning, a leading proponent of the republican hypothesis, has recognized this as the nub of the issue: "The irreducible difference between a strictly liberal interpretation of Jeffersonian ideology and a republican hypothesis may lie in our understanding of the way in which the Jeffersonians related the public and private spheres of life." For the liberal, the sum of private transactions produced a close approximation of the public good; for classical republicans, a commitment to the public weal was necessary to achieve the public good. Classical republicanism taught that the citizenry's commitment to the community would suffer if individuals devoted themselves to private gain; the doctrine of liberalism denied any conflict between the pursuit of private enterprise and the health of society ("Jeffersonian Ideology Revisited: Liberal and Classical Ideas in the New American Republic," *William and Mary Quarterly* [January 1986]: 3-19, quotation on p. 17). In sum, the argument between Banning and Appleby is whether the Jeffersonians were competitive individualists or egalitarian collectivists.

Phrased in terms of cultural categories (rather than, say, in terms of attitudes toward the past and future), an important area of agreement between the two views can be seen. Whether one adopts the portrait presented by Banning or Appleby, the Jeffersonians come across as fundamentally antihierarchical. The republican school draws attention to Jeffersonian opposition to high finance, executive influence, standing armies, central government, and so on. The Jeffersonians, in this view, were opposed not to commerce but to concentrated power and wealth. The liberal Jeffersonian ideology presented by Appleby accents opposition to government regulation of individual behavior. Like classical Republicans, liberal Republicans are thus characterized chiefly by their antipathy to hierarchy.

To point out this area of agreement is not to minimize the important differences between these two viewpoints. There is a world of difference between an interpretation depicting Jeffersonians as adherents of self-regulation—"it was the economy's ordering of society with minimal compulsion that stirred the Jeffersonian imagination," writes Appleby ("Republicanism in Old and New Contexts," *William and Mary Quarterly* [January 1986]: 33)—and one that portrays them as egalitarians who feared that "a spirit of commerce . . . [would promote] inequality of fortunes" and subvert the equality of social conditions necessary to preserve a republic (Banning, "Jeffersonian Ideology Revisited," p. 16; see also Ashworth, "The Jeffersonians," pp. 430-32; Robert E. Shalhope, "Republicanism and Early American Historiography," *William and Mary Quarterly* [April 1982]: 347-49).

Conceptualizing this debate in political cultural terms allows us to see the questions that future research on the ideology of the Jeffersonian party must ask. Were these conflicting ideals held by the same people or did different members of the party hold to opposing versions of an antiauthority ethos? What beliefs or events allowed Jeffersonians to reconcile egalitarian, participatory doctines and individualistic doctrines of self-regulation? What proportion of the party inclined to an egalitarian way of life and what proportion favored individualism? The only book to give systematic attention to ideological divisions within the Republican party is Richard E. Ellis's *The Jeffersonian Crisis: Courts and Politics in the Young Republic* (New York: Oxford University Press, 1971). Ellis distinguishes between radical and moderate Jeffersonians, and finds that the former were much more opposed to authority. But because he does not probe attitudes to egalitarianism, collectivism, or commerce, it is difficult to ascertain whether this division corresponds to an egalitarian-individualist split. We expect that the radical wing would be disproportionately made up of egalitarians (Banning-style Republicans) and that the moderate wing of the party was predominantly drawn from individualists (Appleby Republicans), but at present there is insufficient evidence to judge if this proposition is correct.

2. Lance Banning, *The Jeffersonian Persuasion: Evolution of a Party Ideology* (Ithaca: Cornell University Press, 1978), p. 273. Similarly, Forrest McDonald has observed, "Republican theory was wondrous potent as an ideology of opposition. It remained to be seen whether it was a sound basis for administration" (*The Presidency of Thomas Jefferson* [Lawrence: University Press of Kansas, 1976], p. 27).

3. Jefferson to Elbridge Gerry, January 26, 1799, quoted in Robert M. Johnstone, Jr., *Jefferson and the Presidency: Leadership in the Young Republic* (Ithaca: Cornell University Press, 1978), p. 45.

4. Ibid., p. 51.

5. Quoted in Banning, *Jeffersonian Persuasion*, p. 275. See also Robert Kelley, *The Cultural Pattern in American Politics: The First Century* (New York: Knopf, 1979), p. 118.

6. McDonald, *Presidency of Jefferson*, p. 52.

7. James Sterling Young, *The Washington Community, 1800-1828* (New York: Columbia University Press, 1966), p. 207; Alexander Lacy, quoted in Johnstone, *Jefferson and the Presidency*, p. 119; Wilfred E. Binkley, *President and Congress* (New York: Vintage, 1962), pp. 61-62; Leonard D. White, *The Jeffersonians: A Study in Administrative History, 1801-1829* (New York: Macmillan, 1951), p. 31.

8. Griswold to John Rutledge, December 14, 1801, cited in Noble E. Cunningham, Jr., *The Jeffersonian Republicans in Power: Party Operations, 1801-1809* (Chapel Hill: University of North Carolina Press, 1963), p. 74; Sullivan to William Eustis, January 13, 1802, cited in Ellis, *Jeffersonian Crisis*, p. 23. See also Wilson Cary Nicholas to Madison, May 1, 1801, ibid., pp. 23-24.

9. Jefferson to Caesar Rodney, February 24, 1804, cited in Cunningham, *Republicans in Power*, p. 76. See also Johnstone, *Jefferson and the Presidency*, p. 118. On the anarchic social organization of Capitol Hill, see Young, *Washington Community*, especially pp. 186, 210, 215.

10. See Young, *Washington Community*, esp. pp. 63, 206-7; Johnstone, *Jefferson and the Presidency*, p. 77.

11. Dumas Malone, *Jefferson the President: First Term, 1801-1805* (Boston: Little, Brown, 1970), p. 112; Dumas Malone, *Thomas Jefferson as Political Leader* (Berkeley: University of California Press, 1963), p. 34. Similarly, Noble Cunningham remarks that "the dilemma of trying to provide leadership without being charged with dictation became painfully clear to Jefferson in the course of his presidency" (*The Process of Government under Jefferson* [Princeton: Princeton University Press, 1978], p. 193).

12. Cunningham, *Jeffersonian Republicans*, p. 94; Malone, *First Term*, p. 110.

13. Cunningham, *Process of Government*, ch. 9, esp pp. 189-93; Cunningham, *Jeffersonian Republicans*, ch. 4, esp. pp. 96-98.

14. Johnstone, *Jefferson and the Presidency*, p. 128.

15. Malone, *First Term*, p. 95; Edward S. Corwin, *The President: Office and Powers, 1787-1957* (New York: New York University Press, 1957), p. 18.

16. Malone, *First Term*, pp. 92-93. See also James Hart, *The American Presidency in Action* (New York: Macmillan, 1948), pp. 28-33.

17. Johnstone, *Jefferson and the Presidency*, p. 129.

18. Ibid., pp. 144-48, quotation on p. 129. Henry Adams described Jefferson as "a gentle leader, not a commander" (cited in Banning, *Jeffersonian Persuasion*, p. 279).

19. Jefferson to David Williams, January 31, 1806, cited in Cunningham, *Jeffersonian Republicans*, p. 95.

20. Johnstone, *Jefferson and the Presidency*, p. 147. See also McDonald, *Presidency of Jefferson*, p. 39; Cunningham, *Jeffersonian Republicans*, p. 96.

21. Jefferson to Destutt de Tracy, January 26, 1811, cited in White, *The Jeffersonians*, p. 5; Jefferson to Edward Rutledge, December 27, 1796, cited in Malone, *Jefferson as Political Leader*, p. 21.

22. Johnstone, *Jefferson and the Presidency*, p. 34.

23. Ibid.

24. Fred I. Greenstein, *The Hidden-Hand Presidency: Eisenhower as Leader* (New York: Basic Books, 1982). On Jefferson's attempts quietly to undercut Randolph, see Dumas Malone, Jefferson the President: Second Term, 1805-1809 (Boston: Little, Brown, 1974) pp. 108-9, 161-62; Cunningham, *Republicans in Power*, pp. 86-88.

25. Dumas Malone, "Presidential Leadership and National Unity: The Jeffersonian Example," *Journal of Southern History* (February 1969): 16; Johnstone, *Jefferson and the Presidency*, pp. 95-98; Cunningham, *Process of Government*, pp. 60-71, 319-20.

26. White, *The Jeffersonians*, p. 80.

27. Johnstone, *Jefferson and the Presidency*, p. 86.

28. McDonald, *Presidency of Jefferson*, p. 38.

29. Johnstone, *Jefferson and the Presidency*, pp. 58-60. James Thomas Flexner, *George Washington and the New Nation* (Boston: Little, Brown, 1969), p. 208. Malone, *First Term*, pp. 93-94. Malone, "Presidential Leadership," pp. 14-15.

30. Jefferson to Comte Diodate, March 29, 1807, cited in Johnstone, *Jefferson and the Presidency*, pp. 65-66; Jefferson to Thomas Cooper, November 29, 1802, cited in Malone, *First Term*, p. 137.

31. Doris A. Graber, *Public Opinion, the President, and Foreign Policy: Four Case Studies from the Formative Years* (New York: Holt, Rinehart & Winston, 1968), pp. 134-35.

32. Alexander DeConde, *This Affair of Louisiana* (New York: Scribner's, 1976), p. 127.
33. Jefferson to Thomas Cooper, November 29, 1802, cited in Henry Adams, *History of the United States of America during the Administrations of Jefferson and Madison* (New York: Scribner's, 1921), p. 74.
34. Quoted in Graber, *Public Opinion, the President, and Foreign Policy*, p. 137.
35. Hamilton, quoted ibid., p. 137; and DeConde, *Affair of Louisiana*, p. 128.
36. Hamilton, quoted in Gerald Stourzh, *Alexander Hamilton and the Idea of Republican Government* (Stanford: Stanford University Press, 1970), p. 194.
37. See Gilbert L. Lycan, *Alexander Hamilton and American Foreign Policy* (Norman: University of Oklahoma Press, 1970), p. 17.
38. See Drew R. McCoy, *The Elusive Republic: Political Economy in Jeffersonian America* (Chapel Hill: University of North Carolina Press, 1980), esp. pp. 200-4. Federalists, while supportive of the purchase of New Orleans and guaranteed American navigation of the Mississippi, did not share the Republican enthusiasm for westward expansion (ibid., pp. 199-200). Federalists saw this "vast wilderness world" as threatening to undermine order and authority. For Hamilton and his fellow hierarchs, it was essential that the government's means of coercion keep abreast with any increases in territory. See the excellent discussion of Hamilton's and Jefferson's contrasting conceptions of empire in Stourzh, *Alexander Hamilton*, pp. 191-95.
39. Hamilton, quoted in McCoy, *Elusive Republic*, pp. 199-200.
40. The phrase "noble bargain" is from Talleyrand (cited in McDonald, *Presidency of Jefferson*, p. 72).
41. Adams, *History of the United States*, p. 89; Johnstone, *Jefferson and the Presidency*, p. 74. See also Dumas Malone, *Jefferson and the Ordeal of Liberty* (Boston, Little, Brown, 1962), esp. pp. 395-409.
42. Jefferson to Wilson Cary Nicholas, cited in Malone, *First Term*, p. 318.
43. Jefferson to Madison, August 18, 1803, cited in Johnstone, *Jefferson and the Presidency*, p. 73. Nathan Schachner writes: "Jefferson was following the proceeding with the keenest interest and anxiety. Overtly, he could do nothing; but he tried to hold the sagging lines intact, and sought indirectly to bolster the faithful and overcome the recalcitrants" (cited in Graber, *Public Opinion, the President, and Foreign Policy*, p. 145).
44. Jefferson to Levi Lincoln, August 30, 1803, cited in Graber, *Public Opinion, the President, and Foreign Policy*, p. 144. Jefferson sent the same message to Nicholas, asking him that Congress do its duty "with as little debate as possible, and particularly so far as respects the constitutional difficulty" (September 7, 1803, ibid., p. 145).
45. Jefferson to Gallatin, August 23, 1803, cited in Johnstone, *Jefferson and the Presidency*, pp. 72-73.
46. DeConde, *Affair of Louisiana*, p. 187.
47. John Locke, *Second Treatise of Government*, ch. 14, para. 160. Jefferson's reliance on Lockean principles is pointed out both in Johnstone, *Jefferson and the Presidency*, pp. 71-72, and Arthur M. Schlesinger, Jr., *The Imperial Presidency* (Boston: Houghton Mifflin, 1973), pp. 23-25.
48. Johnstone, *Jefferson and the Presidency*, p. 72. See also Jefferson to John B. Colvin, September 20, 1810, in Malone, *First Term*, p. 320; Jefferson to John Adams, in Graber, *Public Opinion, the President, and Foreign Policy*, p. 144; Jefferson to Claiborne, February 7, 1807, in Johnstone, *Jefferson and the Presidency*, p. 198.

49. Taylor, cited in Graber, *Public Opinion, the President, and Foreign Policy*, p. 145.
50. See Schlesinger, *Imperial Presidency*, p. 10.
51. Ibid., p. 9.
52. White, *The Jeffersonians*, p. 424.
53. Johnstone, *Jefferson and the Presidency*, p. 260. See also Banning, *Jeffersonian Persuasion*, p. 292.
54. McCoy, *Elusive Republic*, passim; William Branch Giles quoted on p. 141.
55. Johnstone, *Jefferson and the Presidency*, p. 266.
56. Ibid., p. 45.
57. Leonard W. Levy, *Jefferson and Civil Liberties: The Darker Side* (Cambridge: Harvard University Press, 1963), pp. 109-20, esp. pp. 114, 119.
58. Malone, Second Term, pp. 476, 484, 489, 583-89.
59. Levy, *Jefferson and Civil Liberties*, p. 96.
60. Ibid., pp. 93-141, esp. pp. 96, 104. Graber, *Public Opinion, the President, and Foreign Policy*, p. 153.
61. Malone, *Second Term*, p. 576.
62. Barent Gardenier, cited in Levy, *Jefferson and Civil Liberties*, p. 98.
63. Ibid., p. 102. Johnstone, *Jefferson and the Presidency*, pp. 274-75.
64. Malone, *Second Term*, p. 576; see also p. 623.
65. Ibid., p. 610; Levy, *Jefferson and Civil Liberties*, p. 110.
66. Malone, *Second Term*, p. 589; Johnstone, *Jefferson and the Presidency*, p. 281.
67. Levy, *Jefferson and the Civil Liberties*, pp. 95, 104, 113, 126; Johnstone, *Jefferson and the Presidency*, p. 275; Malone, *Second Term*, p. 579.
68. Levy, *Jefferson and Civil Liberties*, pp. 93-96; Johnstone, *Jefferson and the Presidency*, p. 269; Malone, *Second Term*, pp. 489-90.
69. Malone, *Second Term*, p. 576.
70. Johnstone, *Jefferson and the Presidency*, pp. 286-87. Jefferson labored under the illusion that in abdicating leadership he was doing Madison a favor. To Levi Lincoln, he explained that he thought it "fair to leave to those who are to act on them, the decisions they prefer, being to be myself but a spectator. I should not feel justified in directing measures which those who are to execute them would disapprove" (November 13, 1808; cited on p. 286).
71. Levy, *Jefferson and Civil Liberties*, p. 105; Johnstone, *Jefferson and the Presidency*, p. 297.
72. Johnstone, *Jefferson and the Presidency*, pp. 305-6.
73. Cunningham, *The Process Of Government*, p. 188; see also Jefferson to William Duane, March 22, 1806, cited on p. 193.
74. See Randolph's letter to James Monroe, March 20, 1806, cited in Cunningham, *Republicans in Power*, p. 85; Norman K. Risjord, *The Old Republicans: Southern Conservativism in the Age of Jefferson* (New York: Columbia University Press, 1965), p. 38, and passim; Banning, *Jeffersonian Persuasion*, pp. 281-84.
75. Ellis, *Jeffersonian Crisis*, p. 20; Kelley, *Cultural Pattern*, p. 133.
76. Kelley, *Cultural Pattern*, p. 133; George Dangerfield, *The Era of Good Feelings* (New York: Harcourt, Brace, 1952), pp. 19-20.
77. Ellis, *Jeffersonian Crisis*, pp. 25-30.
78. Taylor to Monroe, October 26, 1810, cited in Banning, *Jeffersonian Persuasion*, p. 282.
79. Banning, *Jeffersonian Persuasion*, ch. 10, esp. p. 290.
80. Kelley, *Cultural Pattern*, p. 116.
81. Merrill D. Peterson, "Henry Adams on Jefferson the President," *Virginia*

Quarterly Review (Spring 1963): 187-201, at p. 194. See also Kelley, *Cultural Pattern*, p. 117.

82. Banning, *Jeffersonian Persuasion*, p. 298.
83. McDonald, *Presidency of Jefferson*, p. 43.
84. Banning, *Jeffersonian Persuasion*, p. 298.
85. Robert Smith to W. C. Nicholas, January 9, 1807, cited in White, *The Jeffersonians*, p. 75.
86. Thomas A. Bailey, *Presidential Greatness: The Image and the Man from George Washington to the President* (New York: Appleton-Century, 1966, p. 273); Bailey ranks Madison as "little better than [a] Near Failure." White, *The Jeffersonians*, p. 36.
87. April and December 1812, cited in Ralph Ketcham, *James Madison: A Biography* (New York: Macmillan, 1971), p. 532.
88. Forrest McDonald, *The Presidency of George Washington* (Lawrence: University Press of Kansas, 1974), p. 68. See also Noble E. Cunningham, Jr., *The Jeffersonian Republicans: The Formation of Party Organization, 1789-1801* (Chapel Hill: University of North Carolina Press, 1957), esp. p. 88; Irving Brant, *James Madison: Father of the Constitution, 1787-1800* (Indianapolis: Bobbs-Merrill, 1950), chs. 30, 32, 33, 34.
89. Wilson Cary Nicholas to James Madison, May 1, 1801, cited in Ellis, *Jeffersonian Crisis*, pp. 23-24.
90. Stephen Skowronek, "Notes on the Presidency in the Political Order," *Studies in American Political Development*, 1:296. Skowronek's theory is discussed in more detail in chapter 10.
91. Banning, *Jeffersonian Persuasion*, p. 283; see also Dangerfield, *Era of Good Feelings*, pp. 190-93.
92. Young, *Washington Community*, p. 209.
93. March 17, 1809, in White, *The Jeffersonians*, p. 35; see also Young, *Washington Community*, pp. 182-86.
94. Young, *Washington Community*, p. 185.
95. Gallatin to Jefferson, March 12, 1812, cited in Banning, *Jeffersonian Persuasion*, p. 299.
96. Ketcham, *James Madison*, p. 585.
97. Ibid., pp. 585-86, quotation on p. 586; Ralph Ketcham, "James Madison: The Unimperial President," *Virginia Quarterly Review* (Winter 1978): 116-36, esp. p. 130; Irving Brant, *The Fourth President: A Life of James Madison* (Indianapolis: Bobbs-Merrill, 1970), p. 599.
98. Johnstone, *Jefferson and the Presidency*, p. 117.
99. Ibid., p. 310.
100. "The power he [Jefferson] wielded," explains Dumas Malone, "was to an exceptional degree personal and little institutionalized" (*Second Term*, p. xxiii).
101. Madison continued, "In war a physical force is to be created; and it is the executive will, which is to direct it. In war, the public treasuries are to be unlocked; and it is the executive hand which is to dispense them. In war, the honors and emoluments of office are to be multiplied; and it is the executive patronage under which they are to be enjoyed" (Ketcham, "Unimperial President," p. 116). On Republican fears of the effects of war, see Banning, *Jeffersonian Persuasion*, p. 292.
102. George Dangerfield, *The Awakening of American Nationalism, 1815-1828* (New York: Harper & Row, 1965), p. 8.

103. Craig L. Symonds, *Navalists and Antinavalists: The Naval Policy Debate in the United States, 1785-1827* (Newark: University of Delaware Press), pp. 198-99.

104. Shaw Livermore, Jr., *The Twilight of Federalism: The Disintegration of the Federalist Party, 1815-1830* (Princeton: Princeton University Press, 1962), pp. 14-15. Dangerfield, *Awakening of Nationalism*, pp. 6-7.

105. Quoted in Livermore, *Twilight of Federalism*, p. 15.

106. This theme is pursued in Roger H. Brown, *The Republic in Peril: 1812* (New York: Columbia University Press, 1964); and Richard Buel, Jr., *Securing the Revolution: Ideology in American Politics, 1789-1815* (Ithaca: Cornell University Press, 1972).

107. Charles D. Lowery, *James Barbour, A Jeffersonian Republican* (Alabama: University of Alabama Press, 1984), p. 90. The words are Lowery's, not Madison's. See also Madison's letter to William Eustis, May 22, 1823, cited on p. 107.

108. Symonds, *Navalists and Antinavalists*, p. 212.

109. Ibid., p. 208.

110. Lowery, *James Barbour*, p. 90.

111. Washington Irving, quoted in Dangerfield, *Era of Good Feelings*, p. 20.

112. Dangerfield, *Awakening of Nationalism*, pp. 8-10.

113. Symonds, *Navalists and Antinavalists*, pp. 199-200, 213-16; quotations on pp. 199-200.

114. The term "frontlash effect" is borrowed from Richard M. Pious, *The American Presidency* (New York: Basic Books, 1979), p. 50.

5

Two Varieties of Cultural Fusion:
James Monroe
and John Quincy Adams

The period extending from the Revolution to the War of 1812 was marked by extraordinarily bitter cultural conflict. With the war now at an end, many politicians, as well as citizens, looked for a respite from the uninterrupted battle of principles that had been waged over the past four decades. Our fifth and sixth presidents, James Monroe and John Quincy Adams, in their different ways, would try to minimize, obscure, and even deny cultural conflict.

Cultural (Con)fusion:
James Monroe and the "Era of Good Feelings"

James Monroe's overriding aim as president was to bring about a fusion of cultures. All political cultures, Monroe hoped, would forget past animosities and join under a single banner. Having been swept into office against only token Federalist opposition, he was confident that the time was ripe for cultural amalgamation. "Discord," Monroe declared in his inaugural address, "does not belong to our system," for the American people are "one great family with a common interest." The president issued heartfelt praise for the "increased harmony which pervades our Union."[1]

Although these sentiments differed little from Jefferson's conciliatory gesture at his inaugural—"we are all Republicans, we are all Federalists"—it soon became evident that Monroe actually intended to realize this cultural fusion. Soon after his inauguration, Monroe embarked on a goodwill tour of New England—the very heart of Federalism—that would give Federalists an opportunity to "get back into the great family of the union."[2] The president visited the homes of a number of prominent Federalists, while publicly reaffirming his desire to promote national harmony.[3] Federalists and Republicans joined in celebrating their chief executive in what Harry Ammon has described as "a love feast of unparalleled enthusiasm."[4] So great was the outpouring of support for Monroe that a Federalist newspaper wrote that the president's visit had ushered in an "Era of Good Feelings." Whatever the descriptive validity of the phrase, it does aptly describe the objectives of President Monroe.[5]

In a letter to Andrew Jackson, written soon after Monroe's election, the new president expressed a determination to test his "hypothesis" that "the existence of parties is not necessary to free government."[6] Monroe's antiparty beliefs are well known, yet they are too often considered apart from his cultural aims.[7] Monroe's denigration of parties, we contend, was strongly motivated by a desire to continue the move away from "pure" Republicanism. Rather than merely reflecting an abstract distrust of parties, Monroe's actions stemmed from his desire to see the Republican party recast in a less antiauthority form.

In order to promote a "union of the community," Monroe warned Boston Republicans, he would "be careful to avoid such measures, as may, by any possibility, sacrifice it."[8] Monroe's goal was to pursue policies that would attract Federalists without repulsing Republicans. Before the War of 1812, writes Robert Kelley, "the Jeffersonians had been libertarian and egalitarian; the Federalists nationalist." What Monroe proposed to do, Kelley suggests, was inject nationalism into the Republican political culture, thereby transforming the Republican party while also undermining Federalism.[9] If, for nationalism, one substitutes respect for national authority, the cultural connection is complete.

Monroe's inaugural address and first annual message outlined what Ammon has described as a program of "moderate nationalism." The most striking departure from Republican orthodoxy came in the realm of national defense; here, Monroe expressed firm support for a larger military establishment and stronger fortifications. To counterbalance this proposal (politically though not financially), Monroe recommended repeal of the internal taxes levied during the war. The president also sought a middle ground on federally sponsored internal improvements. He appealed to orthodox Republicans by denying that such government action was then constitutional, while courting neo-Federalists by proposing a constitutional amendment that would make it constitutional.[10]

Federalists were favorably impressed with Monroe's words and deeds. Throughout his two terms, Federalists were to give Monroe steady support in Congress. "The nearer the Democratic administration and party come up to the old federal principles and measures," wrote one Federalist editor in 1819, "the better they act and the more we prosper—that is the reason that every body is contented with President Monroe's administration, which is in system and effect strictly federal."[11] Federalist support, however, constituted only one leg of Monroe's tricultural program.

By moderating the antiauthority ethos of Republicans, Monroe hoped to gain widespread acceptance for the second national bank, tariffs, and internal improvements. He was eager to demonstrate that these policies, traditionally anathema to Jeffersonians, were in fact compatible with a relatively egalitarian and individualist way of life. All cultures, Monroe argued, could be served by taking the middle road.

Although Monroe's presidential messages constituted a valiant effort to balance competing cultures, he failed to come up with a genuinely integrative solution—i.e. a policy that all cultures could agree on, even if for different reasons. "Good feelings" were consequently short-lived. There was little in Monroe's statements or actions to attract egalitarians, though with egalitarianism weakened in the immediate aftermath of the war this shortcoming of his strategy was not immediately evident. During the flush of postwar prosperity one could call for lower taxes and increased defense spending, thereby courting adherents of individualism and hierarchy, but the panic of 1819 impelled policymakers to choose between the individualist preference for lower taxes and the hierarchical preference for military spending.

Up until the panic of 1819, the first peacetime depression to confront the new nation, Monroe's nonpartisan strategy was relatively effective. The ensuing chaos and hard times, however, emboldened spokesmen for Jeffersonian political culture to decry the postwar departure from Republican principles. In the frantic search for someone or something to blame, the second national bank presented a natural target.[12] The Pennsylvania legislature, for instance, called on other states to join in enacting a constitutional amendment to terminate the national bank—to "vote the monster to the tomb."[13] Monroe's rapprochement with hierarchy brought forth accusations of apostasy from those interested in preserving the Jeffersonian alliance of egalitarianism and individualism.

Proponents of government retrenchment were greatly strengthened by the deficit that the depression produced. Enthusiasm for internal improvements rapidly waned, as did support for a formidable national defense.[14] Sensing that the drive for economy might undermine defense, Monroe reminded Congress of the disastrous consequences of national unpreparedness during the recent war. "One of the best features in our Government," retorted Charles Fisher of North Carolina, "is our unfitness for war." In congressional debates, Carlton Smith observes, the army was portrayed as "naturally anti-republican because of its hierarchical organization and . . . [because it] encouraged men to think in terms of rank and privilege, [and] . . . promoted feelings of inequality." The traditional Jeffersonian fear of a peacetime standing army supplemented with the argument for economy, resulted in Congress's reducing the size of the army by 40 percent and significantly cutting appropriations.[15]

Monroe's amalgamation policy did away with the common enemy—the hierarchical Federalists—that had kept the coalition of egalitarians and individualists together. Each culture takes on its coloration from its opposition; an individualist regime opposing hierarchy looks different from an individualist regime contending against egalitarianism. Only in opposition to hierarchy do those who favor an individualist political culture mute their hostility to equality. Consequently, with the disintegration of the Federalist party, the Republican alliance of egalitarians and individualists began to unravel.

Many within the Republican party had foreseen this. One week after Monroe's inaugural, William Crawford forecast that "the great depression of the Federal party . . . cannot fail to relax the bonds by which the Republican party has been hitherto kept together."[16] The Republicans having "lost the cement given to their union by the rivalship of the Federal party," Madison, too, anticipated that their party would produce "schisms."[17] Monroe, however, adamantly rejected the notion that "the existence of the federal party is necessary to keep union and order in the republican ranks."[18]

When the War of 1812 ended, individualists turned increasingly to the business of making money. Kim Phillips's study of postwar Pennsylvania politics documents the growing estrangement between the egalitarian-inclined "Old School Democrats" and the "New School of entrepreneurial Democrats" created by the postwar boom. To Democrats of the Old School, writes Phillips, the second Bank of the United States "was a monument to the spirit of selfishness gradually overwhelming the egalitarian ideal."[19] Egalitarians saw speculation as greed, and the scramble for riches as fostering inequality and corrupting republican fraternity.[20] "Banks," proclaimed an egalitarian spokesman, "are now to swarm upon us like locusts did over the face of Egypt," and "our substance is to be eaten out by them."[21] This new breed of entrepreneurial Democrat, argued the Old School Democrats, was "woefully lacking in egalitarian convictions."[22]

As the rift between egalitarians and individualists widened, Monroe's amalgamation program came under increasingly severe attack from those who wanted to restore the old Jeffersonian alliance. Many Republicans viewed the entire notion of a politics of "Good Feelings" as "a Federalist plot" hatched in order "to abolish the old political distinctions . . . [and] destroy the Democratic party."[23] Federalism has "changed its name and hidden itself among us," brooded Jefferson; it is "as strong as it ever has been."[24] The former president wondered whether the "civil revolution of 1801" had been subverted by the "surrender of our [Federalist] opponents" and "their reception into our camp."[25]

Monroe's fusion policy had produced cultural confusion. With all cultures going under the same name, it was difficult to determine who were enemies and who were allies. Lacking party cues, politics degenerated into myriad local competitions among rival personalities and factions. The result, observes historian Joel Silbey, "was large-scale confusion and uncertainty over what politics was about, how it was to be carried on, and why it was important."[26] At the best of times it is hard to gain support for presidential leadership in an antiauthority context; without the backing of an organized political party, executive leadership was to prove well nigh impossible.

The amalgamation of cultures meant that Monroe would have to lead without the benefit of party loyalty enjoyed by his predecessors.[27] An alternative to the party leadership practiced by Jefferson was necessary in order for Monroe to exercise effective executive leadership. In searching for a viable substitute, Monroe did not stray far from the covert path established by Jefferson and Madison; he did not try, for instance, to exploit his personal popularity by appealing over the head of legislators.[28] Instead, the president's strategy was to lead Congress by forging a consensus on policy within a prestigious cabinet.

"Taken man for man," writes Leonard White, "Monroe's Cabinet was one of the strongest that any President had assembled."[29] Three of the five who were to be presidential candidates in 1824 sat in that cabinet—John Quincy Adams as secretary of state, William Crawford as secretary of the Treasury, and John Calhoun as secretary of war—and a fourth, Henry Clay, had been offered the War Department but turned it down. Some commentators have mistakenly assumed that during Monroe's tenure the cabinet "took over the presidency."[30] Rather, the cabinet was a tool that Monroe used to achieve his objectives in a Congress that not only lacked party structure but resented direct presidential involvement in legislative deliberations. By selecting cabinet members with significant congressional followings, agreements hammered out in the cabinet stood a good chance of getting through Congress.[31]

The need for agreement within the cabinet accounts for the administration's slowness in reaching decisions—a characteristic often mistakenly attributed to Monroe's alleged indecisiveness. The lengthy and frequent cabinet meetings were not primarily for gathering advice but, rather, to build and solidify commitment among cabinet members to the president's preferred policy objectives. Monroe carefully avoided discussing those issues (e.g. slavery in Missouri and internal improvements) on which there were irreconcilable differences within the cabinet. On most matters, however, the administration was able to hammer out an agreement and was usually quite successful in obtaining congressional approval of the president's policies.[32]

The strategy succeeded, for instance, in stemming the move in Congress to censure Andrew Jackson for unauthorized seizure of the Spanish posts at St. Marks and Pensacola during the 1818 campaign against the Indians. Congress was outraged, believing that Jackson's actions not only had been an invasion of the congressional power to declare war but also had risked precipitating war with Spain. The cabinet was sharply divided on the issue; Adams argued that the president should approve Jackson's actions and retain the seized posts until Spain ceded Florida, while Crawford and Calhoun urged that the general be publicly reprimanded for exceeding orders. According to Ammon, President Monroe "had long before made up his mind to take a stand short of full endorsement, and . . . used the Cabinet discussions to reach a consensus midway between the extremes advocated by the Secretaries.'' Having hammered out an agreement within the cabinet, Monroe was able to check the attempt in Congress, led by Clay, to condemn Jackson as well as to discredit the administration's decision to invade Florida.[33]

The limitations of Monroe's leadership strategy and, by implication, his goal of cultural fusion became evident during his last three years in office. The struggle over who would succeed Monroe made agreement within the cabinet increasingly difficult to achieve. The secretaries' political ambitions dictated that they attack administration policies associated with their rivals.[34] "Mutual vituperation and character assassination,'' writes James Young, "reached a new low in newspapers each of the three secretaries used to promote his candidacy.'' In his diary, John Quincy Adams confided that the administration "is at war with itself.''[35]

The close connections between the department heads and Congress, which had hitherto served Monroe so well, now proved a drawback as congressional partisans maneuvered to embarrass rival candidates. In a bid to discredit Adams and Calhoun, Crawford encouraged his supporters to attack the president's program.[36] The most notable casualty of this jockeying for position within the administration was an agreement with Britain to suppress the international slave trade. Submitted by Monroe to the Senate on April 30, 1824, the treaty was jeopardized by opposition among Crawford partisans to the prospect of having British officers search American ships. Monroe appealed to Crawford to intercede in behalf of the agreement that the Treasury secretary had supported in cabinet meetings the year before, but Crawford, sensing an opportunity to discredit Secretary of State Adams, denied ever having approved the scheme and refused to intervene. The administration, consequently, could not prevent the Senate from modifying the original agreement. Because the Senate's alterations proved unacceptable to the British, the agreement was killed.[37]

"After 1822,'' writes Harry Ammon, "it can be justly said that an 'Era of Bad Feelings' totally eclipsed the harmony evident during his first term.''[38] Without parties to institutionalize cultural disagreement, politics proved far more acrimonious than had politics with parties. The prevailing "state of irritation,'' Crawford estimated, "greatly exceeds anything which has occurred in the history of this government.''[39] Rather than promoting national unity, Monroe's policy of cultural fusion had spawned "a bewildering array of elite personalities, factions, cliques, and juntos.''[40]

Looking back, one can see that the "formless confusion'' of this period was not inevitable.[41] Rather than strive for a cultural union, Monroe could have attempted to forge a new dominant cultural alliance of hierarchy and individualism. In terms of cabinet formation this would have meant jettisoning Crawford, leader of the Old Jeffersonians, in favor of Clay, spokesman for the neo-Federalist program of improvements, tariffs, and a national bank—

thereby signaling his intention to court individualists away from the Jeffersonian alliance in favor of what would later become the Whig alliance of hierarchy and individualism. This path would have been hazardous; Monroe would have been excoriated as a Federalist, a monarchist, and worse. Yet, by making such enemies, the president might have been able to unite his friends around a political program of defense, tariffs, and improvements.

The president's unwillingness to clarify the cultural battle lines by repudiating the Crawfordite ''Radicals'' reflected, in part, the conflict within Monroe between the old republican creed of his youth—emphasizing states' rights, laissez faire, and so on—and the postwar, ''modern'' republicanism that stressed nationalism in the form of defense, internal improvements, tariffs, and acceptance of the national bank. Monroe's reluctance to choose between these cultural alliances was manifest in his refusal to support any candidate in the presidential election of 1824, thereby abandoning the precedent, begun with Jefferson, of naming a successor.[42] The desire to earn the applause of both groups paralyzed Monroe.

During his second term Monroe could create agreement only by avoiding issues. In his annual message in December 1822, the president limited himself to vague and inoffensive generalities.[43] Unwilling to alienate any culture, Monroe immobilized his administration. He refused, for instance, to exert influence in the selection of the speaker of the House for fear that he would appear to favor one faction over another. A Crawford ally, James Barbour, narrowly gained the post and selected enemies of the administration for vital committee chairmanships, such as Military Affairs and Foreign Affairs. As a result, the Radicals were able to gut the defense program upon which Monroe had placed such a high priority.[44]

The fractiousness and paralysis of Monroe's second term led many to question the wisdom of his policy of amalgamation. Van Buren assailed ''the Monroe heresy.'' Not only ''must [we] always have party divisions,'' contended Van Buren, but ''the old ones are best.''[45] Even those who did not attack Monroe personally were coming to doubt the wisdom of cultural fusion. Jefferson, for one, now believed that the ''wholesome . . . party divisions of whig and tory'' served to ''keep out those of a more dangerous character,'' i.e. those with hierarchical propensities.[46] While others were abandoning the notion of the possibility and desirability of a permanent cultural union, Monroe remained wedded to the notion that a single party could encompass all political cultures.

In view of the administration's failure to develop an integrative solution that could sustain ''Good Feelings,'' it is ironic that Monroe's name is linked with a policy that stands as a classic example of a successful integrative solution, the Monroe Doctrine. Future generations of Americans would pledge allegiance to the doctrine, even though, or more accurately, because they all had something different in mind. Underlying disagreements on foreign policy were papered over because different cultures could agree on the policy for different reasons.

Monroe, no doubt, would be highly gratified by the unanimity that until recently has surrounded the Monroe Doctrine. With the passage of time, concludes Dexter Perkins, the document's most distinguished historian, the Monroe Doctrine has won "widespread, indeed almost unanimous, support in American public opinion."[47] So perfectly has the Monroe Doctrine matched the American society's ethos," comments Cecil Crabb, that "it has come to be viewed . . . as an integral part of 'the American way of life.' "[48] But Crabb misses the essential point: the Monroe Doctrine has enjoyed such unanimity not because it coincides with *the* American ethos but because it was tailored to fit different American ethoses.

Throughout his term Monroe had tried to lead without identifying himself with any single culture, but not until the Monroe Doctrine (issued on December 2, 1823) did the president find the type of integrative solution that might have made this possible. Like Washington's Farewell Address, Monroe's message produced agreement despite underlying cultural disagreement. His decision to turn down the British offer of a joint declaration was especially important in giving the message an appeal that bridged different political cultures.

To some, Monroe's message reaffirmed isolationism—a pledge to avoid "European entanglements." Had the message been issued jointly, as Monroe initially had wanted, it would have appeared that the United States was entering into the European system of alliances and balance of power politics. As it stood, however, Monroe's promise not to involve the country in the European sphere satisfied those "Radicals" who favored reducing the military establishment.[49] Yet, if the Monroe Doctrine was a commitment to isolationism, it was also a promise to intervene in areas within the United States sphere of influence.[50] To those in favor of flexing United States might and building up a military establishment, this commitment would serve as an excellent pretext.

Moreover, by avoiding a joint declaration, the Monroe Doctrine satisfied Americans with expansionist ambitions. A joint Anglo-American statement of nonintervention in the Americas would have restricted the freedom of the United States to acquire, for example, Cuba, or Texas.[51] Others saw the doctrine's noncolonization principle as an affirmation of national self-determination. Monroe issued an explicit, ideological challenge to "the political system" of the Old World monarchies, which all Americans could agree were fatalist regimes.[52] Meanwhile, business and commercial interests celebrated the assurance of continued American access to Latin American markets.[53] Finally, the Monroe Doctrine, issued without any consultation with Congress, powerfully affirmed executive authority in foreign policy.[54]

The Monroe Doctrine, cracked one pundit, is "as elastic as india Rubber."[55] Vagueness is a prerequisite to an effective integrative solution because different people must be able read into it their differing cultural predilections. The more precisely the policy is spelled out, the more difficult it becomes to attach conflicting interpretations to it. Yet, if an integrative solution is to generate support for the president, it must not be widely perceived as having avoided the issues. Although scholars have drawn attention to how little was settled by Monroe's message,[56] his contemporaries viewed it as a decisive, bold stroke. Across the political spectrum, elites joined in "the general glow of exultation."[57] The result of the Monroe Doctrine, concludes Ernest May, "was to make foreign policy less a matter of controversy than it might otherwise have been."[58] The bitter conflict over domestic policy, however, continued to escalate. Only in foreign policy, then, could Monroe's successor, John Quincy Adams, hope to cut through the cultural confusion bequeathed him.

Denying Cultural Conflict: John Quincy Adams

The 1824 election came down to a four-way contest between Monroe's Secretary of the Treasury William Crawford, Secretary of State John Quincy Adams, Speaker of the House Henry Clay, and the military hero, Andrew Jackson. Crawford carried the Old Republican banner, but he was burdened by ill health and by the Republican caucus nomination, which, as one historian remarks, hung "like an albatross around his neck."[59] Clay's close identification with his "American System" of protective tariffs, internal improvements, and centralized banking made that candidacy anathema to many. By leaving his domestic views vague and basing his appeal primarily on accomplishments in foreign policy, Adams was able to broaden his appeal. All three, however, stood at a disadvantage relative to Jackson, who benefited from his image as an outsider. Because he was not one of "those creatures that derive their nurture about the public dunghill," many voters looked to Jackson as the man to cleanse "the Great Augean Stables at Washington."[60]

Although Jackson won pluralities in the popular and electoral vote, the crowded field kept him from securing a majority.[61] The election was consequently thrown into the House, where Clay delivered his support to Adams; this gave Adams a victory on the first ballot. Adams's presidency was to be severely hampered by the perception that his election, like "King Caucus"— the epithet given to the practice of Senate nomination of presidential candidates—was another instance of Washington politicians thwarting the will of the country. An early indication of Adams's lack of sensitivity to popular suspicions about the national government was his decision to select Clay as secretary of state, which raised the charge of "bargain and corruption" that would carry Jackson into the White House four years later.

In his inaugural address President Adams announced his intention to continue the cultural fusion policy of his predecessor, James Monroe.[62] "My great object," Adams explained to the Federalist John Reed, "will be to break up the remnants of old party distinctions and bring the whole people together in sentiment as much as possible.''[63] The success of a strategy of cultural amalgamation depends on the political leader's pursuing a course that satisfies competing political cultures. Though Monroe did run into severe difficulties in his last two years, his nonpartisan assertions had been made credible because he had looked for a common policy ground, and had included leaders of various factions in his cabinet. Adams hoped to retain Monroe's cabinet, to offer the vacant War Department to Jackson, and to bring in Clay to head the State Department. With Crawford in the Treasury Department, and two supporters of Vice President John Calhoun—Samuel Southard and John McLean—in the administration, Adams could legitimately declare that his presidency encompassed all political cultures.[64]

Adams's plans were quickly dashed, however, by Crawford's immediate refusal and by the news that Jackson would decline any offer. Rather than a cabinet representing all cultures, Adams wound up forming a cabinet that basically shared his own cultural propensities. Later all of them would join the Whig party. This fundamental agreement, especially on the issue of internal improvements, explains the much more harmonious relations of Adams's cabinet compared with Monroe's cabinet.[65] Harmony within the cabinet, however, was purchased at the price of undermining Adams's claim to be a partisan of no single culture. Because he excluded influential leaders of opposing factions, Adams could not mobilize support in Congress, as had Monroe.

Having failed to emulate Monroe's fusion strategy in his cabinet, Adams proceeded also to depart dramatically from his predecessor's policy proposals. Nine months after issuing a call for an umbrella regime comprising all political cultures, Adams delivered his infamous first annual message to Congress, in which he outlined a program unequivocally endorsing the hierarchical agenda. The president urged Congress to establish a department of the interior, a national naval academy, a national university, a national astronomical observatory, a uniform national militia law, a uniform system of weights and measures, and most important, a national system of internal improvements.[66]

Although Adams's predecessors, Monroe and Madison, had favored federally sponsored internal improvements, they had always tempered this with the belief that a constitutional amendment was a prerequisite to such action. Requiring a constitutional amendment was sound political strategy, for it insured that widespread support for government action would be obtained before the government proceeded. One could construe Adams's inaugural address as indicating a willingness to abide by this compromise formula. He acknowledged existing differences in opinion concerning the national government's power to legislate upon internal improvements, and pledged to act ''within the limits of the constitutional power of the Union.''[67] In the December message, however, Adams forsook his predecessors' policy of muddling through, and announced that government not only had the constitutional right to underwrite the nation's highway and waterway systems but that to fail to do so "would be treachery to the most sacred of trusts." The president lectured Congress on the "sacred and indispensable" duty of government to exercise its powers for "the progressive improvement of the condition of the governed." "Moral, political, [and] intellectual improvement," he explained, were "duties assigned by the Author of Our existence to social no less than to individual man."[68]

The address starkly revealed the cultural chasm between Adams and the Jeffersonian Republicans. To Jeffersonians, improvement sponsored by the government would drive out individual initiative. The central premise of Jeffersonian republicanism was that liberty and power, the individual and the central government, were engaged in a perpetual, antagonistic struggle. For Adams, however, writes George A. Lipsky, "government . . . was not . . . an unfriendly, inimical force to be kept at a minimum. There was much that was dramatic and good, and even magnificent, that government should do, in fact must do, if it was to fulfill its purpose."[69] Adams instructed the nation that "liberty is power" and urged Congress "to give efficacy to the means committed to you for the common good."[70] To a people that looked on foreign governments as corrupt monarchies, Adams spoke of the need to emulate the "gigantic strides . . . in public improvements" being made by foreign nations; he chided congressmen not to be "palsied by the will of our constituents."[71]

Adams saw no inconsistency between the antiparty theme of his inaugural address and the nationalistic program of his December message to Congress. Championing the cause of the Union, Adams assumed, demonstrated that as president he was above party and section. Forceful advocacy of internal improvements, the president believed, would place him before the country as "the Man of the Whole Nation."[72] Like his father, Adams saw himself sitting atop a hierarchy at the head of the nation, rather than down in the arena of competing cultures. Denying cultural conflict, however, did not allow Adams to escape it. His presidency was immediately buried under an avalanche of criticism for what was widely perceived as a blatant revival of the Hamiltonian agenda.[73]

Adams's message helped clarify the cultural confusion that had accompanied Monroe's amalgamation policy. Recognizing in Adams a cultural foe, supporters of Jackson, Crawford, and Calhoun groped toward an antiauthority alliance. To combat this opposition, it was imperative for Adams to build up those who were willing to support the cultural agenda that Adams was advancing.

Executive patronage was the most important tool available to Adams in securing political support for his program and person. The Tenure of Office Act of 1820, by limiting the terms of many federal officeholders to four years, had made it easier for presidents to remove executive officers. Government supporters repeatedly urged the administration that "if [it] . . . would have friends, it must make friends," but Adams was unwilling to countenance the partisan means necessary to secure his partisan ends.[74] The president refused to remove government officials for partisan reasons, and available posts were not dispensed with an eye to creating political support for his policy agenda. Most damaging was Adams's refusal to remove John McLean, a Calhoun-Jackson partisan, who, as postmaster general, dispensed patronage to Adams's opponents. Increasingly aware that a nonpartisan appointment policy was undermining the administration's activist agenda, Clay tried to impress upon Adams the need to adhere to the principle "of appointing only friends to the Administration in public offices."[75]

The president's resistance to building the political-partisan support necessary to establish his program and secure reelection stemmed, in large part, from his hierarchical conception of government and society. In Adams's view, a subordinate in the government should carry out policy that flowed down from the apex of the hierarchy. Believing policy to be agreed upon, and implementation a matter of neutral competence, Adams saw his subordinates as above or apart from politics. In the absence of subversion or malfeasance, qualified officials should be retained. Adams was reluctant to dismiss McLean because he believed the postmaster general to be "an able and efficient officer." At all levels of the executive branch, Adams believed that continuity in office fostered expertise and stability, and would therefore be of great value in implementing the activist government he envisioned.[76]

To appoint on the basis of partisan policy also conflicted with Adams's hierarchical conception of society. Where there is more than one party, partisanship is in continual tension with hierarchy. Accepting the validity of parties—which institutionalize conflict by setting parts in competition with one another—calls into question the hierarchical assumption that the parts of the whole are in harmony. In a hierarchical social order, to pit one part of the body politic against another is perceived as unhealthy, even perverse. A hierarchical leader perceives his role as speaking for the whole, not adopting the cause of a part.[77] Refusing to acknowledge that his program advanced a particular cultural agenda, Adams was reluctant to use the partisan policies necessary to gain political support for his vision.

Historians continue to debate whether Adams's failures as president resulted from circumstance or personality, situation or political ineptitude. While acknowledging the difficulties of the times, one view nevertheless focuses on the president's alleged personal rigidity, his uncompromising personality. The drawback with this view is that Adams often showed himself to be a proficient politician, and quite amenable to compromise. In a chapter entitled "John Quincy Adams, Nonpartisan Politician," Daniel Walker Howe demonstrates Adams's considerable political skill as diplomat, secretary of state, and congressman.[78] A recent biographer writes that in his pursuit of the presidency, Adams displayed "a natural aptitude for political maneuvering that was as inspired as some of his diplomatic efforts."[79] If the stereotype of Adams as a blundering politician is faulty, perhaps the situation is to blame.

Stephen Skowronek suggests that Adams was "caught in the crisis of the old order," and therefore—like Jimmy Carter, Herbert Hoover, and Franklin Pierce—faced an "impossible leadership situation."[80] This conclusion, however, understates Adams's naiveté as a political leader. Sensitive to the nation's bias against authority, President Monroe had settled for a relatively low-key leadership role. By concentrating his energies on a few issues about which he felt most strongly, particularly national defense, he was able to achieve some of his objectives. Adams lacked Monroe's appreciation for the antileadership nature of American political culture. Believing government was a force for good, and that the leader's duty was to offer active direction for society, Adams rejected the covert leadership style of Jefferson, Madison, and Monroe. Treating support for authority as nonproblematic, Adams bombarded Congress with every good idea he had for the improvement of society. Rather than argue with the president's suggestions, Congress simply ignored them.[81] Adams's difficulty was less that the Jeffersonian regime was crumbling, as Skowronek contends, but rather that the hierarchical style and substance of Adams's leadership were out of touch with the antiauthority dispositions of Jeffersonian political culture—soon to be revitalized under the banner of Andrew Jackson.

Adams's cultural dilemma stemmed from the contradiction between needing to behave like a hierarchical leader and carrying out a hierarchical agenda. His hierarchical propensities kept Adams from embracing the role of party leader that was necessary for him to realize his political program. Accepting the legitimacy of partisanship conflicted with hierarchical assumptions about the nature of social organization. If competition between parties was beneficial, the hierarchical metaphor for society as an organic body must be false. Adams was unable or unwilling to retreat from playing "the Man of the Whole Nation" to acting as leader of one party, for this would have entailed sacrificing his conception of himself as a hierarch and his conception of society as hierarchical. Assimilation was the price of adaptation.

The covert, limited leadership practiced by his predecessors also violated Adams's conception of how a political leader was supposed to behave. Benevolent and wise, authority was to be asserted not hidden. Insofar as this constituted a public teaching on the need for authority, it had positive aspects. But if all the public learned was that efforts to exercise leadership were futile, it did no good. Adams had failed to solve the cultural dilemma of being a hierarch in a nonhierarchical context, and so, unresolved, it was passed on for the entire Whig party to wrestle with.

Notes

1. Richard Hofstadter, *The Idea of a Party System: The Rise of Legitimate Opposition in the United States, 1780-1840* (Berkeley: University of California Press, 1969), p. 197.
2. Harry Ammon, "James Monroe and the Era of Good Feelings," *Virginia Magazine of History and Biography* (October 1958): 395.
3. Shaw Livermore, Jr., *The Twilight of Federalism: The Disintegration of the Federalist Party, 1815-1830* (Princeton: Princeton University Press, 1962), pp. 48-49; Ammon, "Good Feelings," p. 394; Harry Ammon, *James Monroe: The Quest for National Identity* (New York: McGraw-Hill, 1971), pp. 374-77.
4. Ammon, *James Monroe*, p. 374.
5. George Dangerfield, *The Era of Good Feelings* (New York: Harcourt, Brace, 1952), p. 95; Ammon, *James Monroe*, p. 366.
6. Monroe to Jackson, December 14, 1816, cited in Hofstadter, *Idea of a Party System*, p. 196.
7. See, for example, Ralph Ketcham, *Presidents above Party: The First American Presidency, 1789-1829* (Chapel Hill: University of North Carolina Press, 1984).
8. Livermore, *Twilight of Federalism*, p. 48.
9. Robert Kelley, *The Cultural Pattern in American Politics: The First Century* (New York: Knopf, 1979), p. 137.
10. Ammon, *James Monroe*, pp. 370, 387.
11. Ibid., p. 378.
12. Ibid., pp. 463, 465. Dangerfield, *Good Feelings*, p. 179.
13. Kim T. Phillips, "Democrats of the Old School in the Era of Good Feelings," *Pennsylvania Magazine of History and Biography* (July 1971): 379.
14. Ammon, *James Monroe*, p. 392; Carlton B. Smith, "Congressional Attitudes toward Military Preparedness during the Monroe Administration," *Military Affairs* (February 1976): 22-25.
15. Smith, "Attitudes toward Military Preparedness," p. 24.
16. Crawford to Albert Gallatin, March 12, 1817, in Charles S. Sydnor, "The One-Party Period of American History," *American Historical Review* (April 1946): 450.
17. Madison to Monroe, May 17, 1806, in J.C.A. Stagg, *Mr. Madison's War: Politics, Diplomacy and Warfare in the Early American Republic, 1783-1830* (Princeton: Princeton University Press, 1983), p. 53. See also Jefferson's prescient observation in Robert M. Johnstone, Jr., *Jefferson and the Presidency: Leadership in the Young Republic* (Ithaca: Cornell University Press, 1978), pp. 155, 223-24.
18. Monroe to Jackson, December 14, 1816, cited in Hofstadter, *Idea of a Party System*, p. 196.
19. Phillips, "Democrats of the Old School"; quotation on p. 377. Also see Kim Tousley Phillips, "William Duane, Revolutionary Editor" (Ph.D. diss., University of California, Berkeley, 1968).
20. Phillips, "Democrats of the Old School," pp. 364, 370, 377.
21. Ibid., p. 367.
22. Ibid., p. 373; see also pp. 365, 370.

23. Quoted in Joel H. Silbey, "The Incomplete World of American Politics, 1815-1829: Presidents, Parties and Politics in 'The Era of Good Feelings,' " *Congress and the Presidency* (Spring 1984): 9-10.

24. Jefferson to Gallatin, August 2, 1823, cited in Arthur M. Schlesinger, Jr., *The Age of Jackson* (Boston: Little, Brown, 1945), p. 26.

25. Jefferson to W. T. Barry, July 3, 1722, cited in Kim T. Phillips, "The Pennsylvania Origins of the Jackson Movement," *Political Science Quarterly* (Fall 1976): 500.

26. Silbey, "Incomplete World of American Politics," p. 3; see also Phillips, "Democrats of the Old School," p. 363.

27. Harry Ammon, "Executive Leadership in the Monroe Administration," in *America: The Middle Period*, ed. John B. Boles (Charlottesville: University Press of Virginia, 1973), pp. 117-18; Ammon, *James Monroe*, p. 380.

28. Ammon, "Executive Leadership," p. 118.

29. Leonard D. White, *The Jeffersonians: A Study in Administrative History, 1801-1829* (New York: Free Press, 1951), p. 81.

30. Edward Corwin, quoted in Richard F. Fenno, Jr., *The President's Cabinet* (New York: Vintage Books, 1959), p. 255.

31. Ammon, "Executive Leadership," esp. pp. 120-21; Ammon, *James Monroe*, pp. 384-85. On congressional resentment of executive interference, see Ammon, "Executive Leadership," pp. 115-17, 119-20.

32. Ammon, "Era of Good Feelings," pp. 388-89, 397; Ammon, *James Monroe*, pp. 384-85, 362, 410.

33. Ammon, *James Monroe*, pp. 421-31, quotation on p. 423; Ammon, "Executive Leadership," pp. 122-24.

34. Ammon, "Executive Leadership," pp. 124, 130-31.

35. James Sterling Young, *The Washington Community, 1800-1828* (New York: Columbia University Press, 1966), p. 235.

36. Ammon, *James Monroe*, p. 360.

37. Ammon, "Executive Leadership," pp. 124-26; Ammon, *James Monroe*, pp. 385, 526-27.

38. Ammon, *James Monroe*, p. 529.

39. Young, *Washington Community*, p. 235.

40. Ronald P. Formisano, *The Birth of Mass Political Parties: Michigan, 1827-1861* (Princeton: Princeton University Press, 1971), pp. 3-4.

41. Quotation is from Silbey, "Incomplete World of American Politics," p. 4.

42. Ammon, *James Monroe*, p. 529; Robert V. Remini, *Martin Van Buren and the Making of the Democratic Party* (New York: Columbia University Press, 1959), p. 24. Monroe was also apparently torn between whether to model his presidency on the presidency of George Washington or that of Jefferson. On Monroe's efforts to model himself after Washington, see, e.g., Ammon, "Era of Good Feelings," p. 392; and Ammon, *James Monroe*, 396-97.

43. Ammon, *James Monroe*, p. 509.

44. Ibid., pp. 498-99.

45. Remini, *Van Buren and Democratic Party*, pp. 12-29. Silbey, "Incomplete World of American Politics," p. 8.

46. Phillips, "Origins of Jackson Movement," p. 500.

47. Dexter Perkins, cited in Cecil V. Crabb, Jr., *The Doctrines of American Foreign Policy* (Baton Rouge: Louisiana State University Press, 1982), p. 33.

48. Ibid., pp. 9-10.

49. Doris A. Graber, *Public Opinion, the President, and Foreign Policy: Four Case*

Studies from the Formative Years (New York: Holt, Rinehart & Winston, 1968), p. 269.

50. Crabb, *Doctrines of Foreign Policy*, pp. 18, 24.
51. Ibid., p. 17; Graber, *Public Opinion, the President, and Foreign Policy*, p. 269.
52. Crabb, *Doctrines of Foreign Policy*, pp. 17-20.
53. Ibid., p. 33.
54. Ibid., pp. 29-32.
55. Cited ibid., p. 11.
56. See, e.g., Ernest R. May, *The Making of the Monroe Doctrine* (Cambridge: Harvard University Press, 1975), pp. 217-18, 228, 240. Also see Graber, *Public Opinion, the President, and Foreign Policy*, pp. 293-94.
57. Daniel Webster, quoted in Graber, *Public Opinion, the President, and Foreign Policy*, p. 294; see also Madison's comments on p. 281.
58. May, *Making of Monroe Doctrine*, p. 253.
59. George Dangerfield, *The Awakening of American Nationalism, 1815-1828* (New York: Harper & Row), p. 218.
60. Quoted in Phillips, "Origins of the Jackson Movement," pp. 501-2.
61. The popular vote was Jackson 153,544, Adams 108,740, Clay 47,136, Crawford 46,618; and the electoral count was Jackson 99, Adams 84, Crawford 41, Clay 37.
62. Mary W. M. Hargreaves, *The Presidency of John Quincy Adams* (Lawrence: University Press of Kansas, 1985), pp. 41-42; Samuel Flagg Bemis, *John Quincy Adams and the Union* (New York: Knopf, 1956), pp. 55-56; Hofstadter, *Idea of a Party System*, pp. 233-35. Monroe's tenure, Adams wrote in November 1823, would be remembered as "the golden age of this republic."
63. Bemis, *Adams and the Union*, p. 44.
64. Hargreaves, *Presidency of Adams*, p. 48.
65. Michael J. Birkner and Robert Thompson, "The Pre-Civil War Cabinet's Role in Presidential Policy Making, with a Special Focus on the Administration of John Quincy Adams" (Paper delivered at the 1985 Annual Meeting of the American Political Science Association), p. 9. See also Charles D. Lowery, *James Barbour: A Jeffersonian Republican* (University: University of Alabama Press, 1984), p. 153. On James Barbour, Adams's secretary of war, see Lowery, *James Barbour*, pp. 150, 154, 168, 172-73, 179-81, 228, and passim. On the secretary of the navy, Samuel Southard, see Michael Birkner, *Samuel L. Southard: Jeffersonian Whig* (Rutherford, N.J.: Fairleigh Dickinson University Press, 1984), esp. p. 88. Though he thought Adams's first annual message "excessively bold," the attorney general, William Wirt, told Adams, "There is not a line in it which I do not approve" (Bemis, *Adams and the Union*, p. 68). The shared outlook of Clay and Adams was almost immediately apparent (Hargreaves, *Presidency of Adams*, pp. 38, 65). Adams's choice as secretary of the Treasury, Richard Rush, was the firmest proponent of national authority of the group (Hargreaves, *Presidency of Adams*, p. 49). Postmaster General John McLean did not share Adams's policy preferences, but he was not a member of the official cabinet.
66. Bemis, *Adams and the Union*, p. 69.
67. Hargreaves, *Presidency of Adams*, p. 41.
68. Ketcham, *Presidents above Party*, p. 136. Hargreaves, *Presidency of Adams*, pp. 165-66. See also Daniel Walker Howe, *The Political Culture of the American Whigs* (Chicago: University of Chicago Press, 1979), p. 48.
69. George A. Lipsky, *John Quincy Adams: His Theory and Ideas* (New York: Crowell, 1950), p. 140; see also Ketcham, *Presidents above Party*, p. 133.

70. Adams, quoted in Bemis, *Adams and the Union*, p. 69; Hargreaves, *Presidency of Adams*, p. 208. See also Richard Latner. *The Presidency of Andrew Jackson: White House Politics, 1829-1837* (Athens: University of Georgia Press, 1979), p. 27.
71. Hargreaves, *Presidency of Adams*, p. 166.
72. Bemis, *Adams and the Union*, p. 65.
73. On the hostile reaction to Adams's message, see Remini, *Van Buren and the Democratic Party*, pp. 101-5; Birkner, *Samuel Southard*, p. 73; and Lowery, *James Barbour*, pp. 169-71, 173-74.
74. Hargreaves, *Presidency of Adams*, pp. 258-61; Nathaniel Greene Cleary quoted on p. 259.
75. Ibid., pp. 259-61; Clay, quoted on p. 261. On McLean, see pp. 50-53, 239-40. During his four-year tenure, Adams removed only twelve persons from office (Bemis, *Adams and the Union*, p. 65).
76. Hargreaves, *Presidency of Adams*, pp. 50-61, 65, 236-37; Adams quoted on p. 52. Also see Birkner, *Samuel Southard*, p. 76.
77. See Howe, *Political Culture of Whigs*, pp. 51-52. See also Sydney Nathans, *Daniel Webster and Jacksonian Democracy* (Baltimore: Johns Hopkins University Press, 1973), esp. pp. 5-6.
78. Howe, *Political Culture of Whigs*, esp. pp. 46-47, 60, 64.
79. Marie B. Hecht, cited ibid., p. 46.
80. Stephen Skowronek, "Presidential Leadership in Political Time," in *The Presidency and the Political System*, ed. Michael Nelson (Washington, D.C.: Congressional Quarterly Press, 1984), p. 129; Skowronek, "Notes on the Presidency in the Political Order," *Studies in American Political Development*, 1:292.
81. Bemis, *Adams and the Union*, pp. 75-76.

6

Building Up Presidential Authority
to Tear Down Hierarchy:
Andrew Jackson Creates
the Whig Dilemma

The Jacksonian movement was a self-conscious revival of Jeffersonian political culture. Many were alarmed by the retreat from Jeffersonian orthodoxy that dated from the conclusion of the War of 1812. Amos Kendall, an influential member of Andrew Jackson's "kitchen cabinet," found Monroe's principles closer to "federal republicans than republicans of the Jeffersonian school."[1] But if the Monroe administration's policies raised doubts about its fidelity to the Jeffersonian heritage, John Quincy Adams's administration signaled an even more ominous revival of Federalist hierarchy. Adams's presidency, John Randolph declared, "is the last four years of the Administration of the father renewed in the person of the son . . . . I bore some humble part in putting down the dynasty of John the First, and . . . I hope to aid in putting down the dynasty of John the Second."[2]

Deeply disturbed by Adams's premise that liberty and power were not necessarily antagonistic, egalitarians and individualists issued a call for a rededication to the Jeffersonian principles of limited government coupled with hostility to special privilege.[3] Improving the condition of the governed was to be achieved not, as Adams contended, through the central government but, rather, by liberating individuals from hierarchical institutions like the government.

Acute observers saw past the personalities of the 1828 presidential campaign to an underlying cultural conflict. On the day of his death, DeWitt Clinton wrote to a political ally assuring him that Jackson's victory would mean "the restoration of pure, republican principles," i.e. minimal central government.[4] Although many were not exactly sure what Jackson represented, they were convinced that to keep Adams meant an increase in government authority and binding prescriptions, and a corresponding decrease in liberty.

Martin Van Buren took it upon himself to insure that Jackson's victory would be not merely personal but would engender a restored two-party system with a Republican party devoted to Jeffersonian principles.[5] From the outset of his national political career, Van Buren had labored for a "resuscitation of the old democratic party," which he thought required a revival of a competitive two-party system.[6] Monroe's attempt to incorporate all elements of society under a single cultural umbrella, believed Van Buren, had produced a concentration of power in Washington and a Republican party permeated with Federalist principles.[7] Confident that in a battle of principle history would repeat itself and Jeffersonians would defeat the Federalists, Van Buren conceived of the two-party system as a means of keeping hierarchy from creeping into the ruling coalition.

The apprehensions of Van Buren and others concerning the depth of Jackson's commitment to Jeffersonian principles and a competitive two-party system were understandable,[8] but an attentive observer could have detected Jackson's identification with Jeffersonian political culture.[9] As a young congressman, Jackson had had his political beliefs significantly shaped by such old Republican ideologues as John Randolph, Nathaniel Macon, and Henry Tazewell.[10] "My political creed," Jackson proudly reported to James Polk in 1826, "was formed in the old republican school."[11] His political views were, as Richard Latner concludes, "basically Jeffersonian in origin," and reflected his preeminent "concern for preserving liberty . . . from the perilous influences of power and corruption."[12]

Jackson interpreted his election as a mandate to restore antiauthority principles to government.[13] By selecting Van Buren for the most prestigious cabinet post, secretary of state, Jackson signaled his intention to formulate a program devoted to Jeffersonian ends. The administration chose to veto the Maysville Road bill—requiring the federal government to buy stock in a corporation that was to extend the National Road from Maysville to Lexington, Kentucky—in order to take an early stand in favor of "reform, retrenchment and economy in the administration of Government."[14] A collaborative effort on the part of Van Buren and Jackson, the Maysville veto was designed, in Robert Remini's words, to allow "people, through their states, to conduct their own affairs."[15] That "true believer" of republicanism, John Randolph, rhapsodized that the veto "fell upon the ears like the music of other days."[16]

Jackson's Indian-removal policy reflected, ironically, the rigorous application of antihierarchical principles. As John Quincy Adams brooded over passage of the Indian-removal bill, he had correctly identified the measure "as part of a concerted effort to diminish the power of the federal government to do good." Only with government protection, as wards of the state, reasoned Adams, could the Indian hope to survive; only in a mansion with many rooms would the Indian be given a place. An individualist culture required Indians to compete. "The Indians are already sacrificed," lamented Adams; "domestic industry and internal improvement will be strangled; and when the public debt will be paid off and the bank charter expired, there will be no great interest left upon which the action of the General Government will operate."[17] The thrust of Jacksonian policy was, as Adams so clearly saw, to reduce the need for governmental authority.

The emerging cultural alignment was further crystallized by Jackson's veto of the bill to recharter the national bank. As the most visible concentration of financial and political power, the bank provided a compelling symbol around which to unite the two antiauthority cultures. Jackson's veto message was carefully crafted to fuse the individualist concern with economic competition with the egalitarian fear of inequalities. "The rich and powerful," Jackson declared, "too often bend the acts of government to their selfish purposes." "Distinctions in society will always exist under every just government," Jackson acknowledged, but when "the laws undertake to add . . . artificial distinctions, to grant titles, gratuities, and exclusive privileges, to make the rich richer and the potent more powerful, the humble members of society— the farmers, mechanics, and laborers—who have neither the time nor the means of securing like favors to themselves, have a right to complain of the injustice of their Government."[18] By conferring exclusive privileges on selected institutions, Jackson believed, the government was thwarting economic competition and opportunity, and thereby fostering inequalities. If government would leave individuals alone, not only liberty but also equality would increase. The belief that increased economic opportunity would produce greater equality of condition allowed egalitarians to unite with individualists—a fusion of cultures nicely captured by Charles Sellers's label "egalitarian enterprise."[19]

Because the central government created inequalities and suppressed competition, Jacksonians tried to limit strictly the scope of government activity. They agreed with their Jeffersonian predecessors that "government, like dress, is the badge of lost innocence." The world is governed too much" announced the lodestar on the Jackson administration mouthpiece, the *Washington Globe*. "The best government," agreed the influential *Democratic Review*, "is that which governs least."[20]

While committed to reclaiming the Jeffersonian heritage of minimal government, Jacksonians did soften somewhat the Jeffersonian antipathy to national defense. Jackson and his followers supported a positive role for government in the realm of foreign affairs, where it might serve its sole legitimate function of "keeping off evil."[21] Though government intervention in the domestic sphere created special privileges, in the foreign arena Jacksonians did not see government activity as unfairly advantaging one group at the expense of another. By promoting commerce with other nations, government could expand opportunities for everyone. Territorial expansion, they believed, maintained equality by opening up new opportunities. The West Point military academy, by contrast, because it was a symbol of special privilege, remained vulnerable to Jacksonian hostility.[22]

The Jacksonian aversion to central authority created the same presidential dilemma—reconciling individualistic and egalitarian dispositions with the exercise of authority—that the Jeffersonians had had to face.[23] In a culture that, as Rush Welter notes, often "carried [its] antipathy toward power to the point of casting opprobrium on the whole range of activities traditionally associated with governing," how could one govern?[24] How, as John Ashworth asks, "was the obedience of the people to government and to law to be secured in a society which had so undermined the claims, and therefore weakened the grip, of authority?"[25] Clearly, leadership in a culture of autonomous equals would demand great imagination and innovation if it were to avoid the fate—an ideology of inaction strangling a government that had to act—that befell Jefferson's successors.

The Mandated Presidency

In large part Andrew Jackson's historical significance rests on his success in providing an enduring solution to the problem of presidential leadership in an antiauthority culture. Jackson and his allies forged a justification of presidential power in a culture severely distrustful of the exercise of power. Unlike Jefferson's, Jackson's solution did not depend on the personal qualities of the officeholder and therefore was capable of sustaining successors.[26]

The Jacksonian justification of presidential power was closely tied to a defense of political parties. In the New York constitutional convention of 1821, Martin Van Buren defended the idea of extending the governor's power to appoint local officials on the grounds that this would strengthen the parties, which would in turn empower the majority. "That power," argued Van Buren, "would be put in the hands of the executive, not for himself, but to secure to the majority of the people that control and influence . . . to which they are justly entitled."[27] Van Buren's reasoning anticipated basic doctrines of Jacksonian Democracy in which executive leadership was justified as the instrument of the majority.

Democrats commonly sought to allay fears of executive power, finds M. J. Heale, "by making the president the obedient servant of the party, and hence of the people." A Democratic president, continues Heale, was to be "a servant rather than a leader, dutifully carrying out the wishes of his electoral masters."[28] Consequently, the Democrats preferred loyal party servants as presidential candidates, a preference not shared by the Whig party. A campaign biography of Van Buren proudly broadcast that the Democrats—in contrast to the Whigs, who "cast around for great men"—"want, for public office, servants and not masters; agents who will execute their will and not dictators to control it."[29] The Democratic flagbearers who followed Jackson—Van Buren, James Polk, Lewis Cass, Franklin Pierce, and James Buchanan—were above all "regular and reliable party men."[30]

The Whigs disagreed with the Democratic view that a political leader should be a mere "specimen of his constituents." The president, Whigs believed, should be a man of special talent and wisdom, set off from the common crowd. They could not understand how a Democratic editor could praise Polk for being "a man whose virtues are more conspicuous than his talents." But the Democrats wanted a leader who was like those he represented, "an equal among equals."[31] The successful Democratic leader had to have the ability, which Jackson had, to lead men and yet appear as one of them. In Jacksonian thought, explains John William Ward, "the vertical distance that separates the leader from the led must be denied." One of the easiest ways to shrink the distance while also swelling follower allegiance is through a nickname. Not surprisingly, "Old Hickory" was the first president to be accorded a nickname.[32]

Whigs felt no such need to lessen the distance between leader and follower. In fact, the further the leader was from the pressure of the follower, the more "disinterested" was the leadership. Only the leader unfettered by commitments and pledges could be trusted to deliberate in the national interest. Political leaders, in the Whig mind, were to be "trustees," not agents.[33]

Whigs celebrated "that lofty independence and integrity of mind which should characterize representatives of the people." They saw the practice of instruction as "totally irreconcilable to the first principles of Representative Governments." A political leader should be left "entirely free to act after thorough discussion and mature deliberation, as his best judgement shall dictate." In a public letter, Millard Fillmore explained that he was "opposed to giving any pledges that shall deprive me hereafter of all discretionary power. My own character must be the guaranty for the general correctness of my legislative deportment." In a similar vein, Zachary Taylor wrote to his son that, if chosen to occupy the White House, "I must be untrammeled and unpledged, so as to be president of the nation and not of the party."[34]

The Democratic view could hardly have been more different. Being pledged to the party and instructed by the people was what legitimized Democratic presidents' role as leaders. Only because they were executing the public will and (therefore exercising minimal discretion) could they justify their leadership. The political leader was a "delegate" who, according to the *Democratic Review*, "should have no will of his own which is independent of that of his constituents." Democrats defended the right of constituents to instruct their representatives, and the propriety of leaders making pledges to their constituents. for this was "the only safeguard of the people against the encroachments of power."[35]

The "delegate" theory of representation provided an effective cover under which leaders could exercise power while denying they were doing anything more than carrying out the popular mandate. If the president had a mandate to carry out a policy, there was no reason to fear "executive usurpation." Jackson insisted that he could hear not only the voice of the people in his elections but their precise words. The 1832 election, for instance, Jackson construed as popular vindication of his bank veto and a mandate to continue his financial policies.[36]

After his reelection, Jackson decided to step up the Bank War by removing all government deposits from the "Monster Bank." Jackson publicly defended his action by drawing attention to the "solemn decision of the American people" expressed in the recent election. To his cabinet, he explained that he "had felt it his duty to exert the power with which the confidence of his countrymen had clothed him." In moving "to check and lessen its [the bank's] ability to do mischief," Jackson argued, he was only following the popular will.[37] Thus a concept—that the citizenry instructed or mandated public officials to act—originally designed to increase popular control over legislative elites became, in the hands of Jackson, a means of empowering leaders.

The corollary to the mandate theory, as articulated by Jackson, was that the president, rather than Congress, was "the tribune of the people." The president, Democrats agreed, was "the very point where the popular will is most potently concentrated." "The President," Jackson thundered, "is *the* direct representative of the American people."[38] Polk, Jackson's protègè, would later make the same point even more bluntly: The president, "Young Hickory" brashly asserted, "is more representative than Congress of the whole people."[39]

Jackson's preference for appealing directly to the people and over the head of Congress was well suited to his negative policy aims. Lacking, for the most part, a positive legislative program that would require the support of a majority, he could afford to alienate Congress. And alienate Congress he did. Angered by Jackson's removal of the deposits by executive order and his firing of Treasury Secretary William Duane—who refused to carry out Jackson's order—the Senate took the unprecedented step of censuring the president for what Henry Clay labeled "open, palpable and daring usurpation."[40] Jackson's successors, Van Buren and Polk, both of whom needed congressional cooperation to enact legislation, would find real limitations in Jackson's confrontational leadership strategy.

It is a great irony that the party that most distrusted power contributed so much to its justification. But while the Democrats did create a compelling defense of assertive presidential action, it must be remembered that for the most part it was the veto power that Democrats were defending. "Whig efforts to equate the power to nullify legislation with the power to rule,"[41] observes Rush Welter, were consistently rejected by Democrats.

The negative power of the veto, which Jackson employed more than all his predecessors combined, and more than any other pre-Civil War president, fit well with Democratic political culture. It was exercised in the name of curbing power, checking the wasteful expenditures produced by the corrupting mix of public and private power in the halls of Congress. Because the veto could "only be exercised in a negative sense," Democrats reasoned that it posed no danger to liberty.[42] Originally designed by the Federalists as a check upon democracy, the executive veto was now portrayed as the people's main weapon in the battle to promote equality by limiting government.

The Jacksonians' defense of the presidency was thus more limited than is commonly assumed. Given their ingrained distrust of power it could not have been otherwise. Though willing to defend the veto, they clung to a haunting fear of the "alluring and corrupting influence of the Executive patronage."[43] In his final major address to the Senate in 1828, Van Buren identified himself with those who preferred to "limit the extent of executive authority" and criticized those who sought to "condense . . . all power [in] a single head."[44] Fifteen years later Van Buren was still worrying about the president's power of appointment, which was "peculiarly adapted to the sinister purposes of ambitious and selfish aspirations" (as opposed to the veto power that he viewed as having been "uniformly exercised for the public advantage").[45] Welter concludes that "the portrait Democrats typically drew of executive power was unflattering and apprehensive except when they were able to visualize an incumbent as the tribune of the people."[46] The *Democratic Review*'s proclamation to its readers—"We are no friends to strong government action. We are no friends to powerful executive influence"[47]—captures the tenuous and limited nature of the Jacksonians' support for executive leadership.

Jackson's political genius consisted in fusing an energetic chief executive with the cause of limited central government. Presidential activism was justified in the name of limiting the activities of hierarchical institutions, the "Monster Bank," "King Caucus," even government itself. Presidential powers were to be enlisted in the battle to remove institutional impediments to freedom and equality. Extending the franchise, overthrowing the caucus system, and instituting rotation in office would increase public participation. Terminating the privileges conferred by government upon private industry through charters and franchises would permit the unfettered operation of free enterprise and, thereby (in their view) promote equality.

Since its founding the presidency had been regarded with widespread suspicion as the institutional representation of hierarchy. Jefferson, Madison, and Monroe all were troubled by the sense that to act openly would constitute betrayal of their antiauthority ideals. By demonstrating that the executive could be used to undermine hierarchy, Jackson smashed the link in the popular mind between the presidency and hierarchy. Where Jefferson, for instance, fearing cries of executive "corruption," had carefully masked the removal of Federalists from public office, Jackson trumpeted his removals in full view of the public, thus elevating the principle of rotation in office to a positive good.[48] Now that the presidency was perceived to be in the service of "the people"— flattening the hierarchy by increasing popular control over those in positions of authority—presidential leadership no longer needed to be hidden. In solving the leadership dilemma for the alliance of egalitarianism and individualism, however, Jackson added an extra twist to the dilemma facing adherents of hierarchy, for they were now torn between their hierarchical inclination to support authority and fear that the presidency would destroy their hierarchical way of life.

The Whig Dilemma: Hierarchy without a Hierarch

Though the term *Whig* was not formally used to designate the party until 1834, the party's origins go back to the commencement of Jackson's bank war. The dominant element of this new party came from the Clay-Adams coalition that had been operating under the label of "national republican." Opposition to Jackson's "usurpation" became the party's primary issue in the 1832 presidential campaign that followed on the heels of the bank veto.[49] In defining itself in opposition to "King Andrew," the Whig party created a cultural anomaly: a hierarchy without a hierarch.

Those who wanted to sustain hierarchy by building respect for authority turned naturally to the Whig party. The Whigs shared with the Democrats an "entrepreneurial temperament,"[50] i.e. an individualistic orientation, but differed in their selection of cultural allies. Rush Welter captures the Whig alliance of individualism and hierarchy in his characterization of "the Whig ethic" as "property and paternalism."[51] And John Ashworth contrasts the Democrats' vision of "a society of independent equals" with that of the Whigs, who "in advocating individuality . . . stressed both the differences between men and their mutual dependence."[52]

The difference between Whig and Democratic cultures was reflected, among other places, in their divergent conceptions of the role of government.[53] Whigs rejected the Democratic premise that the interests of government and the governed were in conflict. Horace Greeley articulated the Whig belief that "government need not and should not be an institution of purely negative, repressive usefulness and value, but . . . should exert a beneficent, paternal, fostering usefulness upon the Industry and Prosperity of the People."[54] The Whig party was committed to the belief that "energy in government promoted economic development;'' because all groups shared a natural ''harmony of interests,'' government action would ''lift up all classes together to prosperity.''[55] Whigs wanted to use government power not only to foster economic growth but also, as Ronald Formisano points out, to ''protect the weak and disabled and to guide the more dependent members of society.''[56]

The Whig vision of a positive, paternal government became even more appealing during the economically hard times of Van Buren's presidency.[57] While Democrats offered little but ''cupping and bleeding,''[58] the Whigs promised not only prosperity but also care for those in need. When Van Buren lectured the nation that people ''looked to the government for too much,'' Henry Clay retorted that people were ''entitled to the protecting care of a paternal government.''[59] Van Buren was attacked by Daniel Webster for leaving the people to ''take care of themselves,'' and Clay ridiculed the president, who, ''lifting his umbrella over his head, tells them, drenched and shivering as they are under the beating rain and hail and snow falling upon them, . . . that they must look out for their own shelter, and security, and salvation!''[60]

The Whigs' ''paternal sympathy'' fit with their tendency to view government as the ''parent of the people.''[61] Leaders, believed the Whigs, should have the same attitude toward the citizenry that ''a parent holds to a child, or a guardian to a ward.''[62] The nation, in the words of Daniel Webster, ought to be a ''family concern.''[63] Daniel Barnard, a follower of Millard Fillmore, identified the patriarchal family as the origin of the state.[64] This analogy of the nation as a family implied not only that government should take care of the governed but also that the latter should show deference to the former. Whig paternalism taught that ''there must be a prevalent spirit of subjection to established law and constituted authority.''[65]

In sum, the Whigs spoke for authority. They had little sympathy for Democratic doctrines that denigrated the art of governing. Democratic beliefs and practices, they feared, fostered ''a wild spirit of insubordination to established authority.''[66] If support for political leadership was to be forthcoming in the antebellum United States, one would think it would have to come from the Whig party. But, although common sense would lead us to expect defenders of hierarchy to defend the hierarch, defenders of paternalism to defend the patriarch, and defenders of government to defend the executive, the Whigs' prolonged period in opposition placed the presidency in an anomalous position in Whig thought and experience.

Exponents of Whiggery tirelessly preached the virtues of positive government while simultaneously warning of the dangers of presidential power. They affirmed the principles of hierarchy but maintained a running battle against the hierarch—''King Andrew.'' Given the apparent incongruity between Whig political culture and Whig attitudes toward the presidency, one is tempted to dismiss Whig accusations of "executive usurpation" as "a cynical effort to discredit Democratic candidates."[67] But the fact that "executive despotism" provided a "fresher and far more popular issue" under which to unite those factions opposed to Jacksonian policies, we believe, should not obscure the sincerity and conviction of the Whig assault on the executive.[68]

If it is inappropriate to treat Whig attitudes toward the presidency as essentially a partisan fraud, it is even more so to view the dispute as primarily an abstract constitutional debate over the proper role of the presidency in the U.S. political system.[69] We contend that Whig attitudes toward executive power were derived from primary cultural values and beliefs. The venomous Whig attacks on the presidency are therefore best understood as a defense of the Whigs' hierarchical way of life.

The Jacksonian president presented two distinct challenges to Whig political culture. First, by appealing directly to voters over the heads of established elites, the Jacksonian style of leadership threatened to undermine the Whig hierarchical pattern of deference in politics. Lynn Marshall has suggested that the Whigs' "chief objection" to Jackson's bank veto was that its direct appeal to the electorate made for a "short-circuiting of established political leaders."[70] Jackson's mode of governing promised to level the hierarchy by eliminating the need for intermediaries essential to a hierarchical structure.[71] Whigs were impelled to attack the president so as to resist the leveling thrust that endangered the very existence of the hierarchy.

The other threat that Whigs perceived, particularly in Jackson's presidency, was the substitution of personal will for law. Adherents of a hierarchical order particularly fear the rise of a charismatic leader who substitutes his will for established precedent. After Jackson's bank veto, Daniel Webster, who most eloquently expressed Whiggery's fear that Jackson would substitute himself for the law, announced that the issue before the nation was whether "the people of the United States are mere . . . man-worshippers."[72] At stake, when Jackson removed government deposits from the national bank, asserted Webster, was the "SUPREMACY OF THE LAWS."[73] "To make the law, as far as possible, everything, and the individual will, as far as possible, nothing," was, in Webster's view, the essence of American government.[74] Years later, reflecting on the presidencies of Jackson, Van Buren, and Tyler, Webster deplored the "strong tendency" for those occupying the presidential office to think of themselves as "above the Constitution."[75] The Jacksonian presidency, modeled as it was in the image of "King Andrew," was perceived by hierarchically oriented Whigs such as Webster to institutionalize the danger of a charismatic demagogue placing himself above the laws.

This attack on the Jacksonian presidency was an integral part of the defense of Whig culture, but their antiexecutive stance involved Whigs in a deep contradiction that ultimately debilitated their political culture. By "clamoring against executive despotism,'' Welter shows that ''Whig spokesmen also called into question the very concept of an effective national government.''[76] Whig opposition to the executive veto, for instance—initially ''a defense of the authority of the national legislature to shape the national economy''—in later years ''came close to being an attack on authority itself.''[77] In attacking the hierarch, the Whigs, writes Welter, ''acquiesced in Democratic fantasies about power,''[78] thus aiding and abetting in destroying the very hierarchical political culture their ideology embraced.

Perhaps sensing this self-destructive contradiction, Daniel Webster found it hard to embrace the Whig standard of ''executive usurpation.''[79] As a former Federalist, Webster was not uncomfortable with the concept of an energetic executive; he had in fact defended Jackson's use of presidential power in meeting the nullification crisis. After Jackson's forceful exertion of national authority in response to South Carolina's declaration that a state had the right to nullify a federal law, Webster briefly flirted with the idea of a permanent political alliance with Jackson, but the cultural chasm separating the two men quickly reasserted itself, for although both Webster and Jackson rejected the doctrine of nullification, they articulated very different defenses of Union. Whereas ''Jackson based the Union on the will of the majority,'' according to historian Major Wilson, ''Webster invoked the will of all generations.''[80] It soon became apparent to Webster that Jackson's vigorous exercise of presidential power during the nullification controversy was not being used to further hierarchy but, as during the bank war, for the purpose of thwarting an undemocratic minority.

The most hierarchical Whigs tried to resolve their cultural dilemma by restoring the hierarch to his position atop the hierarchy in such a manner that he would no longer pose a threat to the hierarchy. They attempted to remind other Whigs that the fault lay not in executive power per se but in the Jacksonian executive. Noah Webster proposed changing the Constitution to create a chief executive almost entirely independent of the people. More moderate, but with the same aim of loosening the connection between president and populace, was Charles Mercer's proposal to elect a president for an eight-to-ten-year term.[81] These proposals offered, logically speaking, ''solutions'' to the Whig dilemma, but public advocacy would, of course, have been political suicide. Instead, the Whig party followed down the politically successful but culturally disastrous path of the 1840 presidential campaign.

Part of the tragedy of Whiggery was that the party could gain the presidency only by muting traditional Whig concerns, and by jettisoning its regular party leaders. Three times Henry Clay lost in the general election: in 1824 to John Quincy Adams, in 1836 to Martin Van Buren, and in 1844 to James Polk. The two elections in which Whigs did win control of the White House (1840 and 1848) were those in which the party ran popular war heroes not closely identified with orthodox Whiggery. Indeed Zachary Taylor, the Whig candidate in 1848, had never voted in his life.

In the election of 1840 Whigs echoed the Democratic theme of the encroaching nature of power. In a campaign speech, Clay instructed his audience that "the pervading principle of our system of Government . . . is not merely the possibility but the absolute certainty of infidelity and treachery with even the highest functionary of the State."[82] If the listener could find little here that was recognizably Whiggish, the listener could find even less in the campaign statements of the presidential candidate, William Henry Harrison. The "Old Hero" told audiences that he had been reared on the "doctrines of '98"—the essence of which had been strict construction of the Constitution, states' rights and limited government—and that he agreed with those Jeffersonians that "the seeds of monarchy were indeed sown in the soil of our Federal Constitution."[83] "The old-fashioned Republican rule," continued Harrison, "is to watch the Government. See that the Government does not acquire too much power. Keep a check upon your rulers. Do this, and liberty is safe."[84]

One of the ways by which Harrison and the Whigs promised to reduce the "vast power" of the presidency was to limit presidents to a single term. A one-term pledge, they reasoned, was "our only security against treachery and inordinate ambition." Whig party platforms endorsed the idea of a single term for the presidency.[85] The distrust of power manifested in these one-term pledges was perfectly compatible with the Democratic party's antipower predilections. In fact, Andrew Jackson had indicated his support for the one-term presidency in his 1828 campaign and in each of his annual messages to Congress. James Polk in 1844 and Lewis Cass in 1848 both pledged to serve only a single term if elected.[86]

This competition over who could distrust power more signaled a cultural victory for the Jacksonians.[87] What had begun as an attack on a particular mode of executive leadership broadened into an attack on all executive power, until finally Whig views about authority seemed almost indistinguishable from Democratic assumptions. The Whigs, argues Welter, "ended by embracing most of the ideas their fathers had condemned. By 1850 it was difficult for most Americans to think [about power] in other [than Democratic] terms."[88] Whig capitulation to Democratic categories of thought badly weakened hierarchy. It meant, Major Wilson suggests, that the nation had lost "for a generation at least . . . an effective corporate vision of its destiny."[89] It had proved impossible for Whigs to adapt to the antebellum cultural context without transforming Whiggery in the direction of the dominant antiauthority culture. Hierarchy without a hierarch, strong government without a strong executive, had proved an unviable cultural experiment.

Notes

1. *Argus of Western America*, February 22, 1822, cited in Richard B. Latner, *The Presidency of Andrew Jackson: White House Politics, 1829-1837* (Athens: University of Georgia Press, 1979), p. 21.
2. Samuel Flagg Bemis, *John Quincy Adams and the Union* (New York: Knopf, 1956), p. 132.
3. Latner, *Presidency of Jackson*, pp. 7-30; Robert V. Remini, *Andrew Jackson and the Course of American Freedom. 1822-1832* (New York: Harper & Row, 1981), pp. 12-155. See also Major L. Wilson, *The Presidency of Martin Van Buren* (Lawrence: University Press of Kansas, 1984), p. 29.
3. Daniel Walker Howe, *The Political Culture of the American Whigs* (Chicago: University of Chicago Press, 1979), pp. 181-82.
4. Remini, *Jackson and American Freedom*, pp. 129-30, quotation on p. 130; Latner, *Presidency of Jackson*, p. 23. Also see Kim T. Phillips, "The Pennsylvania Origins of the Jackson Movement," *Political Science Quarterly* (Fall 1976): 489-508.
5. Remini, *Jackson and American Freedom*, pp. 113-14.
6. Donald B. Cole, *Martin Van Buren and the American Political System* (Princeton: Princeton University Press, 1984), pp. 101-81; Van Buren quoted on p. 104. See also Robert V. Remini, *Martin Van Buren and the Making of the Democratic Party* (New York: Columbia University Press, 1959); Latner, *Presidency of Jackson*, pp. 126-27.
7. Remini, *Jackson and American Freedom*, p. 114.
8. Latner, *Presidency of Jackson*, pp. 24-25.
9. Ibid., pp. 23-27; Remini, *Jackson and American Freedom*, pp. 129-31. Also see Charles G. Sellers, "Banking and Politics in Jackson's Tennessee, 1817-1827," *Mississippi Valley Historical Review* (June 1954): 61-84.
10. Remini, *Jackson and American Freedom*, p. 32; Latner, *Presidency of Jackson*, p. 25.
11. Remini, *Jackson and American Freedom*, p. 32.
12. Latner, *Presidency of Jackson*, pp. 23-24. See also Remini, *Jackson and American Freedom*, pp. 31-34.
13. Latner, *Presidency of Jackson*, p. 50.
14. Jackson, quoted in Latner, *Presidency of Jackson*, p. 101. See also Remini, *Jackson and American Freedom*, p. 252.
15. Remini, *Jackson and American Freedom*, pp. 252-56, quotation on p. 255. See also Latner, *Presidency of Jackson*, pp. 101-3.
16. Randolph, cited in Remini, *Jackson and American Freedom*, p. 254. For reaction to the veto, see ibid., pp. 254-55, and Latner, *Presidency of Jackson*, pp. 103-7.
17. Latner, *Presidency of Jackson*, p. 95. See also Howe, *Political Culture of Whigs*, pp. 40-42.
18. Remini, *Jackson and American Freedom*, pp. 367-69.
19. Charles Sellers, "Introduction" in *Andrew Jackson: A Profile*, ed. Charles Sellers (New York: Hill & Wang, 1971), p. xvi. The Jacksonians, agrees Daniel Walker Howe, preached both "individualism and egalitarianism" (Howe, *Political Culture of Whigs*, p. 22).
20. Remini, *Jackson and American Freedom*, pp. 29, 298; John Ashworth, *'Agrarians' and 'Aristocrats': Party Political Ideology in the United States, 1837-1846*

(Atlantic Highlands, N.J.: Humanities Press, 1983), p. 18. See also Latner, *Presidency of Jackson*, p. 121. The phrase "badge of lost innocence" is from the opening page of Thomas Paine's *Common Sense*, published originally in 1776.

21. Amos Kendall, quoted in Latner, *Presidency of Jackson*, p. 121. On Jackson's foreign policy, see John M. Belohlavek, *"Let the Eagle Soar!" The Foreign Policy of Andrew Jackson* (Lincoln: University of Nebraska Press, 1985). Also see David Resnick and Norman C. Thomas, "Reagan and Jackson: Parallels in Political Time" (Paper presented at the Annual Meeting of the Midwest Political Science Association, Chicago, April 9-11, 1987, typescript), pp. 20-22.

22. Samuel P. Huntington, *The Soldier and the State: The Theory and Politics of Civil-Military Relations* (Cambridge: Harvard University Press, 1957), pp. 203-11.

23. Ashworth writes that "the pre-occupation with power was in some respects even more marked in the Jacksonian era than in the revolutionary age" (*Agrarians and Aristocrats*, p. 17).

24. Rush Welter, *The Mind of America, 1820-1860* (New York: Columbia University Press, 1975), p. 171.

25. Ashworth, *Agrarians and Aristocrats*, p. 15. The Jacksonian dilemma was acutely perceived by Orestes Brownson, and led to his conversion from radical Jacksonian Democrat to conservative Roman Catholic. Bownson wrote, "We are the children of revolution in the State and of dissent in religion. We see nothing sacred in government, we feel nothing binding in ecclesiastical establishments. Our youth are early imbued with a sense of the supremacy of the individual; and . . . [we] grow up with the conviction that our own judgement is in all cases to be our rule of action" (ibid., p. 109).

26. Clinton Rossiter makes a similar point in *The American Presidency* (Harcourt, Brace & World, 1960), pp. 94-98.

27. Cole, *Martin Van Buren*, p. 75.

28. M. J. Heale, *The Presidential Quest: Candidates and Images in American Political Culture, 1787-1852* (New York: Longman, 1982), pp. 156, 176.

29. Ibid., p. 185.

30. Ibid., pp. 171-77, quotation on p. 177.

31. Ashworth, *Agrarians and Aristocrats*, pp. 14, 57; Heale, *Presidential Quest*, pp. 178-86.

32. John William Ward, *Andrew Jackson: Symbol for an Age* (New York: Oxford University Press, 1953), pp. 55-56, quotation on p. 55.

33. On "delegates" and "trustees" as role orientations in the legislative process, see Heinz Eulau et al., "The Role of the Representative: Some Empirical Observations on the Theory of Edmund Burke," *American Political Science Review* (September, 1959): 742-56. Also see Hanna Fenichel Pitkin, *The Concept of Representation* (Berkeley: University of California Press, 1967).

34. Ashworth, *Agrarians and Aristocrats*, pp. 57-58; K. Jack Bauer, *Zachary Taylor: Soldier, Planter, Statesman of the Old Southwest* (Baton Rouge: Louisiana State University Press, 1985), p. 232.

35. Ashworth, *Agrarians and Aristocrats*, p. 19.

36. Latner, *Presidency of Jackson*, p. 165; Robert Remini, "The Election of 1832," in *History of American Presidential Elections, 1798-1968*, ed. Arthur M. Schlesinger, Jr. (New York: Chelsea House, 1971), 1:516. The *Washington Globe* reported: "We rejoice to witness with what an intelligent and fortunate unanimity the people have ratified the sound, wise and healthy principles of *public policy* adopted and avowed by the present administration" (November 15, 1832, empha-

sis added). See also Wilfred Binkley, *President and Congress* (New York: Vintage Books, 1962), p. 83; Latner, *Presidency of Jackson*, p. 50.

37. Robert V. Remini, *Andrew Jackson and the Bank War* (New York: Norton, 1967), pp. 119, 142. Clay countered: "I am surprised and alarmed at the new source of executive power which is found in the result of a presidential election. I had supposed that the constitution and the laws were the sole source of executive authority . . . that the issue of a presidential election was merely to place the Chief Magistrate in the post assigned to him . . . But it seems that if, prior to an election, certain opinions, no matter how ambiguously put forth by a candidate, are known to the people, those loose opinions, in virtue of the election, incorporate themselves with the constitution, and afterwards are to be regarded and expounded as parts of the instrument!" (p. 138).
38. Ashworth, *Agrarians and Aristocrats*, p. 35; Remini, *Jackson and the Bank War*, p. 143 (emphasis added). See also Remini, *Jackson and American Freedom*, pp. 350-51.
39. Charles Sellers, *James K. Polk: Continentalist, 1843-1846* (Princeton: Princeton University Press, 1966), p. 324.
40. Remini, *Jackson and the Bank War*, pp. 137-41; Clay quoted on p. 138.
41. Welter, *Mind of America*. p. 175.
42. Ashworth, *Agrarians and Aristocrats*, p. 35.
43. James Polk, quoted in Welter, *Mind of America*, p. 171.
44. Cole, *Martin Van Buren*, p. 114.
45. Welter, *Mind of America*, pp. 175-76.
46. Ibid., p. 171.
47. Ibid., p. 241.
48. Jackson, according to Arthur Schlesinger, Jr., "ousted no greater a proportion of officeholders than Jefferson" (*The Age of Jackson* [Boston: Litle, Brown, 1945], p. 47).
49. Lynn L. Marshall, "The Strange Stillbirth of the Whig Party," *American Historical Review* (January 1967): 445-47.
50. Robert Kelley, *The Cultural Pattern in American Politics* (New York: Knopf, 1979), p. 143.
51. Welter, *Mind of America*, p. 99. See also Howe, *Political Culture of Whigs*, pp. 31-32 and passim; Kelley, *Cultural Pattern*, esp. p. 163.
52. Ashworth, *Agrarians and Aristocrats*, pp. 61-62.
53. The hierarchical propensities of the Whig party are also evident in its attitudes toward the past (and future). In contrast to the Democrats, who agreed with Thomas Paine that "every age and generation must be free to act for itself," Whiggery, writes Daniel Walker Howe, "maintained the right and duty of one generation to bind another." While Democrats asserted that "the things of the past have but little interest or value for us," Whigs insisted on the need "to honor the past." "Our American liberty," declared Daniel Webster, "has an ancestry, a pedigree, a history." "Human nature is . . . so strongly inclined to go astray," another Whig reminded his audience, "that it is safer to rely on the power of habit to keep it on a path approximate to the parallel of rectitude, than to give it unlimited freedom to go right or wrong" (Howe, *Political Culture of Whigs*, pp. 70-72; Ashworth, *Agrarians and Aristocrats*, pp. 59-60).
Daniel Walker Howe has isolated three major preoccupations that exponents of Whiggery shared. Each of these is evidence of a hierarchical belief system. First, "Whigs were much more concerned than Democrats with providing conscious direction to the forces of change." Second, "while Jacksonian rhetoric emphasized

'equality' . . . Whig rhetoric emphasized 'morality'—or 'duties' rather than 'rights.' Third, "whereas Jacksonians spoke of conflicting interests, . . . a recurring theme in Whig rhetoric was the organic unity of society" (Howe, *Political Culture of Whigs*, p. 21).

Like their Federalist predecessors, Whigs drew an analogy between the human body and the social and political system. Just as there was a need in the body for the higher faculties of conscience and reason to restrain the lower animal passions, so in society it was necessary for the more responsible at the upper end of the social stratum to discipline and regulate the profligate at the lower end (Howe, *Political Culture of Whigs*, pp. 29-30). That different members of society performed unequal functions need not produce conflict any more than the different functions carried out by the head and hands produced discord in the body. Harmony, the Whigs believed, came out of diversity. Conflict between different parts of society, Clay argued, "would be just as unnatural and absurd as between the members of the human body." "The fact is," repeated another, "that the whole body of society is woven together as it were, each individual and each profession being mutually dependent on others and mutually employing each other. . . . An injury to one does not help the others, but affects them injuriosly" (Ashworth, *Agrarians and Aritocrats*, p. 69).

Whigs looked to public education (as well as the family and religion) as a means of instilling internal restraints, thereby making external restraint less necessary. Thus could Daniel Webster liken public education to a "wise and liberal system of police" (Welter, *Mind of America*, p. 284; Howe, *Political Culture of Whigs*, p. 218). When Democrats defended public education, in contrast, it tended to be as a vehicle for redistributing knowledge, and hence power, on a more equal basis. Thus, agreement on policy disguised underlying cultural disagreement (Welter, *Mind of America*, ch. 11, esp. 289-90, 292-93; Howe, *Political Culture of Whigs*, p. 36).

54. Ashworth, *Agrarians and Aristocrats*, pp. 54-55.
55. Ronald P. Formisano, *The Transformation of Political Culture: Massachusetts Parties, 1790s-1840s* (New York: Oxford University Press, 1983), pp. 275-76; see also Melvyn Dubofsky, "Daniel Webster and the Whig Theory of Economic Growth: 1828-1848," *New England Quarterly* (1969): 551-72.
56. Formisano, *Transformation of Political Culture*, p. 268.
57. Major L. Wilson, *The Presidency of Martin Van Buren* (Lawrence: University Press of Kansas, 1984), p. 143.
58. Azariah Flagg to Van Buren, April 10, 1837, cited in Wilson, *Van Buren*, p. 51.
59. Howe, *Political Culture of Whigs*, p. 19.
60. Donald B. Cole, *Martin Van Buren and the American Political System* (Princeton: Princeton University Press, 1984), p. 331; Wilson, *Van Buren*, p. 143.
61. John Davis and Horace Mann, quoted in Formisano, *Transformation of Political Culture*, pp. 271, 458.
62. Quoted in Ashworth, *Agrarians and Aristocrats*, p. 55.
63. Ibid., p. 55. See also Howe, *Political Culture of Whigs*, p. 45.
64. Howe, *Political Culture of Whigs*, p. 86. On Barnard's political activities, see Sherry Penney, *Patrician in Politics: Daniel Dewey Barnard of New York* (Port Washington, N.Y.: Kennikat Press, 1974).
65. Barnard, quoted in Ashworth, *Agrarians and Aristocrats*, p. 59.
66. Quoted ibid., p. 114. See also Welter, *Mind of America*, p. 171. The Jacksonian Amos Kendall, for instance, declared that public officers "should be considered [as] having nothing of dignity, or power, or splendor about them, beyond that

which belongs to honest men representing others in the private walks of life. . . . The world will not be governed as it ought to be, until government shall be stripped of the majesty with which the arts and errors of the ages have clothed it, and come to be considered as a part of the ordinary business of society'' (Ashworth, *Agrarians and Aritocrats*, p. 15).

67. Welter, *Mind of America*, p. 192.
68. Quotations are from Schlesinger, *The Age Of Jackson*, p. 276. Howe points out that Whigs distrusted executives at both the state and federal levels (*Political Culture of Whigs*, p. 20).
69. See, for example, William S. Stokes, "Whig conceptions of Executive Power," *Presidential Studies Quarterly* (Winter and Spring 1976): 16-35.
70. Marshall, "Stillbirth of Whig Party," quotation on p. 449. Also see Sydney Nathans, *Daniel Webster and Jacksonian Democracy* (Baltimore: John Hopkins University Press, 1973), pp. 45-46.
71. See Jackson's parallel request that all "intermediate" agencies be removed in the election of the president (Remini, *Jackson and American Freedom*, p. 225).
72. Sydney Nathans, *Daniel Webster and Jacksonian Democracy* (Baltimore: Johns Hopkins Press, 1973), p. 46.
73. Ibid., p. 77.
74. Binkley, *President and Congress*, p. 101. Webster continued. "We have endeavored by statute upon statute, and by provision following provision, to define and limit personal authority; to assign particular duties to particular public servants; to define those duties; to create penalties for their violation; to adjust accurately the responsibility of each agent with its own powers and its own duties" (p. 100).
75. Howe, *Political Culture of Whigs*, p. 89.
76. Welter, *Mind of America*, p. 193. Marshall makes the same point: in forcing the issue of executive usurpation, the Whigs ended up "emasculating their ideology in the process" ("Stillbirth of Whig Party," p. 448).
77. Welter, *Mind of America*, p. 210.
78. Ibid., p. 194.
79. Nathans, *Daniel Webster*, p. 74.
80. Major L. Wilson, " 'Liberty and Union': An Analysis of Three Concepts Involved in the Nullification Controversy," *Journal of Southern History* (August 1967): 331-55, quotation at p. 349. On Webster's flirtation with Jackson during the nullification crisis, see Norman Brown, *The Politics of Availability* (Athens: University of Georgia Press, 1969).
81. Merrill D. Peterson, *The Jeffersonian Image in the American Mind* (New York: Oxford University Press, 1962), p. 104. Ashworth, *Agrarians and Aristocrats*, pp. 122-23.
82. Welter, *Mind of America*, p. 195.
83. Peterson, *Jeffersonian Image*, p. 109.
84. Welter, *Mind of America*, p. 195.
85. Ibid., p. 193. Heale, *Presidential Quest*, pp. 150-54; Millard Fillmore quoted on p. 151.
86. Latner, *Presidency of Jackson*, p. 34; Heale, *Presidential Quest*, pp. 150-52.
87. Welter, *Mind of America*, p. 195.
88. Ibid., p. 331.
89. Major L. Wilson, "The Concepts of Time and the Political Dialogue in the United States, 1828-1848," *American Quarterly* (1967): pp. 619-44, quotation on p. 644.

7

The Limits of Jackson's Solution: Martin Van Buren, John Tyler, and James Polk

A common enmity toward hierarchy held together the Jacksonian coalition of individualists and egalitarians. Andrew Jackson's leadership of the Democratic party had hinged on the ability to identify and dramatize hierarchical enemies, from "King Caucus" to the "monster Bank." The heroic battle with the second Bank of the United States had been particularly significant in keeping the attention of Jackson's followers fixed upon hierarchical abuses. Focusing Democratic eyes upon the dangers of concentrated political and economic power muted conflict between egalitarianism and individualism.

By slaying the "monster Bank," however, Jackson left his successors without a visible hierarchical target around which to keep individualists and egalitarians united. Having destroyed the powerful central bank that had regulated the economy, the individualist wing of the Democratic party (labeled by contemporaries as "Conservative") hoped to call off the bank war and unleash the nation's entrepreneurial energies. Because hierarchy no longer threatened their preferred way of life, many individualists ceased to see the value of an alliance with egalitarian, hard-money Democrats who were calling for restrictions on credit and banking. Conservative Democrats, as historian John Ashworth argues, "had begun to dilute equality of conditions into equality of opportunity."[1]

The egalitarian wing of the Democratic party, meanwhile, was dissatisfied with what happened after Nicholas Biddle's bank was destroyed. Rather than decreasing inequality and privilege, Jackson's action seemed to have both fueled speculation and caused a proliferation of banking, furthering the individualist life of bidding and bargaining while retarding egalitarianism. "Equality," warned Pennsylvania Democrat Charles Ingersoll, "is rapidly disappearing in the possession, distribution, and transmission of [property]." William Leggett, editor of the *New York Evening Post* was another who was worried by the "vast disparity of condition" that was opening up in society between the "vast numbers of men" doomed to "groan and sweat under a weary life" of "incessant toil" and those speculators who grew rich without laboring.[2] These egalitarians demanded the president declare war on all banks in order to arrest this alarming increase in "artificial inequality."

Managing the Jacksonian Coalition by Forsaking the Jacksonian Solution: Martin Van Buren

The most troublesome decision facing Martin Van Buren when he assumed office was whether to uphold or repudiate Jackson's specie circular. Designed to curtail speculation and restrict credit, this executive order provided that government agents would accept only specie—gold and silver—as payment for public lands. This decision aggravated the division between egalitarianism and individualism. The *New York Journal of Commerce*, which had been mildly antibank, voiced the individualist indictment of the specie circular: "We do not elect a President to control speculation in land. We have not submitted to the degradations of permitting government to investigate and direct the affairs of private business. . . . Is it any of his business that the people speculate?"[3] Yet, egalitarian Democrats such as Thomas Hart Benton and William Gouge believed the directive did not go far enough in restraining speculation.[4] The success of Van Buren's presidency would depend on how well he was able to manage the tug of these opposing cultural forces within his own party.

Spurred by mounting currency contraction, Congress had passed a measure (sponsored by Conservative Democrat William Rives) in the closing days of Jackson's term that would amend, if not repeal, Jackson's circular. The House vote revealed the sharp division within the Democratic party: 59 Democrats voted to retain the circular; 54 Democrats joined Whigs in supporting the bill.[5] Jackson's pocket veto of the bill left Van Buren in a bind. The entrepreneurial wing of the Democratic party informed Van Buren that repudiation of Jackson's order was a condition of its support, and others warned Van Buren of the danger of "any measure which could be construed into a departure from the policy of the late administration."[6]

After much agonizing, Van Buren decided to retain the circular, but carefully avoided interpreting this act as favoring either wing of the Democratic party. He sought to persuade Rives, a vigorous foe of the national bank under Jackson, that the aim of the circular was to prevent Whigs from restoring the national bank. Retaining the circular, Van Buren argued, was motivated not by a commitment to hard-money policies but as a means of saving the deposit banks. Their goal, the president assured Rives, was the same. Yet the method Van Buren had selected—retaining the order—won him enthusiastic applause from those hard-money proponents who wanted to destroy the banking system.[7]

Van Buren's overriding aim here as elsewhere was to mediate between the egalitarian and individualist elements of the Jacksonian coalition. To maintain the Jacksonian coalition in the absence of a powerful hierarchical enemy entailed, ironically, leading in non-Jacksonian ways. By stressing what he was opposed to, Jackson led by polarizing cultural battle lines; Van Buren tried to hold the coalition together by remaining ambiguous as to what policies he favored and what they meant. At the same time, however, Van Buren's leadership of the Democratic party was constrained by the need to be seen as sustaining Jackson's policy commitments.

Within one week of Van Buren's making public his decision to retain the specie circular, New York's banks closed their doors, precipitating a financial panic. To assign blame for the onset of the panic and the contraction of the economy became the central political issue. Had the national bank retained its great power over the economy, Van Buren would not have found it hard to convince his followers that blame lay with the "Monster Bank." The panic might thus have cemented the cultural coalition of egalitarianism and individualism even tighter. Lacking this hierarchical villain, however, the debate over who was to blame for the panic accented the cultural division within the Democratic party.[8] Thus, Jackson's solution—destroying the bank—was the source of Van Buren's dilemma: keeping individualists and egalitarians together in the absence of a hierarchical enemy.

To egalitarian-inclined Democrats, suspension of specie payments by the banks demonstrated the perfidy of the "money power." Blame for the panic was laid at the doorstep of speculators and state bankers. Hard-money Democrats had always been uneasy with the pet bank system, hence suspension not only vindicated their contention that bankers could not be trusted but also enabled them to return to the more familiar posture of denouncing the "banking interest." Believing that banks were "bastions of inequality and not unlike cancerous growths, working their profound and corrupting change," these Jacksonians looked for a remedy that would allow the government to separate itself from this source of corruption.[9]

Conservative Democrats countered by blaming the panic on radical, hard-money policies (particularly the specie circular) that attempted to restrict the expansion of credit. By draining state banks of their specie holdings, they argued, the circular had forced state banks to suspend specie payments. The specie circular "struck at the very vital of public confidence," a correspondent wrote to Van Buren, by "saying to the people, beware of the Banks, . . . they are not to be trusted."[10] To publicize their version of the causes of, and remedies for, the panic, Conservative Democrats formed a new paper, the *Madisonian*. Its aim was to prevent radical Jacksonians from initiating a "war . . . against all our banking institutions . . . to prostrate our whole credit system, which has done so much for the prosperity of the country."[11]

In defending the state banks, these Democrats were doing far more than defending the interests of banks; they were defending the individualist way of life. Egalitarian rantings about increasing inequality were misguided, they believed, for the fluidity of American society meant that "one generation . . . [was] enough to bring those now at the bottom of the wheel of fortune to the top." But only with credit available to those who wanted it would "every man who bears a tolerable character, coupled with industry . . . [have an opportunity] of bettering his condition."[12] Restricting or eliminating banks, these Democrats argued, would only rigidify class lines and generate mass discontent.

Van Buren's primary task as president was to prevent the Jacksonian coalition of individualists and egalitarians from tearing itself apart under the pressure of the economic panic. Van Buren had long attempted to situate himself midway between individualist Democrats who promoted investment and speculation, and egalitarian Democrats who tried to restrict credit for fear speculation would increase inequalities.[13] At the outset of his presidency, Van Buren had hoped to keep the peace by remaining reticent in those areas where differences of opinion were great. In contrast to the stirring rhetoric that had marked Jackson's messages, Van Buren's inaugural address gave no indication of the direction the administration desired to take.[14] Fear of aggravating divisions within the Democratic party also motivated Van Buren's decision to retain Jackson's cabinet and make no immediate removals at lower levels of administration.[15] This allowed Van Buren to claim Jackson's mantle without having to decide which wing of the party had the better claim to the legacy of the "Old Hero."

But the worsening financial crisis, focusing the nation's attention on banking and currency, impelled Van Buren to address publicly these divisive issues. Many Democrats, Van Buren included, feared that the Whigs would capitalize on the collapse of the state bank system by trying to reestablish a national bank. The administration was urged by its supporters to come up with a plan of its own "in order that the advocates of a National Bank may be met in argument."[16] Although Democrats could agree on the need to avoid a return to the bank they deemed hierarchical, they disagreed heatedly about what should take its place. Van Buren therefore had to devise a program that would forestall Whig efforts to restore the Bank of the United States without tearing apart the Democratic party.

Van Buren spent the summer sounding out leading Democrats and crafting a program that could satisfy both egalitarians and individualists.[17] On September 5, 1837, he unveiled his solution to the special session of Congress. Its centerpiece—presented as an expedient remedy for the current crisis rather than a fundamental institutional reform[18]—was a proposal to make the federal Treasury independent of the banks. By portraying the independent-treasury scheme as the only viable alternative to a revived national bank, Van Buren hoped to win support from both wings of the Democratic party.[19]

The message was balanced to appeal equally to antibank and probank Democrats. Van Buren's indictment of the "spirit of reckless speculation" was tempered by reference to credit as a "just reward of merit and an honorable incentive to further acquisition."[20] Van Buren faulted state banks rather than Jacksonian policies for the panic, but his relief measures, designed to help overextended merchants and bankers, testified that he had no desire to punish banks.[21] On the highly controversial issue of whether the government should receive funds in specie, as hard-money Democrats desired, or bank notes, as soft-money Democrats wished, Van Buren was silent.[22]

Though opposed to granting relief to banks and speculators and disappointed at the absence of a specie clause, the egalitarian wing of the Democratic party was delighted by Van Buren's independent-treasury proposal.[23] Persuaded that the president was a convert to their antibank doctrines, a number of dissident egalitarian factions, including the Locofoco or Equal Rights party in New York, now returned to the Democratic fold.[24] Why did egalitarians regard this proposal—which, as one skeptical scholar has written, amounted to "nothing more than a new way of storing public monies"—as "a question of . . . paramount importance to the democracy?"[25]

Radical Democrats had always been uncomfortable with the unholy alliance between government and banking that had resulted from Jackson's decision to withdraw all federal funds from the national bank and place them in "pet banks" throughout the country. To restrain speculation and limit the expansion of credit had required negotiation with these deposit banks, but to cooperate with, rather than berate, the "money power" threw many egalitarians off balance.[26] Van Buren's action seemed to egalitarians an admission by the administration that banks were an evil, corrupting influence upon government. By severing all connections between the national government and banking, the independent-treasury scheme would restore the purity of the Democratic party while providing a noble example to be followed by state governments.[27] Interpreted by radical Democrats like William Gouge as an opening salvo against credit banking, its end result would be, many hoped, that individual states would outlaw the banking system entirely, for it was this system, egalitarian Democrats believed, that was directly responsible for the "artificial inequality of wealth, much pauperism and crime, the low state of public morals, and many of the other social evils."[28]

In large part because of the enthusiasm for an independent treasury displayed by hard-money Democrats, reactions of soft-money Democrats ranged from wary to hostile. The governor of New York, William Marcy, strongly objected to a proposal that he believed elevated Locofoco demands to the status of national policy. The proposal to divorce government from banking, contended Democratic Senator Nathaniel Tallmadge, "strikes at the very foundation of the Credit System. . . . Disguise it as you may it is no more nor less than a war upon the whole banking system." Thomas Ritchie, editor of the influential *Richmond Enquirer*, echoed the individualist fear that Van Buren's decision not only would destroy public confidence in state banks but also constituted a first step in an attack on the entire credit structure. The result, individualist Democrats concurred, would be to eliminate "the great lever of our advancement as individuals, and as a nation in wealth and prosperity."[29]

Aware that this interpretation of the independent-treasury proposal—as an endorsement of egalitarian hard-money principles—would tear the party apart and insure the measure's defeat in Congress, the president labored to persuade probank Democrats that the proposal was neither motivated by a hostility to banking nor did it adversely affect bankers. Van Buren pointed to the firm support given the proposal by John Brockenbrough, president of the Bank of Virginia, who defended the scheme on the grounds that it would leave banking reform to the states.[30] The federal government's divorce plan, the administration assured Marcy and others, did not indicate a preference for divorce at the state level.[31] Rather, Van Buren explained, the plan's virtue was that it left reform of banks to "the proper tribunal—the people of the states."[32] Cultural conflict was not so much resolved as (it was hoped) diffused to the state level. By separating the national government from state banking, the independent-treasury proposal deflected disagreements between egalitarians and individualists to the state level, thus preserving national party unity. Soft-money Democrats like Marcy could support the proposal and remain within the Democratic party without capitulating to egalitarian hard-money Democrats at the state level.

Assessing the success of Van Buren's balancing act is complex. On one hand, the independent-treasury proposal precipitated the defection of Rives, Tallmadge, and other Democrats opposed to the egalitarian wing of the party. On the other, it was no small achievement to have fashioned a proposal that held Marcy's support while also satisfying the hard-money Benton.[33] Van Buren's moderate interpretation prevented Rives and Tallmadge from drawing off Democrats like Marcy who were in agreement with their probank, soft-money views. Senate Democrats demonstrated impressive party unity under the skilled guidance of Silas Wright, passing Van Buren's proposal in both the special and regular session. In the House, however, with its slender Democratic majority, Conservative defections were sufficient to defeat the proposal.[34]

The administration's failure to secure immediate passage of the independent-treasury proposal has earned Van Buren low marks for presidential leadership—especially by contrast with the "strong" presidency of his predecessor. Van Buren's "political ineptness," contends Arthur Schlesinger, Jr., "weakened his administration and delayed until 1840 the passage of the independent treasury."[35] How is it, we ask, that the most skilled politician of his generation could exhibit such political ineptitude? More recently, Donald Cole has commented that Van Buren had "lost some of the sharpness that had shaped his reputation," yet Cole never explains where or how the president mysteriously had lost the political skill that had earned him the nickname "Magician." Had the "Magician" run out of tricks or had he been dealt an impossible hand?[36]

We contend that Van Buren's difficulties are better explained by the cultural dilemma that hamstrung the president than by his failings as a politician. Van Buren's central dilemma was how to cope with financial panic and economic contraction without splitting the Jacksonian alliance of egalitarians and individualists. Jackson, whose instinct was to lead through blaming, constantly urged Van Buren to declare war on the state banks. To attack all banks rather than just the national bank, however, was to shift the target from monopoly to credit, from privilege to economic expansion—in short, from hierarchy to individualism.[37] Schlesinger criticizes Van Buren for allowing "the Tallmadge split to grow almost into a rebellion, while similar splits under Jackson never became more than individual desertions,"[38] but if Van Buren had followed Jackson's advice, the individualist exodus out of the Democratic party would likely have been far greater than it was. What is remarkable is not that the Tallmadge-Rives faction quit the Democratic party but that Van Buren prevented more from following. Even the path pursued by Van Buren, moderate as it was, tarred his party with an egalitarian brush that contributed to Democratic defeats in state elections.[39] If the president seemed overly cautious, it was because he was caught in a dilemma in which the inherited solution—Jackson's polarizing style of governing—would have destroyed party unity.[40]

Comparisons that pit Jackson's strength against the weakness of Van Buren are misleading for another reason: Van Buren's independent-treasury proposal required congressional assent; Jackson's major policy goals rarely necessitated constructing a majority coalition in Congress. The national bank had been struck down by presidential veto. In addition, Jackson removed the deposits from the national bank without congressional approval and had managed the pet bank system through executive fiat.[41] Because Van Buren was attempting to lead Congress in a manner that his predecessor had never really tried, Jackson's confrontational style was an inadequate model. If Van Buren were to direct the legislative process, he could not afford the provocative vetoes and the angry battles over appointments that had soured Jackson's relations with Congress.[42]

It is a mistake to equate Van Buren's conciliatory strategy with weak leadership. That the president never vetoed a congressional bill signifies strategy rather than infirmity; Van Buren deemed the veto destructive of the good relations with Congress necessary to cement the Jacksonian alliance. He opted instead for compromise and ambiguity as the means best suited to holding together the Jacksonian coalition of individualism and egalitarianism and keeping the supporters of hierarchy a minority party. Though the worsening depression did sweep the Whigs into power in 1840, Van Buren had prevented the complete unraveling of the alliance forged by Jackson, thereby putting the Democratic party in position to regain power in the subsequent election. In fact, without the late and unexpected intrusion of the Texas question, Van Buren would have been the party's presidential nominee in 1844. By moving out from under the shadow of "Old Hickory," by abandoning his predecessor's confrontational mode of leadership, Van Buren was perhaps better able than Jackson himself to institutionalize the Jacksonian coalition.

Rejecting the Jacksonian Coalition: John Tyler Experiments with a Unicultural Party

The 1840 election gave the Whig party control of the White House for the first time. Eager to translate Whig cultural dispositions into legislative measures, Henry Clay persuaded the newly elected president, William Henry Harrison, to call a special session of Congress to address the nation's pressing financial problems. The first order of business on the Whig agenda was to abolish the independent treasury; the second was to reestablish a national bank.

But the well-laid plans of the Whigs went awry when, one month after assuming office, Harrison died, leaving John Tyler, a former Democrat, as president. Tyler was a Virginia states' rights politician whose primary political concern had been to limit the size and scope of the federal government. In the 1828 election, he supported Andrew Jackson over John Quincy Adams because the latter's vision of a strong central government, as articulated in Adams's first annual message to Congress, had repelled Tyler. Though suspicious of Jackson's populist rhetoric and his emphasis on increasing public participation in government, Tyler—who had spent his many years in public service trying to limit the powers of the national bank and prevent federally sponsored internal improvements—was favorably impressed by Jackson's actions in his first term, particularly by the vetoes of the Maysville Road bill and the bill to recharter the national bank. For these actions, decided Tyler, Jackson deserved a second term.[43]

After Jackson's reelection, however, Tyler became increasingly disenchanted with what he perceived as Jackson's growing power. Tyler began to doubt that Jackson's expansive brand of presidential leadership could be reconciled with limited government. Jackson's confrontational handling of the South Carolina nullifiers followed by his decision to withdraw government funds from the bank convinced Tyler that active presidential leadership would inevitably produce an active federal government. Tyler joined with the Whigs in formally censuring Jackson for converting the federal government into what Tyler termed a "mere majority machine." "What interest is safe," he wondered, "if the unbridled will of the majority is to have sway."[44] The egalitarian preference for majoritarianism, Tyler decided, was incompatible with his individualistic concern for self-regulation.

Having rejected Jackson's solution, President Tyler embarked on an unusual cultural experiment. Forsaking both the hierarchy of Whiggery and the egalitarianism of Jacksonianism, Tyler tried to create a unicultural party consisting solely of individualists. Understanding why Tyler was unable to establish such a party may tell us something about the cultural requisites of presidential leadership.

Tyler's inaugural message called for a cessation of the war against the banks that the Jacksonians had been waging, but the new president revealed little sympathy for the Whig vision of a revived national bank. In his address to the special session of Congress, Tyler indicated his preference for a solution that would fall somewhere between resuscitating the national bank and sticking with the existing independent treasury scheme.[45] Tyler's opposition to both the independent treasury and to a national bank placed him midway between the orthodoxy of both parties.

Twice in the summer of 1841 the Whig-controlled Congress passed bills to establish a national bank, and twice Tyler vetoed them. Tyler's second veto caused an uproar within the Whig party. All but one member of the cabinet resigned, and Tyler was literally read out of the Whig party. Even before this second veto and the subsequent resignations, however, Tyler had determined to reorganize his cabinet and form a new party with himself as leader.[46] Tyler's refusal to approve a bill that would incorporate a new national bank was designed to attract "moderate" opinion within both parties—an alliance of the center against the two extremes of egalitarianism and hierarchy.[47]

Tyler's effort to steer a course midway between the antibank stance of Van Buren Democrats and the national bank advocated by Clay Whigs found a receptive audience among Conservative Democrats. William Rives, leader of the Conservative revolt, became Tyler's spokesman in the Senate.[48] After the rupture with the Whigs, Tyler turned to the *Madisonian* (founded in 1837 as the conservative Democratic newspaper) as official mouthpiece of his administration.[49] The "premier" of Tyler's reconstituted cabinet was the South Carolinian Hugh Legarè, who, like Rives, had moved into the Whig party as a consequence of Jackson's and Van Buren's radical antibank doctrines.[50] In creating his new cabinet, Tyler explained that he had sought "Jackson men [who] . . . fell off"[51]—in other words, Jackson supporters who, like himself, had been repelled by Jacksonian egalitarianism. The opportunity to support minimum government without having to suffer the egalitarianism that had accompanied Jacksonianism was particularly appealing to southerners.

Tyler's appeal to individualists was couched in the language of moderation. "Every Whig is not an ultra-Bank man; nor every Democrat a Bentonian humbugger; . . . [it was] to the moderate men," the *Madisonian* declared, "that the country looks for salvation." Tyler's leading spokesman in the House, fellow Virginian Henry Wise, urged his colleagues to abandon the "dangerous extremes of both parties" in favor of a president who could be trusted to establish "Constitutional Republicanism in the place of Agrarianism on the one hand and of Federalism on the other."[52]

It was a bold strategy with an appealing logic. After all, agreement over individualism did link the Democratic and Whig parties. Initially it appeared that Tyler's strategy of luring individualists away from both parties might pay off. Tyler's plan for a "Board of Exchequer," outlined in his message to the regular session of Congress, aroused considerable interest among those Whigs who were reluctant to reinstate a national bank, as well as tempting Democrats who were uncomfortable with their party's antibank rhetoric.[53]

The *Madisonian* defended the exchequer plan, seeing it as designed to restore stability and faith in the financial system with a minimum of currency management by the Treasury Department. The requirement that states must consent to the establishment of branch banks appealed to those suspicious of the power of the central government.[54] Tyler's scheme, moreover, was free of the crusading antibank animus that pervaded radical Democratic thought. Despite initial interest, however, the Tyler administration was unable to shake enough Democrats and Whigs from their party moorings; and the exchequer plan was decisively defeated.

Though he lacked the party support necessary to push proposals through Congress, Tyler was nonetheless effective in securing his goal of minimizing the powers of the national government. The presidential veto well suited his individualist bias. By using the veto more frequently than had any of his predecessors, Tyler consistently frustrated Whig efforts to increase the scope of the national government.[55] In defending the veto, however, Tyler downplayed the Jacksonian justification of the veto as empowering the people, stressing instead that it was the "great conservative principle of our system."[56] For the individualist, the value of the presidential veto lay not in promoting vicarious public participation but, rather, in creating additional impediments to government action.

Control over executive patronage and extensive popular support for individualism nevertheless proved an insufficient basis on which to build a unicultural party. By the end of 1842, Tyler had only two supporters in the Senate and six in the House.[57] The president's failure came not from miscalculating the support for individualism but from impediments inherent in the existing two-party system. Individualists on both sides were unwilling to defect because to weaken one's own party risked allowing the opposition to gain control. Individualists in the Democratic party were afraid to defect to Tyler because this could allow the hierarchical Whigs to triumph and to reinstate a national bank. By the same token, individualistic Whigs hesitated to defect for fear that it would strengthen the Democratic party, and thus a return to radical antibank policies.[58]

Although he had been unable to establish a viable new party on the basis of banking and finance, Tyler still hoped to use the Texas issue to rehabilitate his cultural strategy and thereby his political fortunes. In the spring of 1843 he began a concerted campaign to push his scheme for annexing Texas to the top of the political agenda.[59] With the leading candidates of both major parties (Van Buren and Clay) opposed to the plan, Tyler calculated that annexation, by fomenting divisions within the two parties, would allow him to attract the individualist center that had eluded him in the banking controversy.

In an attempt to keep expansion—and slavery—off the agenda, both Van Buren and Clay issued public declarations in late April 1844 opposing Tyler's proposal to annex Texas. Delegates to the Democratic presidential convention already had been selected, a majority of whom were pledged or instructed to vote for Van Buren. As Tyler anticipated, Van Buren's stance on the Texas issue aroused intense opposition within the Democratic party, so intense that the convention nominated instead James Polk, who was firmly committed to the "immediate re-annexation of Texas." With the expansionist Polk as the Democratic nominee, Democrats had swiped Tyler's main issue, forcing "His Accidency" to withdraw from the race.[60] Though he had failed to create a new party or to win the Democratic party nomination, Tyler's actions were instrumental in beginning a shift within the Democratic party away from an alliance of individualism and egalitarianism forged on economic issues and toward a party with a more individualistic and less egalitarian hue. The result was that Tyler, like many of his followers, felt able to return to the Democratic fold.

Pushing a Solution to Its Limits: James Polk

The acrimonious struggle over the 1844 Democratic nomination—a marked contrast to the Whig's unanimous nomination of Henry Clay—brought into public view divisions within the Democratic party. Ever since Jackson's retirement, party leaders had labored to contain intraparty disputes between radicals and conservatives, egalitarians and individualists. In almost every state of the Union a battle raged between these two wings of the Democracy.[61] As of 1843 it appeared that Van Buren, the Democratic nominee in 1836 and

1840, again would be the candidate to unite the divided party. The "Little Magician" was supported by the leading party newspapers, including Thomas Ritchie's *Richmond Enquirer* and Francis Blair's *Washington Globe*, and had the backing of the most influential party leaders, including the "Old Hero" himself. But Van Buren's public declaration opposing annexation of Texas snatched defeat from the jaws of victory, inducing many, including Ritchie and Jackson, to withdraw their support. To jettison Van Buren, however, was also to remove the only national figure, other than Jackson, who had proved capable of holding together the competing cultures within the Democratic party.[62]

With Van Buren unable to secure the two-thirds majority required for nomination and with the convention unable to agree on an alternative candidate, prolonged deadlock seemed inevitable. Some egalitarian supporters of Van Buren were threatening to bolt the party; only the prospect that their arch foe, Lewis Cass, might obtain the nomination persuaded them to stay. To many, the Democracy seemed on the verge of dismemberment. Defeat in the general election appeared certain. The ninth ballot, writes Charles Sellers, "began in a pandemonium of angry recriminations" yet "ended in a delirium of joy and brotherly love."[63] In between the Democrats had selected James Knox Polk.

Polk's nomination successfully mediated intraparty conflict, allowing Democrats to enter the general election with a united front.[64] As a Tennessee congressman and a Jackson protégé, Polk had opposed Clay's American system in its entirety: tariffs, internal improvements, a national bank, and high land prices.[65] Polk's labors as chairman of the Ways and Means Committee in behalf of Jackson's bank war and as speaker of the House supporting Van Buren's independent-treasury scheme made him acceptable to Van Burenites. At the same time his vigorous support for "immediate re-annexation of Texas" made Polk attractive to adherents of the "New Democracy" who, like Robert Walker and Cass, were indifferent if not hostile to the egalitarian crusade against paper money.[66]

Polk was committed to holding together the Jacksonian coalition of individualism and egalitarianism. The Democratic party, he believed, was carrying on the same good fight that the Jeffersonian heroes of his youth had waged a generation earlier. If the Democratic coalition collapsed, the Whigs (whom Polk invariably referred to as Federalists[67]) would—through Clay's American system—advance the cause of hierarchy. "I resolved from the beginning," he wrote to Silas Wright, "to know no divisions of the democratic party, as the only means of keeping it *united* & preserving its *strength*."[68] Presidential leadership, as Polk confided to his diary, depended on not "identifying . . . with any faction of the Democratic party."[69]

In December of 1845 Polk presented Congress with an ambitious program that enabled him to seize control of the political agenda. Tariff reform was at the top of Polk's domestic agenda, absorbing four full pages of the address. The president skillfully weaved together egalitarian and individualistic arguments in favor of tariff reduction. The existing Whig tariff of 1842 Polk considered "manifestly oppressive and unjust," for it made "the rich richer and the poor poorer." It burdened "labor and the poorer classes, who are least able to bear it, while it . . . protects the capital of the wealthy manufacturer, and increases his profits." Not only did tariffs increase inequality, however, they also violated competition and self-regulation. The result of a protective tariff, wrote Polk, "was to take the property of one man, and give it to another, without right or consideration." The follow-up report by Secretary of the Treasury Robert Walker further stressed the benefits of free and unrestricted trade among nations.[70]

The one-vote margin by which the Walker tariff passed in the Senate attracts attention to the pivotal role of administration pressure in keeping swing votes in line. Lost sight of, however, is the mix of egalitarianism and individualism with which Polk invested tariff reform to make a high degree of party unity possible. Only the two Democratic senators from Pennsylvania (where manufacturing interests were adversely impacted) and Senator Niles of Connecticut, who regarded tariff reform as a plot to "favour the slave labor [system] of the south," crossed party lines. Championing tariff reduction allowed Polk to join the themes of laissez-faire and reducing differences, appealing to individualists and egalitarians and thereby cementing the Jacksonian coalition.[71]

Of particular importance in selling the Walker tariff as a Jacksonian measure was the egalitarian rhetoric Polk used to justify it. Many radical Democrats were suspicious of tariff reduction, in part because they saw it as advantaging the South, and in part because the bill was so closely identified with the secretary of the Treasury. Caring little for the issues of banking and finance so close to the heart of egalitarian Jacksonians, Walker's consuming passion instead was territorial and commercial expansion. As a congressman, he had fought to have Jackson's specie circular rescinded, and had publicly ridiculed the hard-money doctrines championed by Thomas Hart Benton. At the recent Democratic convention, moreover, Walker had played a leading role in deposing Van Buren. The radicals' distrust of Walker was further fanned by the news that one of Jackson's last acts before his death was to warn Polk about Walker's involvement in speculative schemes.[72]

Although suspicious of Walker and lukewarm about free trade,[73] the egalitarian Van Buren-Benton wing of the party enthusiastically endorsed Polk's proposal to reestablish the independent treasury. In his message (recommending what he preferred to call a "constitutional treasury") Polk pulled out the old, antibank Jacksonian rhetoric. Banks, according to Polk, had proved "faithless." To oppose the constitutional treasury was to put more confidence in "presidents, cashiers, and stockholders of banking corporations" than in "the people."[74] Hard-money Democrats were overjoyed at what they construed as vindication of their position. "Since the President's message," rejoiced Ohio radical Samuel Medary, "soft-ism . . . is the poorest of God's creations."[75] By framing the issue as one of fidelity to the Jacksonian heritage and by identifying the proposal as an administration measure, Polk was able to secure passage of the constitutional treasury bill along strict party lines.[76]

Having successfully managed the Jacksonian domestic program, Polk hoped to further cement party unity by placing territorial expansion at the top of the agenda. Though the controversy over annexing of Texas had precipitated the rejection of Van Buren at the convention and had unleashed bitter personal animosities within the party, expansion now, ironically, seemed to hold out the potential to provide fresh glue for a party divided on issues of finance and banking. In Ohio, for instance, where Democrats remained badly split over economic issues, there was widespread agreement within the party on the desirability of territorial expansion.[77]

Industrialization was perceived by many in the Democratic party to pose a fundamental threat to their preferred way of life. It was widely believed that egalitarianism and individualism could thrive only in an agrarian setting. Britain's "corporate factory system" entailed hierarchy and an erosion of the independence, widespread ownership of property, and social mobility that had made the United States unique.[78] Whig policies—such as the protective tariff, centralized banking, and restrictive land policies—would make the United States become, "like England, a nation of nabobs and paupers."[79] As Democrats saw it, Whig champions of the nascent industrial order, in the spirit of Hamilton, were trying to transform the United States into a British-style alliance of hierarchy and individualism.

Territorial expansion, Democrats believed, was the best way to keep authority widely dispersed.[80] Extending the base of the pyramid horizontally, they believed, would prevent it from growing vertically. Jefferson, by acquiring Louisiana, and Jackson, through Indian removal, had forestalled the emergence of a hierarchical social order. In his final annual address Polk reiterated the Democratic conviction that territorial expansion had allowed the United States to avoid "the tendencies to centralization and consolidation" that plagued other less fortunate nations.[81]

Expansion through space, as an antidote to hierarchical development through time, was a familiar formula, but Polk brought to the White House a zeal for expansion that went far beyond anything hitherto experienced by the nation. Under Jackson the brunt of the battle against hierarchy had been waged on the domestic front in a war on the national bank. Jefferson's eight years in office had been marked by an ambivalence toward expansion that stemmed in large part from the fear that aggression would undermine the country's role as a model republic.[82] For Polk, however, territorial expansion appeared a panacea for not only the nation's but also the party's ills.[83]

Like Jackson's bank war, expansion seemed a way to revitalize the Democratic alliance of egalitarianism and individualism by identifying a hierarchical enemy—abroad as well as at home. Members of the individualistic wing of the party overwhelmingly favored territorial expansion, for they thought the acquisition of additional territory would enable them to escape from central authority. Expansion, in addition, would open up new markets; the prospect of gaining the harbor of San Francisco was particularly attractive. By removing powerful foreign enemies from the nation's borders, individualists hoped to reduce the need for a strong national defense.

Egalitarians could agree on the perils posed by hierarchy. Despite Van Buren's opposition, annexation of Texas had been supported by many from the radical wing of the Democracy, including William Allen, Samuel Medary, Francis Blair, Churchill Cambreleng, and George Bancroft.[84] The crusading quality of expansionism appealed to many of those who, like the editor of the *Daily Plebian*, Levi Slamm, had been crusaders in behalf of Locofocoism, labor-unionism, and Dorrism.[85] Indeed, the phrase "Manifest Destiny" was coined by John O'Sullivan, a Van Burenite editor of the *Democratic Review*. Expansion, O'Sullivan rhapsodized, would promote the "universality of freedom and equality."[86]

If expansion could unite individualists and egalitarians, Polk might avoid Van Buren's fate of being torn between the two political cultures and could emulate Jackson's successful forging of a cultural hybrid. Unfortunately for Polk, however, as expansion became entwined with slavery, the egalitarian wing of the Democracy pulled back from supporting it. Some radical Democrats, like Theodore Sedgwick, Jr., Preston King, John Hale and William Cullen Bryant, had opposed annexation from the outset on the grounds that "it must incalculably increase . . . the slaveholding power."[87] Others, like David Wilmot, having supported the annexation of Texas, now tried to exclude slavery from all the territory acquired in the Mexican War by attaching a proviso—the Wilmot Proviso—to an appropriations bill.[88]

Though Polk continued to assert that he favored no one faction within the Democratic party, his aggressive expansionist policy increasingly alienated him from the party's more egalitarian elements. Their lack of representation within Polk's cabinet hastened egalitarian estrangement from the administration. Only the secretary of the navy, George Bancroft, came from the egalitarian wing of the party, and he was gone by the summer of 1846. The other major appointments—Walker in the Treasury Department, James Buchanan as secretary of state, and William Marcy as secretary of war—went to persons with little sympathy for the Van Buren faction.[89]

The distance between the president and the Van Burenites was further dramatized by Polk's decision to discard Francis Preston Blair's paper, the *Washington Globe*, as the mouthpiece for the administration. A close friend of Jackson and Van Buren, Blair's sympathies were with the radical wing of the Democracy. Already disappointed with Polk's cabinet selections, Jackson was outraged by Blair's removal. In an angry letter to Polk, Jackson predicted "destruction of the democratic party" if Blair were replaced. Polk informed Jackson that "it is impossible for him [Blair] to command the support of the whole party," i.e. that Blair was too closely aligned with the radical Democracy of Benton and Van Buren. Selection of conservative Thomas Ritchie to head the new administration organ, the *Washington Union*, only fueled suspicion of Polk's antiegalitarian bias.[90] On balance, Polk's personnel moves shifted power away from the more egalitarian Jacksonians—Blair, Benton, Van Buren, John Dix—and toward such individualists as Walker, Buchanan, Ritchie, Cass, Daniel Dickinson, and Stephen Douglas.

The shift away from egalitarianism was expedited by the outbreak of war with Mexico in the spring of 1846. The subsequent debate about whether to outlaw slavery in any territory gained from Mexico would irreparably alter the character of the Democratic party. Alarmed at "the spirit and demands of the Slave Power,"[91] the egalitarian wing pressed for the Wilmot Proviso, which would prohibit by federal law the introduction of slavery into any territory gained from the war with Mexico; the individualist wing, however, preferred leaving the decision to local inhabitants. In 1848 many Jacksonian radicals would bolt to the Free Soil party rather than support the party nominee, Lewis Cass, and his doctrine of "squatter sovereignty." With egalitarianism increasingly weak, the Democratic party, drained of the crusading idealism that had characterized it during the 1830s and early 1840s, took on an increasingly southern cast.

Polk's most conspicuous failing as a political leader was an inability to grasp that because of slavery, expansion was creating more problems than it was solving, both for the Democratic party and the nation.[92] "Slavery," Polk confided to his diary, "was one of the questions adjusted in the compromises of the Constitution. It has, and can have no legitimate connection with the war with Mexico."[93] But the sectional cast of the debate over the Wilmot Proviso belied Polk's contention. To the end of his term, he refused to acknowledge the divisive implications of territorial expansion. In his final address to Congress, Polk maintained that expansion had provided an "additional guaranty for the preservation of the Union itself."[94] The president's attempt in the closing days of his term to purchase Cuba, a territory with almost as many slaves as whites, was dramatic testimony to Polk's blindness to the dangers of rapid territorial expansion.[95]

Charles Sellers concludes his definitive biography by arguing that Polk was "the last American president who had any chance to master" the conflict between the slaveholding states of the South and the free states of the North.[96]

The indictment can be extended further, for the inability of Polk's successors to manage the conflict between the North and South peacefully was in large part due to Polk's policy of rapid territorial expansion. The continental impulse that Polk had helped foster between the summer of 1844 and fall of 1846 began to undermine the national character of the political parties, thereby crippling the greatest force for national unity.[97] Though Jacksonian orthodoxy held that each additional state "added another pillar to the temple of liberty," in the changed context of the mid-1840s new states were, as Van Buren, Calhoun, and others saw, becoming arenas for a divisive struggle over the extension of slavery.[98]

Polk never tried to adjust his policies to take into account the transformation in the political landscape wrought by slavery. As others more and more began to ask about the sectional implications of policies, Polk's gaze remained transfixed on the past. Because Polk conceived of tariff reduction solely in terms of past party battles, for instance, he remained insensitive to the sectional implications of the Walker tariff, despite the fact that the measure clearly advantaged southern states. His vigorous promotion of tariff reduction therefore made many northeastern Democrats suspect that the administration harbored prosouthern sympathies.[99]

Polk's veto of the rivers and harbors bill of 1846 provides another instance in which the president adhered to Jacksonian orthodoxy, insensitive to the sectional implications of his action.[100] The primary division over internal improvements now ran along sectional rather than party lines. Believing they had traded support of the administration's tariff bill for administration support of internal improvements, western Democrats were outraged by Polk's veto. To the *Cleveland Plain Dealer*, the veto was definitive proof that "the administration is Southern, Southern, Southern!"[101]

And northern resentment was fanned by Polk's eagerness to provoke Mexico into war over the slaveholding territory of Texas, an action that many in the West contrasted with the president's previous willingness to compromise with Britain over the nonslaveholding Oregon territory.[102] Polk never questioned the Democratic axiom that all new territory not only furthered the national interest but, in Jackson's widely quoted phrase, was also "extending the area of freedom."[103] Those who drew any connection between slavery and expansion, Polk believed, were "not only unwise but wicked."[104] "Young Hickory" lacked the imagination necessary to realize that he faced a new set of dilemmas that could not be resolved by old Jacksonian solutions.[105]

Similarly, Polk did not recognize—as Van Buren did—the limitations of the leadership style inherited from Andrew Jackson. The Jacksonian concept of the popular mandate enabled the chief executive to sustain a relatively wide scope of activity within a generally antiauthority context. But Jackson's style of presidential leadership contained potential pitfalls for an unwary president. The belief that a president was endowed with a popular mandate could tempt him into denigrating Congress for thwarting the popular will. A popular war hero with mostly negative aims could afford to sour relations with Congress; Polk, a politician with little public support and with a legislative agenda that required congressional assent, could not.

"Young Hickory" consciously emulated the leadership style of his political idol.[106] In his last annual message to Congress, Polk explicitly articulated the theory of presidential leadership that Jackson had personified.[107] He lectured Congress on the myriad ways in which the legislative branch distorted the popular will, concluding that the president was more representative than Congress of the wishes of "the whole people." Openly challenging congressional prerogative did little to endear Polk to Congress, but it was less what he said at the close of his term than how he had behaved throughout his four years that precipitated the congressional backlash against Polk and, more generally, presidential leadership.

Believing that his victory over Henry Clay constituted a popular mandate for Jacksonian policies,[108] Polk repeatedly threatened to go over the head of recalcitrant Democratic congressmen. "The people elected a majority of both Houses to sustain my policy," Polk complained in early 1847, "but their Representatives do not do so." Confident that he had it in his power "by communicating the truth to their constituents to destroy them politically," the president vowed, in good Jacksonian fashion, to "fearlessly appeal to the people" for support.[109]

Democrats who resisted administration initiatives, Polk believed, were guilty of putting personal interests ahead of the will of the majority. He lamented "the selfishness of some members of Congress who make their public duties bend to their personal interests."[110] Polk's uncompromising stance on the tariff, for instance, stemmed from his conviction that Democratic opposition was "the work of monied interests, armed with bribes and influence." Similarly, Polk dismissed Democratic support for the rivers and harbors bill as capitulation to "a lobby influence." After the Senate turned down one of his appointments, Polk fumed that the offending Democratic senators were acting like "spoiled children."[111] Emboldened with the belief that he held a mandate from the people, observes historian Thomas Hietala, Polk "treated party members as if they were merely his tools to move the nation's politics toward a Jeffersonian-Jacksonian order."[112]

Polk's confrontational methods produced striking short-term policy successes, but at the high cost of generating great resentment in his own party.[113] By the midpoint of his term virtually every major figure in the Democratic party—John Calhoun, James Buchanan, Thomas Hart Benton, George Dallas, and Van Buren, among others—had distanced himself from Polk.[114] In July 1846 a Calhounite could state that "no President ever lost so much personal popularity in so short a time, or had a smaller remnant left."[115] By his aggressive behavior, Polk made himself the focal point for criticisms of administration policies. From Philadelphia came the opinion, "I never saw an administration that was so little looked to or cared for." A prominent Van Burenite, Churchill Cambreleng, called it a "blundering administration."[116] "All around is dissension and distrust," wrote a Virginia Democrat. "Gloom overspreads the party." Another southern Democrat pronounced the administration "almost unanimously deserted."[117] Despite impressive legislative successes, Polk, like Lyndon Johnson, left office a broken man, highly unpopular within the Democratic party as well as the nation at large. Polk's presidency, which had begun so auspiciously, ended in bitter frustration and mutual recrimination. Having entered office as the youngest chief executive in the nation's history, he died only three months after leaving what he termed "my long confinement" in the presidential office.[118]

In spite of these failings, the 1962 presidential greatness survey conducted by Arthur Schlesinger found Polk to be a "near-great" president, immediately below Theodore Roosevelt and just above Harry Truman. Clinton Rossiter judged Polk "the one bright spot in the dull void between Jackson and Lincoln." Reviewing Polk's governing style, Charles Sellers concludes that Polk "utilized all the tactics for executive leadership of Congress that were eventually to become standard operating techniques of the presidency."[119] Polk's precocious conception of the president as chief legislator has brought accolades from twentieth-century scholars who assume executive initiative in the legislative sphere to be the proper mode of governing.[120] Charles McCoy, for instance, praises Polk for being a president who "regarded it as his duty not merely to recommend legislation to the Congress but to advocate by every means at his disposal the enactment of the Administration's program."[121] But should behaving as presidents are expected to behave today be a criterion for a past leader's greatness?

If greatness is to be measured by the ambitiousness of legislative objectives and success in achieving those objectives, then Polk's high ranking is deserved. At the outset of his term, according to Navy Secretary Bancroft, Polk identified the "four great measures of my administration": reduction of the tariff to a revenue basis, acquisition of California, settlement of the Oregon question, and establishment of an independent treasury.[122] In all four areas his record of accomplishment is impressive. If, however, we evaluate a president's greatness in terms of dilemmas resolved, Polk fares less well.

From his predecessors Polk inherited a set of solutions to antiauthority dilemmas. His failure to perceive the limits and contradictions of these solutions had disastrous consequences for the nation and the Democratic party; this leads us to question whether Polk deserves the relatively high esteem that twentieth-century historians and political scientists have generally paid him. Territorial expansion, Polk learned from Jefferson and Jackson, could keep domestic and foreign hierarchy at bay; by contrast, expansion in the 1840s opened up the wrenching debate over slavery that would end in civil war. Each succeeding president was to try a different cultural combination to resolve the dilemma posed by slavery, but until the outbreak of war none would succeed. Adopting Jackson's conception of the mandated presidency, Polk ended up by souring relations between Congress and the presidency. When Polk left office, argues historian William Brock, "the relationship between Executive and Congress had deteriorated to the point that the capacity to govern had become gravely weakened."[123] Polk left his successors in the unenviable position of trying to cope with the looming division between North and South in an atmosphere of heightened distrust of the executive branch of government.

Notes

1. On the individualist orientation of Conservative Democrats, see John Ashworth, *'Agrarians' and 'Aristocrats': Party Political Ideology in the United States, 1837-1846* (Atlantic Highlands, N.J.: Humanities Press, 1983), pp. 132-46, esp. pp. 138-41; quotation on p. 139. On the egalitarianism of the hard-money Democrats, see James Roger Sharp, *The Jacksonians versus the Banks: Politics in the States after the Panic of 1837* (New York: Columbia University Press, 1970), p. 17, and Ashworth, *Agrarians and Aristocrats*, pp. 87-111.
2. Ashworth, *Agrarians and Aristocrats*, pp. 89, 94.
3. *New York Journal of Commerce*, October 21, 1836, cited in John M. McFaul, *The Politics of Jacksonian Finance* (Ithaca: Cornell University Press, 1972), p. 181.
4. James C. Curtis, *The Fox at Bay: Martin Van Buren and the Presidency, 1837-1844* (Lexington: University Press of Kentucky, 1970), pp. 67, 69.
5. McFaul, *Jacksonian Finance*, p. 182.
6. Ibid., p. 185; Major L. Wilson, *The Presidency of Martin Van Buren* (Lawrence: University Press of Kansas, 1984), p. 50; Curtis, *Fox at Bay*, p. 70; Donald B. Cole, *Martin Van Buren and the American Political System* (Princeton: Princeton University Press, 1984), p. 293.
7. Wilson, *Presidency of Van Buren*, pp. 53-54.
8. Ibid., pp. 55-56. On the divisive impact of the panic on the Democratic party, see Michael F. Holt, "The Democratic Party, 1828-1860," in *History of U.S. Political Parties*, ed. Arthur M. Schlesinger, Jr. (New York: Chelsea House, 1973), 1:510; Sharp, *Jacksonians versus Banks*, p. 14; Cole, *Martin Van Buren*, p. 298.
9. Sharp, *Jacksonians versus Banks*, p. 17. See also McFaul, *Jacksonian Finance*, pp. 85, 96, 188, 189, 207-8, 212-13; Sharp, *Jacksonians versus Banks*, pp. 18-19.
10. P. Lindsley to Van Buren, June 1, 1837, cited in McFaul, *Jacksonian Finance*, p. 188. See also Curtis, *Fox at Bay*, p. 102.
11. Nathaniel Tallmadge to William Rives, May 31, 1837, cited in Sharp, *Jacksonians versus Banks*, p. 12.
12. Ashworth, *Agrarians and Aristocrats*, p. 138.
13. Curtis, *Fox at Bay*, p. 66. Also see Sharp, *Jacksonians versus Banks*, pp. 14-15.

14. Cole, *Martin Van Buren*, pp. 290-91.
15. Wilson, *Presidency of Van Buren*, pp. 38-39. See also Cole, *Martin Van Buren*, pp. 287, 291; Curtis, *Fox at Bay*, pp. 52-63. The only cabinet post open when Van Buren was elected was the War Department, which Van Buren offered first to the leader of the Conservative Democrats, William Rives.
16. Wilson, *Presidency of Van Buren*, p. 62. Also see Curtis, *Fox at Bay*, pp. 75, 84.
17. Cole, *Martin Van Buren*, pp. 300, 304-6; Wilson, *Presidency of Van Buren*, p. 68; Curtis, *Fox at Bay*, pp. 74-85.
18. Curtis, *Fox at Bay*, pp. 97-98; Cole, *Martin Van Buren*, p. 307.
19. Wilson, *Presidency of Van Buren*, p. 79. See also Curtis, *Fox at Bay*, pp. 101, 103.
20. Quoted in Curtis, *Fox at Bay*, p. 89, and Cole, *Martin Van Buren*, p. 303.
21. Wilson, *Presidency of Van Buren*, pp. 71, 74; see also p. 63.
22. Curtis, *Fox at Bay*, p. 89; Wilson, *Presidency of Van Buren*, pp. 64-66, 75.
23. Holt, ''The Democratic Party,'' p. 511; Arthur M. Schlesinger, Jr., *The Age of Jackson* (Boston: Little, Brown, 1945), pp. 236, 241.
24. Wilson, *Presidency of Van Buren*, pp. 71-72. Ashworth, *Agrarians and Aristocrats*, pp. 92-93. Schlesinger, *Age of Jackson*, p. 261. The Locofocos received their name when, on October 29, 1835, they used locofoco matches to light candles in order to continue meeting after the regular Tammany Democrats had declared a party meeting adjourned by turning out the gaslights in the meeting hall.
25. Edward Pessen, *Jacksonian America: Society, Personality, and Politics*, 2d ed. (Homewood, Ill.: Dorsey Press, 1978), p. 186; Theophilus Fisk, quoted in Ashworth, *Agrarians and Aristocrats*, p. 88.
26. McFaul, *Jacksonian Finance*, p. 207; Sharp, *Jacksonians versus Bank*, p. 8.
27. McFaul, *Jacksonian Finance*, p. 97.
28. Wilson, *Presidency of Van Buren*, p. 68; Ashworth, *Agrarians and Aristocrats*, p. 90.
29. Ivor Debenham Spencer, *The Victor and the Spoils: A Life of William L. Marcy* (Providence: Brown University Press, 1959), pp. 91-92; Wilson, *Presidency of Van Buren*, p. 83; Curtis, *Fox at Bay*, p. 93; Ashworth, *Agrarians and Aristocrats*, p. 138.
30. Curtis, *Fox at Bay*, pp. 76-77; Wilson, *Presidency of Van Buren*, pp. 65, 68; Cole, *Martin Van Buren*, p. 299.
31. Curtis, *Fox at Bay*, p. 92.
32. Van Buren, cited in Sharp, *Jacksonians versus Banks*, p. 13. The *Washington Globe*, the administration's paper, similarly pronounced that ''the states only are competent to bring their own institutions under proper subjection'' (Curtis, *Fox at Bay*, p. 81).
33. Cole, *Martin Van Buren*, p. 306.
34. Ibid., pp. 306-7, 311-12, 333-36; Curtis, *Fox at Bay*, pp. 104-5, 109, 124-26, 132-33; McFaul, *Jacksonian Finance*, pp. 204-6.
35. Schlesinger, *Age of Jackson*, p. 264.
36. Cole, *Martin Van Buren*, p. 316; see also p. 287. Chapter 12 is entitled ''The End of the Magic.''
37. Jackson's gravitation toward the egalitarian side of the Democratic party is a major theme in Robert Remini, *Andrew Jackson and the Course of American Democracy, 1833-1845* (New York: Harper & Row, 1984).
38. Schlesinger, *Age of Jackson*, p. 264.

39. Cole, *Martin Van Buren*, pp. 312-14.
40. Cole, for example, criticizes Van Buren for being "too cautious" (ibid., p. 315).
41. James C. Curtis, "In the Shadow of Old Hickory: The Political Travail of Martin Van Buren," *Journal of the Early American Republic* (Fall 1981): 263.
42. Ibid., pp. 258-59.
43. Robert Seager II, *And Tyler Too: A Biography of John and Julia Gardiner Tyler* (New York: McGraw-Hill, 1963), pp. 79-80, 85-90.
44. Ibid., pp. 92, 101.
45. Ashworth, *Agrarians and Aristocrats*, p. 142; Jean E. Friedman, *The Revolt of the Conservative Democrats* (Ann Arbor: UMI Research Press, 1976), p. 106.
46. Glyndon G. Van Deusen, *The Jacksonian Era, 1828-1848* (New York: Harper & Row, 1959), pp. 158-59.
47. Friedman, *Conservative Democrats*, p. 108; Ashworth, *Agrarians and Aristocrats*, p. 171.
48. Ashworth, *Agrarians and Aristocrats*, pp. 142, 172; Friedman, *Conservative Democrats*, pp. 105-6.
49. Friedman, *Conservative Democrats*, p. 110; Ashworth, *Agrarians and Aristocrats*, p. 142.
50. Marvin R. Cain, "Return of Republicanism: A Reappraisal of Hugh Swinton Legaré and the Tyler Presidency," *South Carolina Historical Magazine* (October, 1978): 264-80, esp. pp. 268, 279.
51. Oscar Doane Lambert, *Presidential Politics in the United States, 1841-1844* (Durham: Duke University Press, 1936), p. 83.
52. Ashworth, *Agrarians and Aristocrats*, pp. 171, 143.
53. Van Deusen, *Jacksonian Era*, p. 163; Ashworth, *Agrarians and Aristocrats*, p. 172.
54. Friedman, *Conservative Democrats*, pp. 110, 116.
55. Jackson vetoed twelve bills in eight years, while Tyler vetoed nine during a four-year reign. Madison vetoed seven, Washington two, and Monroe 1. See Carlton Jackson, *Presidential Vetoes, 1792-1945* (Athens: University of Georgia Press, 1967), p. viii. On Tyler's vetoes, see pp. 56-84.
56. Robert J. Morgan, *A Whig Embattled: The Presidency under John Tyler* (Lincoln: University of Nebraska Press, 1954), p. 43.
57. Ashworth, *Agrarians and Aristocrats*, p. 143.
58. Ibid., p. 173.
59. Holt, "The Democratic Party," p. 516; Frederick Merk, *Slavery and the Annexation of Texas* (New York: Knopf, 1972), esp. pp. 1-35, 52.
60. Richard P. McCormick, *The Presidential Game: The Origins of American Presidential Politics* (New York: Oxford University Press, 1982), pp. 193-94; Merk, *Annexation of Texas*, p. 68; Friedman, *Conservative Democrats*, pp. 114-15.
61. Ashworth, *Agrarians and Aristocrats*, pp. 132-34, 143-46.
62. McCormick, *The Presidential Game*, p. 193; Van Deusen, *Jacksonian Era*, p. 184; Remini, *Andrew Jackson and the Course of American Democracy*, pp. 498-99.
63. Charles Sellers, *James K. Polk: Continentalist, 1843-1846* (Princeton: Princeton University Press, 1966), pp. 87-98, quotation on p. 96; Ashworth, *Agrarians and Aristocrats*, pp. 132-33.
64. McCormick, *The Presidential Game*, pp. 194-95. Silas Wright told Cave Johnson that Polk was "the only man he thought the Northern democrats would

support if Van Buren was set aside'' (Remini, *Jackson and American Democracy*, p. 500).

65. Charles Sellers, *James K. Polk: Jacksonian, 1795-1843* (Princeton: Princeton University Press, 1957), p. 152. Sellers places particular emphasis on Polk's ''Old Republican'' loyalties and beliefs. See pp. viii, 6, 92, 105, 112-13, 122, 153-54, 161, 170, 279, 378-79, 489-90; Sellers, *Polk: Continentalist*, pp. v, 6-7, 213, 487.

66. Van Deusen, *Jacksonian Era*, pp. 170-207, esp. pp. 170-71, 185, 192; Schlesinger, *Age of Jackson*, pp. 437-38.

67. William R. Brock, *Parties and Political Conscience: American Dilemmas, 1840-1850* (Millwood, N.Y.: KTO Press, 1979), p. 20. See, for example, Polk's diary entries cited in Norman A. Graebner, *Empire on the Pacific: A Study in American Continental Expansion* (New York: Ronald Press, 1955), pp. 179, 184; and Leonard D. White, *The Jacksonians: A Study in Administrative History* (New York: Free Press, 1954), p. 61.

68. Polk to Wright, July 8, 1845, in Sellers, *Polk: Continentalist*, p. 283 (emphasis in original).

69. Ibid., p. 326.

70. Ibid., p. 343; Charles A. McCoy, *Polk and the Presidency* (Austin: University of Texas Press, 1960), pp. 148-51; Allan Nevins, ed., *Polk: The Diary of a President* (New York: Longmans, Green, 1929), p. 129.

71. Sellers, *Polk: Continentalist*, pp. 457-67, quotation on p. 459.

72. Schlesinger, *Age of Jackson*, p. 443; Van Deusen, *Jacksonian Era*, pp. 198-99; Holt, ''The Democratic Party,'' pp. 517-19; James P. Shenton, *Robert John Walker: A Politician from Jackson to Lincoln* (New York: Columbia University Press, 1961), p. 70.

73. William Nisbet Chambers, *Old Bullion Benton: Senator from the New West* (Boston: Little, Brown, 1956), p. 300; Sellers, *Polk: Continentalist*, p. 459.

74. Sellers, *Polk: Continentalist*, p. 344; Van Deusen, *Jacksonian Era*, p. 204.

75. Samuel Medary to William Allen, December 9, 1845, in Sellers, *Polk: Continentalist*, p. 347.

76. Ibid., p. 469.

77. Stephen E. Maizlish, *The Triumph of Sectionalism: The Transformation of Ohio Politics, 1844-1856* (Kent: Kent State University, 1983); Holt, ''The Democratic Party,'' p. 516.

78. Thomas R. Hietala, *Manifest Design: Anxious Aggrandizement in Late Jacksonian America* (Ithaca: Cornell University Press, 1985), pp. 97, 226, and passim; John O'Sullivan, quoted on p. 100.

79. Alfred Stone, Democratic Congressman from Ohio, quoted in Hietala, *Manifest Design*, p. 106; on this theme see pp. 98-103, 121.

80. Hietala, *Manifest Design*, pp. 6-7, 112-13, 258, 297, and passim. Frederick Merk contrasts the Whigs who ''adhered to the philosophy of concentration of national authority in a limited area . . . with the Democratic philosophy of dispersion of authority over wide spaces'' (Frederick Merk, *Manifest Destiny and Mission in American History* [New York: Vintage, 1963], p. 40). See also Major L. Wilson, ''The Concept of Time and the Political Dialogue in the United States, 1828-1848,'' *American Quarterly* (1967): 619-44; Rush Welter, *The*

81. Hietala, *Manifest Destiny*, pp. 121-22.

82. This was the basis of eighty-seven-year-old Albert Gallatin's opposition to the Mexican War. Gallatin believed that a territorial war jeopardized the status of

the United States as the "Model Republic" (Brock, *Parties and Conscience*, p. 171; Robert W. Johannsen, *To the Halls of Montezuma: The Mexican War in the American Imagination* [New York: Oxford University Press, 1985], pp. 284-87). See also Welter, *Mind of America*, pp. 46-53.

83. Maizlish, *Triumph of Sectionalism*, pp. 49-50, 52-53; Hietala, *Manifest Design*, p. 122. Also see the comments by Polk, Thomas Ritchie, Chesseldon Ellis, Andrew Kennedy, and Robert Walker, cited in Hietala, *Manifest Design*, pp. 185-86, 26-32.

84. Sellers, *Polk: Continentalist*, p. 57; Schlesinger, *Age of Jackson*, p. 428.

85. Merk, *Manifest Destiny*, p. 36. Dorrism was a movement in Rhode Island during the early 1840s, headed by Thomas W. Dorr, protesting the existing government, which denied suffrage to over half the adult male population. The Dorrites drew up a new constitution, submitted it to the state's entire population, and upon ratification pronounced Dorr governor of Rhode Island. Through a show of force, the charter government reestablished its authority, and Dorr eventually was captured and sentenced to life imprisonment. On the different reactions of Democrats and Whigs to the Dorr Rebellion, see Ashworth, *Agrarians and Aristocrats*, pp. 225-31.

86. Schlesinger, *Age of Jackson*, p. 427. On O'Sullivan's attachment to Van Buren, see Sellers, *Polk: Continentalist*, p. 57; and Ashworth, *Agrarians and Aristocrats*, p. 132.

87. Schlesinger, *Age of Jackson*, pp. 429-30; Sedgwick quoted on p. 429.

88. Ibid., pp. 450-51.

89. Van Deusen, *Jacksonian Era*, p. 194; Holt, "Democratic Party," p. 519.

90. Remini, *Jackson and American Democracy*, pp. 512, 515-16, Jackson quoted on p. 516; Schlesinger, *Age of Jackson*, pp. 444-45, Polk quoted on p. 444; Van Deusen, *Jacksonian Era*, pp. 194-95; Holt, "Democratic Party," p. 519. On Ritchie as a representative of "conservative" opinion, see Ashworth, *Agrarians and Aristocrats*, p. 146.

91. David Wilmot, quoted in Holt, "Democratic Party," p. 523.

92. Hietala, *Manifest Design*, pp. 252-54; Maizlish, *Triumph of Sectionalism*, p. 53.

93. January 4, 1847, quoted in Brock, *Parties and Conscience*, pp. 208-9.

94. Polk, quoted in Hietala, *Manifest Design*, p. 122.

95. Frederick Merk, *The Monroe Doctrine and American Expansionism, 1843-1849* (New York: Knopf, 1966), pp. 283-84.

96. Sellers, *Polk: Continentalist*, p. 487.

97. Brock, *Parties and Conscience*, pp. 151-53; Sellers, *Polk: Continentalist*, p. 487; Hietala, *Manifest Design*, p. 203.

98. Andrew Kennedy, Democratic congressman from Indiana, quoted in Hietala, *Manifest Design*, p. 185. On Van Buren and Calhoun, see Hietala, *Manifest Design*, p. 243. Also see Graebner, *Empire on the Pacific*, pp. 187-88.

99. Brock, *Parties and Conscience*, pp. 173-74, 179, 208.

100. Norman A. Graebner, "James Polk," in *America's Ten Greatest Presidents*, ed. Morton Borden (Chicago: Rand McNally, 1961), pp. 121-23; Brock, *Parties and Conscience*, p. 175; Sellers, *Polk: Continentalist*, pp. 473-74.

101. Maizlish, *Triumph of Sectionalism*, p. 56. The *New York Tribune* accused Polk of having "never done anything" for the North: "The subjects which a majority of the people were most interested, [such as] . . . river and harbor improvements, a protective tariff, and all of Oregon, as an offset to an increase of slav-

ery territory, he sacrificed for the South'' (Hietala, *Manifest Design*, p. 250).
102. Hietala, *Manifest Design*, pp. 216-17; Maizlish, *Triumph of Sectionalism*, pp. 57-60; Merk, *Monroe Doctrine*, pp. 282-84; Brock, *Parties and Conscience*, pp. 179-80, 208.
103. John William Ward, *Andrew Jackson: Symbol for an Age* (New York: Oxford University Press, 1953), pp. 133-49; Jackson quoted on p. 136.
104. Polk, quoted in Brock, *Parties and Conscience*, p. 209. See also Graebner, *Empire on the Pacific*, p. 185; Graebner, "Polk," p. 135; Sellers, *Polk: Continentalist*, p. 485.
105. Sellers, *Polk: Continentalist*, p. 487. Polk is commonly described by historians as "unimaginative," "narrow," or "dogmatic." See, for example, Merk, *Monroe Doctrine*, p. 286; Sellers, *Polk: Continentalist*, pp. 208, 214; Hietala, *Manifest Design*, p. 248. Polk was not alone, however, in his dogged adherence to traditional Democratic principles (see Welter, *Mind of America*, pp. 371-72).
106. Sellers, *Polk: Continentalist*, pp. 163-64, 213-14; Hietala, *Manifest Design*, pp. 210, 216.
107. Sellers, *Polk: Continentalist*, p. 324.
108. Hietala, *Manifest Design*, pp. 84, 223. The administration organ, the *Washington Union*, chastised Congress for its inaction in the face of the president's program, which was "in obedience to the popular mandate" (May 9, 1846, in Sellers, *Polk: Continentalist*, p. 446).
109. Polk quoted in Hietala, *Manifest Design*, p. 208; Sellers, *Polk: Continentalist*, p. 447; Graebner, *Empire on the Pacific*, p. 184. Also see McCoy, *Polk and the Presidency*, p. 181.
110. Quoted in McCoy, *Polk and the Presidency*, p. 167. See also Graebner, *Empire on the Pacific*, pp. 145, 183, 185; Sellers, *Polk: Continentalist*, pp. 298-299; Hietala, *Manifest Design*, p. 223; McCoy, *Polk and the Presidency*, p. 182.
111. Brock, *Parties and Conscience*, p. 174 (the words are Brock's, not Polk's); McCoy, *Polk and the Presidency*, p. 181; Hietala, *Manifest Design*, p. 239.
112. Hietala, *Manifest Destiny*, p. 223.
113. Sellers, *Polk: Continentalist*, pp. 476, 478; Hietala, *Manifest Design*, pp. 217, 248-49; Brock, *Parties and Conscience*, pp. 174, 179-80.
114. Hietala, *Manifest Design*, p. 216, and ch. 7 passim. See also Holt, "The Democratic Party," p. 519.
115. Ellwood Fisher to Calhoun, August 20, 1846, cited in Sellers, *Polk: Continentalist*, p. 478.
116. Graebner, *Empire on the Pacific*, p. 180; Sellers, *Polk: Continentalist*, p. 478.
117. Graebner, *Empire on the Pacific*, pp. 179-80.
118. Sellers, *Polk: Continentalist*, p. 484. See also ibid., p. 301; Hietala, *Manifest Design*, p. 251.
119. Thomas A. Bailey, *Presidential Greatness: The Image and the Man from George Washington to the Present* (New York: Appleton-Century, 1966), pp. 24-25; Clinton Rossiter, *The American Presidency* (New York: Harcourt, Brace & World, 1960), p. 106; Sellers, *Polk: Continentalist*, p. 447.
120. This bias is betrayed, among other places, in Charles McCoy's comment that "fortunately this period of congressional leadership [between Jackson and Lincoln] was interrupted by the four years of the Polk administration." McCoy also praises Polk for "expressing the will of the future" (*Polk and the Presidency*, pp. 143, 145).
121. McCoy, *Polk and the Presidency*, p. 182. Polk also receives high marks for im-

posing presidential control of the executive departments, particularly in instituting a form of budgetary control (ch. 3, esp. pp. 74-81).
122. Sellers, *Polk: Continentalist*, p. 213. According to Sellers, it "was indubitably the most impressive record of accomplishment in the history of the presidency thus far" (p. 486).
123. Brock, *Parties and Conscience*, p. 178.

8

Three Failed Cultural Solutions to the Problem of Slavery: Millard Fillmore, Franklin Pierce, and James Buchanan

Millard Fillmore, Franklin Pierce, and James Buchanan remain largely forgotten presidents. When remembered at all, this "drab trio" is maligned for personal inadequacies and failure of leadership. In the 1948 Schlesinger poll, these three presidents were all rated "below average," ranked 24, 26, and 27, respectively (out of 29).[1] Why was the pre-Civil War period beset with a string of ineffective presidencies? Their failures, we contend, had less to do with personal inadequacies than with the intractability of the cultural dilemma posed by the "peculiar institution." Fillmore, Pierce, and Buchanan all were experienced politicians; each offered a credible political solution to the cultural dilemma bequeathed in large part by James Polk's expansionist policies. Each solution failed, however, and three strikes were all the nation was allowed. War alone was left.

On a Collision Course with Slavery: Millard Fillmore and the Whig Party

Members of the Whig party could be excused for thinking the presidency a downright inhospitable place. The first Whig president, William Henry Harrison, died a month after taking office. Harrison's vice president, John Tyler, once ensconced in the White House, blocked the Whig program and was read out of the party. In 1844, Henry Clay, the Whig standard-bearer, went down to his third defeat in a national presidential election. On March 5, 1849, Zachary Taylor was sworn in as president. Sixteen months later the second (and last), president to be elected under the Whig banner was dead. Upon Taylor's death, Millard Fillmore became the thirteenth president of the United States.

With memories of John Tyler's apostasy fresh in their minds, orthodox Whigs expressed understandable anxiety about Fillmore. But after initially proclaiming Zach Taylor's death a "national calamity,"[2] these same Whigs soon recognized that the general's death might have been a rare stroke of luck. Like Harrison, Taylor had been a military hero without a strong sense of party identification.[3] "Old Rough and Ready" had never voted in his life; Fillmore had been a loyal foot soldier of the Whig party from its inception and, as chairman of the House Ways and Means Committee in the early 1840s, had been influential in advancing the Whig economic agenda.[4] Having won the national election by running a nonpartisan military hero and by avoiding the adoption of a party platform, orthodox Whiggery finally had one of their own in the White House.[5]

Taylor's death had been particularly alarming to southern Whigs. Fillmore's place on the Whig ticket had been widely interpreted as an antislavery counterweight to the Louisiana slaveholder, Zachary Taylor. In the national election, southern Democrats repeatedly had branded Fillmore a quasi-abolitionist.[6] By throwing his support behind the Compromise of 1850 measures in Congress—which included a fugitive slave bill, and organization of the New Mexico and Utah territories without the Wilmot Proviso—Fillmore quickly erased this undeserved antislavery image. The new president's firm support was a pleasant surprise for southern Whigs that more than compensated for their disappointment at Taylor's gravitation toward the antislavery orbit of William Henry Seward. With the threat of presidential veto that Taylor had cast over the congressional proceedings removed, and with the administration quietly throwing "its whole weight" into the proceedings, the Compromise of 1850 finally became law.[7]

The solution to the sectional controversy, Fillmore believed, was to revitalize the old Whig coalition of individualism and hierarchy. Zachary Taylor's presidency, short as it was, had been plagued by poor relations with congressional Whigs. Taking office as a political outsider, Taylor had done little to ingratiate himself with the Whig leadership. In disgust, Henry Clay wrote: "I have never before seen such an Administration. There is very little co-operation or concord between the two ends of the avenue. There is not, I believe, a prominent Whig in either House that has any confidential intercourse with the Executive." The administration's political weakness was compounded by the limited clout most members of Taylor's cabinet carried in Congress.[8]

Upon assuming office, Fillmore's first decision was to accept the resignation of the entire Taylor cabinet; he was the only vice-presidential successor ever to do this.[9] The new president recruited old-line Whigs, including the highly respected party leaders John Crittenden, Thomas Corwin, and Daniel Webster. It was a cabinet united by considerable congressional experience, orthodox Whig views on economic questions, and hostility to the newly formed Free Soil party, which was pledged to preventing the spread of slavery into the territories and to admitting new slave states.[10] The appointment of

Webster, a leading advocate of the compromise measures, as secretary of state clearly signaled the president's intention to support the compromise. Fillmore's appointments also gave an early indication of his desire to unite the party around the old Whig issues of promoting internal improvements, domestic industry, and economic development.

After Congress had hammered out an agreement on the status of slavery in the newly acquired territories, Fillmore hoped that divisions within the Whig party and the nation could be healed with the balm of economic growth. In Fillmore's mind, sectional peace, Whig party unity, and economic development were linked. Economic prosperity, he argued, depended on national acceptance of the compromise as "a final settlement." Not only was the cessation of sectional agitation a prerequisite to economic prosperity but, in turn, a burgeoning economy, by binding the nation, would insure sectional peace. As guest of honor at a ceremony celebrating the opening of new railroad lines connecting Boston with the West and Canada, Fillmore praised Massachusetts for having "stretched forth her iron arms to the great West and to the Canadas," thus demonstrating how a nation "can be bound together by the ties of mutual business interests and relations."[11]

Fillmore believed also that economic development would unite the Whig party. The marriage of economic growth and social stability had long constituted the foundation of the Whig coalition of individualism and hierarchy. By pushing national economic development to the forefront of the political agenda, the president hoped to hold together a party that was badly divided on the slavery issue. Antislavery "liberal" Whigs like William Henry Seward were no less ardent champions of Whig economic policies than were such "conservative" Whigs as Fillmore. Seward supported government participation in building railroads and making other internal improvements, government subsidies for American steamship lines, a survey of the Arctic and Pacific Oceans for the benefit of the whaling industry, and expansion of American trade in the Far East—all of which were administration policy.[12] "Liberal" and "conservative" Whigs alike expressed unbounded faith in the benefits of economic development. Popular government, Seward rhapsodized, "follows in the track of the steam-engine and the telegraph."[13] Fillmore therefore had reason to believe his strategy might be successful.

The success of the president's strategy of relegating slavery to a secondary issue rested on the Whig party's accepting the Compromise of 1850 as a final settlement. That settlement, however, included the Fugitive Slave Act, which threatened to keep the question of slavery at the forefront of northern attention. Federal marshals were empowered to require that citizens assist in capturing runaway slaves, and heavy penalties were imposed for harboring or rescuing a fugitive. The law also denied the accused fugitive a trial by jury as well as the right to testify in his or her own behalf. The commissioner charged with deciding the case was to be paid a $10 fee if he found the black to be a slave, but only $5 if the black were set free. This unpopular law, which required continued enforcement, would prove, as Robert Winthrop foresaw, "a constant source of irritation and inflammation."[14]

The Fugitive Slave Act created great strain within the Whig party. Individualists were troubled, for although they had no desire to interfere with existing slave property, neither did they want the federal government to enlist them in a search for runaway slaves. Protecting southern slave property under these conditions came at the expense of abridging the autonomy of northern whites, not to mention endangering the liberty of free blacks. The close regulation of behavior inherent in a slave society was, according to some, being transferred to northern society. "The infamous Fugitive Slave Bill," went one complaint, "is a reproduction, on the soil of Massachusetts, New York and Ohio, of the most diabolical features of the slave code."[15]

Hierarchical Whigs were in conflict. Edward Everett, a leading Massachusetts Whig closely allied with Webster, complained that while the South had the "theoretical right . . . to an efficient extradition law, . . . it is a right that cannot be enforced."[16] Even more troubling to hierarchically inclined Whigs were the arbitrary features of the law, which made a mockery of that core value of hierarchical political culture: equality before the law. After trying in vain to incorporate habeas corpus, trial by jury, and protection for free colored seamen, Robert Winthrop, a political leader of the "Cotton Whigs," reluctantly cast his vote against the bill.[17]

Many Whigs, including Winthrop, swallowed their misgivings; they vowed to uphold the law. Whigs throughout the country were reminded of "the cardinal Whig doctrine" of "obedience to the laws of the land."[18] Addressing a large Boston audience, the hierarchical Whig Benjamin Curtis condemned those who preached resistance to the fugitive slave law. "We have come here," he said,

> not to consider particular measures of government, but to assert that we have a government; not to determine whether this or that law be wise or just; but to declare that there is law . . . not to consult whether this or that course of policy is beneficial to our country, but to say that we yet have a country, and intend to keep it safe.

Rufus Choate told the same gathering that every citizen "according to his measure, and in his place, in his party, in his social, or his literary, or his religious circle, in whatever may be his sphere of influence, [should] set himself to suppress the further political agitation of the whole subject."[19]

Though Fillmore welcomed public support for the Compromise of 1850, willing as he was to "bring the whole force of the government to sustain the [fugitive slave] law," he was disturbed by the direction in which many conservative Whigs were headed.[20] Rather than working to restore Whig unity, they seemed determined to create a new Union party. The meeting at which Choate and Curtis spoke was advertised as a bipartisan "Union meeting." In Fillmore's native New York there was a similar "Union meeting" in which people were urged "without distinction to party" to voice approval of "peace measures" and to take action "best calculated to avert the further progress of political agitation in the north." Fillmore's friends intervened and headed off the call for a "Conservative Union Party" because a union with procompromise Democrats around the issues of law and order and preservation of the Union was at odds with Fillmore's economically oriented solution.[21] Fillmore wanted the nation to accept the Compromise of 1850, but he did not want to make the compromise the basis of a new party system. Webster, on the other hand, was staking his presidential ambitions on a Union party. "There is but one all-absorbing question," Webster insisted, "and that is the preservation of the Union."[22]

Webster's position threatened to bring to the surface the submerged tension within Whig ranks between order and growth. The Whigs, as Major Wilson argues, had long assumed "a Janus-like pose." The more hierarchical members, best represented by Webster, stood as the "party of memory or order." Their emphasis, notes Wilson, "was ever on the importance of the judiciary, established constitutions and the educating effect of the law." The other side of Whiggery, in the words of its leading spokesman, William Seward, represented "the party of hope, progress, and of civilization."[23] Fillmore tried in vain to unite the two faces of Whiggery by focusing on finance, commerce, manufacturing, and transportation, issues that had long been the Whig stock in trade. Webster's course, however, was pulling apart the proponents of social order and economic growth, hierarchy and individualism.

Webster's strategy required focusing national attention on resistance to the fugitive slave law. But Fillmore, aided by a booming economy and a nation tired of slavery agitation, was relatively successful at temporarily keeping the fugitive slave law off the national agenda, thus undermining the basis for Webster's Union party. The slavery question, writes historian Thomas O'Connor, "seemed virtually forgotten as the country plunged into a round of building and spending."[24] Only once in the second session of the 31st Congress did Seward refer to the slavery question.[25] For all the tension between Fillmorites and Sewardites, New York Whigs were united in the 1851 elections.[26] As agitation over the compromise settled down and Webster's hopes for a Union party died, Fillmore's stock rose appreciably.[27]

Although the Fugitive Slave Act created severe strains within Whig ranks, the Compromise of 1850 for the most part did what Fillmore had hoped, namely, deflect the country's attention from slavery to economic development. However, because it reproduced the cultural contradiction within

Whiggery, Fillmore's strategy could not halt the gradual disintegration of the Whig party. How could the Whig party celebrate industrial capitalism as the highest stage of civilization without viewing southern slavery as a blight on the economic potential of the nation? If, as Henry Adams recalled being taught, "bad roads meant bad morals," then it followed that the economically underdeveloped South was morally benighted. It was only a short step from the Whig celebration of industry and growth to the Republican pledge to "northernize the South."[28] By the same token the position of southern Whiggery became increasingly untenable, for how could one embrace economic development while defending slavery?

Perhaps more than any other president, Fillmore can be said to have faced an insoluble cultural dilemma. The very economic policies that had united the Whigs now deepened the wedge dividing North and South. Economic dynamism, upon which the Whig party had staked its identity, was disrupting the carefully crafted sectional balance. Fillmore correctly saw that so long as slavery was atop the national agenda, the Whig party could not remain united. What he failed to see was that the Whig ideology celebrating economic growth, capitalist enterprise, and industrial manufacturing was on a head-on collision course with the South's "peculiar institution."

In the presidential election of 1852, the Whig party ruptured along sectional lines and a massive Democratic landslide swept Franklin Pierce into office. Conciliating the South had left Fillmore with no significant base of support in the North. Had he condemned slavery in the territories or refused to sign the Fugitive Slave Act, however, his actions would have left him without political support in the South and might very well have precipitated civil war.[29] The issue of slavery had made it impossible for Fillmore to reconstitute the old Whig coalition of hierarchy and individualism; now Pierce would discover whether slavery also had made untenable the old Jacksonian coalition of individualism and egalitarianism.

Living up to Jackson while Living with Slavery: Franklin Pierce

The received image of Franklin Pierce, writes his biographer Roy Nichols, is "a picture of more or less unrelieved weakness." Allan Nevins describes Pierce as "one of . . . the weakest of the men who have held his high office." Manufactured during his lifetime, the stereotype of Pierce as a "putty man" has never been erased.[30] Alexander Stephens, a southern Whig, accused Pierce of "fickleness, weakness, folly and vacillations." According to the Connecticut Democrat Gideon Welles, Pierce was a "pliant man . . . [who] by his errors and weakness broke down his Administration, and his party." The "anybody-but-Pierce" sentiment of 1856, believed another, was due to the fact that "there is so much weakness in him *personally*."[31]

Yet, if the fault lies within Pierce, how do we explain his past successes? His previous political career had, according to Nichols, been "phenomenal." "In New Hampshire politics," writes Nichols, "his leadership was decisive and effective."[32] Pierce had played a pivotal role during the 1840s in keeping the New Hampshire Democratic party united.[33] Never defeated for office, Pierce was elected to the state legislature at age 24; at 26 he was speaker, presiding over 229 other legislators; three years later he went to the U.S. House of Representatives; by 36 he was a United States senator; and at 48 he was elected president, the youngest chief magistrate in the Republic's history. As Pierce prepared to assume the presidency, his friend Nathaniel Hawthorne confided to a correspondent that he believed Pierce "has in him many of the chief elements of a great ruler. His talents are administrative, he has a subtle faculty of making affairs roll onward according to his will, and of influencing their course without showing any trace of his action. . . . [He] has the directing mind, and will move them about like pawns on a chess-board, and turn all their abilities to better purpose than they themselves could do."[34]

Although we do not take this partisan assessment at face value, we contend nonetheless that Pierce's personal inadequacies alone cannot explain his weak presidential performance. Pierce was no Jefferson, but neither did he lack political skill. As Nichols correctly points out, Pierce "did not suffer from any illusions as to his power over Congress."[35] Pierce placed the highest priority upon establishing good relations with the Senate, whose support would be especially important to his foreign policy and the appointments necessary to secure control over the party.[36] He well understood the necessity of going along to get along. Moreover, Nichols argues, Pierce's handling of his cabinet demonstrated considerable "tact and leadership."[37] Pierce's cabinet—according to Nichols, "one of the most compact and smoothly operating small groups which American politics had ever known"—is the only presidential cabinet to remain intact for a four year term.[38]

Nichols accounts for Pierce's lack of success as president in terms of the personal: the tragic death of his only child in a train wreck en route to the inauguration, which left him entering the office "deprived of the capacity for leadership."[39] But this explanation, as Nichols himself seems to recognize, is insufficient—Lincoln, after all, also lost a son during his term in office. A few pages later he hits closer to the mark: "It was Pierce's misfortune to be elected to the chief-magistracy at a moment when probably no one was prepared for it or when no one could have occupied it successfully. Today, it is difficult to discover any formula of success which Pierce and his associates might have created and applied."[40] In our terms, Pierce found himself in a binding cultural dilemma from which there was no easy avenue of escape. We turn now to delineating the dilemma that hamstrung Pierce's presidency.

When Franklin Pierce assumed office in 1852, the slavery issue was transforming the cultural universe. The Democratic party under Jackson had fused individualism and egalitarianism into a virulently antihierarchical party. For Jacksonians, all past history presented the same sordid spectacle of the few seeking to "pervert the laws and institutions of society to their own temporary aggrandizement and to the permanent oppression of the mass of their fellow creatures."[41] The perceived threat to their way of life, Jacksonians thought, stemmed from privileged minorities, who could be combated only by mobilizing the majority. Majority rule therefore created liberty, i.e. freedom from the oppression of the few.

Slavery presented an intractable dilemma to a party that defined itself in opposition to hierarchical institutions and privileged minorities. Although the institution itself might be rationalized in terms of black inferiority, the Slave Power (i.e. Southern domination of national political life) could not be so easily dismissed. Eric Foner and John Ashworth, among others, have shown that the wing of the Democratic party that was most hostile to banks, corporations, monopolies, and tariffs also was the most attracted to the free soil cause, and was the faction most likely to defect to the Republican party.[42] To the radical antibank wing of the Democratic party, the Slave Power was analogous to the Money Power: both demonstrated that "privilege never restrains its ambition to rule."[43] Among radical Democrats the Slave Power presented a

> struggle between those who contend for caste and privilege and those who neither have nor desire to have privileges beyond their fellows. It is the old question that has always, in all free countries, subsisted—the question of the wealthy and the crafty few endeavoring to steal from the masses of the people all the political power of the government."[44]

Many Democrats, North and South, had long been suspicious of the virulent anti-institutional ethos produced by the fusion of individualism and egalitarianism. Although they favored minimal central government, these Democrats had never been comfortable with the crusading, Jacksonian, antibank rhetoric. Extreme Democratic hostility to banks, for instance, led to a demand for strict regulation of banking that individualists found unappealing. The "despotic, monopolizing interest" that radical Democrats had seen in "the paper money interest" and now saw in "the slave interest" left individualistic Democrats like Stephen Douglas uneasy.[45]

Rather than advancing liberty through a war on the Slave Power, Douglas preferred to foster freedom by leaving control over decisions at the local level. "Each locality having different interests, a different climate and different surroundings," maintained Douglas, "required different local laws, local policy and local institutions, adapted to the wants of that locality."[46] For Congress to exclude slavery from the territories, Douglas contended, deprived people of the right to regulate their own affairs. Douglas's laissez-faire approach to slavery was consistent with Democratic antipathy to government regulation of the economy, religion, education, and drinking.[47]

The Kansas-Nebraska Act made Douglas's principle of "popular sovereignty" the law of the land. But "Bleeding Kansas" revealed the limits of the Democratic policy of self-regulation. With land claims unsettled and without rules that defined voter qualification, registration, jurisdiction over disputed ballots, and control of the polls, popular sovereignty invited widespread fraud and violence. Without an external authority to handle disputes, the locals settled competing claims by resorting to intimidation and murder.[48]

Slavery was rending asunder the Jacksonian fusion of egalitarianism and individualism. Southerners were particularly quick to see that majoritarianism and egalitarianism endangered their way of life. The Democratic rallying cry of majority rule threatened to deprive the South of property rights in the territories. Under the intellectual leadership of Calhoun, the South developed a defense of minority rights sharply at odds with Jacksonian political culture.

The South's interest in preserving slavery made the crusading quality of Jacksonian political culture increasingly intolerable. The same crusading spirit that animated the war on the national bank could, and was, being converted into a war against the Slave Power. Egalitarianism also had become increasingly suspect on account of abolitionist activities. To retain southern support, the Democracy was impelled to jettison its egalitarianism and to moderate its attacks on hierarchical institutions. If the Slave Power replaced the "Monster Bank" as the Democratic Party's "master symbol," the Democracy would cease to exist as an intersectional party.[49] Thus, Pierce faced the dilemma of discarding the Jacksonian fusion or turning his back on the South. Neither choice looked promising.

Pierce's dilemma was to live up to Jackson while also having to live with slavery. "Old Hickory" left a legacy of presidential activism in the name of combating hierarchy. Though Pierce wanted to measure up to Jackson's activist legacy, if his party were not to take on hierarchical institutions, what could the president do? Lacking hierarchical institutions to attack, other than the Slave Power, what justification for presidential leadership remained?

Jackson had been Pierce's political idol from the earliest stages of the latter's career.[50] During the 1852 campaign, Pierce was hailed as Jackson's successor, "Young Hickory of the Granite Hills."[51] Having carried twenty-seven of thirty-one states and 254 of 296 electoral votes, and with overwhelming majorities in both Houses of Congress, Pierce tried, under presidential auspices, to engineer a revival of the united Democratic party he so fondly remembered from Jackson's day.[52] By placing himself at the head of the party, Pierce hoped, in the words of Stephen Skowronek, "to claim the mantle of Andrew

Jackson."[53] Testimony to Jackson's influence was Pierce's decision to abandon the emerging one-term tradition and instead to follow Jackson's precedent of seeking a second term.

Why did it prove impossible for Pierce to lead the Democratic party in the way that Jackson had done? Jackson had mobilized his followers in a war against the "Monster Bank." William Cullen Bryant, a radical Democrat who moved into the Republican party, recalled how when faced with "the paper money interest, . . . Andrew Jackson came into office for a second term, like a mighty conqueror."[54] What powerful vested interest was Pierce going to slay? Apparently Pierce could emulate the presidential leadership of Jackson only by leading a crusade against the Slave Power. To do so, however, would have torn apart not only his party, but the nation as well.

Pierce saw no contradiction between being a president in the mold of Andrew Jackson while heading a Democratic party that retained support from the slaveholding South. After all, Jackson had done both. Like Fillmore, Pierce hoped to unite both party and nation by keeping slavery off the national agenda. National cohesion, Pierce told the nation in his first annual message, depended on "the strictest fidelity to the principles of the constitution . . . the minimum of federal government . . . strict deference to the sovereign rights and dignity of every state."[55] But what role, then, was there for presidential leadership? Unless Pierce could identify a threat to their way of life how could he mobilize his followers behind presidential leadership? If the aim of government was to leave people alone and the government was already doing that, what was there for the president to do?

Pierce hoped to resolve this dilemma through an aggressive, expansionist foreign policy.[56] The cultural propensities of Pierce and his followers prohibited an expansive domestic program but, as Nichols remarks, "diplomacy offered an unhampered field for constructive achievement."[57] In his inaugural address, Pierce pledged that "my administration will not be controlled by any timid forebodings of evil from expansion."[58] As under Polk, foreign policy was to provide the avenue for presidential leadership. Cuba, Hawaii, Alaska, the Dominican Republic, and Northern Mexico were all viewed by the Pierce administration as legitimate spheres for expansion.

Expansion would permit Pierce to emulate the leadership styles of Polk and Jackson, while uniting the party and the nation. Pierce was confident that social equality and economic opportunity also would be served because acquisition of new territory would create a Union with many more free states than slave states. An aggressive foreign policy coupled with popular sovereignty would therefore both expand the sphere of freedom and remove the debate over slavery from the halls of Congress.[59]

Pierce's decision to support the Kansas-Nebraska Act must be understood against this backdrop. Secretary of War Jefferson Davis (future leader of the

Confederate states), Stephen Douglas, and five influential southern senators visited Pierce at the White House, asking for his support of a bill to organize the Kansas and Nebraska territories on the principle of popular sovereignty—thereby repealing the Missouri Compromise of 1820, which had excluded slavery north of the Missouri Compromise line. Under the terms of the Compromise of 1820, slavery would be excluded from both Kansas and Nebraska. Although Pierce was reluctant to reopen the slavery issue recently settled by the Compromise of 1850—though that compromise had applied the principle of popular sovereignty to the Utah and New Mexico territories, both lay west of the Missouri Compromise line, thereby avoiding direct repeal of the Missouri Compromise—he did pledge to support the bill.[60]

Many historians have construed Pierce's decision to support the Kansas-Nebraska Act as compelling evidence of personal weakness. We contend that in hindsight the decision may have been a blunder, but it was not a blunder attributable to lack of spine. Pierce believed that support of the Kansas-Nebraska Act not only was sound public policy but also was necessary for presidential leadership. The administration's active use of patronage and persuasion to insure passage of the bill should alone give pause to the "putty-man" view of the Pierce presidency.[61] Like Douglas, Pierce fully believed that popular sovereignty would mean a free Kansas, so he viewed the concessions to the South as essentially symbolic. More important, Pierce recognized that Senate support was essential to secure the appointments necessary to control the party and ratify the expansionist foreign policy of which he dreamed.[62] In lending his support to the Kansas-Nebraska bill, Pierce had grabbed one horn of a dilemma, but the alternative—turning his back on the South—probably would have left Pierce, like Tyler, a president without a party.[63]

New dilemmas required creative solutions. Pierce was not the incompetent political weakling portrayed by most historians, but neither was he an innovative leader. On the assumption that what had worked in the past would work in the present, Pierce relied on old formulas to solve new problems.[64]

In good Jacksonian tradition, Pierce preached "rigid economy" at home and expansion abroad. Six internal improvements bills met with Pierce's emphatic veto. Jackson's internal improvements vetoes had mobilized and unified the party around an antipathy to the inequalities produced by governmental interference in the economy. But Pierce's vetoes had the opposite effect of splintering the party, making few friends and many enemies. Congress sustained Pierce's first veto but by overwhelming majorities overrode the next five. Most members, as we shall see, no longer viewed internal improvements in the former cultural terms.[65]

The changing times were apparent also in the realm of foreign policy. Early in its term, the Pierce administration had succeeded in negotiating the purchase from Mexico of the land that is now Arizona and southern New Mexico.

When the administration submitted the Gadsden Treaty to the Senate, however, it had to *give up* 9,000 square miles of the acquired land in order to get the Senate to accept the treaty.[66] With expansion inextricably entwined with the debate over slavery, it was no longer possible "to do a Texas."[67]

The Jacksonian program of territorial expansion and domestic economy, so successful in the past, could no longer mobilize and unify the party faithful. Pierce had kept faith with Jacksonian policies, but the cultural significance of those policies had been transformed by slavery. In the age of Jackson, for example, government subsidies for internal improvements had been anathema to Democrats, who viewed such action as unfairly advantaging privileged minorities. By contrast, opposition to federal governmental assistance for Western economic development in the 1850s was construed by many northern Democrats as evidence that the Pierce administration was under the sway of a privileged southern minority, the Slave Power. Thus, the kind of presidential actions that had galvanized the Democrats under Jackson now, under Pierce, divided the party. That Pierce never recognized how changing times were making old solutions counterproductive indicates the limits of his leadership.

To identify, and channel, the direction of cultural change while still living through it is the mark of greatness. That Pierce was not a great president we already know; that others would have performed better is less clear. James Buchanan's lack of success in grappling with the same dilemma lends added credence to our contention that the intractable nature of the cultural dilemma, rather than the personal inadequacies of the president, best explains the ineffectiveness of presidential leadership during the 1850s.

Individualists and Egalitarians Are Different: The Cultural Failure of James Buchanan

The new president, James Buchanan, having watched Fillmore's vain efforts to revive the Whig party and Pierce's failure to resuscitate the old Democratic coalition, offered a new solution: unite elements of both parties. Buchanan was one of the most politically experienced men ever to occupy the presidential office. No one in either party could match his breadth of experience in foreign and domestic affairs. Over the previous forty years he had served in national public office almost without interruption: as representative and then senator; as minister to Russia under Jackson; as Polk's secretary of state; and as minister to Great Britain during the Pierce administration.[68]

Party leaders turned to Buchanan in 1856 in the belief that this experienced politico could negotiate among the treacherous shoals of competing factions on which Pierce's presidency had foundered.[69] A long and successful career in Pennsylvania politics had demonstrated Buchanan's skill in balancing issues and groups. Amid the crossfire of warring factions, the "circumspect and sagacious'' Buchanan had a remarkable knack for landing on his feet.[70] He was the only member of the bitterly divided Polk administration who had not incurred any serious political handicaps; and his position as minister to Great Britain had conveniently kept him free from all "Kansas-Nebraska taint."[71]

Buchanan was supremely confident that he could avoid the mistakes made by his inexperienced predecessor.[72] Chief among Pierce's errors, Buchanan believed, had been the attempt to reconstitute the old Jacksonian alliance. More specifically, Pierce had erred in trying to reach out to those Democrats who had defected to the Free Soil party in 1848. In contrast, Buchanan determined to form a cabinet that while incorporating men from different sections, would not attempt to include all the diverse elements of the old Democratic party.[73] A former Federalist, Buchanan had always been deeply suspicious of the egalitarian, hard-money, antislavery wing of the Democratic party. His aim was "a national and conservative government" that would unite like-thinking Democrats and Whigs against northern fanatacism.[74]

Pierce had relied primarily on past Jacksonian formulas of economy and expansion; Buchanan offered a new cultural solution. Buchanan's vision was of an establishment Union party united against radical egalitarianism. The unity of the nation, and the dominance of the Democracy, could be preserved, Buchanan believed, by drawing the battle lines between an establishment party that stood for order and stability against the fanatical "Black Republicans." Although Buchanan's strategy failed, scholars have not adequately appreciated the innovative nature of the new cultural alliance of individualism and hierarchy that Buchanan was proposing.

Stephen Maizlish has shown that in the years immediately preceding the Civil War, many northern Democrats expressed a preoccupation with stability, order, and "the peace and quiet" of the nation.[75] Under Republican rule, charged the *New York Herald*, "the laws will be violated, . . . and the Union brought into contempt." Republican doctrines were "dangerous in their tendencies to the peace of the Union, the supremacy of the law, and the safety of society."[76] Buchanan wanted to mobilize the North by appealing to its fear of anarchy and disunion and its concomitant enthusiasm for stability and harmony.

Throughout the 1856 campaign Buchanan focused almost exclusively on "the question of Union or Disunion." All other issues, he explained, were "of little importance . . . when compared with the grand and appalling issue of Union or Disunion."[77] After his election Buchanan affirmed that "the great object of my administration will be to arrest, if possible, the agitation of the slavery question at the North . . . [and] restore harmony to the Union." Could he achieve no more than this, he wrote, "I shall feel that I have not lived in vain."[78]

Buchanan viewed the Republican party as indistinguishable from abolitionism;[79] he was to see Lincoln's election in 1860 as "the final triumph of [the northern Abolitionist] cause."[80] Buchanan's plan to forge an establishment alliance depended on blurring the distinction between the predominantly individualist Republican party and the egalitarian abolitionists. During the campaign he advised others that "the Black Republicans must be, as they can be with justice, boldly assailed as disunionists, and this charge must be reiterated again and again." The Democracy's best defense, Buchanan believed, was to publicize the sentiments of "the abolitionists, free soilers and infidels against the Union."[81] Once people perceived that "this Northern abolition party" was endangering peace and order in the Union, the "silent majority" would rally around Buchanan's conservative administration.

Buchanan's veneration of the Union echoed the teachings of the most hierarchical Whigs. "Disunion is a word which ought not to be breathed amongst us even in a whisper," warned Buchanan solemnly. "Our children ought to be taught that it is a sacrilege to pronounce it. . . . There is nothing stable but Heaven and the Constitution."[82] Little wonder that many prominent Whigs, including the arch-conservative Rufus Choate, and the sons of Henry Clay and Daniel Webster, gravitated toward Buchanan.[83] Conservative Whigs recognized a cultural affinity in Buchanan's campaign themes of respect for law, national unity, and harmony. Choate, for instance, believed that Buchanan's candidacy offered the best prospect "to restore the good temper and generous affection of the parts and the whole."[84]

After the election Buchanan moved immediately to implement his strategy of cementing an establishment alliance to oppose egalitarian fanaticism. The Dred Scott case before the Supreme Court offered an early opportunity. Believing that a definitive decision by the Court would present a rallying point for the establishment, Buchanan wrote to his fellow Pennsylvanian, Justice Robert C. Grier, urging him to tackle the question of the rights of slave property in the territories in order to halt the agitation over slavery. According to historian Roy Nichols, Buchanan's "may well have been the deciding voice" in determining the decision.[85] Whatever Buchanan's influence, Grier then informed Buchanan that the Court had decided not to avoid the broad questions and would rule that Congress could not interfere with slaveholding in the territories—in effect, thereby ruling the Missouri Compromise to be unconstitutional. With this knowledge in hand, Buchanan pledged in his inaugural address that "in common with all good citizens, I shall cheerfully submit . . . to their decision, . . . whatever this may be."[86]

Neither the propriety nor duplicity of Buchanan's behavior concern us here. We are interested, however, in Buchanan's assumption (shared by other Democratic leaders) that the Supreme Court decision would diminish slavery agitation. It was hoped that adherents of individualist and hierarchical cultures would unite behind the Court—for individualists required the sanctity of contract, and supporters of hierarchy the adjudicating of who had the right to do what—thereby isolating and weakening those egalitarians who claimed to follow some higher law. Ignoring the immense electoral support given to Fremont and the Republicans in the 1856 election, Buchanan acted as if antislavery sentiment were the product of a relatively small number of egalitarian abolitionists.[87] The northern outcry against the Dred Scott decision gave an early indication of the error of Buchanan's premise and the consequent weakness of his strategy.

To argue that the strategy was flawed is not to imply that it was born of weakness. By analyzing the cultural context within which Buchanan announced that slavery was ''a judicial question which legitimately belongs to the Supreme Court,'' we can see the fallacy of the view that cites this incident as an example of Buchanan's ''abdication'' of presidential leadership.[88] This conventional view of Buchanan results from an exclusive focus on institutional prerogatives divorced from both political strategy and cultural dilemmas. Buchanan did not abdicate leadership to the Supreme Court; rather, he tried to manipulate a Court decision in order to galvanize his followers and to disorient his enemies.

Buchanan's action did, however, signal a clear retreat from the Jacksonian coalition of individualism and egalitarianism. Antipathy to the judiciary, that bastion of Federalism, had long been a defining feature of Jeffersonian and Jacksonian political culture. ''Judges and clergymen,'' remarked Van Buren, are the ''two classes in every community, whose interference in politics is always and very naturally distasteful to sincere republicans.''[89] Jackson had consistently denied the courts any right to speak for the people on questions of public policy. ''The Congress, the Executive, and the Courts,'' he said in his bank veto, ''must each for itself be guided by its own opinion of the Constitution.''[90]

An alliance of individualism and hierarchy could be maintained, as Buchanan well understood, only if the relative merits of slave and free society were not discussed. In the territories, where people were being asked to choose the way of life they preferred, Buchanan recognized that his establishment coalition was threatened. The president thus placed the highest priority on settling the Kansas question, as demonstrated by his selection of a leading Democrat, Robert Walker, to be governor of the territory.[91] Buchanan labored to convert the issue of slavery or no slavery into the issue of Union or disunion. Faced with the first pair, individualists must opt against slavery; faced with the second, they would prefer protecting slave property where it existed.

Congressional approval of the LeCompton Constitution (a proslavery document that would protect already-existing slave property in the Kansas territory), Buchanan believed, would switch national attention away from the territories—together with the concomitant question of slavery versus free society—and would isolate abolitionists by focusing on the question of Union versus disunion. Having carefully canvassed Congress, the president sent the LeCompton Constitution to the two houses accompanied by a strongly worded message urging congressional approval. Hoping to lay the Kansas question to rest, Buchanan boldly staked his prestige on the question, pledging "to stand or fall" on the issue.[92] Making admission of Kansas under the LeCompton Constitution a litmus test of party loyalty, Buchanan mobilized all his presidential resources to drive wavering votes into the fold. The president, writes Buchanan's biographer Philip Klein, "used every means he could to pick up the few votes needed, dismissing friends of Douglas wholesale, holding up new appointments, and offering patronage, contracts, commissions, and in some cases cold cash."[93]

Despite conducting the fight "shrewdly and ably,"[94] the administration lost. To explain why the administration came to grief over LeCompton sheds light on its failure to establish a dominant establishment alliance. The usual personal characteristics trotted out to explain Buchanan's failure—"weak," "timid," "vacillating," "indecisive"—are inaccurate.[95] Buchanan's attempt to drive the bill "naked" through the House revealed a resoluteness bordering on the stubborn. His behavior could hardly be construed as exemplifying personal timidity.[96] Opposition congressmen, far from seeing Buchanan as infirm, branded the president as "a dictator, a tyrant, a James the First."[97]

Why was Buchanan's plan for an establishment alliance shattered by the controversy over the LeCompton Constitution? Buchanan's strategy failed in part because of southern behavior over which he had little control. The battle over LeCompton provided a national stage on which to air the developing southern ideology of slavery as a "positive good." Before the rise of an organized abolition movement in the North, southerners had mostly agreed with the North that slavery was a "necessary evil." By the 1850s, however, with their way of life under attack, southerners increasingly defended the virtues of the slave-master relationship and struck out at the "free labor" society in the North.[98] On the floor of the Senate, for instance, James Hammond of South Carolina announced that the North had abolished "the name slavery, but not the thing itself." This speech, along with northern rebuttals, was circulated widely throughout the North, and thousands of copies were issued in pamphlet form in the South.[99] With southerners telling the North that the market way of life was equivalent to slavery, there was little chance that northern individualists could succeed in forging an establishment alliance.

Buchanan could not see that opposition to slavery in the territories was an individualist, as well as an egalitarian, position. Individualists could agree not to touch slavery where it already existed, but in the territories their stance was essentially indistinguishable from that of egalitarians. Because he never appreciated the immense popular support in the North for the Republican rallying cry of "free soil, free labor, free men," Buchanan failed to understand the tremendous demand he was imposing on northern Democrats in asking them to support a proslavery constitution, especially with an election approaching.[100] With the Douglas wing of the Democratic party alienated, passage of the LeCompton Constitution was impossible and there could be no cross-sectional alliance of individualism and hierarchy.

Because Buchanan himself never perceived (or did not wish to perceive) the important distinction between abolitionism and Republicanism, egalitarianism and individualism, he was unable to teach it to southerners. After John Brown's raid, for instance, southerners portrayed Brown as the modal Republican. Even anti-LeCompton, Douglas Democrats were cast as the "Black Republican Reserve."[101] In his annual message President Buchanan only fueled southern fears when he warned that the raid was symptomatic of "an incurable disease in the public mind, which may . . . terminate . . . in an open war by the North to abolish slavery in the South."[102] Civil war would be precipitated not by a northern assault on southern slavery, however, but by a South that could not distinguish between John Brown and Abraham Lincoln, that is, between egalitarian abolitionism and the predominantly individualistic Republican party. The success of Buchanan's strategy of uniting individualism and hierarchy hinged on recognizing and exploiting the points of disagreement between the egalitarians and individualists. Unable to recognize this distinction, Buchanan's actions defeated his aims.

The Democrats' "crushing defeat" in the midterm election registered Buchanan's failure.[103] When Buchanan came into office, there had been in the House of Representatives fifty-three free-state Democrats and seventy-five slave-state Democrats. After the 1858 elections, only thirty-two free-state Democrats remained, twelve of whom were anti-LeCompton Democrats. With sixty-nine slave-state Democrats, the party for the first time was dominated by southerners.[104] A Democratic president who now neglected the interests of the South was committing political suicide.

Southern secession, which followed Lincoln's election, left Buchanan conflicted. The lynchpins of his establishment strategy had been reverence for the Union and obedience to law. But now disunion was being advocated not only by egalitarian abolitionists but by the entire southern establishment. To champion Union and the primacy of federal law entailed coercing the South; to acknowledge the South's right to secede meant forsaking the establishment union.

Buchanan's last message to Congress reveals a president being gored on the horns of a dilemma, pitching this way then that, unable to extricate himself. Buchanan denied the federal government's right to coerce a state, but then denied the right of a state to secede from the Union. The president repeated and vindicated southern arguments used to justify secession, yet argued that "the injured States" first had to use "all peaceful and constitutional means to obtain redress" before they "would be justified in revolutionary resistance to the government of the Union." The South was angry that Buchanan denied states the right to secede; Republicans were outraged that he blamed secession on the North's "incessant and violent agitation of the slavery question"; and Douglas Democrats were appalled that Buchanan appeared to countenance peaceable secession.[105]

The commonplace evaluation of Buchanan as an indecisive and weak president "who would hardly cross the street without congressional approval," stems largely from his behavior during his last four months in office.[106] This makes for a misleading view of the Buchanan presidency, because southern secession had exploded the political strategy upon which Buchanan had staked his administration. No longer could his aim of constructing a conservative alliance of individualists and hierarchs be served by a resounding appeal to Union, for the enforcement of federal laws would repel the South. Nor could his goal be served by sanctioning secession, and the dissolution of the Union, for this would repel the North. Buchanan's indecision in the face of southern secession is better explained, we contend, by this intractable dilemma than it is by focusing on his alleged "weakness." In short, the presidency of James Buchanan was immobilized because his cultural solution had failed.

By 1860 it appeared that every peaceful solution to the dilemma posed by slavery had failed. Neither the Whig alliance of individualism subordinated to hierarchy, nor the Democratic fusion of egalitarianism and individualism, nor Buchanan's antiegalitarian Union party had succeeded in containing slavery. The question now facing the nation was what Lincoln and the Republican party could offer that was different.

Notes

1. Thomas A. Bailey, *Presidential Greatness: The Image and the Man from George Washington to the Present* (New York: Appleton-Century, 1966), p. 285. In the 1962 poll, the results were essentially the same except Pierce and Buchanan swapped positions (pp. 24-25).
2. Thomas H. O'Connor, *Lords of the Loom: The Cotton Whigs and the Coming of the Civil War* (New York: Scribner's, 1968), pp. 85-86; Abbott Lawrence quoted on pp. 85-86.
3. K. Jack Bauer, *Zachary Taylor: Soldier, Planter, Statesman of the Old Southwest* (Baton Rouge: Louisiana State University Press, 1985), pp. 215-55.
4. Robert J. Rayback, *Millard Fillmore: Biography of a President* (Buffalo: Henry Stewart, 1959), pp. 69-90, 122-36. Fillmore, records Rayback, "participated in nearly every significant deed of the . . . [Whig party] from its birth—even conception—to its death" (p. viii). Also see Joel H. Silbey, *The Shrine of Party: Congressional Voting Behavior, 1841-1852* (Pittsburgh: University of Pittsburgh Press, 1967), p. 160.

5. Glyndon G. Van Deusen, "The Whig Party," in *History of U.S. Political Parties*, ed. Arthur M. Schlesinger, Jr. (New York: Chelsea House, 1973), 1:356.
6. David M. Potter (completed and edited by Don E. Fehrenbacher), *The Impending Crisis, 1848-1861* (New York: Harper & Row, 1976), p. 109; Van Deusen, "The Whig Party," p. 356; Rayback, *Fillmore*, pp. 186-87.
7. William Alexander Graham, Fillmore's secretary of the navy, quoted in Allan Nevins, *Ordeal of the Union* (New York: Scribner's, 1947), 1:342. On Fillmore's role in the adoption of the compromise, see Holman Hamilton, *Prologue to Conflict: The Crisis and Compromise of 1850* (Louisville: University of Kentucky Press, 1964), esp. pp. vii, 107-8, 157-58; Rayback, *Fillmore*, pp. 247-53; Potter, *Impending Crisis*, pp. 110, 120; and Robert F. Dalzell, Jr., *Daniel Webster and the Trial of American Nationalism, 1843-1852* (Boston: Houghton Mifflin, 1973), pp. 196-222, esp. pp. 208-9.
8. Bauer, *Zachary Taylor*, pp. 250, 262, 265-66, 297, 308; Clay to James Harlan, March 16, 1850, cited on p. 265.
9. Potter, *Impending Crisis*, p. 110.
10. Rayback, *Fillmore*, pp. 243-45. Five of the seven cabinet members had served in the United States Senate.
11. Ibid., pp. 289-90. Fillmore, quoted in Potter, *Impending Crisis*, p. 121; and Rayback, *Fillmore*, p. 294.
12. Glyndon G. Van Deusen, *William Henry Seward* (New York: Oxford University Press, 1967), p. 140.
13. Seward, quoted in Eric Foner, *Free Soil, Free Labor, Free Men: The Ideology of the Republican Party before the Civil War* (New York: Oxford University Press, 1970), p. 39. On the "liberal" Whigs, see John Ashworth, *'Agrarians' and 'Aristocrats': Party Political Ideology in the United States, 1837-1846* (Atlantic Highlands, N.J.: Humanities Press, 1983), pp. 147-70, esp. 148-49; and Daniel Walker Howe, *The Political Culture of the American Whigs* (Chicago: University of Chicago Press, 1979), pp. 181-209.
14. Potter, *Impending Crisis*, pp. 130-31; Kenneth M. Stampp, *The Imperiled Union: Essays on the Background of the Civil War* (New York: Oxford University Press, 1980), p. 237; Martin B. Duberman, *Charles Francis Adams, 1807-1886* (Boston: Houghton Mifflin, 1961), pp. 169-170, Robert Winthrop quoted on p. 170.
15. Quoted in Larry Gara, *The Liberty Line: The Legend of the Underground Railroad* (Lexington: University of Kentucky Press, 1961), p. 129.
16. Quoted in Jean V. Matthews, *Rufus Choate: The Law and Civic Virtue* (Philadelphia: Temple University Press, 1980), p. 194. See also Potter, *Impending Crisis*, p. 133.
17. Duberman, *Charles Francis Adams*, p. 170.
18. O'Connor, *Lords of the Loom*, pp. 96-98; Stephen E. Maizlish, *The Triumph of Sectionalism: The Transformation of Ohio Politics, 1844-1856* (Kent: Kent State University Press, 1983), pp. 167-68, *Cleveland Herald*, October 5, 1850, quoted on p. 167.
19. Matthews, *Choate*, pp. 195-96.
20. Fillmore, quoted in Rayback, *Fillmore*, p. 271.
21. Matthews, *Choate*, p. 194; Rayback, *Fillmore*, p. 266.
22. Rayback, *Fillmore*, p. 263. Dalzell, *Daniel Webster*, pp. 223-258; Webster quoted on p. 237. Webster hoped to emulate the success of the Union party in Georgia that had been forged under the leadership of Alexander Stephens, Robert Toombs, and Howell Cobb (Dalzell, *Daniel Webster*, p. 235; see also

Arthur Charles Cole, *The Whig Party in the South* [Washington, D.C.: American Historical Association, 1914]).

23. Major L. Wilson, "The Concept of Time and the Political Dialogue in the United States, 1828-1848," *American Quarterly* (1967): 624-25.
24. O'Connor, *Lords of the Loom*, p. 94.
25. Van Deusen, *Seward*, p. 135.
26. Dalzell, *Daniel Webster*, p. 236.
27. Ibid., pp. 234-51.
28. Foner, *Free Soil*, p. 54 and passim; Adams quoted on p. 39.
29. After carefully weighing the evidence, the distinguished historian David Potter concludes "that by 1850 southern resistance to the free-soil position was so strong and widespread that if the Union were to be preserved, the South had either to be conciliated or to be coerced" (*Impending Crisis*, p. 118).
30. Roy Franklin Nichols, *Franklin Pierce: Young Hickory of the Granite Hills* (Philadelphia: University of Pennsylvania Press, 1958), pp. 533-34; Bailey, *Presidential Greatness*, p. 286.
31. Nichols, *Franklin Pierce*, pp. 452, 533, 454 (emphasis in original).
32. Ibid., p. 536.
33. Donald B. Cole, *Jacksonian Democracy in New Hampshire, 1800-1851* (Cambridge: Harvard University Press, 1970), pp. 216-33, esp. p. 232.
34. Nichols, *Franklin Pierce*, p. 217.
35. Ibid., p. 302.
36. Ibid., p. 217.
37. Ibid., p. 247.
38. Ibid., p. 540.
39. Ibid., p. 536.
40. Ibid., p. 544.
41. Cited in John Ashworth, "The Democratic-Republicans before the Civil War: Political Ideology and Economic Change," *Journal of American Studies* (December 1986): 375-90, at 379.
42. Foner, *Free Soil*, esp. p. 169; Ashworth, "Democratic-Republicans." See also Arthur M. Schlesinger, Jr., *The Age of Jackson* (Boston: Little, Brown, 1945), pp. 433, 450-83.
43. Kinsley Bingham quoted in Ashworth, "Democratic-Republicans," p. 380.
44. Ashworth, "Democratic Republicans," p. 381.
45. William Cullen Bryant cited ibid., pp. 380-81.
46. Bruce Collins, "The Ideology of the Ante-bellum Northern Democrats," *Journal of American Studies* (April 1977): 103-21, at 108.
47. Ibid., pp. 107-9, 119. See also Harry V. Jaffa, *Crisis of the House Divided: An Interpretation of the Issues in the Lincoln-Douglas Debates* (Garden City, N.Y.: Doubleday, 1959). Douglas viewed the Kansas-Nebraska Act as an opportunity to purge the crusading egalitarian element from the Democratic party. Threatening to "shoot the deserters," Douglas insisted that "the principle of this bill will form the test of Parties" (Foner, *Free Soil*, p. 158).
48. Philip Shriver Klein, *President James Buchanan: A Biography* (University Park: Pennsylvania State University Press, 1962), p. 290; Nichols, *Franklin Pierce*, pp. 407-15, 441-45, 473-83, esp. p. 477.
49. The term "master symbol" comes from Marvin Meyers, *The Jacksonian Persuasion: Politics and Belief* (Stanford: Stanford University Press, 1960), p. 254. Also see Foner, *Free Soil*, p. 91.

50. See Nichols, *Franklin Pierce*, pp. 29-30, 33; Cole, *Jacksonian Democracy*, p. 60.
51. Nichols, *Franklin Pierce*, p. 208; Cole, *Jacksonian Democracy*, p. 243.
52. Nichols, *Franklin Pierce*, p. 292; Stephen Skowronek, "Presidential Leadership in Political Time," in *The Presidency and the Political System*, ed. Michael Nelson (Washington, D.C.: Congressional Quarterly Press, 1984), p. 118.
53. Skowronek, "Political Time," p. 118. On Pierce's conception of himself as leader of the Democratic party, see Nichols, *Franklin Pierce*, pp. 308, 429-34.
54. Bryant, cited in Ashworth, "Democratic-Republicans," p. 381.
55. Nichols, *Franklin Pierce*, p. 300.
56. Ibid., pp. 270, 325, 376, 539.
57. Ibid., p. 325.
58. Ibid., p. 235. See also Potter, *Impending Crisis*, pp. 181-82.
59. Collins, "Ante-Bellum Northern Democrats," pp. 105-7; Cole, *Jacksonian Democracy*, p. 217; Jaffa, *Crisis of House Divided*, pp. 41-103, esp. p. 48.
60. Potter, *Impending Crisis*, pp. 145-76.
61. Nichols, *Franklin Pierce*, pp. 333-38; Skowronek, "Political Time," p. 120.
62. Nichols, *Franklin Pierce*, pp. 287, 323, 544; Michael Holt, "The Democratic Party, 1828-1860," in *History of U.S. Political Parties*, ed. Arthur M. Schlesinger, Jr. (New York: Chelsea House, 1973), 1:526-27.
63. Nichols, *Franklin Pierce*, pp. 544-45.
64. Ibid., pp. 298, 545; Cole, *Jacksonian Democracy*, pp. 245, 246; Carlton Jackson, *Presidential Vetoes, 1792-1945* (Athens: University of Georgia Press, 1967), pp. 105-6.
65. Jackson, *Presidential Vetoes*, pp. 99-106; Nichols, *Franklin Pierce*, pp. 354-55, 377-78.
66. Potter, *Impending Crisis*, pp. 178, 182-83.
67. Nichols, *Franklin Pierce*, p. 399.
68. Potter, *Impending Crisis*, p. 297; Roy Franklin Nichols, *The Disruption of American Democracy* (New York: Macmillan, 1948), p. 11.
69. Nichols, *Disruption of Democracy*, pp. 11-12, 42.
70. Martin Van Buren, cited in Elbert B. Smith, *The Presidency of James Buchanan* (Lawrence: University Press of Kansas, 1975), p. 11; see also pp. 18, 31.
71. Nichols, *Disruption of Democracy*, p. 11; Smith, *Presidency of Buchanan*, p. 12.
72. Potter, *Impending Crisis*, p. 297; Nichols, *Disruption of Democracy*, p. 54. Buchanan's overconfidence, Nichols argues, was in fact a liability (pp. 75, 81).
73. Nichols, *Disruption of Democracy*, p. 56. Buchanan had advised Pierce that "he who attempts to conciliate opposing factions by placing ardent and embittered representatives of each in his Cabinet will discover that he has only infused into these factions new vigor and power for mischief" (quoted in Richard F. Fenno, Jr., *The President's Cabinet* [Cambridge: Harvard University Press, 1959], p. 182).
74. Buchanan, quoted in Philip Shriver Klein, *President James Buchanan: A Biography* (University Park: Pennsylvania State University Press, 1962), p. 262. Also see Ashworth, *Agrarians and Aristocrats*, p. 145.
75. Stephen E. Maizlish, "Race and Politics in the Northern Democracy: 1854-1860," in *New Perspectives on Race and Slavery in America*, ed. Robert H. Abzug and Stephen E. Maizlish (Lexington: University Press of Kentucky, 1986), pp. 79-90, esp. p. 85.

76. *New York Herald*, November 1, 1854, and October 19, 1858, cited in Maizlish, "Race and Politics," p. 85.
77. Buchanan to J. Glancy Jones, June 29, 1856, cited in Klein, *President Buchanan*, p. 257; Buchanan to Nahum Capen, August 27, 1856, cited in Potter, *Impending Crisis*, p. 264.
78. Buchanan to John Y. Mason, December 29, 1856, cited in Klein, *President Buchanan*, pp. 261-62. See also Nichols, *Disruption of Democracy*, p. 54; Potter, *Impending Crisis*, p. 297.
79. Smith, *Presidency of Buchanan*, p. 6.
80. Buchanan, cited ibid., p. 193.
81. Klein, *President Buchanan*, p. 257; also see p. 366.
82. Ibid., p. 253.
83. Potter, *Impending Crisis*, p. 263. On Rufus Choate's decision to support Buchanan, see Mathews, *Rufus Choate*, pp. 220-26. Also see Klein, *President Buchanan*, pp. 259, 263.
84. Choate, cited in Mathews, *Rufus Choate*, p. 224.
85. Nichols, *Disruption of Democracy*, p. 66.
86. Potter, *Impending Crisis*, p. 287.
87. Smith, *Presidency of Buchanan*, p. 26. See also Nichols, *Disruption of Democracy*, p. 61.
88. See, for example, Wilfred E. Binkley, *President and Congress* (New York: Vintage Books, 1962), p. 131. Buchanan, cited in Potter, *Impending Crisis*, p. 287.
89. Van Buren, cited in Schlesinger, *The Age of Jackson*, p. 17.
90. See Robert V. Remini, *Andrew Jackson and the Course of American Democracy, 1833-1845* (New York: Harper & Row, 1984), pp. 317, 339-40, quotation on p. 340. On Jeffersonian hostility to the judiciary, see Richard E. Ellis, *The Jeffersonian Crisis: Courts and Politics in the Young Republic* (New York: Oxford University Press, 1971).
91. Potter, *Impending Crisis*, pp. 297-98.
92. Buchanan to Robert Walker, quoted in Klein, *President Buchanan*, p. 295. Also see Potter, *Impending Crisis*, p. 316.
93. Klein, *President Buchanan*, pp. 308-11, quotation on p. 311; Potter, *Impending Crisis*, pp. 318-23; Smith, *Presidency of Buchanan*, p. 44.
94. Potter, *Impending Crisis*, p. 319.
95. Theodore Roosevelt called the fifteenth president "Buchanan the little" (Potter, *Impending Crisis*, p. 517). In Charles Francis Adams's view, Buchanan was "timid and vacillating" (Potter, *Impending Crisis*, p. 520), and Allan Nevins accuses Buchanan of "feeble pliancy" (Donald V. Weatherman, "James Buchanan on Slavery and Secession," *Presidential Studies Quarterly* [Fall 1985]: 796-805, at 802). The southerners, argues Gerald Caspers, "bent the president at will" (Klein, *President Buchanan*, p. 308). This stereotype is convincingly challenged in Smith. *Presidency of Buchanan*, p. 11 and passim; Klein, *President Buchanan*, p. 308 and passim; and David E. Meerse, "Presidential Leadership, Suffrage Qualifications, and Kansas: 1857," *Civil War History* (December 1978): 293-313. See also Thomas A. Bailey, *Presidential Greatness: The Image and the Man from George Washington to the Present* (New York: Appleton-Century, 1966), p. 288.
96. Buchanan, quoted in Potter, *Impending Crisis*, p. 323.
97. Klein, *President Buchanan*, p. 337.

98. Richard J. Ellis and Aaron Wildavsky, "A Cultural Analysis of the Role of the Abolitionists in the Coming of the Civil War" (typescript).

99. Smith, *Presidency of Buchanan*, pp. 43-44.

100. Potter, *Impending Crisis*, p. 319.

101. Klein, *President Buchanan*, pp. 336-37.

102. Smith, *Presidency of Buchanan*, p. 95; see also pp. 26, 148, 161.

103. Buchanan, quoted ibid., p. 81.

104. Potter, *Impending Crisis*, p. 326.

105. Ibid., pp. 520-21; Smith, *Presidency of Buchanan*, pp. 149-51; Klein, *President Buchanan*, p. 363.

106. Arthur Schlesinger, Jr., *The Imperial Presidency* (Boston: Houghton Mifflin, 1973), p. 297. See Bailey, *Presidential Greatness*, p. 290.

9

Subordinating Hierarchy
to Individualism:
Abraham Lincoln

In his pioneering study *Psychopathology and Politics*, Harold Lasswell identified the successful politician as one who is able to elevate his personal problem to match the solution required by the nation. Lincoln's psyche we leave to those who declare they understand it. But we agree that his lifelong political problem—to reconcile being a Whig with being a successful politician—did call for a national as well as a personal solution.

From early manhood Lincoln had identified with and participated in a political party. But Lincoln's political ambition, that "little engine that knew no rest,"[1] was thwarted by adherence to the Whig party. The Whigs, as we have seen, were a cultural alliance, predominantly hierarchical, yet with a strong admixture of individualism. When economic times were hard—as in 1840—the paternalism of the party served them well, but for the most part Whiggery appeared too restrictive to a nation eager to exploit the resources of a seemingly boundless continent. Henry Clay, the Whig standard-bearer and Lincoln's political idol lost all three presidential elections in which he participated. The only Whig successes in presidential contests, William Henry Harrison in 1840 and Zachary Taylor in 1848, had depended on submerging party principles and policies.

From the sobering experience of Clay's defeats in 1836 and 1844 as well as from the victories of the apolitical generals in 1840 and 1848, Lincoln learned that his own personal advancement would depend on creating a party that could elevate not only famous military heroes but an Illinois party politician to the presidential office. To make the Whig party a majority party required subordinating hierarchy to individualism. Lincoln was instrumental in creating a new Republican party in which individualism was tempered but not led by hierarchy. He thus helped to give the majority culture—individualism— the dominant place in governing the nation. The Republican amalgam of economic individualism and social hierarchy was to dominate American politics for the next fifty years, in the same way that Jefferson's and Jackson's alliance of egalitarianism and individualism had dominated the previous half century.

The Whigs' only popular cause had been the cry of executive usurpation. In the Whig mind, "King Andrew" signified the degeneration of egalitarianism into the charismatic leader whose aim was to replace the law with his personal wishes. In an 1837 address before the Young Men's Lyceum of Springfield, Abraham Lincoln delivered a typical Whig warning against the charismatic leader.[2] Firmly grounded in the legal tradition of conservative Whig jurisprudence, with its respect for law and belief in strong government,[3] Lincoln admonished his young audience not to be seduced by the "towering genius" who "disdains a beaten path." Such a demagogue, warned Lincoln, would disregard precedent and convention, trample on established laws, and tear down the careful work of the founding fathers. In words that could have been spoken by the leading Whig exponent of hierarchy, Rufus Choate, Lincoln pleaded for the American people to make "reverence for the laws . . . the political religion of the nation."[4]

Whigs were torn between their hierarchical inclination to support central authority and their fear of the disruptive potential of presidential power. The result was that they wanted an anomalous executive, one who stood for but did not actually exercise authority. The chief executive was to enforce the laws of the land but otherwise to be confined within narrowly circumscribed limits: no veto power, no congressional influence. As president, Lincoln had to reconcile this Whig doctrine with his will to exert power, to restore the Union, and to establish the Republican party.

Had the Whigs been faced only with what they considered a degeneration of democracy—a lawless executive pandering to the populace—they might have managed or, at least, survived. In the South, however, Whigs confronted something worse, the ultimate degeneration of hierarchical principles in the form of the master-slave relationship. Unable to abide its arbitrariness or to condone upsetting its legal status, they floundered, split not only between northern and southern Whigs but also (and more importantly) between the apparent necessity to give up either their individualistic adherence to free labor or their hierarchical attachment to patriarchy. Before Lincoln freed the slaves, he had to free his party from being immobilized by this dilemma: an immoral legality through acceptance of slavery, or an illegal moralism through its abolition.

From Whig to Republican

What was the relationship between the Lincoln of the Lyceum speech and Lincoln the president? Was he, as David Donald maintains, essentially a "Whig in the White House" or, as Stephen Oates contends, had Lincoln jettisoned his Whig past in becoming a "Republican in the White House?"[5] How did Lincoln reconcile his career as an orthodox conservative Whig in the

1830s and 1840s with his subsequent identity as a Republican proponent of free soil, free labor, and free men? Lincoln struggled with the question of what it meant to be a Republican. "I think I am a whig," he mused, "but others say there are no whigs, and that I am an abolitionist."[6] During the course of the 1858 campaign Lincoln began to formulate an individualist identity shorn of much of the hierarchy of the Whigs, yet without adopting the egalitarianism of the abolitionists.

Daniel Walker Howe has identified Lincoln as a central figure in Whiggery's metamorphosis. In a brilliant final chapter entitled "Abraham Lincoln and the Transformation of Northern Whiggery," Howe traces the changes in Lincoln's thought through his relationship to the Whig tradition. Lincoln, contends Howe, "avoided both the Jacksonian zero-sum game (seeing one person's gain as another's loss) and Whiggish condescension. In place of these alternatives, he glorified upward social mobility and made himself its greatest archetype."[7] Lincoln synthesized Whiggery and Democracy by stressing the market individualism that these two cultures shared, while minimizing the egalitarianism of Jacksonianism and the hierarchy of Whiggery.

"The old Whig political culture," explains Howe, "had been an unstable compound of modernization with paternalism. . . . The new party of Abraham Lincoln left paternalism behind."[8] Howe goes on to observe that "the old hierarchical idea of a harmony of interests between classes was not encouraged by the Republicans. Instead they argued that America ought to become a classless society, in which individual initiative and hard work received their just reward when the laborer became a capitalist in his own right."[9] This move away from hierarchy and toward individualism manifested itself in a number of specific policy areas. The Whigs had promoted mixed public-private corporations; the Republicans opted for a system of free enterprise aided by subsidies. The Republican party also overcame the Whig fear of western expansion, and many—like Lincoln—reversed their previous opposition to free land for homesteaders.[10] What differentiated the Republican party from the Whig party was that, in the former, hierarchy was clearly subordinate to individualism. Authority might be imposed as a last resort, but self-regulation, the ideal of individualists, came first.

The subordination of paternalism to self-help in the views of Lincoln and the Republican party generally is in large part attributable to the rise of the debate over slavery. When southerners defended slave labor as a positive good, most northern Whigs responded by playing up the virtues of a system of competitive individualism while downgrading their hierarchical vision.[11]

The move away from hierarchy was furthered by the migration of a sizable segment of former Democrats into the Republican party. With hierarchy subordinated to individualism, the Republican party could attract antislavery

Democrats; by the same token the antihierarchical leanings of these former Jacksonians contributed to the individualist flavor of the new Republican party. As president, Lincoln promoted the individualist cast of the Republican party by inviting a number of former Democrats into his cabinet.[12]

The political isolation and confusion of the more hierarchical Whigs during the 1850s was evidence of the extent to which the Republican party had transformed its cultural principles. Rufus Choate, who had so much in common with the Lincoln of the Lyceum address, now turned to the Democratic party of James Buchanan. Other leading spokesmen for Whig hierarchy, such as Josiah Quincy and Edward Everett, felt they were left without a party with which they could identify.[13]

Still, Lincoln did retain some of the hierarchical elements of Whiggery. The hierarch's sense of a "duty to posterity" to preserve and transmit the work of past generations, expressed so vividly by Lincoln in the Lyceum speech, remained with him as president. "Fellow citizens, we cannot escape history," he declared in his annual message to Congress in 1862. "The fiery trial through which we pass will light us down, in honor or dishonor, to the latest generation."[14] Two years later Lincoln told the nation that "we are striving to maintain the government and institutions of our fathers, to enjoy them ourselves, and transmit them to our children and our children's children forever."[15]

Lincoln's rhetoric during the Civil War, moreover, expressed the hierarchical conception of the need for the parts to sacrifice for the whole. Lincoln, Howe points out, "fulfilled the hopes of Whig conservatives like Webster and Choate, who had wanted to endow American nationality with a sacrosanct aura."[16] Having elevated the Union, in Alexander Stephens's words, "to the sublimity of a religious mysticism,"[17] "Father Abraham" called on individuals and states to sacrifice life and limb for the good of the collectivity in a way that no pure individualist would have.

"When Lincoln confronted the secession crisis as president-elect," observes historian George Fredrickson, "he presented himself primarily as defender of law and order, a champion of the procedural community against those who refused to abide by a public decision constitutionally arrived at."[18] There appears here a recognizable continuity with the prescription of the Lyceum speech "never to violate in the least particular, the laws of the country; and never to tolerate their violation by others."[19] But Fredrickson points out correctly that "the Lincoln of the 1850s was not purely and simply what he had been in the late 1830s—a conservative of the rational-legalistic persuasion."[20] In the hierarchical view, the true object of war with the South was "maintenance of the idea of Government."[21] By contrast, Lincoln explicitly defined the Civil War as a struggle "to elevate the condition of men—to lift artificial weights from all shoulders—to clear the paths of laudable pursuit for all—to afford all, an unfettered start, and a fair chance, in the race of life."[22] For Lincoln, the purpose of the war was not only to reaffirm authority but also to vindicate a competitive economic and political system.

Leadership in an Antileadership System

Downplaying the hierarchy of Whiggery while stressing the individualism of the Republican party helped make Lincoln the sixteenth president of the United States. But shackled with the Whig antiexecutive tradition, the slavery issue, and an antileadership system, the prospects for presidential leadership looked bleak. The presidencies of James Buchanan, Franklin Pierce, and Millard Fillmore were grim reminders of the extraordinary impediments to effective leadership.

Although we will never know whether Lincoln desired the onset of war in order to resolve the dilemmas handcuffing his party,[23] there is no doubt that a Lincoln presidency apart from the Civil War is inconceivable. The firing on Fort Sumter provided Lincoln with an opportunity to avoid his predecessors' fate, for now the slavery issue, which had shackled presidents in the previous decade, actually served as a means for expanding presidential power. A widespread perception of crisis empowered the presidency, permitting Lincoln to reconcile personal ambition and Whig theory.

Support for authority, however, even during war, was far from automatic. Lincoln's behavior as president reflected his acute awareness that support for leadership in the United States was very meager. Better than any previous president disposed toward hierarchy, Lincoln understood its weakness and the need to act accordingly. Though Lincoln occupied an office of great formal power, observes biographer J. G. Randall, "it was a power that had to be exercised with deference. He could govern, but only if his governing voice was not too bluntly audible." To counteract the political system's inherent tendency to dissipate power, Randall concludes, Lincoln had to act "with the tact of a moderator instead of the scowl of a dictator."[24]

The willingness of a predominantly individualist population to trust in government, even during wartime, was sharply limited. Military setbacks were blamed not on the North's lack of military preparedness but on the "fixed belief that the managers . . . at Washington are incompetent."[25] The government's demands for additional material sacrifices were met with skepticism from individualists who wanted some indication that their sacrifices would not again be wasted.[26]

The weakness of hierarchy in the North was underlined by the utterly inadequate method of raising troops. It took two years to set up a system of national conscription. Even then a drafted man could gain exemption from service by either raising $300 or furnishing an acceptable substitute. "Bounty brokers" flourished as a result of the elaborate system of bounties designed to encourage volunteering. The individualists' preferred way of life, bidding and bargaining, proved to be a very expensive and inefficient way to fight a total war.[27]

Given the antiauthority cultural context, popular wrath was bound to strike the national government. One of Lincoln's tasks, therefore, was to set up lightning rods that could deflect the full brunt of popular anger when the Union army suffered reverses. To shield himself from the torrent of abuse, Lincoln skillfully used the old Whig executive doctrine. Lincoln's need to exert leadership in an antileadership system, in our opinion, explains that "peculiar paradox" of his presidency first pointed out by David Donald in his seminal essay, "Whig in the White House."[28]

Donald contrasts Lincoln's vigorous extralegal use of executive authority in regard to his war power with the timid, obsequious, virtual nonuse of presidential resources to influence domestic policy. "Were I president," Lincoln had written in 1848, "I should desire the legislation of the country to rest with Congress, uninfluenced by the executive in its origin or progress, and undisturbed by the veto unless in very special and clear cases."[29] And Donald contends that Lincoln, as president, showed little interest over a wide range of domestic policies, including tariffs and banking; the introduction of the first income tax; creation of the Department of Agriculture, and land-grant colleges.[30] "Less than any other major American President," concludes Donald, "did Lincoln control or even influence the Congress."[31] Indeed, when his proposed appointees were turned down by the Senate, Lincoln thought it improper even to resubmit their names.[32]

How does Donald resolve the paradox of a chief executive simultaneously strong and weak? Not lack of time for domestic policy but rather an inability to "rid himself of the political ideas with which he had been raised," Donald argues, explains the "puzzling ambiguity of his presidency." "Both in strongly asserting his war powers and in weakly deferring to Congress," continues Donald, "he was following the Whig creed in which he was raised."[33]

Though not explicitly taking issue with Donald's thesis, G. S. Boritt's interpretation of Lincoln's behavior in the White House undercuts Donald's contention that Lincoln's "political education" explains the paradox of his presidency.[34] Lincoln, points out Boritt, faced a Congress dominated by a Republican party that was in essential agreement with Lincoln's preferred economic policies. Therefore, argues Boritt, "there was little call for Lincoln to pressure Senators and Congressmen, to use those 'certain indirect influences' on behalf of 'sound' economics."[35] Lincoln did not have to work so hard because Congress was disposed to do much of what he liked with regard to tariffs, internal improvements, finance, and homestead legislation. Boritt concludes that "Lincoln thus had the pleasure of signing into law much of the program he had worked for through the better part of his political life," legislation that amounted to what historian Leonard Curry has called a "blueprint for modern America."[36]

Boritt shows also that Lincoln was much more active in domestic policy than he appeared to Donald, as well as to contemporaries. When it came to establishing a national banking system, Lincoln did attempt to influence Congress. He sent one of his private secretaries to sway wavering senators, persuaded influential senators to go to bat for him, talked the matter up in the cabinet, and even seems to have cashed in on patronage, all the while exclaiming to New York financiers, "Money, I don't know anything about 'money.' "[37]

Lincoln, writes Boritt, "took up a Whiggishly circumspect championship of almost the full range of his old economic policies. He felt free to follow such a . . . course because to the country it could appear as part of the war effort."[38] Put another way, the sharp distinction that Donald draws between domestic and war measures was in fact quite blurred, at least in Lincoln's mind. "A sound and stable financial system" was, in the view of Lincoln and his fellow Republicans, essential to the Northern war effort.[39]

"The Whig in the White House," observes Boritt, "knew when to apply his theory of the executive, and also when to discard it."[40] One realm in which Lincoln completely disregarded Whig theory was Reconstruction of the South. His pocket veto of the Wade-Davis bill—a radical Reconstruction measure endorsed by virtually the entire Republican party—violated the most hallowed Whig precept. Lincoln's "political education," which taught him of the "despotism" of the veto power, proved to be much less restraining than Donald assumed.[41] Reconstruction did not come prelabeled as a war issue or domestic issue. Here as elsewhere this ambiguity gave Lincoln a great deal of scope in deciding what he would consider within his purview while still nominally adhering to Whig doctrine.

That Lincoln was not the enthralled captive of Whig doctrine that Donald portrays is indicated by Lincoln's active involvement on behalf of the Thirteenth Amendment.[42] Jackson-like, Lincoln informed the lame-duck session of Congress that in the recent election "the voice of the people" had been expressed in favor of the proposed amendment.[43] He did not, however, rest content with a firm message urging its passage. The president worked hard, using his considerable powers of persuasion and patronage to enlist conservative Republicans as well as wavering Democratic members to back the amendment.[44]

Given the lack of support for substantial executive leadership among political elites as well the public at large, Lincoln knew he had to rest content with the fewest possible priorities: unity to win the war, and to achieve whatever national economic policy was possible without making a target of himself.

When Lincoln overstepped the bounds of "the light-handed Whig executive," Congress often subjected him to "contemptuous treatment."[45] A Whiggish deference toward Congress, as Boritt observes, "helped cultivate the goodwill of Capitol Hill."[46] Lincoln's Whiggish behavior as president was not simply dictated by early political education but, rather, was a conscious political strategy, an adaptive response to an antileadership system.

What about Lincoln's "curious failure" to control his cabinet, which Donald sees as compelling evidence of the grip the Whig view of the presidency had on Lincoln.[47] This interpretation neglects the advantages Lincoln reaped by distancing himself from the cabinet. "When Congress showed unhappiness with executive direction," points out Boritt, "the separation between the President and his official family often diverted the legislators to attacking the latter. With the Cabinet absorbing much of the fire, the White House could often escape unscorched." When Lincoln decided not to enforce congressional acts confiscating the property of slave owners, for example, Attorney General Edward Bates took most of the heat from the radicals.[48]

Likewise, the relatively free hand given to Salmon Chase as secretary of the Treasury was well suited to deflecting criticism away from the president. As Lincoln knew full well, to raise the financial resources necessary to support a war was not likely to be easy. Getting individualists to fight was often easier than getting them to pay. By leaving the obligation of raising taxes to the Treasury secretary and Congress, Lincoln was able, as Boritt puts it, to take "refuge in his Whiggishness," letting public displeasure at higher taxes fall on other heads.[49]

We may be excused for believing that this man, whose intellect was as formidable as any this nation has produced, was fooling his fellow Americans by his avowals of naivete or disinterest about such matters as banking, finance, and foreign affairs—"you understand these things. I do not," Lincoln told Chase.[50] Allowing his cabinet members to think themselves superior may have given Lincoln protection against what would otherwise have been a crescendo cry of usurpation. His humble posture, the log cabin stories, and the like served as a shield against the pervasive antiauthority bias.

Crisis Leadership

War creates a severe dilemma for those political cultures not designed to support authority. The heavy emphasis on individual rights in an individualist culture is ill-suited to wartime demand of sacrifice for the collectivity. A crisis requiring extensive mobilization and coordination of persons and resources jeopardizes individualist principles of self-regulation.

Adherents of an individualist culture hope that temporary but extraordinary grants of power to the leader will allow society to survive the crisis without creating a permanently strengthened authority structure. Power granted to leaders in emergencies, individualists fear, may subsequently be cited as a precedent for more hierarchical social relations in future noncrisis situations. We would therefore expect the ideal typical individualist leader repeatedly to reassure his followers that his power is justified only by the exceptional nature of the situation. For fear of establishing precedents and alienating wary followers, the individualist leader may resist attempts to have his powers codified or systematized. The paradigmatic formulation of individualist leadership in crisis situations is John Locke's understanding of the executive's emergency powers as an undefined extraconstitutional weapon that the law of necessity and self-preservation periodically forces upon the nation.

We would expect the purely hierarchical leader faced with a crisis of similar proportions to try squeezing maximum mileage from existing roles and functions. Expansion of the office's authority would be perceived not as a threat but as an opportunity to permanently strengthen hierarchical social relations. Indeed, hierarchists may welcome wars they think they can win in the hope that a successful collective effort will reflect positively on those in leadership positions and thus increase support for authority in peacetime.

Lincoln's behavior in office reflected his fusion of hierarchy and individualism. He appealed both to the situation and the role, stressing the exceptional nature of the circumstance as well as the enduring institutional prerogatives of the executive office. He voiced the hierarchical hope that the Civil War would strengthen and enoble the collectivity, but also expressed the individualist concern that war would transform American institutions.

Fearing perhaps that Congress would not grant him the power to deal effectively with the crisis, Lincoln delayed calling the legislature into session for several months after the firing on Fort Sumter. Upon meeting Congress on July 4, 1861, Lincoln articulated the individualist definition of the nation's dilemma: "Must a Government, of necessity, be too strong for the liberties of its own people, or too weak to maintain its own existence?" He explained to Congress that his sweeping actions of the previous three months, "whether strictly legal or not," had been thrust upon him by "public necessity."[51] Lincoln appealed to Congress to ratify presidential actions taken in the name of national self-preservation.

Lincoln elaborated on his individualistic justification of emergency leadership in a letter to A. G. Hodges, dated April 4, 1864. In words that directly echoed Jefferson's, Lincoln explained that just as "often a limb must be amputated to save a life," so "measures, otherwise unconstitutional, might become lawful by becoming indispensable to the preservation of the Constitution through the preservation of the nation."[52] Because the life of the nation was at stake, Lincoln argued, he had no choice but to assume the powers he did.

Although Lincoln's individualist propensities led him to accent the extraordinary nature of the situation, his hierarchical background inclined him to turn also to established roles and offices for sanction of his authority. As the war continued, Lincoln increasingly used the role of commander in chief to justify his unprecedented exercise of presidential power: he did so in large part because invoking the law of self-preservation did not address the question of why decisions about public safety should rest with the president rather than with Congress. "When rebellion or invasion comes," reasoned Lincoln, "the people have, under the Constitution, made the commander-in-chief of their army and navy . . . the man who holds the power and bears the responsibility of . . . [deciding what] the public safety requires." Lincoln's Emancipation Proclamation, for instance, began by invoking "the power in me vested as Commander-in-Chief of the Army and Navy."[53]

Whereas for Locke and Jefferson the executive's emergency power had been, as Arthur Schlesinger, Jr., explains, "a weapon outside and beyond the Constitution," Lincoln's innovation was "constitutionalizing the law of necessity." He wrung authority from the commander-in-chief role, and the presidential oath to "preserve, protect, and defend the Constitution of the United States," as well as from the constitutional injunction that the President "shall take Care that the Laws be faithfully executed."[54]

In Whig thought, presidential power had been suspect because of its association with the subversion of law. By presenting the president as upholding the supreme law in the face of lawless Southern secession, Lincoln managed to attract political support from legal-minded former Whigs. Despite his own frequent disregard for the legal limits on presidential authority, Lincoln was able to place himself on the side of law and order by sustaining the assertion that "the Constitution invests its commander-in-chief clause with the law of war, in time of war."[55] On the basis of power invested in him through the role of commander in chief, Lincoln distinguished his emancipation proclamation—which he termed "a fit and necessary war measure"—from General John Fremont's declaration of emancipation, which Lincoln condemned as "simply 'dictatorship.' "[56]

If the hierarchical culture feared that a charismatic president would substitute his personal will for the law, the primary concern of the individualist was that Lincoln's personal power would become institutionalized. A central authority thus strengthened might permanently restrict individual autonomy. To assuage such individualist fears, Lincoln justified the Emancipation Proclamation—which would result in the confiscation of millions of dollars' worth of what was still commonly conceived to be private property—as an act of military necessity. The implication was that the act was warranted only because emancipation was necessary to defeat the South, and therefore would not constitute a precedent as to the central government's powers in peacetime. Lincoln's disregard for formality, system, and ceremony perhaps served as further reassurance to individualists concerned that his wartime leadership would establish precedents for peacetime governing.

From the individualist perspective, Lincoln's greatness consisted in showing that an individualist regime could cope with large-scale crises without undergoing a transformation of its cultural identity. Lincoln's example offered hope that individualist regimes were not subject to an "inherent and fatal weakness"; such a regime could be strong enough to function successfully in an emergency without permanently altering internal social relations in a hierarchical direction. Temporary emergency leadership in times of total war, individualists now knew, did not lead inexorably to permanent dictatorship in peacetime.

Lincoln's leadership was equally exemplary from the hierarchical standpoint, but for very different reasons. In Woodrow Wilson's view, Lincoln's greatness lay in moving the United States "from a divided, self-interested contractual association to a unified, spiritual, organic state."[57] Also, his presidency had rebuilt the alliance of strong government with a strong executive that had been rent assunder by the party battles of the 1830s and 1840s.

By elevating the prestige and expanding the prerogatives of the presidential office Lincoln had left a permanent legacy on which future hierarchs could try to build. But if adherents of hierarchy thought that they need only invoke the authority of the office they were very much mistaken. Apart from a wartime emergency, Lincoln's legacy was bound to be ambiguous. Were it not deemed a war in defense of union (i.e., self-defense) on which all other rights, including property rights, depended, individualists might be unwilling to suspend self-regulation. If hierarchical authority depended not on a war against that epitome of inequality, slavery itself, but rather on humankind's allegedly natural inequalities, egalitarians surely would demur.

How did egalitarians view Lincoln? The Civil War had elevated egalitarian abolitionists from a despised, fringe minority to a respected and influential group at the center of the political process.[58] Under the pressures of war, immediate emancipation of slaves—the central abolitionist demand for three decades—became an increasingly popular policy option. As the idea of abolition grew in popularity, so too did the prestige of abolitionists. This newfound popularity of egalitarian forces greatly complicated Lincoln's leadership task, for he had to resist the abolitionist desire to invest him with charismatic qualities, making him purely good and the South purely evil. Framing the struggle in this way would simultaneously weaken the Northern war effort by alienating the border states and northern Democrats, and dash hopes of eventual national reconciliation. Balancing the zeal of the egalitarians against the caution of the establishment cultures constituted perhaps the central cultural dilemma of Lincoln's leadership. The next section explores in depth this critical relationship between Lincoln and the egalitarian abolitionists.

The Egalitarian Challenge to Lincoln's Establishment Vision

To win egalitarians' support for the Civil War it was necessary to show that the war's chief aim was to abolish slavery. Only such a lofty goal could justify jettisoning their pacifist and antimilitarist principles. The prospect of emancipation enabled even those who believed "all war to be wicked and unchristian" to "delight that this conflict is upon us."[59] Slavery, after all, was "perpetual war . . . a single day of Slavery . . . witnesses more wrong, violence, corruption, more actual war, than all that civil war ever could bring."[60] Wendell Phillips agreed that "the bloodiest war ever waged is infinitely better than the happiest slavery which ever fattened men into obedience."[61]

In a speech announcing his support for the war, Phillips justified his decision by drawing attention to the glorious ends that would be served. Following the bloodletting and atonement, "the world will see under our banner all tongues, all creeds, all races,—one brotherhood."[62] Yesterday, reasoned Phillips, the government had been an agreement with Hell; today it was "the Thermopylae of Liberty and Justice."[63] Phillips's speech made it clear that egalitarian support depended on the government's transforming the war into a crusade against slavery.

William Lloyd Garrison advised his fellow abolitionists to mute their criticisms of the government. This was no time, he explained, "for minute criticism of Lincoln, Republicanism, or even the other parties, now that they are fusing for a death-grapple with the Southern slave-oligarchy."[64] But the abolitionist press made clear, if the g overnment demonstrated a lack of moral purpose, then "the time of criticism and censure will have come again."[65]

Egalitarians were divided over whether or not to support the war. The most extreme, like Parker Pillsbury and Stephen Foster, were, in the words of James McPherson, "incapable of supporting any government."[66] They opposed Garrison's call for a temporary cessation of criticism of the government.[67] At a July 4th gathering of Garrisonian abolitionists, Foster proposed a resolution stating that until the administration proclaimed emancipation to be the aim of the war, abolitionists would "give it no support or countenance in its effort to maintain its authority over the seceded States."[68] And on August 1, Pillsbury introduced another resolution denouncing the Lincoln administration. "I have no higher opinion," declared Pillsbury, "of Abraham Lincoln, and his Cabinet . . . than I have of the President and Cabinet . . . of the Confederate States."[69] "Abraham Lincoln," proclaimed Foster, "is as truly a slaveholder as Jefferson Davis."[70]

These extreme resolutions were defeated, however; most abolitionists pre-ferred to follow the lead of Garrison and Phillips, supporting the war while pressing the North to embrace emancipation. But having overridden their firmly held objections to coercion in any form, egalitarians engaged in a des-perate search for signs that "the Cause of the North will become the Cause of Truth."[71] The trouble was that the Lincoln administration was giving few visi-ble signs of such inner grace.

More and more it was beginning to seem that the Lincoln administration had no intention of declaring a holy war on slavery. "If there is one point of honor upon which more than another this administration will stick," the *Springfield Republican* assured the nation, "it is the pledge not to interfere with slavery in the states."[72] Lincoln's July 4th message to Congress reaf-firmed the administration's pledge not to interfere with slavery in the Southern states. At the end of July, the House and Senate passed near-unanimous reso-lutions stating that "this war is not waged upon our part . . . for any purpose . . . of overthrowing or interfering with the rights or established institutions of . . . southern States."[73] Restoration of the Union, not emancipation of slaves, clearly and unmistakably was being proclaimed as administration pol-icy. Such a policy was consistent with the establishment cultures—for whom maintenance of national institutions and concern for property rights, order, and liberty were high priorities—but not with a culture in which equality was the guiding norm.

In view of the abolitionists' enthusiastic embrace of the war, the refusal by the government to call it a war for emancipation left a stain on the moral pu-rity of the abolitionists.[74] Their early hope for a war to redeem a guilty nation redoubled their sense of betrayal. By September 1861, haunted by the unbearable thought that they were supporting a bloody war that might leave slavery untouched, egalitarians began to retreat from their tenuous truce with Lincoln.

Fearing that a speedy end to the war would leave slavery in place in the South, abolitionists now prayed for defeat of the impure Union forces. "God grant us so many reverses," Phillips prayed, "that the government may learn its duty."[75] In the same vein, Charles Sumner admitted, "I fear more from our victories than our defeats. There must be more delay and more suffering."[76] The defeat of the Union army at Bull Run was greeted as "the first step to-ward emancipation."[77] Because only a prolonged war seemed capable of con-verting the North to emancipation, abolitionists were in the awkward position of simultaneously demanding a more vigorous prosecution of the war while withholding full support until the administration adopted its antislavery cause.

But to the abolitionists there was no contradiction between effective prose-cution of the war and morality. They were convinced that emancipation was necessary to inspire the North. The knowledge that they were fighting on the side of justice would impart "superhuman strength" to Union soldiers. "The strongest battalions," insisted the abolitionists, "are those on the side of God."[78] After the war Lydia Maria Child attributed the North's early military setbacks to the "want of moral grandeur" in the government during those first years of the war.[79]

On August 30, 1861, General John C. Fremont issued a proclamation freeing the slaves of every rebel in the state of Missouri. Here finally was a leader willing to give to the war a great, moral purpose that could justify the carnage.[80] Lincoln's modification of Fremont's order, to conform to the Confiscation Act of August 6, left the abolitionists aghast. Garrison charged Lincoln with a "serious dereliction of duty"; revoking Fremont's order was "timid, depressing, suicidal." Privately, Garrison fumed that Lincoln was "only a dwarf in mind."[81] Edmund Quincy believed it to be "one of those blunders which are worse than crimes."[82] Another abolitionist lamented the president's "pigheaded stupidity."[83] The limited armistice between the abolitionists and the administration seemed to have been terminated by Lincoln's act.

The president's annual message in December, warning against degeneration of the war "into a violent and remorseless revolutionary struggle," met with widespread abolitionist condemnation. In the *Liberator*, Garrison characterized Lincoln's message as "feeble and rambling." Garrison privately confided his belief that Lincoln "has evidently not a drop of anti-slavery blood in his veins," and concluded by lamenting that Lincoln was "a man of very small calibre."[84] Gerrit Smith publicly assailed the president's address as "twattle and trash."[85] An even more hostile critic called it a "timid, timeserving, commonplace sort of an abortion of a message, cold enough . . . to freeze h-ll over."[86] In the fight against evil, moderation was no virtue.

Throughout 1862 the abolitionists rode a roller coaster of hope and despair. A wave of optimism swept over them in the early spring of 1862 after Lincoln signed legislation abolishing slavery in the District of Columbia.[87] The *National Anti-Slavery Standard* heralded this as "the Beginning of the End of Slavery."[88] With Edwin Stanton installed as the new secretary of war and with growing popular support for ending slavery, abolitionists seemed confident of Lincoln's intentions and capacity.[89]

But events of late May 1862 led abolitionists to despair once again of the Lincoln administration, and their criticism of the government mounted. Within the span of a few weeks, Lincoln had revoked General David Hunter's military order proclaiming emancipation in Georgia, South Carolina, and Florida; a bill to emancipate all slaves of rebel masters was defeated in the House; and the administration was firmly enforcing the fugitive slave law in the District of Columbia.[90] In the pages of the *Liberator* Garrison scolded Lincoln: "Shame and confusion to the President for his halting, shuffling, back-ward policy."[91] Anna Dickinson pronounced the president as "not so far from . . . a slave-catcher after all."[92]

More abolitionist criticism was prompted by Lincoln's appointment of General Henry Halleck (who, while in command of the Western Department, had tried to exclude fugitive slaves from the area under his jurisdiction) as general-in-chief of the U.S. Army; and by the president's refusal to issue a proclamation ordering his generals to enforce the second Confiscation Act. The administration, Garrison despaired, "is blind as a bat to its true line of policy." "Stumbling, halting, prevaricating, irresolute, weak, besotted" were the only words he could find to describe Lincoln's policy.[93] To demon-strate that the cause of the North was just, abolitionists wanted a ringing dec-laration that called for the immediate freedom of all slaves.

Lincoln's preliminary Emancipation Proclamation, issued on September 22, won fervent applause from abolitionists.[94] In a letter to Garrison, Theo-dore Tilton confessed himself to be "half crazy with enthusiasm."[95] Frederick Douglass, who only two weeks before had expressed his "ineffable disgust" with Lincoln's behavior, declared, "We shout for joy that we live to record this righteous decree."[96] "Joy, gratitude, thanksgiving, renewed hope and courage fill my soul," echoed Samuel May, Jr.[97] "God bless President Lin-coln," declared another abolitionist. "He may yet be the Moses to deliver the oppressed."[98] Seeking deliverance from oppression, egalitarians earnestly sought the inspired leadership necessary to reach the promised land.

The leadership dilemma posed by the egalitarians can be seen most starkly in the career of Wendell Phillips. Across the nation and throughout the war, Phillips preached that the nation needed decisive and bold national leadership; in speech after speech he told his audiences that the country was suffering from a crisis of leadership. But while demanding stronger leadership, Phillips was simultaneously engaging in sustained, ruthless criticism—at one point damning Lincoln as an "unlimited despot"—that sought to undermine the president's leadership.

During the election of 1860 Phillips had refused to support Lincoln or any other candidate. He denounced Lincoln as the "Slave-Hound of Illinois."[99] After the nomination Phillips asked, "Who is this huckster in politics? . . . Who is this who does not know whether he has got any opinions?"[100] Over the next four years Phillips vigorously criticized the Lincoln administration, as George Fredrickson writes, "for its failure to give wholehearted support to the ideals of egalitarian democracy."[101]

In a letter to Charles Sumner, Phillips expressed his belief that Lincoln "is doing twice as much today to break this Union as [Jefferson] Davis is." Lin-coln was "a timid and ignorant President."[102] Phillips urged the radicals in

Congress to withhold money and supplies until Lincoln redefined the war aims. On August 1 Phillips publicly expressed the view that if Lincoln had been a "traitor," he could not have been of more aid to the South.[103]

Phillips oscillated between periods of scathing denunciation and of guarded approval. After Lincoln's preliminary Emancipation Proclamation in September and the dismissal of McClellan a few weeks later, Phillips publicly announced that he would no longer criticize the president. "I trust the President," he informed a Boston gathering in November.[104] But only three days after Lincoln issued the Emancipation Proclamation, Phillips was calling it a "reluctant gift,"[105] and once again stepped up his attacks on the Lincoln administration. He refused to support Lincoln in the 1864 election, and his attacks on Lincoln persisted to the point where by the end of the war Garrison was accusing Phillips of being "a bayoneter of presidents."[106]

Those willing to take decisive, dramatic action against slavery earned Phillips's impassioned gratitude. Like many other abolitionists, Phillips idolized General John C. Fremont, who, after declaring martial law in Missouri, had issued a proclamation freeing the slaves of every rebel in the state of Missouri.[107] Benjamin F. Butler was another of Phillips's heroes. Butler declared all fugitive slaves who came into his lines to be "contraband" and put them to work for the Union cause. As military governor of New Orleans, writes Irving Bartlett, Butler acted "almost as a law unto himself. . . . Butler assumed the entire financial control of the city, [and] hanged a man for hauling down the American flag."[108] Though long an opponent of capital punishment, Phillips was so enamored with Butler's decisive leadership that he told a crowd that if "I were he and were to die soon, I would have a tombstone inscribed 'I was the only Major General of the United States that ever hung a traitor; that ever, by the boldness of my action, and the method of the death, told the world it was a Government struggling with rebels, with the right and purpose to put them beneath its laws, at any cost.' "[109] For Phillips, attention to legality was timidity; in essence he desired a charismatic leader who would substitute his will for the law in order to achieve an exalted objective.

Phillips's attitude toward Fremont and Butler reveals that at issue was not only an imbalance between demand for and support of leaders but the type of leadership desired. Phillips demanded men with "wills hot enough to fuse the purpose of nineteen millions of people into one decisive blow for safety and union."[110] No leader who wanted to please a national constituency encompassing a wide array of interests was going to find it easy to meet Phillips's standards.

The conflict between Lincoln and Phillips can be conceived as a conflict between what James MacGregor Burns has called "transactional" and "transforming" leadership styles.[111] Phillips desired a thoroughgoing social revolution: "The whole social system of the Gulf states is to be taken to pieces; every bit of it."[112] A revolutionary transformation of Southern society required leadership willing to disregard convention, law, and precedent. The compromises and half measures that Lincoln engaged in to keep his party together could not satisfy Phillips's demand for charismatic leadership. Their different goals—revolutionary transformation of the Southern social structure versus conciliation with Southern elites—required different modes of leadership.

Perhaps because of his establishment vision—the attempt to find a meeting ground between self-regulation and collective authority—Lincoln would neither replace nor abandon the law. More than any other president before or since, Lincoln tried to distinguish a president with emergency powers from a charismatic leader. Much is made of Lincoln's suspension of habeas corpus, but often lost sight of is the extent to which Lincoln went to avoid substituting his personal preferences regarding slavery for the written law.

Lincoln admitted on occasion that he considered slavery to be morally wrong.[113] Given this admission, abolitionists believed that Lincoln was obligated to do everything in his power to abolish slavery. They could not understand Lincoln's hesitancy to act publicly on his private conviction. "If all earthly power were given me," Lincoln had stated in 1854, "I should not know what to do" about slavery.[114] During the war years the abolitionists hoped Lincoln would assume such earthly power and abolish slavery. But Lincoln's comment, in the last months of his presidency, indicated that he never came around to the abolitionist conception of leadership. "I am naturally anti-slavery. If slavery is not wrong, nothing is wrong. . . . And yet I have never understood that the Presidency conferred upon me an unrestricted right to act officially upon this judgement and feeling."[115]

Cultural Unity: All Things to All Men

During the 1860 election Wendell Phillips had ridiculed those who "rejoice that [Lincoln] can ride on two horses,"[116] but to ride horses that are charging in divergent directions is no small accomplishment. Lincoln's achievement was to reconcile conflicting demands for union, opportunity, and abolition (hierarchy, individualism, and egalitarianism). If Lincoln is famous and enigmatic (or perhaps more accurately, famous *because* enigmatic), this is precisely because all the main political cultures perceive him to be infused with their cause.

How did Lincoln as a political leader hold his followers together? As president, Lincoln had to appeal to three distinct cultures, each of which was making contradictory demands. Egalitarians pressured him to convert the war into a crusade against slavery. But any signs of administration hostility toward slavery could alienate critical border states and swing the balance of military power to the South. Support from the egalitarians was premised on the war's being a morally just war against slavery; establishment support entailed limiting the war aims to restoration of the Union with the minimum of tampering with Southern property rights. To reconcile the competing cultural claims of order, liberty, and justice was Lincoln's central cultural dilemma.

Emancipation coupled with confiscation created a thorny problem for an individualist culture. Did the war make it legitimate for the government to do that which all Republicans agreed it could not do in time of peace, namely, take away Southern property? Lincoln's proclamation calling for 75,000 troops to suppress the rebellion explicitly promised "to avoid any destruction, or interference, with [Southern] property."[117] In 1863 Lincoln told a Baptist delegation: "When brought to my final reckoning, may I have to answer for robbing no man of his goods."[118] Even Henry Ward Beecher, while declaring his strong hate for slavery, insisted that "ours is not an army of liberation . . . because the fifteen states of the South are guaranteed security in their property, and we have no right by force to dispossess them of that property."[119]

But this is precisely what egalitarians were demanding. Only one month after the firing on Fort Sumter, the abolitionist William Goodell called for confiscation of rebel land and redistributing it among freed slaves. Abolitionists, in the words of historian James McPherson, pressed for "full-scale expropriation."[120] After emancipation had been adopted as the official war aim, abolitionists stepped up these demands for redistribution of Southern land.

The debate that persists to this day about Lincoln's intentions vis-á-vis slavery testifies to his skill in bridging the competing cultural visions of the Civil War. If modern historians, well-versed in Lincoln's private correspondence, have been unable to decide whether Lincoln was a cautious conservative or champion of racial justice, the confusion of Lincoln's contemporaries is very understandable. And, just as scholars today seem to see in Lincoln a reflection of their own preferences, so during the Civil War Lincoln managed to be different things to different people.

Richard Hofstadter has written that the Emancipation Proclamation "had all the moral grandeur of a bill of lading." Hofstadter cites the *London Spectator's* jibe that "the principle is not that a human being cannot justly own another, but that he cannot own him unless he is loyal to the United States." Yet James McPherson dismisses the "the old cliché" that the proclamation did not free a single slave because it applied only to those states where the government had no power, as completely missing the point. "From the time the Emancipation Proclamation went into effect at the beginning of 1863," McPherson argues, "the North fought for the revolutionary goal of a new Union without slavery." Scholars' continued debate over the true meaning of the proclamation serves to highlight the vexing ambiguity of the proclamation that enabled groups with widely divergent goals to support it.[121]

If, as Hofstadter claims, Lincoln's message "contained no indictment of slavery," it is all the more remarkable to find some of the most morally exacting abolitionists enthusiastically hailing it. "All . . . trials . . . are swallowed up in the great deep joy of this emancipation," wrote a correspondent of Garrison's; another abolitionist rejoiced, "This is a great Era! A sublime period in history! The Proclamation is grand. The President has done nobly."[122] Garrison himself publicly hailed it as "a great historic event, sublime in its magnitude, momentous and beneficent in its far-reaching consequences."[123]

Perhaps the most impressive aspect of Lincoln's leadership was the way in which he persuaded many egalitarians that his heart was with them when his public behavior told a different story. Even after Lincoln revoked General Hunter's order, Carl Schurz remained confident of Lincoln's good intentions. After meeting with Lincoln, Schurz wrote to the president: "After you had explained your policy to me the other day I left you perfectly happy and contented, fully convinced that, in spite of appearances to the contrary, you were determined to use all your constitutional power to deliver this country of the great curse, and so I would receive all your acts and manifestations with the utmost confidence."[124]

A striking example of Lincoln's ability to persuade antislavery advocates of his good intentions in the face of contrary or ambiguous public evidence is Sydney Gay's reaction to Lincoln's famous public letter to Horace Greeley in which the president announced that "my paramount object in this struggle is to save the Union, and is not either to save or to destroy slavery." A Garrisonian abolitionist and editor of the *Anti-Slavery Standard* for fourteen years, Gay had become managing editor of Horace Greeley's *New York Tribune* in the spring of 1862. Gay met with Lincoln in the summer of 1862 and argued for emancipation; although Lincoln made no promises, Gay was favorably impressed by Lincoln's antislavery convictions.[125] A few weeks later, when Greeley's "Prayer of Twenty Million" demanding emancipation was published, Lincoln's prompt reply to Greeley apparently disavowed emancipation as a war aim. Yet, clinging to Lincoln's promise that "if I could save it [the Union] by freeing all the slaves I would do it," Gay wrote Lincoln that "your letter to Mr. Greeley has infused new hope among us . . . I think that the general impression is that . . . you mean presently to announce that the destruction of Slavery is the price of our salvation."[126]

Lincoln also persuaded the highly influential chairman of the Senate Foreign Relations Committee, Charles Sumner, that they both had the same goals. In December 1861 Sumner confidently reported that the "the Presdt. tells me that the question between him & me is one of 4 weeks or at most 6 weeks, when we shall all be together."[127] A frequent visitor at the White House, Sumner came to have not only a "profound pity" for Lincoln but also a belief that the president wanted "to do right & to save the country."[128] Sumner's trust in Lincoln's intentions enabled Lincoln to act in ways that otherwise he would have found difficult to sustain politically.

Despite moments of doubt and despair, Garrison supported Lincoln's reelection in 1864. At the annual meeting of the Massachusetts Anti-Slavery Society in January 1864, Garrison, although willing to criticize certain features of Lincoln's policy, refused to question the president's good intentions. He defended Lincoln by arguing that the president had moved as fast as public opinion had allowed him.[129] After meeting with Lincoln in June, Garrison pronounced the interview "very satisfactory." "There is no mistake about it in regard to Mr. Lincoln's desire to do all that he can . . . to uproot slavery, and give fair-play to the emancipated. I was much pleased with his spirit."[130] Indeed, to Garrison, something in their struggle had seemed to rub off on the president. Most abolitionists would have agreed with Owen Lovejoy that although "he does not drive as fast as I would, he is on the right road, and it is only a question of time."[131]

Although Garrisonian abolitionists were evenly divided over the question of Lincoln's renomination, it was an impressive achievement to have won over about half of the most radical of the abolitionists. In the general election all but a few abolitionists followed Garrison rather than Phillips in supporting Lincoln.[132] It is not surprising, as McPherson writes, that "the very nature of the presidency compelled Lincoln to proceed more cautiously than radicals desired."[133] What is impressive is that Lincoln convinced ardent abolitionists that this necessary deference to public opinion, rather than his personal motives, explained why his actions diverged from their desires.

The extent to which Lincoln was able to gain the support of radical abolitionists is amazing in view of the fact that many "conservative" and border-state Republicans counted the Kentucky-born Lincoln on their side.[134] Up until late 1863 even the arch-conservative New York Herald was calling on all "the conservative Union men of Congress and the country" to support Lincoln.[135] The attorney general from Missouri, Edward Bates, considered Lincoln "an excellent man," although Bates sensed and feared a lack of "will and purpose."[136] Joshua Speed, a longtime friend of Lincoln, worried that a "large and powerful party of . . . ultra men" was "being formed to make war upon the President and upon his conservative policy."[137] While the moderate and conservative elements of the Republican party periodically doubted Lincoln's ability, they rarely questioned his motives.[138]

How was Lincoln able to keep the support of such radically divergent groups? His strategy was to convey different intentions to the different sides. "My policy," Lincoln was fond of telling people, "is to have no policy."[139]

Just as he used the political pressure of conservatives to temper or thwart radical demands, Lincoln skillfully manipulated and even fabricated egalitarian pressure to move the border states and conservatives from their seemingly intransigent position (thereby converting egalitarian moral pressure into a chip comprehensible to those accustomed to the language of political bargains).[140] In effect, Lincoln argued that his actions were resultants, a product of external pressures, rather than a reflection of his intentions, which, he assured both sides, were fully in sympathy with them. Both sides could thus believe they had a sympathetic friend in the White House.

Aimed at maintaining a governing coalition, Lincoln's strategy risked courting a reputation for vacillation and weakness. Repeatedly charging him with indecision and of lacking control of men or events, many critics disparaged Lincoln's policy as "muddy."[141] Another typical, if somewhat harsh, criticism of Lincoln began by admitting that "Mr. Lincoln may mean well," but went on to condemn him for being "vacillating in policy, undecided in action, weak in intellectual grasp."[142]

To the extent that Lincoln's leadership style contributed to an appearance of not being in control, it may have drawn into question his ability to lead, and encouraged those looking for "strong" leaders to condemn the president. But, given the often disastrous Northern war effort, the substantial criticism and unpopularity of Lincoln is not what was remarkable; rather, it was his ability to maintain sufficient support to become the first president since Andrew Jackson to gain reelection. We would argue that more often than not his strategy helped him by diverting attention from his actions (which inevitably had to alienate one faction) to his intentions (which could be all things to all people). This rainbow strategy enabled him to avoid becoming identified exclusively with any one culture and thus maintain the political support of all three. Lincoln's success is attested by the fact that today individualists, hierarchs, and egalitarians alike claim Lincoln as one of their own.

All three cultures now claim Lincoln, but it does not follow that each has an equally legitimate claim. Because he led during a civil war in which he needed political support from all three cultures, Lincoln left his cultural commitments partly ambiguous. Yet President Lincoln's vision of reconstruction ("with malice toward none; with charity for all") was couched not in the egalitarian language of justice but rather in the establishment language of mercy. Lincoln envisioned no sweeping revolution in Southern social relations—as did Wendell Phillips or Thaddeus Stevens.[143] Lincoln spoke not of reducing distinctions or of confiscating and redistributing property but, rather, of social mobility, opportunity, and economic growth. Lincoln was thus the ideological architect of the modern Republican party in which individualist themes of competition and self-regulation would be raised to a preeminent position.

Notes

1. William H. Herndon, cited in Richard Hofstadter, *The American Political Tradition* (New York: Vintage Books, 1973), p. 118.
2. See George Fredrickson, "The Search for Order and Community," in *The Public and Private Lincoln*, ed. Cullom Davis et al. (Carbondale: Southern Illinois University Press, 1979), pp. 92-93.
3. Daniel Walker Howe, *The Political Culture of the American Whigs* (Chicago: University of Chicago Press, 1979), p. 269.
4. Ibid., pp. 269, 271; Fredrickson, "Order and Community," p. 92.
5. David Donald, "Abraham Lincoln: Whig in the White House," in *The Enduring Lincoln*, ed. Norman Graebner, (Urbana: University of Illinois Press, 1959), pp. 47-66; Stephen B. Oates, "Abraham Lincoln: Republican in the White House," in *Abraham Lincoln and the American Political Tradition*, ed. John L. Thomas, (Amherst: University of Massachusetts Press, 1986), pp. 98-110.
6. Lincoln to Joshua F. Speed, August 24, 1855, cited in Howe, *Political Culture of Whigs*, p. 278.
7. Howe, *Political Culture of Whigs*, p. 291. Rush Welter similarly concludes that "the speeches of Abraham Lincoln document the reorientation in conservative values" (*The Mind of America, 1820-1860*, [New York: Columbia University Press, 1975], p. 350).
8. Howe, *Political Culture of Whigs*, p. 280.
9. Ibid.
10. Ibid. Also indicative of the move away from hierarchy is Howe's finding that "with their new emphasis on Locke and natural rights, the Republicans were moving away from the adulation of Burke that had characterized the Whigs" (p. 291).
11. See Welter, *Mind of America*, p. 355; Howe, *Political Culture Of Whigs*, p. 280; Fredrickson, "Order and Community," pp. 94-97; Yehoshua Arieli, *Individualism and Nationalism in American Ideology* (Cambridge: Harvard University, 1964), pp. 297-322.
12. Lincoln's first cabinet contained four former Democrats: Montgomery Blair, Salmon Chase, Simon Cameron, and Gideon Welles. Edwin Stanton who soon replaced Cameron as secretary of war was also a former Democrat. Other prominent Democratic Republicans included Benjamin Butler, John Niles, Preston King, David Wilmot, Lyman Trumbull, William Cullen Bryant, John Hale, Kinsley Bingham, Nathaniel Banks, Lot Morrill, James H. Lane, John Logan, and Lincoln's two vice presidents, Hannibal Hamlin and Andrew Johnson. On the impact of the Democratic-Republicans on the Republican party, see Eric Foner, *Free Soil, Free Labor, Free Men: The Ideology of the Republican Party before the Civil War* (New York: Oxford University Press, 1970), ch. 5.
13. Howe, *Political Culture of Whigs*, p. 277.
14. Ibid., p. 295. Although egalitarians reject "ancestors" as imposing the inequalities of a less enlightened age, and individualists do not wish to be bound by precedent, supporters of hierarchy try to demonstrate an unbroken succession—it was ever thus—to legitimate the inequalities and coercion that mark their regime.
15. George B. Forgie, *Patricide in the House Divided: A Psychological Interpretation of Lincoln and His Age* (New York: Norton, 1979), p. 285. See also Howe, *Political Culture of Whigs*, p. 271.

16. Howe, *Political Culture of Whigs*, p. 296.

17. Quoted, ibid.

18. Fredrickson, "Order and Community," p. 95.

19. "Address to the Young Men's Lyceum of Springfield," in *Abraham Lincoln: Selected Speeches, Messages and Letters*, ed. T. Harry Williams (New York: Holt, Rinehart & Winston, 1957), p. 10.

20. Fredrickson, "Order and Community," p. 95.

21. James Russell Lowell, cited in George M. Fredrickson, *The Inner Civil War: Northern Intellectuals and the Crisis of the Union* (New York: Harper & Row, 1965), p. 120. Slavery, contended Lowell, was the side issue; the real issue was "the reestablishment of order" (p. 60).

22. Lincoln, cited in Welter, *Mind of America*, p. 350.

23. Lincoln, it appears, harbored doubts about his own intentions. Kenneth Stampp has remarked that it may well be that Lincoln's "effort to treat the South with the utmost generosity reflected, in part, his desire for personal absolution" (*The Era of Reconstruction, 1865-1877*) [New York: Vintage Books, 1965], p. 37). This theme is pursued in Michael Paul Rogin, "The King's Two Bodies: Lincoln, Wilson, Nixon, and Presidential Self-Sacrifice," in *Public Values and Private Power in American Politics*, ed. J. David Greenstone (Chicago: University of Chicago, 1982), pp. 71-108. On Lincoln's role in the firing on Fort Sumter, see Charles W. Ramsdell, "Lincoln and Fort Sumter," *Journal of Southern History* (1937):359-88; David M. Potter, *Lincoln and His Party in the Secession Crisis* (New Haven: Yale University Press, 1942); Kenneth M. Stampp, "Lincoln and the Strategy of Defense in the Crisis of 1861," *Journal of Southern History* (1945):297-323; and Richard N. Current, "The Bringer of War" in *The Lincoln Nobody Knows* (New York: Hill & Wang, 1958), pp. 104-30.

24. J. G. Randall, *Lincoln the President: Springfield to Gettysburg*, 2 vols. (New York: Dodd, Mead & Co., 1945), 2:238.

25. John Baldwin to Sumner, December 30, 1862, cited ibid., p. 241.

26. Ibid., p. 240.

27. See J. G. Randall and David Donald, *The Civil War and Reconstruction*, 2d ed. (Lexington, Mass.: Heath, 1969), pp. 313-15, 328-29.

28. Donald, "Whig in White House," p. 47.

29. G. S. Boritt, *Lincoln and the Economics of the American Dream* (Memphis: Memphis State University Press, 1978), p. 195. After his election, Lincoln explained that although under the Constitution the executive may recommend some measures, veto others, and employ "certain indirect influences to affect the action of congress," "my political education strongly inclines me against a very free use of any of these means" (p. 195).

30. Donald, "Whig in White House," pp. 52-53.

31. Ibid., p. 51.

32. Ibid.

33. Ibid., pp. 60, 65.

34. Stephen Oates is mistaken, in our view, in seeing Boritt as having "carried the Donald thesis to almost absurd lengths" (Oates, "Republican in White House," p. 100). Boritt's disagreements with Donald are perhaps disguised by the fact that he uses essentially the same title, "The Whig in the White House" (Boritt, *Lincoln and American Dream*, pp. 195-231).

35. Boritt, *Lincoln and American Dream*, pp. 196-97; see also pp. 203, 209.

36. Ibid., p. 197; see also p. 226; Leonard P. Curry, *Blueprint for Modern America:*

Nonmilitary Legislation of the First Civil War Congress (Nashville: Vanderbilt University Press, 1968).

37. Boritt, *Lincoln and American Dream*, pp. 201-3.
38. Ibid., p. 198.
39. Senator John Sherman, quoted ibid., p. 197; see also pp. 201, 203.
40. Ibid., p. 229.
41. On the widespread support for the Wade-Davis bill among congressional Republicans, see Hans L. Trefousse, *The Radical Republicans: Lincoln's Vanguard for Racial Justice* (Baton Rouge: Louisiana State University, 1968), p. 287. During the Mexican War Lincoln had accused Polk of "high-handed and despotic exercise of the veto power, and . . . the utter disregard of the will of the people in refusing to give assent to measures which their representatives passed for the good and prosperity of the country" (quoted in Donald, "Whig in White House," p. 58).
42. Donald writes that Lincoln "was never able to disenthrall himself from his own political education" ("Whig in White House," p. 66).
43. Quoted in J. G. Randall and Richard N. Current, *Lincoln the President: Last Full Measure* (New York: Dodd, Mead, 1955), p. 308.
44. Trefousse, *Radical Republicans*, p. 299; Current, *Lincoln Nobody Knows*, p. 230; Randall and Current, *Last Full Measure*, p. 309; Oates, "Republican in White House," p. 106.
45. Boritt, *Lincoln and American Dream*, pp. 196, 201.
46. Ibid., p. 227. Boritt goes on, "Lincoln understood that the average solon was more likely to take offense if the executive arm denied certain economic benefits for his constituents, than if it took upon itself the direction of Reconstruction for example. Indeed, giving Congress a free rein on the one hand probably gave the President a firmer grasp on the other" (ibid.); see also pp. 198, 229.
47. Donald, "Whig in White House," p. 59.
48. Boritt, *Lincoln and American Dream*, p. 228.
49. Ibid., p. 203; see also pp. 199, 204-5.
50. Quoted ibid., p. 199.
51. Arthur M. Schlesinger, Jr., *The Imperial Presidency* (Boston: Houghton Mifflin, 1973), pp. 58-59.
52. Wilfred E. Binkley, *President and Congress* (New York: Vintage Books, 1962), pp. 154-55; Schlesinger, *Imperial Presidency*, pp. 59-60. Lincoln also assured the nation "the Executive power itself would be greatly diminished by the cessation of actual war" (quoted in Schlesinger, *Imperial Presidency*, p. 66).
53. Schlesinger, *Imperial Presidency*, pp. 62-63.
54. Ibid., pp. 60-61.
55. Lincoln, quoted ibid., p. 62.
56. Randall, *Springfield to Gettysburg*, 2:22, 165-66.
57. Rogin, "King's Two Bodies," p. 80.
58. On the wartime popularity and prestige of the abolitionists, see James M. McPherson, *The Struggle for Equality: Abolitionists and the Negro in the Civil War and Reconstruction* (Princeton: Princeton University Press, 1964), pp. 81-90, 127-32, 299-320. Once abolition of slavery had been achieved, however, the egalitarian forces went into a rapid decline. Usually egalitarians craft their demands in such a manner that they cannot be met: total justice, perfect safety, and so on. By formulating their demands so they could be met, abolitionists laid the ground for emancipation's being perceived as the final victory and thereby removing the purpose for their existence.

59. William Lloyd Garrison, Jr., to Edward S. Bunker, Jr., April 28, 1861; quoted in McPherson, *Struggle for Equality*, p. 52. On the pacifism and antimilitarism of Radical Republicans, see Trefousse, *Radical Republicans*, p. 23.

60. Moncure Conway, quoted in McPherson, *Struggle for Equality*, p. 55.

61. McPherson, *Struggle for Equality*, p. 55.

62. Phillips, quoted in Irving H. Bartlett, *Wendell Phillips: Brahmin Radical* (Boston: Beacon Press, 1961), p. 239. George Fredrickson writes that the "belief that an affectionate society of free individuals would somehow emerge out of the bloodshed and hatred of war, was characteristic of the thinking of many abolitionists in 1861" (*Inner Civil War*, p. 69). Radical Republicans, like Charles Sumner, also tended to glorify the ends of the war. Sumner grandiloquently proclaimed that "slavery will give way to freedom; but the good work will not stop here. . . . As the whole wide-spread tyranny begins to tumble, then, above the din of battle, sounding from the sea and echoing along the land . . . will ascend voices of gladness and benediction" (Allan G. Bogue, *The Earnest Men: Republicans of the Civil War Senate* [Ithaca: Cornell University Press, 1981], p. 154). Only a few weeks after Fort Sumter fell, William Goodell trumpeted the war as "the glorious second American Revolution" (McPherson, *Struggle for Equality*, p. 65).

63. Bartlett, *Wendell Phillips*, p. 238. Excellent discussions of the abolitionists' embrace of "righteous violence" can be found in Lewis Perry, *Radical Abolitionism: Anarchy and the Government of God in Antislavery Thought* (Ithaca: Cornell University Press, 1973), pp. 231-67; and Lawrence J. Friedman, *Gregarious Saints: Self and Community in American Abolitionism, 1830-1870* (New York: Cambridge University Press, 1982), pp. 196-222. See also Fredrickson, *Inner Civil War*, esp. pp. 68-69.

64. Garrison to Oliver Johnson, April 19, 1861, cited in McPherson, *Struggle for Equality*, p. 55. Garrison gave Lincoln's call for troops firm support. "All my sympathies and wishes are with the government," announced Garrison, "because it is entirely in the right." By abolishing slavery, the war would "bring with it inconceivable blessings" (Garrison to T. B. Drew, April 25, 1861, cited ibid., p. 52).

65. *Anti-Slavery Standard*, quoted ibid., pp. 55-56.

66. Ibid., pp. 103-104; see also p. 10.

67. Ibid., p. 56.

68. Ibid., p. 59. In May of the following year Foster introduced another set of resolutions committing the abolitionists to give no more support to the Union than to the Confederate government (p. 103).

69. Ibid., pp. 59-60.

70. ibid., p. 103.

71. Gerrit Smith to Garrison, September 2, 1861, quoted ibid., p. 60.

72. *Springfield Republican*, June 8, 1861, quoted ibid., pp. 57-58.

73. Ibid., p. 70.

74. In the pages of the *Liberator*, Wendell Phillips warned that unless the war was prosecuted for the purpose of removing slavery it would leave the "bloodiest stain of the century" (July 12, 1861, cited in Bartlett, *Wendell Phillips*, p. 241).

75. *New York Tribune*, May 12, 1863, cited in T. Harry Williams, *Lincoln and the Radicals* (Madison: University of Wisconsin Press, 1941), p. 13.

76. Sumner to John Bright, July 21, 1863, cited in McPherson, *Struggle for Equality*, p. 124. See also ibid., p. 107; Williams, *Lincoln and Radicals*, p. 13.

77. George L. Stearns, quoted in McPherson, *Struggle for Equality*, pp. 70-71.

78. Moncure D. Conway, quoted ibid., p. 64.
79. Lydia Maria Child to George W. Julian, April 8, 1865, cited in T. Harry Williams, "Lincoln and the Radicals: An Essay in Civil War History and Historiography," in *Grant, Lee, Lincoln and the Radicals*, ed. Grady McWhiney (Evanston, Ill. Northwestern University Press, 1964), pp. 102-3.
80. It was Phillips's view, writes Bartlett, that "here was a man who deserved to be a leader because he was willing to 'launch a thunderbolt' and proclaim emancipation" (*Wendell Phillips*, p. 245). Fremont's proclamation, Gerrit Smith wrote to Lincoln, was "the first unqualifiedly and purely right" step that had taken place during the war. Governor Andrew of Massachusetts believed the order gave "an impetus of the grandest character to the whole cause," and Garrison hailed it as "the beginning of the end" (McPherson, *Struggle for Equality*, pp. 72-73).
81. *Liberator*, September 20, 1861, and Garrison to Oliver Johnson, October 7, 1861, cited ibid., p. 73.
82. *National Anti-Slavery Standard*, September 28, 1861, quoted ibid.
83. B. Rush Plumly to Salmon Chase, October 19, 1861, cited ibid., p. 74.
84. *Liberator*, December 6, 1861, and Garrison to Oliver Johnson, December 6, 1861, cited ibid., p. 94.
85. Gerrit Smith to Thaddeus Stevens, December 6, 1861, cited ibid., p. 94.
86. S. York to Lyman Trumbull, December 5, 1861, quoted in Randall, *Springfield to Gettysburg*, 2:27.
87. McPherson, *Struggle for Equality*, pp. 95-98, 106-7.
88. *National Anti-Slavery Standard*, April 26, 1862, cited ibid., p. 98.
89. Bartlett, *Wendell Phillips*, p. 251.
90. McPherson, *Struggle for Equality*, pp. 103-4, 108-9.
91. *Liberator*, May 23, 1862, cited ibid., p. 108.
92. *Liberator*, June 6, 1862, cited ibid., p. 108. Privately, Dickinson condemned Lincoln as "an Ass . . . for the Slave Power to ride" (Anna Dickinson to Susan Dickinson, May 27, 1862, ibid.).
93. *Liberator*, July 25, 1862, cited ibid., p. 112.
94. Ibid., p. 117.
95. Tilton to Garrison, September 24, 1862, quoted ibid., p. 118.
96. Douglass to Gerrit Smith, September 8, 1862, and *Douglass' Monthly*, October 1862, cited ibid., pp. 117, 118.
97. May to Richard Webb, September 23, 1862, cited ibid., p. 119.
98. Joseph Emery to Salmon Chase, September 29, 1862, quoted in Randall, *Springfield to Gettysburg*, 2:169.
99. Bartlett, *Wendell Phillips*, pp. 221-22.
100. *Liberator*, June 8, 1860, cited in McPherson, *Struggle for Equality*, p. 12. Garrison believed "The Republican party means to do nothing, can do nothing, for the abolition of slavery" (*Liberator*, July 20, 1860, cited ibid., pp. 12-13).
101. Fredrickson, *Inner Civil War*, p. 127.
102. Phillips to Charles Sumner, June 29, 1862, quoted in Bartlett, *Wendell Phillips*, p. 252.
103. Ibid., p. 253.
104. Ibid., p. 254.
105. Ibid., p. 255.
106. Ibid., p. 290.

107. In the election of 1864, Phillips supported Fremont over Lincoln, for, as Bartlett explains, Phillips thought he saw in Fremont a "man who might be able to control events and lead the nation along righteous paths" (ibid., p. 270). Phillips was willing to support Fremont despite the fact that a Fremont candidacy would divide the antislavery vote and perhaps allow McClelland to gain the presidential office because that would mean "a live Republican party opposing McClellan in the chair" (ibid., p. 272).

108. Ibid., p. 261.

109. Ibid., p. 262.

110. Phillips, quoted ibid., pp. 246-47.

111. James MacGregor Burns, *Leadership* (New York: Harper & Row, 1978).

112. Williams, *Lincoln and the Radicals*, p. 9.

113. Trefousse, *Radical Republicans*, p. 238; McPherson, *Struggle for Equality*, p. 11.

114. Lincoln, "Speech at Peoria, Illinois," October 16, 1854, in Williams, *Abraham Lincoln: Selected Speeches*, p. 44.

115. James MacGregor Burns, *Presidential Government: The Crucible of Leadership* (New York: Avon, 1965), p. 56.

116. Bartlett, *Wendell Phillips*, p. 222.

117. April 15, 1861, cited in McPherson, *Struggle for Equality*, p. 56.

118. Boritt, *Lincoln and American Dream*, p. 250.

119. June 23, 1861, cited in McPherson, *Struggle for Equality*, p. 58.

120. Ibid., pp. 246-59; quotation on p. 247.

121. Hofstadter, *American Political Tradition*, pp. 169-70; James M. McPherson, "Abraham Lincoln and the Second American Revolution," in Thomas, *Abraham Lincoln*, p. 151.

122. Rev. Charles E. Hodges to Garrison, January 2, 1863, cited in Randall, *Springfield to Gettysburg*, 2:169; Reverend R. C. Waterston to Sumner, January 2, 1863, cited in McPherson, *Struggle for Equality*, p. 121.

123. *Liberator*, January 2, 1863, cited in McPherson, *Struggle for Equality*, p. 121.

124. Schurz to Lincoln, May 19, 1862, cited in Trefousse, *Radical Republicans*, p. 215.

125. McPherson, *Struggle for Equality*, pp. 86, 114-16.

126. Ibid., p. 116.

127. David Donald, *Lincoln Reconsidered* (New York: Vintage Books, 1961), pp. 121-122.

128. Sumner, quoted in ibid., pp. 119-21.

129. McPherson, *Struggle for Equality*, pp. 260-61.

130. Garrison to Helen Garrison, June 9, 11, 1864, cited ibid., p. 272.

131. *New York Tribune*, June 13, 1862, cited in Williams, *Lincoln and the Radicals*, p. 3.

132. McPherson, *Struggle for Equality*, p. 285.

133. Ibid., p. 117.

134. Williams, "Civil War History and Historiography," p. 93; Randall, *Springfield to Gettysburg*, 2:220; 1:6.

135. Randall, *Springfield to Gettysburg*, 2:220; Randall and Current, *Last Full Measure*, pp. 42-45.

136. Bates, diary, December 31, 1861, cited in Randall, *Springfield to Gettysburg*, 2:28.

137. Speed to Joseph Holt, December 8, 1861, cited ibid., p. 217.
138. We have in mind here such senators as Edgar Cowan, Orville Browning, Jacob Collamer, John Henderson, and James Doolittle.
139. Donald, *Lincoln Reconsidered*, p. 131.
140. Lincoln's use of egalitarian pressure to move the conservatives in an emancipationist direction is a major theme in Trefousse's *The Radical Republicans*.
141. A. Wattles to Horace Greeley, February 6, 1864, cited in Randall and Current, *Last Full Measure*, p. 112. See Donald, *Lincoln Reconsidered*, pp. 128-29; J. G. Randall, "The Unpopular Mr. Lincoln," in *Lincoln: The Liberal Statesman* (New York: Dodd, Mead, 1947), pp. 65-87.
142. S. Wolf to Rev. Dr. McMurdy, March 7, 1864, cited in Randall and Current, *Last Full Measure*, p. 112.
143. See Richard Hofstadter, "Wendell Phillips: The Patrician as Agitator," in *American Political Tradition*; Eric Foner, "Thaddeus Stevens, Confiscation and Reconstruction," in *The Hofstadter Aegis: A Memorial*, ed. Stanley Elkins and Eric McKitrick (New York: Knopf, 1974), pp. 154-83.

10

Rummaging, or Redeeming, History?

The skeptical reader may wonder whether we have not been guilty of
rummaging history: picking the pieces of historical evidence that fit our theory
while discarding other, more inconvenient facts? To those who might say that
we have read history, or historians, through the eyes of cultural theory, we
must plead guilty. Believers in the pristine fact will find this a heinous sin.
Yet, one cannot look at everything at once. All perception is selective. The
question that should be asked is not whether our version of American history
is category-laden (of course it is), but whether propositions that emerge are
accurate or, less ambitiously, more accurate than those generated by rival theories. We therefore conclude by asking what negative evidence would look
like (that is, what kind of fact or occurrence would surprise us), and how our
theory fares against others.

How Would One Know If We Were Wrong?

In using cultural categories to characterize presidents and their parties, we
have relied upon the judgment of historians. Some readers might feel more
comfortable had we used primary sources, letting the historical actors speak
directly to us, rather than relying on portraits drawn by present-day historians.
In our view, the danger of distorting history through selective quotation was
greatly minimized by basing our conclusions on the findings of cultural historians who, besides specializing in the values and beliefs of a particular political party, came to their evaluations quite unaware of our categories.

There still remains the temptation of listening only to those who support
one's preconceived notions. To guard against this, we have sought books that
the historical profession considers to be the leading works on early American
political culture. Our portrayal of the Whig party as importantly hierarchical,
for instance, rests heavily, though not solely, on the interpretation presented
in Daniel Walker Howe's *The Political Culture of the American Whigs*,[1]
widely regarded as the best exposition of Whig beliefs and values. Were future research to contradict Howe's claims, we would then have to reappraise
our interpretation in light of the new evidence. This means only that all hy-

potheses are tentative until new theories and data arise that are more persuasive.

Where possible, we have searched for a consensus among historians. Our characterization of Federalist political culture as predominantly hierarchical, for example, is based on conclusions reached in major works on the Federalist party by David Hackett Fischer, James Banner, and Linda Kerber.[2] Each of these authors describes the Federalist worldview as structured by a belief in society as a collectivity of harmonious and mutually interdependent parts, with a premium placed on social solidarity and order.

In other areas, ongoing historical controversy prevented us from finding a consensus. Historians, for instance, have been unable to settle the question of whether the Jacksonian movement is better characterized as egalitarian, as Arthur Schlesinger, Jr., contends, or individualist, as Bray Hammond and Richard Hofstadter have maintained.[3] Our solution was to designate the Jacksonian movement as an amalgam of the two political cultures. The Jacksonians were able to combine an individualist concern for expanding economic opportunity with an egalitarian concern for decreasing differences, we contend, because they believed that expanding opportunity would reduce differences.

If the historiography upon which we rely were shown to be faulty, it might disconfirm our characterization of the cultural propensities of a particular president or party. Can our assertions about the relationship between culture and leadership also be disproved? Our aim, after all, has been not only to categorize political parties and individuals in terms of our cultural typology but also to account for presidential behavior.

What would count as evidence against our thesis that scope and style of leadership is a function of culture? We have suggested that hierarchical cultures will reject charismatic leaders because charismatics attempt to substitute themselves for the written law. If, therefore, we found a hierarchical regime—such as the Federalist or Whig party—promoting charismatic leaders, we would be surprised. If such an anomaly recurred with any frequency, and assuming our characterization of the party as hierarchical was correct, it would constitute disconfirmation.

Other examples of negative evidence running counter to the predictions of our theory would include an egalitarian president who makes no effort either to hide his leadership or justify it in the name of decreasing inequalities; egalitarian followers who support overt leadership without any promise of increasing equality; an individualist president who tries to expand the scope of leadership and/or to make his authority permanent; individualist followers who support a leader in trying to enlarge permanently the scope and duration of his leadership; a hierarchical president who feels authority should be minimized or apologized for; or hierarchical followers who criticize, berate, and tear down their leaders.

Do the Whigs, a hierarchical party that tried to limit presidential power, count as evidence against our cultural theory? From a distance it might seem so, but upon closer inspection we see that their traumatic experience with Andrew Jackson—whom Whigs feared was, or would become, a charismatic leader—accounts for their distrust of executive power. Indeed this conflict between propensities, instructing them to support authority, and experience, teaching them to beware the presidency, was the source of the Whigs' defining cultural dilemma: a hierarchy without a hierarch. Because Whigs in some sense represented a cultural anomaly, they serve the valuable function of indicating that the cultural propositions we have advanced are not tautological.

We have attempted to account for presidential behavior by situating presidents within cultural dilemmas, but it is worth reiterating that the theory is not deterministic. We cannot predict what a president will do only from knowing his or even his followers' preferred political culture. Presidents respond strategically to a given cultural configuration. The concept of strategy implies human choice. But though the leader chooses a strategy, he is not free to adopt just any strategy. Cultures constrain leaders by attaching costs to certain leadership behaviors. The costs of acting in certain ways will be so prohibitive that we can rule them out as options available to the president. For Jefferson, for instance, the bias against overt leadership was so high that one could expect him to hide his leadership, which he did; justify his leadership in the name of limiting authority and furthering equality, as Jackson did; or be passive, i.e., fail to lead.

Because we cannot rerun the reel of history, propositions about the past are not strictly disconfirmable. Most explanations remain little more than plausible hypotheses.[4] Rather than letting the researcher off the hook, however, this imprecision makes it all the more imperative that the researcher try to devise tests that could undermine one's explanation. Counterfactual or "what-if" history can be a helpful tool in this respect.

We could ask, for instance, what would have happened had Jefferson, rather than dissemble, openly flaunted his leadership of Congress? We contend that if Jefferson had done so, his party would have savaged him, his popular support would have plummeted, and his presidency would have been much less successful than it was. By examining the egalitarian reaction to situations in which Jefferson's leadership was inadvertently exposed to public scrutiny, one might begin to assess this counterfactual hypothesis. A case in point is the embargo; there, despite Jefferson's efforts to conceal the power he exercised, the unprecedented concentration of authority in the hands of the executive became increasingly apparent to informed members of the public.

Similarly, one might investigate the reaction of both parties to Jackson during the nullification crisis when assertive presidential leadership was used to sustain central authority. If we are correct, this episode should have caused significant confusion within the major political parties. Jackson should have received praise and criticism from unfamiliar quarters. In particular, hierarchical Whigs should have become attracted to Jackson, and egalitarian-individualist Jacksonians should have felt uneasy with Jackson's behavior.

Alternatively, one might test some of the propositions we offer by looking at regional variations. In our study of Washington's presidency, for instance, we suggest that the variation by region in reaction to the administration's response to the Whiskey Rebellion provides a partial test of our cultural theory. Had Massachusetts, where hierarchy was strong, shared Pennsylvania's dismay at President Washington's show of power, then we would know that either our theory, or our characterization of Massachusetts as predominantly hierarchical, was wrong.

The decision to look at Revolutionary governors was motivated in large part by the sense that here was a crucial test for our theory. The process of constitution-making gave each state a chance to enact its vision of desirable executive leadership. Aware that New York, Virginia, and Pennsylvania varied significantly in political culture, we anticipated (predicted, or more exactly, retrodicted) that the type of governor created by each of the states also would vary. Variations between types of governors allowed us to evaluate our hypothesized relationships between culture and leadership more precisely than was possible with a single president.

Ultimately, however, the question is not whether our theory is totally true but whether it is "truer" or more persuasive than existing alternatives. By comparing our cultural theory of presidential dilemmas with alternative ways of looking at the presidency, the reader will be better able to evaluate the relative strengths of our approach. Which theory, our reader should ask, better resolves long-standing historical puzzles, leads to more interesting research questions, and produces more powerful predictions (or retrodictions)? We shall argue that our approach is better or, perhaps more accurately, less worse than alternative theories.

Competing Ways of Studying the Presidency

Psychological

Psychological analyses of the presidency have always flourished. In contrast to those who study the Congress, political parties, interest groups, or courts, observers of the presidency are invariably interested in the question: "What manner of man?" We care about this question because the presidency, despite all the loose talk about "institutionalization," remains a very personal office.[5] Because the chief executive is a single individual, it is not unreasonable to expect that personality will be more important in understanding the behavior of presidents, and therefore the presidency, than the behavior of other major institutions.

The psychological analyst looks at presidential actions for the ways in which they help the president in coping with internal psychological conflicts. Not conflicts between people but the conflicts within one individual's psyche are the focus of this mode of analysis. It has been argued, for instance, that Woodrow Wilson's stubborn and self-defeating behavior in the battle over the League of Nations resulted from a "fear of being dominated," an insecurity rooted in his childhood experience with an overbearing and perfectionist father. To take another example, Andrew Johnson's "scandalous harangues" delivered during his famous "Swing Around the Circle"—in which he went to the people to defend his reconstruction policies—have been attributed to an effort to "compensate for the needs left from his traumatic childhood."[6]

As these examples indicate, the psychological perspective tends to emphasize irrational behavior, that is, behavior that is counterproductive from the point of view of the president's own professed aims. This pathological orientation results in a pronounced bias toward studying presidents who have failed. A psychobiography, explains Erik Erickson, characteristically "gives an account of what went wrong with a person and of why the person fell apart or stopped developing."[7] Hence the attraction of a Richard Nixon, Lyndon Johnson, or Woodrow Wilson. The utility of psychological analysis of those presidents who lack a debilitating neurotic conflict remains relatively unexplored.

To note that the relevance of psychological analysis to successful presidents has not been demonstrated, however, is not to concede that presidential failures are always well explained by psychology. In those case where there is a recurrent pattern of self-defeating behavior on the part of the leader, as is true for Wilson, the prospects for a psychological explanation are promising. But a focus on the leader's personality fares less well when failure in the White House follows on the heels of success. In the period that we studied, we were struck not by "self-defeating patterns"[8] but by how often failure in the White House stood in stark contrast to repeated successes earlier in a president's political career.

Take for instance, James Madison, so successful as a congressional leader and constitution maker, yet considered by many to be a flop as president. The usual explanations—personal timidity, compliancy, a need for affection—cannot explain his bold maneuvering in Congress and at the Constitutional Convention. Or, take John Quincy Adams; as diplomat and secretary of state, he ranks among the most successful this nation has produced, yet as president he was a disappointment. Again, explanations that focus on personality—

psychological rigidity, compulsiveness—leave us wondering how such an inflexible, uncompromising man could have been the most successful American diplomat of his age.

We believe that the cultural approach presented in this book allows one to resolve these sorts of historical puzzles better than can competing modes of analysis. Not John Quincy Adams's prickly personality but his hierarchical propensity best explains why he could succeed so spectacularly in the realm of diplomacy yet be such an ineffective president. The hierarch's forte, negotiating jurisdictions—who has the right to do what—and adjudicating statuses, although valuable assets for a diplomat, are ill-suited to the president's inevitably competitive relationship with Congress and his position as the leader of a political party. Madison's difficulties in the presidency, we contend, had more to do with the antiauthority cultural propensities of his followers than any features of Madison's personality. Where no one is disposed to follow, no one, no matter how psychologically "healthy," can lead. In the aftermath of the War of 1812, when people were more disposed to support authority, Madison performed ably.

Assessing the impact of personality on politics, of course, presents a thorny problem.[9] How are we to determine, for instance, how much of Andrew Jackson's leadership style was due to personality and how much can be accounted for by political culture? Was his conception of the office, as some assert, simply "an expression of temperament?"[10] That Jackson reveled in confrontation, and Thomas Jefferson tried always to avoid conflict, help explain why Jackson justified his leadership as mandated by the people to expand popular participation and check concentrations of political and economic power whereas Jefferson practiced a covert, hidden-hand mode of leadership. But if personality explains the choice of styles, it is culture that determines the available options. Culture tells us what modes of leadership (in these cases, visible action to increase the size and scope of government) are foreclosed to leaders because they will be rejected by their followers. Jefferson and Jackson each selected a style of governing that fitted his temperament, but also both adopted styles that would be accepted by the antiauthority political cultures they led.

In *Andrew Jackson and the Search for Vindication*, James Curtis argues that Jackson's behavior in the bank war constituted a reflexive lashing out at those whom he perceived as wishing to impugn his reputation. How are we to choose between Curtis's interpretation of Jackson's behavior, and our own thesis that Jackson's attack on the national bank represented a political strategy that united his egalitarian and individualist followers against a visible symbol of hierarchy? Perhaps the galvanizing effects of Jackson's actions on the Democratic coalition were entirely fortuitous; perhaps the "Old Hero" was doing no more than exorcising personal demons in his vitriolic denunciations of the bank. But the fact that Jackson's attacks on the "Monster Bank" resonated with the desires of his followers lends support to our view that at issue was not personal psychosis but cultural symbiosis.[11]

Our mode of analysis treats political leaders as primarily purposive and rational. Seeking to achieve those purposes, we see presidents, in Herbert Simon's terms, as "intendedly rational."[12] Rather than first examining the ways in which political behavior serves unconscious needs, we study how making decisions helps or hinders a president in furthering his preferred way of life by governing effectively. Not individuals at war with themselves but cultures competing with one another provides our point of departure. In studying these early administrations we have not found presidents to be too incapacitated by inner psychological conflict to pursue solutions to cultural dilemmas. They may not succeed in solving the problem facing them, but they try. The difference is that some—for example, Washington and Lincoln—were more aware than others (say, the two Adamses) that they faced cultural dilemmas that needed to be resolved.

We stress leadership strategy as a response to cultural dilemmas, but this does not mean we assume leaders to be free agents. We accept the insights of cognitive psychology, that the individual is not free to adapt to the world in any way he wishes. Cultural propensities, we contend, provide filters through which people look at the world. A president's self-image, shaped by the way of life he supports, can lead to counterproductive behavior.

Witness John Adams, who, trying to behave as he thought a hierarch should, ended up by severely limiting his effectiveness as president. As vice president, also, Adams's attempt to endow the executive office with ceremony and dignity ended up embarrassing himself and his party. Because many people rejected his hierarchical assumptions about power, Adams's efforts were counterproductive from the point of view of his own stated goal: to create a government supported with "dignity and splendor."[13] Presidents can be more or less conscious of the cultural spectacles through which they view the world. In contrast to Adams, Washington tended to understand that many people did not share his hierarchical assumptions. It is not surprising, therefore, that Washington was more successful than his Federalist successor; an accurate appraisal of constituents' desires, after all, is a prerequisite to consistently effective political action.

John Quincy Adams's attempt to bolster the hierarchical way of life repeatedly handicapped his efforts as president. Refusing to accept the cultural context as a given, he strove to instruct the nation in the virtues of hierarchy, efforts that won him mostly scorn and derision. Because patronage violated the universalistic criteria appropriate to hierarchy, he ignored his advisers' warnings that if he failed to utilize the available patronage, it would severely reduce his political support and probably would cost him the election. That there is a penalty for "countercultural" behavior is evident from Quincy Adams's failures; true to himself, he could not be true to enacting his hierarchical vision.

The psychological literature has given us a number of persuasive studies of individual presidents—such as James David Barber's essay on Andrew Johnson or the Georges' analysis of Woodrow Wilson[14]—but the fascinating search for the ultimate motives and nature of the man has tended to impede comparison of presidents. Each president stands alone, making it difficult to relate the insights gained in one psychobiography with conclusions reached in another.

The now-famous typology developed by Barber in *The Presidential Character* was a pioneering attempt to introduce comparability to the psychological study of presidents.[15] Barber suggests, for example, that when energy invested in the office is high but affect toward the job is low—the "active-negative" president—self-destruction in office is the likely outcome. We have put forth a counterhypothesis: different personalities will self-destruct or succeed in different cultural contexts. George Washington, we contend, disliked his tenure in office less because of a "passive-negative" personality than because he did not receive the respect he felt was due his station. Perhaps, absent respect, he would have been satisfied with support for his policies, but most often that was not forthcoming either. Had Washington operated in a hierarchical system, where respect rather than criticism inhered in the job, his attitude toward politics would have been much more positive. Seeking a fit between leaders and cultures may make it possible to combine the insights of personality theory and cultural theory.

Institutional

An antidote to the tendency to focus exclusively on the person is provided by an alternative theoretical tradition that focuses on the institution of the presidency. Clinton Rossiter, Edward Corwin, and Wilfred Binkley are among the best-known practitioners of this venerable mode of analysis.[16] This literature tends to be heavily descriptive, concerned as it is with recounting the evolution over time in the roles and functions of the presidential office. A primary focus is on the precedents that presidents set for future incumbents.

From this perspective, a president's performance can be evaluated by weighing his "contributions to the presidency." "We are not likely to rate a President highly," explains Rossiter, "if he weakens the office through cowardice or neglect. A place at the top of the ladder is reserved only for those Presidents who have added to the office by setting precedents for other Presidents to follow."[17] Lincoln's expansion of the chief executive's war powers or

Jackson's democratization of the office stand out as prime examples of institution building. Lesser lights, too, may receive praise for defending presidential prerogatives. John Tyler, for instance, is congratulated by Binkley for having "saved the presidency from suffering a backset," and Polk wins plaudits for having "carried it deliberately forward to a more firmly established place in our constitutional system."[18] Rossiter lauds Andrew Johnson, "whose protests against the ravages of the Radicals in Congress were a high . . . point in the progress of the Presidency."[19] Defense of institutional prerogative, we contend, is not an adequate guideline for evaluating presidencies.

The distortions that result from reducing political-cum-cultural conflict to a dispute over institutional prerogatives can be illustrated by recalling the experience of James Buchanan. Buchanan's decision to leave determination of the status of slavery in the territories to the Supreme Court is construed by Binkley as an instance of "abdication of executive claims."[20] Far from being an abnegation of leadership, however, we argue that this episode represented an effort on Buchanan's part to forge an establishment alliance and thereby resolve the cultural dilemma posed by slavery. Buchanan gambled that a decision by the Court protecting slavery as a form of private property would give him the opportunity to unite adherents of individualism and hierarchy against egalitarians who declared they followed a higher law. By looking at conflict solely through the lens of institutional conflict, the significance of Buchanan's political strategy is missed.

To analyze institutional struggles apart from their political and cultural roots also makes a hash out of the Whig view of the presidency. The battle between Jackson and the Whigs is portrayed by institutionalists primarily as an exercise in constitutional theory, i.e., a debate over the proper roles of Congress and the presidency in the political system. Presidents are, to be sure, constantly engaged in an unresolvable struggle over the scope of their institutional prerogatives; missing from the institutional perspective, however, is an understanding of why the Whigs felt so deeply threatened by Jackson's exercise of executive powers. We have argued that Whig attitudes toward the executive were derived from their attempt to defend their hierarchical way of life. Such Whig leaders as Henry Clay and Daniel Webster viewed Jackson as a charismatic leader who was substituting himself for the law. Moreover, Jackson's proclivity to appeal directly to the people over the heads of elite intermediaries would, Whigs feared, erode the pattern of deference upon which their hierarchical way of life rested.

A focus on the linear development of the institution of the presidency has the further drawback of shifting attention away from types of presidencies comparable across time. If, as Corwin argues, "Jackson's presidency was no mere revival of the office; it was a remaking of it," then how could Jackson's successors be compared with his predecessors? Or if, as Binkley writes, by 1860 "the presidency of the United States . . . bore only slight resemblance to the office forty years before," then one cannot draw intelligible comparisons between Lincoln and our early presidents.[21] Put another way, the institutional literature is historical without being comparative.

Central to the institutional approach, particularly as elaborated by Rossiter, is the concept of role. Although the precise list of presidential roles varies with the author, a contemporary inventory would probably include chief of state, chief executive, commander in chief, chief legislator, chief diplomat, and party chief.[22] Rossiter defines the president's roles as "those tasks we call upon the President to perform."[23] The presidential role is defined by what Americans, elite and mass, expect of the office's incumbent. A good start. To specify more precisely what followers in fact do expect of presidents should—because it would let us delineate the varying contexts in which presidents act—be at the top of the presidency research agenda.

Though the empirical evidence concerning what is expected of a president is sparse, claims abound. One recent book, for instance, asserts that

> we expect our presidents to engage in . . . crisis management, symbolic and morale-building leadership, priority setting and program design, recruitment leadership, legislative and political coalition building, program implementation and evaluation, and general oversight. . . . He must be an expert on everything from clean air to neutron bombs. . . . Our demands on him are extraordinary. We require him over and over again to prove himself to us, to be 'all things to all men.'[24]

The assertion that too much is expected of the president is as old as the office itself. Shortly after his inauguration, George Washington worried "that my countrymen will expect too much from me." Fifty years ago the Brownlow Committee concluded that "the nation expects more of the President than he can possibly do."[25] Observers have been concerned not only with the sheer number of demands made upon the president but also with the conflicting nature of those expectations—how, for instance, can a president be both nonpartisan chief of state and leader of his party?

Our purpose here is not to enter into the argument about whether expectations of the presidency are or are not too high but to suggest that *expectations may vary by political culture*. Our study of presidencies in the antebellum period persuades us that future research would profit from being more attuned to the possibility that different groups of people may have different expectations of the president. Rather than talk about the expectations of "the public" or "the nation," we would do well to break down these amorphous designations into competing political cultures. Claims about "public expectations," as if egalitarians expected the same scope or style of leadership as did hierarchs, are bound to be confused.

In the one study that does separate expectations of the presidency according to political ideology, we find something remarkably like political cultures. In a sample of "attentive citizens," Bruce Buchanan finds that self-described moderates, liberals, and conservatives hold contrasting visions about the functions of the presidency, and how it should work. Liberals, Buchanan finds, downplay the importance of strength and dominance as strategies of presidential leadership. Rather, they look for high moral purpose. Conservatives, in contrast, look for a president who displays dominance, consistency, and potency. In this vision, presidents are expected to exercise political power in the service of a clear-cut, planned-out strategy. Moderates are not particularly impressed by either displays of high moral purpose or dominant leadership; instead they give top priority to a presidency that avoids disasters and crises. Theirs is, in Buchanan's words, a "damage control" vision of the presidency.[26]

Buchanan's findings suggest that rival expectations about the president's role may be due not, as most commentators have assumed, to individuals holding contradictory ideas about the type of presidential leadership they want but, as we have argued, to disagreements between adherents of different cultures.[27] Our contention is that the conflict over the proper scope and mode of presidential leadership does not occur only (or even primarily) within individuals but between individuals. The nation is conflicted about presidential power because adherents of the three political cultures disagree about power. By focusing on the way in which expectations about leadership vary by political culture, we have retained the focus on role—"who expects whom to do what"[28]—while recasting it in a way that we believe will facilitate comparison of presidents.

Political Power

Where the institutionalist perspective talks of presidential powers, the political approach refers to presidential power in the singular. Edward Corwin's magisterial study of the presidency was entitled *The President: Office and Powers*. The first chapter of Clinton Rossiter's influential work, *The American Presidency*, is "The Powers of the Presidency." In contrast, Richard Neustadt gave his great book the title *Presidential Power*. The basis of that power, Neustadt argues, is "the power to persuade." This semantic change indicated a fundamentally different way of thinking about the presidency. To the institutionalist, power inhered in the president's formal powers; for Neustadt " 'powers' are no guarantee of power."[29]

Neustadt's core insight, translated into the language of political culture, is that where hierarchy is weak, power does not inhere in position. We would add to this that not all presidents are equally likely to assume that power does inhere in the office. Presidents with a hierarchical propensity, we maintain, are more inclined to assume that an order will be obeyed. The major challenge facing hierarchical presidents is how to reconcile their culture preferences with the fact that the national government does not operate entirely, even largely, on the principle of hierarchy. As the experiences of John Adams and John Quincy Adams demonstrate, the cost of failing to take this into account is high—the destruction of party for Adams the father, and the inability to gain support for programs for Adams the son.

One of the differences between Neustadt's approach and ours is where we cut into the problem. Neustadt is not interested in explaining why a particular president behaves in certain ways. Rather, he is concerned with predicting the effects that different modes of presidential behavior will have on the president's effectiveness. We share this concern, but also desire to understand *why* presidents behave as they do. That is, we wish to make leadership a dependent as well as an independent variable, something to be explained as well as something explaining how well presidents do.

To posit that presidential power is a function of a leader's bargaining skills is to take for granted the attributes of his followers. Leadership thereby becomes an act of will. Neustadt's premise appears to be that leaders are not significantly constrained by their followers in adopting a leadership style. A president's mode of leadership is treated as an overcoat to be put on or discarded at will—subject only to the constraints of the leader's personal characteristics. In this book we have tried to address the prior question of what types of political cultures promote or reject what forms of leadership. From time to time, for instance, Thomas Jefferson was disposed to provide vigorous public leadership. Doing this on a regular basis, however, would have deeply discomforted his egalitarian followers. George Washington would have loved a more active foreign policy and a fancy title, but not in America where hierarchy had been weak from the beginning. To his everlasting credit, Washington decided not to try to impose his personal cultural preferences on an unwilling citizenry but rather, albeit sadly, to accept the limitations imposed by his recalcitrant countrymen.

Divorcing leaders from followers obscures the possibility that the key to presidential failure (and success) may reside as much in the followers as in the leader. Will it do, for instance, to explain the troubled presidencies of Lyndon Johnson, Richard Nixon, Gerald Ford, Jimmy Carter, and now Ronald Reagan solely in terms of their personal shortcomings?[30] Do we wish to argue that our wonderful people mysteriously keep getting terrible presidents? Is the historical reading of the United States as a land particularly favored by providence now to be replaced by a new myth of Americans as an unlucky people done in by unworthy presidents?

In our study of early presidencies we found that being an accomplished politician was insufficient to guarantee success in office. Martin Van Buren, for instance, was perhaps the most adroit politician of his day. Contemporaries marveled at his "powers of persuasion."[31] His various nicknames—the "Little Magician," the "Sly Fox"—testified to his substantial reputation. A lack of political acumen, in short, was not Van Buren's problem. Rather, his difficulties stemmed from the fact that with the national bank destroyed, he lacked a visible hierarchical target around which to unite egalitarians and individualists.

Nor can it be said that the three failed presidencies prior to the Civil War— those of Millard Fillmore, Franklin Pierce, and James Buchanan—can be attributed to a lack of political skill. This is particularly true with respect to Buchanan, one of the most politically experienced men ever to occupy the White House. The troubles these men faced cannot be explained without looking beyond presidential behavior to the cultural context within which each operated (just as Franklin Roosevelt's successes cannot be understood apart from the context of economic crisis within which he led). Hamstrung by the cultural dilemma posed by slavery, the opportunities for successful presidential leadership were very few in the years immediately prior to the Civil War.

Obviously not all presidents face the same situation.[32] What Harry Truman had to do to succeed as president was, as Fred Greenstein points out, different from what Dwight Eisenhower had to do. Truman needed to impress his Democratic followers, especially liberals, that he remained true to Roosevelt's activist legacy; Eisenhower was compelled, if he were to succeed, to avoid overt demonstrations of presidential leadership that, in the eyes of the Taft wing of the Republican party, were inextricably bound up with the Democratic agenda of increasing the scope and size of government.[33] One of the major intellectual challenges facing those who write after Neustadt is attempting to link types of situations to leadership.

The assumption of a generic leadership situation must be abandoned, but without retreating to the chaos of historical narrative—from which Neustadt rescued us—in which it is assumed there are as many situations as there are presidents. For if all presidents face dissimilar situations, we will be still further than before from our goal of comparing presidents. If, as Thomas Bailey contends, "no two incumbents were ever dealt the same hand," then comparison is impossible. How can we compare presidents "confronted in different eras by different tasks that called for different skills exercised at different tempos?"[34] If we concede that each historical situation is unique, then it is impossible to study leadership, presidential or otherwise. Comparing presidents therefore depends on being able to make situations comparable. We now turn to the few gallant efforts that have been made to do just this.

Cyclical

Interestingly, every one of the attempts to categorize situations faced by leaders have had one feature in common: all try to compare presidencies by situating presidents within a recurring cycle, whether an "election cycle," "policy cycle," or "regime cycle." The logic of the argument is that presidents can be compared by virtue of parallel situations within these cycles.

James David Barber has hypothesized "a steady, recurrent rhythm" between politics as conflict, politics as conscience, and politics as conciliation. The motor driving the "pulse of politics," Barber argues, is "the climate of expectations" that shifts every four years. Barber's explanation goes roughly like this: people grow tired of conflict for its own sake and want uplift; having been uplifted, they want a rest from moralism and thus slip into conciliation; then the "itch for adventure" and "blood-and-guts" political conflict sets in, and so on.[35] Although we wonder why people would want to reject institutions or leaders or parties who have served them well, there is a fruitful idea here, namely, that presidents can be compared on the basis of the climate of expectations they face. Rather than assume that everyone in the nation shares the same expectations of leaders, we have hypothesized that people who identify with different cultures expect different things from presidents. Indeed, Barber's categories—conflict, conscience, and conciliation—can, we believe, be derived from cultural categories. Individualists prefer a politics of conflict, egalitarians a politics of conscience, and hierarchs a politics of conciliation.

Michael Nelson and Erwin Hargrove posit a policy cycle consisting of a presidency of preparation, a presidency of achievement, and a presidency of consolidation. Presidents can thus be compared on the basis of how well they understand and perform their "function in the policy cycle."[36] We have little difficulty with their idea that some presidents are blessed with a period historically ripe for policy breakthroughs, and that it requires different skills to pass legislative programs than to administer them. A fundamental difficulty with this formulation, however, is that the stage of the cycle is identified and defined in terms of presidential behavior. A presidency of achievement is defined as the stage "in which reforms are enacted," and a presidency of consolidation is the period "in which reforms are rationalized."[37] We are being offered not propositions but definitions. How can we distinguish a president who achieves in spite of the cycle from a president who achieves because of the cycle? We are unable to do so because both situations are defined as presidencies of achievement. Lyndon Johnson's, for example, is identified as a presidency of achievement because of the many programs enacted during his administration—Medicare-Medicaid, the Voting Rights Act of 1965, Older Americans Act, and so on—yet the stage in the policy cycle is identified by these very same accomplishments. Without a way to identify situations—the stage in the cycle—apart from presidential behavior, the exercise of deducing behavior from situations lapses into tautology. Indeed, the great advantage of Nelson and Hargrove's innovative effort to compare presidencies is that it does reveal the importance of trying to separate the situation from the presidential behavior that responds to or creates it.

An alternative cyclical interpretation of U.S. political history, grounded in the theory of periodic party realignment, is offered by Stephen Skowronek. The generation and degeneration of electoral coalitions provide the dynamic that creates four different leadership situations. His typology is based on two variables: "the president's relationship to the regime (i.e., previously dominant) party" and "the standing of the regime party's commitments in the nation at large."[38] A president may be either opposed to or affiliated with the regime party, while the standing of the regime party's commitments varies from vulnerable to resilient. This is good; here presidencies are related to something important outside themselves, something political, something variable, something that may be measurable, and something that brings followers into the act.

At its best, Skowronek's typology of situations provides criteria for evaluating presidential performance. He suggests, for example, that we look beyond personal incompetence to explain the failed presidencies of John Quincy Adams, Pierce, Buchanan, Hoover, and Carter. All of these men, submits Skowronek, were presidents allied with a vulnerable regime party, and therefore they faced "the very definition of the impossible leadership situation." These presidents, he argues, faced a no-win situation in which the leader is confronted with the choice of "upholding the integrity of the old order . . . [and becoming] stigmatized as a symptom of the nation's problems and a symbol of the failure of the entire regime . . . [or] repudiating its basic commitments . . . [and becoming] isolated from his most natural allies and rendered politically impotent."[39] Thus, Skowronek persuasively roots his explanation of presidential failures outside the idiosyncrasies of individual presidents.

Not all the categories, however, are so satisfying. Particularly troubling is the category Skowronek labels the politics of articulation, i.e. the president in alliance with a resilient regime party. The president in this situation, argues Skowronek, is "*propelled* to complete the unfinished business of the regime's political agenda." As examples Skowronek has selected Theodore Roosevelt, James Polk, James Monroe, John Kennedy, and Lyndon Johnson. But why not Ulysses Grant, Warren Harding, and Calvin Coolidge, all of whom were affiliated with a resilient regime party? The latter three presidents fit the category without seeming to fit Skowronek's description of the politics of articulation as a time when presidents "think about completing the unfinished business of national politics and realizing the regime's highest moral vision for the nation."[40] This leads us to ask whether the "politics of articulation" is derived from the dimensions—affiliation with a resilient regime—or from ad hoc observation of presidents who did well when allied with a dominant party. Of course, like those who precede us, we have found it easier to spot deficiencies in other scholars' theories than to avoid our own.

The virtue of Skowronek's framework (and of a cyclical approach in general) is that it makes it possible to begin to compare modern presidents with premodern presidents.[41] Other approaches to studying the presidency have succeeded only in erecting walls between what happened before the advent of the modern presidency and what occurred after. Representative of the accepted wisdom in political science is Fred Greenstein's conclusion that "the transformation of the office has been so profound that the modern presidencies have more in common with one another in the opportunities they provide and the demands they place on their incumbents than they have with the entire sweep of traditional presidencies from Washington's to Hoover's"[42] Yet, Greenstein's brilliant evocation of Eisenhower's hidden-hand presidency would persuade anyone familiar with Jefferson that the two men did share political styles despite the vast differences in their institutions and times. Skowronek's contribution is to challenge this assumption by accenting those "problems of political action that distinguish modern presidents from one another and link them individually across historical periods to their counterparts in political time."[43]

Although in these pages we have not undertaken to compare modern and premodern presidents, our research has convinced us that such comparisons are both possible and fruitful. Nineteenth-century presidents, we find, did a great deal more leading than social scientists commonly give them credit for.[44] Though convention prevented early presidents from initiating a legislative program in the way that presidents do today, nineteenth-century presidents, like modern chief executives, did actively manage the competition between rival ways of life. If this is so, then situating presidents within their cultural context should make it possible for us to begin systematically comparing nineteenth- and twentieth-century presidents.

The Value Added: Or, What Have We Learned?

What have we learned from applying our theory of political culture to early American presidencies? What, can we hope, has the reader gained from the preceding pages that could not have been found elsewhere?

Individualism Is Necessary but Not Sufficient to Govern:
Hartz's Liberal Tradition Revisited

We have learned of the pivotal role individualism played in the American experience. To be sure, this is not new; students of American political culture have long recognized its central importance. Indeed, according to Louis Hartz's seminal study, *The Liberal Tradition in America* (as well as Richard Hofstadter's *The American Political Tradition*), individualism has been the only significant political tradition in the American past.[45]

Hartz's thesis is that the United States, because it lacked the feudal institutions of Europe, has been characterized by a consensus on liberal values. Hartz uses the term *liberal* in "the classic Lockian sense," shorn of "all sorts of modern social reform connotations." The essence of Lockean liberalism, as conceived by Hartz, is the placing of limits upon the state to keep it from interfering with the pursuits of private persons. "The master assumption of American political thought," writes Hartz, is "atomistic social freedom."[46] Indeed, American Lockeans could be more consistent in opposing a powerful central government than Locke himself, for whom the state was a weapon to destroy the preexisting hierarchical order.[47] Liberalism, as conceptualized by Hartz, is thus roughly equivalent to the way of life we have designated as individualism.

As Hartz's analysis would lead us to expect, every major cultural alliance studied in this book included individualism. What we find surprising is not that individualism was incorporated in every political party but, rather, that individualism did not become the dominant partner in any major political party until Lincoln, who, by subordinating hierarchy to individualism, forged a Republican coalition that has persisted in recognizable form down to the present day. Within the Federalist party, individualism had remained subordinate to hierarchy; and the Whigs inclined at least as much toward hierarchy as individualism. Moreover, both the Jeffersonian and Jacksonian alliances were characterized by a rough equivalence of egalitarianism and individualism. Neither culture could claim a clear upper hand.

The importance of individualism helps explain why the hierarchical Federalist party collapsed so suddenly, but not why our first two presidents were Federalists. If individualism was as hegemonic as Hartz contends, Jefferson and Madison (not Washington and Adams) should have been our first presidents. Why, to take another example, were the Articles of Confederation scrapped in favor of the Federal Constitution? Individualist proponents of minimal central authority, their laissez-faire preferences discredited by events under the Articles, found themselves losing out to advocates of a more hierarchical way of life. Far from being an unquestioned axiom, individualism, at least in the early republic, was repeatedly challenged by rival ways of life. For the period between the Revolution and the Civil War, our research indicates that Hartz has exaggerated the sway of individualism while underestimating the role of egalitarianism and hierarchy. Only in the 1850s, after the Jacksonians shed their egalitarian cast and the Republican party replaced the Whig party, does the United States, at least in the North, begin to resemble the consensual society posited by Hartz.

Although prior to the 1850s individualism never dominated a political party, the balance of power within the party system always hinged on whether individualists leaned toward egalitarianism or hierarchy. Among early presidents, James Madison most clearly reveals an individualist disposition. Sufficiently long-lived and flexible in his views, Madison serves as a weather vane for the changing course of individualism. Struggling against the hierarchical authority of King George III, Madison had little trouble seeing that the cause of individualism was best served by breaking away from the crown. Sensing that the coalition of egalitarianism and individualism that animated the Articles of Confederation was not enough to hold the republic together, however, Madison supported an increase in central authority at the Constitutional Convention. After the new Constitution had been established, fearing that Hamilton was attempting to greatly increase the scope and power of central government, Madison reached out in favor of an alliance with the egalitarians. Not until the last years of his second term—after having witnessed the destruction of the nation's capital during the War of 1812—did Madison lean back in the direction of shoring up central authority.

But though individualism may have been essential to a governing coalition, it could not rule alone, as John Tyler's trying experience in the presidency confirmed. Tyler's attempt to govern without the support of either adherents of hierarchy or egalitarianism floundered, both because individualism's strength was divided between the two major parties and because egalitarian and hierarchical preferences were stronger and more widespread than he had estimated. We learn from this little-remembered president that although individualism may be a necessary component of a governing coalition in the United States, it is not by itself sufficient.

Individualism Is Different from Egalitarianism

We hope also that this study has helped to clear up the common confusion between competitive individualism and egalitarian collectivism. To be sure, in the years between the Revolution and the Civil War we often find the two cultures so closely allied that it becomes difficult to separate them, but even during this period there is enough evidence to distinguish egalitarians from individualists.

When persuaded that hierarchy posed the severest challenge to their preferred way of life, individualists and egalitarians in the early republic often joined sides. But when the hierarchical threat seemed to wane, divisions between the two antiauthority cultures immediately opened up. The split can be seen, for instance, immediately after the defeat of the British in the war for independence; in the bitter political battles in Pennsylvania after the War of 1812; and, especially, in divisions within the Democratic party after Jackson's departure. Once the hierarchical bank had been slain, an irreparable fissure opened up between Jacksonian individualists like William Marcy, who wanted now to unleash the entrepreneurial energies of the nation (the Democratic party as described by Bray Hammond and Richard Hofstadter), and egalitarians like William Cullen Bryant, who, seeing that destroying the central bank had fueled speculation and increased inequalities, hoped to extend the bank war to all banks (the Democratic party as described in Arthur Schlesinger's *Age of Jackson*).

The unfortunate effects of this confusion of the two cultures can be seen most vividly in Samuel Huntington's otherwise splendid book, *American Politics: The Promise of Disharmony*,[48] thus far the most creative attempt to reconcile Hartz's consensus theory with the deep conflicts that have periodically punctuated American history.[49] How is it, Huntington asks, that a consensual society can be the "disharmonic polity par excellence"?[50]

Following Hartz, Huntington argues that "a broad consensus exists and has existed in the United States on basic political values and beliefs. . . . The values of this Creed," Huntington continues, "are liberal, individualistic, democratic, egalitarian, and hence basically antigovernment and antiauthority in character." But because political practice invariably must fail to measure up to the values espoused in this creed, the consensus stands as a permanent indictment of existing institutions. Periods of bitter disagreement—"creedal passion periods"—stem from periodic attempts to put into practice the nation's liberal-democratic values. Everyone believes in the creed, Huntington suggests; some just believe more passionately in its values than do others.[51]

Did Lincoln believe any less intensely in American political values than William Lloyd Garrison? We think not. Rather, they held different political values. Garrison, like other abolitionists, believed slavery to be morally wrong because it violated the principle that "each human being is invested with sovereignty over himself—and no one over another." Lincoln, like other Republicans, objected to slavery because it denied individuals the opportunity to compete and improve their condition. Though both men often appealed to a common document—the Declaration of Independence—each attached a very different meaning to the phrase "all men are created free and equal" because Lincoln and Garrison meant very different things by the term *equality*.[52]

Failing to sort out the various meanings attached to the word *equality* is the most common cause of the confusion of egalitarianism and individualism. Americans can agree about the desirability of equality only because they mean different things by it. Both Ronald Reagan and Ralph Nader, for instance, without sharing a common political culture, profess a deep commitment to equality. For Reagan, as an individualist, equality means equality of opportunity; for Nader, the egalitarian, it means more equal results. There is a world of difference between those who wish to reduce authority so as to create opportunities and promote individual differences, and those who reject authority so as to diminish differences among people.

The four periods that Huntington identifies as creedal passion periods—the Revolutionary, Jacksonian, and Progressive eras, and the 1960s—were all associated with an upsurge in egalitarian forces. Huntington himself recognizes that reducing differences was a central feature of all these movements: "Each was in some measure a period in which distinctions—whether based on status, occupation, knowledge, or position—were denigrated, in which there was a stress on homogenization, on 'the great principle' (in the words of Jacksonians) 'of amalgamating all orders of society.' "[53]

But is American society characterized by agreement on the proposition that distinctions among people should be reduced? The answer is clearly no. Indeed, the principle of reducing differences is antithetical to core values of the liberal ethos. It is the principle of differences, not similarities, that animates "Lockean liberalism." That vision is one of a social order based on exchange, implying differences and differentiation rather than similarity and likeness.[54] Lockean political values (re individualism) include equal treatment and expansion of opportunities, but not a communitarian equality dedicated to reducing differences.

Having assumed a consensus on radical egalitarianism, Huntington then arrives at the conclusion that "the legitimacy of American government varies inversely with belief in American political ideas."[55] But one can offer a more plausible (if less striking) proposition by abandoning the assumption of consensus: the legitimacy of American institutions varies inversely with the strength of egalitarianism. The denigration of authority so characteristic of creedal passion periods comes not from the consensus "coming alive"[56] but from the rise of egalitarian forces.

The period after the Civil War, when egalitarianism was at an all-time low, corroborates our proposition. During no time in our history, as Hartz recognizes, was the Lockean ethic more triumphant.[57] The doctrine of equal opportunity was triumphant as individuals pursued life, liberty, and happiness with a minimum of government intervention—except, of course, when they could get government to intervene on their side. Untempered by egalitarianism, individualism had no tolerance for the moral crusades engaged in by the Jacksonians. With egalitarianism relatively quiescent, the burning antiauthority animus—characteristic of both the Jacksonian period and the 1960s—subsided.[58] The scope of the national government, and of the chief executive, was, to be sure, circumscribed, and a lively skepticism about politicians prevailed, but authority was not denigrated nor actively undermined.

We contend that the egalitarian instinct is to tear down authority; the individualist instinct is to limit it. These differing expressions of an "antipower" ethic can be illustrated by comparing the egalitarian Thomas Paine with the individualist James Madison. Paine gloried in berating authority, ridiculing its pomp, and stripping away its secrecy. Madison's forte, in contrast, was in devising ways to check and limit power. In those spheres where he deemed government authority appropriate, however, Madison gave government complete backing. Paine's ideas were fashioned to bring down government; Madison's to establish a limited one.

James Buchanan's presidency serves to remind both theorists and politicians of the costs of missing this distinction. Buchanan's failure as president, we have seen, stemmed from an inability to distinguish egalitarian abolitionists from individualist Free Soilers. Unable to grasp this distinction, and thus to exploit the two cultures' points of disagreement, Buchanan's strategy of creating an establishment alliance of hierarchy and individualism was foiled. Also, he was unable to teach the South the important distinction between Garrisonian abolitionism and Lincoln's Republican party. Similarly, Huntington, by conflating egalitarianism and individualism, leaves himself ill equipped to distinguish between those who today wish to limit the scope of government and those who desire to denigrate all authority.[59] An understanding of political culture thus enables us to call on the experience of past presidents to help us interpret our own.

Remembering Past Presidents

One of our aims in writing this book was to recover our early presidents. They seemed to be remembered, when at all, only by superficial catch-phrases and caricatures—"Tippecanoe and Tyler too," "King Andrew," "Polk the mendacious," the "Corrupt Bargain," the "Era of Good Feelings," and so on. Some textbooks on the presidency allot a stray sentence or paragraph to the more prominent among them, but the rest have been consigned to oblivion.

The dichotomy between modernity and tradition justifies this neglect by instructing political scientists that the early presidents are irrelevant to their concerns. Typical is Richard Neustadt's comment that only Lincoln and Wilson faced "conditions something like our own."[60] Historians, by contrast, tend to judge the past as not so very different from the present. Arthur Schlesinger, Jr., for instance, pleads with political scientists and other pundits to "avoid the fallacy of self-pity that leads every generation to suppose that it is pecul-iarly persecuted by history.'' Historical forces, he concludes, ''have always conspired against the Presidency.''[61]

Historians provide valuable perspective on the present, but they have not succeeded in convincing political scientists that there is anything to learn from paying attention to early presidents—except perhaps in understanding how the institution evolved into its present form. Unwilling to try constructing theoret-ical frameworks that might lift past administrations out of the realm of histori-cal narrative, historians have made those presidencies seem irrelevant to those of us concerned with a more recent historical period. That we remember so little about early presidents may be in large part because historians require us to remember so much.

If Jackson's presidency is to be remembered only for tales of myriad past political conflicts, or his contribution to the office's development, then it is not surprising that those interested in the presidency in the here and now don't see the need to remember it. If, however, as we have argued, Andrew Jackson's tenure was about exercising presidential power in the name of reducing the size and scope of government, then his presidency suddenly be-comes relevant to today's presidency. Parallels with Ronald Reagan, for in-stance, immediately suggest themselves. Through the cultural theory pre-sented in these pages, we have tried to provide not only the means but also the motive for remembering what Jackson's presidency was about, for we be-come willing to remember past presidents as they become relevant to present concerns.

If Jefferson's presidency is merely about how the conflict between Federal-ists and Republicans worked itself out, then who but historians of the period should care about it? If, on the other hand, it is about hiding leadership from antiauthority followers, perhaps Jefferson's tenure becomes relevant to to-day's age, in which distrust of authority is again on the rise. By studying the successes and failures of Jefferson's ''hidden-hand'' leadership style, future presidents might improve upon their own performance.

Why should we bother to remember John Adams's tenure in office if it is only about the treachery of Timothy Pickering, the duplicity of Alexander Hamilton, or Adams's own obstinacy? His presidency might seem less arcane if we were to conceptualize it not as a collection of personages and events but as an instance of a larger set: the hierarch without a hierarchy. The intrigues and maneuvers of the day might then recede as we focused on the predicament he shares with other hierarchical presidents. From Adams, moreover, we can learn the importance of accurately appraising one's cultural context.

If asked to think on James Monroe, we are likely to recall the ''Era of Good Feelings.'' We have all heard the phrase, but what it actually means has al-ways remained something of a mystery. When we have learned that this era was about cultural fusion—the attempt to join all three political cultures under a single political banner—we come to have a much better idea of what Monroe was about. Remembering his presidency as an attempt at cultural fusion raises it out of the realm of historical trivia, and makes it potentially relevant to other, later administrations. Franklin Roosevelt's initial attempts to respond to the depression, for example, were marked by elements of this same strategy.[62] And some future president, following an era of intense partisan strife or facing a severe crisis, might want to try it again.

John Tyler is remembered, if at all, as "his Accidency," or as the latter half of the famous 1840 campaign slogan, "Tippecanoe and Tyler too." Historians remember his reign as a period of internecine conflict between various stubborn Whig leaders. Others might recall that as the first vice president to assume the presidency upon the death of a president, Tyler set the important precedent of assuming the title of president when the Constitution stipulated only that the vice president should take over the *duties* of the president. If this is all there is to Tyler's term then perhaps it is best to leave Tyler to the historians. But if, as we contend, Tyler's presidency represented an historic experiment to govern without the aid of egalitarianism or hierarchy, then the results of that experiment become relevant to contemporary concerns.

Early presidents should not be left to gather dust. By orienting presidencies around cultural dilemmas, we have sought to show that students of the presidency—political scientists in the current division of academic labor—can profit from comparing early presidents with modern presidents. Our aim, in short, is not only to remember past presidents but to reorient the future of presidential research.

A Research Agenda

A theory should be judged not only for what it says but for where it leads. What questions most need answering? What sort of research program emerges from this mode of theorizing? What might this program tell us that we don't already know?

Recommendations as to what should be done to improve the study of the presidency are legion, reflecting a widespread feeling that the quality of presidential research is subpar, particularly when contrasted to the body of knowledge regarding Congress or voting behavior. In the past decade the field of presidential studies has been flooded with essays telling others what or how they should be studying.[63] We worry that telling others what they ought to do is often a substitute for, rather than being a prelude to, research. Nevertheless, we hope that by presenting our ideas at the end of a substantive piece of work, we will be forgiven the hubris of telling others how they might profitably spend their time. We intend to follow a few of these leads ourselves. More to the point, the fruitfulness of our cultural approach will be judged in significant part by the richness of the research projects it generates.

Future research on the presidency, we believe, must bring followers into the act. We are not the first to suggest the need for "moving beyond the Oval Office,"[64] but the cultural approach does allow us to specify more precisely how to do so.

It is not that no one has thought to study what the public expects of presidents but, rather, that lacking theoretical guidance, interviewers have not known what are the appropriate questions to ask. A 1979 Gallup poll, for instance, offered respondents a list of attributes people might look for in a president; the poll found that 82 percent want a president with intelligence, 81 percent a president with sound judgment in a crisis, 74 percent a president with the ability to get things done, and 66 percent a president with high ethical standards. These data are used by at least one scholar to show that Americans expect superhuman presidents.[65] Yet, because the questions offered positively valenced words (without asking respondents to rank-order the attributes), the responses tell us very little about the shape of public expectations of the presidency. Who, after all, is going to prefer a president lacking in intelligence, judgment, competence, or virtue?

Research on public expectations of the president has yielded a hodgepodge of findings: 50 percent feel it is important to have a president with a sense of humor, 33 percent would strongly object if he used profane language in private, 35 percent think the president should have the major responsibility for setting economic policy; 36 percent would strongly object if the president used tranquilizers occasionally, and so on.[66] This line of inquiry—adding up what "the public" expects without specifying what kind of whole it adds up to—has not proven fruitful, we contend, in large part because variations in attitudes among different sectors of the public have been neglected. Our hope is that cultural theory will prompt researchers to probe the ways in which attitudes toward the presidency vary by culture or ideology. Bruce Buchanan's work, relating public attitudes to types of presidencies (referred to earlier), constitutes a first step in this direction.

A cultural approach, moreover, tells us that expectations of presidential behavior (the demand side) are only half of the equation. The supply side (support for presidents) also must be taken into account. Those who expect much of a president but match their demands with a willingness to support a wide variety of presidential actions may not be a "drag" on presidential popularity. Scholars concerned with low presidential support, our theory suggests, need to look to that segment of the population that does not match high demands with high support. Our hypothesis is that this unbalanced pattern of support and expectations is characteristic of egalitarians.[67]

As students of the presidency, we are interested in the content of public expectations only insofar as those expectations impact upon presidential behavior. At present, a battle rages about whether the present string of troubled presidencies is due to the public's contradictory and unrealistic expectations or to a failure in our leaders. Those who would argue the former thesis must come to grips with public opinion research documenting that most people most of the time don't care much about politics. Not only does the mass public not think about politics much, but also most members of the public rarely involve themselves in it, except to vote.[68] It seems implausible, therefore, that the unsophisticated American public—those least well informed about, and involved in, politics—is the constraint upon presidents.

Equally unsatisfactory is the contrary position; this view would absolve the followers entirely, pinning all blame on leaders. A cultural approach allows us to resolve this impasse by focusing on those followers who hold relatively enduring cultural preferences. If one is interested in finding out what constraints followers impose on presidents, we suggest the researcher study relatively attentive publics—the political stratum—not the relatively inattentive mass public.

Putting leaders and followers into the same picture means investigating not only the impact that followers have on leaders but also the effect leaders have on followers. We need to know more about how and when leaders can transform the values and beliefs of followers. It may prove helpful to distinguish two kinds of presidents: those who take the cultural propensities of followers as they find them; and those who attempt to transform them.[69] Fillmore, for instance, tried to hold together the existing Whig alliance of hierarchy and individualism; Lincoln, by contrast, helped to transform Whiggery in the direction of greater individualism by subordinating the hierarchy that had made Whiggery unpalatable to much of the country.

But leadership alone cannot explain cultural change. How is it—if, as we contend, cultural propensities are relatively enduring orientations toward the world—that the strength of cultures wax and wane? While this subject cries out for further theorizing, our research on early presidents does suggest a partial answer. Adherence to a culture is not unlike adherence to a theory.[70] Although every attempt is made to fit events into one's culture, occasionally there are anomalies—occurrences that cast doubt upon the wisdom of one's preferred way of life. The social and economic disorder under the Articles, for instance, discredited somewhat the antiauthority ethos that had prevailed during the Revolution. Similarly, the War of 1812 undermined many people's confidence in the egalitarian-individualist belief that the nation was safest with a minimal national defense. When things go wrong, in short, the prevailing cultural orientation tends to receive the brunt of the blame, at least where there is vigorous competition between cultures. Those less well integrated into a specific culture—who identify with it but are not unshakeable true-believers—will be particularly inclined to treat their adherence to the culture as a hypothesis to be tested. Although few of those who are deeply committed to a particular way of life actually will convert to another culture, events may leave them much less certain, and therefore less assertive, about their way of life. This is what seems to have happened to the Democratic party, for instance, in the late 1970s and early 1980s.[71]

How does thinking about the presidency in terms of political culture affect how one might approach some of the old favorites of presidential research, such as president-cabinet relations? Rather than ask only about the quality of advice or the range of opinions that the president gets from his cabinet and staff, important as that is, we might also investigate how presidents use advisers to help them deal with their cultural context. So, for instance, we not only look at the quality of Hamilton's advice to Washington but explore also how Hamilton may have acted as a lightning rod to deflect criticism away from the president. Lincoln, we suggest, used cabinet members in a similar fashion. Culture thus helps us to move "beyond the Oval Office" without actually forsaking it.

A cultural perspective injects new meaning, too, into the familiar subject of president party relations. Parties stand as the organized expressions of cultural preferences. A cultural approach instructs researchers to focus on the effects of presidential actions on the cultural balance within the president's party. To focus a cultural lens on Ronald Reagan's presidency, for instance, would immediately sensitize us to (among many possible divisions) the split within the Republican party between social hierarchs and economic individualists. One aspect of our evaluation of Reagan's presidency would focus on his success (or lack thereof) in keeping these cultures together. His strategy might very well be relevant to future presidents.[72] By the same token, this implies that Reagan himself could have benefited from looking at how past presidents coped with cultural splits—Jackson, for example, who fused two competing cultures; or Van Buren, who tried to be an egalitarian to egalitarians and an individualist to individualists.

If the three political cultures that we have described can be found in all times and places, then we can begin to compare presidents not only with one another but with executives of other countries. All executives, whether prime ministers, governors, or presidents, we hypothesize, must manage the competition between the three rival ways of life. The concept of culture, which has hitherto been the greatest obstacle to cross-national comparisons could now, redefined as competing ways of life within nations, serve to facilitate comparison.

We suggest also that all presidents, not just the past six or seven, be made subjects of study. The modern/tradition dichotomy that justifies the exclusive focus on those presidents that came after Franklin Roosevelt is filled with holes. What will we do in another fifty years, when what is now modern has become traditional? Will we invent a third category, postmodern, to indicate the institutional and technological changes that will inevitably happen? If we persist in holding up this distinction between what is past and what is currently significant, we are forever limiting our sample to a handful of presidents. By using political culture categories, we open the door to studying past presidents, and thereby hold out the promise of a sample sufficiently large so that we may, at long last, begin to discern patterns of presidential behavior.

If all we did, however, was to prescribe comparing all presidents, we wouldn't be saying much. To recommend studying everything is hardly a helpful guide; a principle of selectivity is required. Enter cultural dilemmas. These dilemmas delimit our subject matter by isolating the interaction between a president's cultural identification, the cultural context (what rival cultures will allow), and the demands of the historical situation.

Comparing and evaluating presidents according to the cultural dilemmas they face casts fresh light, for instance, on the age-old question of why presidents succeed (or fail).[73] We suggest that if a president does not understand his dilemma, he will fail no matter how healthy his personality. This may help explain why Jimmy Carter, despite an "active-positive" character,[74] shared the fate of the supposedly "active-negative" John Adams, for we assert that neither understood his cultural context. Both failed because they acted as if authority inhered in position.

Nor is political skill always an accurate predictor of success in the White House. Although poor politicians have rarely, if ever, been successful presidents, faltering presidencies have often been the fate of accomplished politicians—James Madison, Martin Van Buren, James Buchanan, Lyndon Johnson, Richard Nixon, to name a few. Future research might profit from comparing the presidents who, despite success as politicians, had unending troubles as chief executives. To pose this comparison forces one to look beyond the attributes of the leader. A comparison of the string of skilled politicians who failed as president prior to the Civil War with post-1964 presidents who failed, for instance, might provide clues about the constraints that followers and situations exert upon leaders.

Our analysis suggests also that to an extent not previously recognized, presidential failure is closely bound up with the success of predecessors. That is, one president's solution becomes the source of another president's dilemma. Thus, presidents might be compared by how they manage a dilemma bequeathed by a dominant predecessor. Both Truman and Van Buren, for example, were torn between Democratic activists who demanded the president be true to what was perceived as their hero's inspirational spirit and style and

Congress, which demanded more respect for its institutional prerogatives than it had received under the domineering leadership of Jackson and Roosevelt. Presidents taking over from the opposite party also may inherit dilemmas. Just as Whigs formed their conceptions of appropriate presidential leadership in reaction to "King Andrew," so Taft Republicans demanded Dwight Eisenhower reject not only New Deal policies but also the activist style of presidential leadership that they identified with Roosevelt. Eisenhower's solution was a hidden-hand style that allowed him to avoid appearing like another FDR to his Republican followers while still achieving his own political objectives.

A common denominator in our recommendations for improving the study of the presidency is the idea that presidents should be studied in relationship to followers. We believe this idea is fundamental to future progress. A decade ago, in the *Handbook of Political Science*, Anthony King suggested that the difficulties of executive research were due largely to the fact that "it has been less clear (than, say, in voting behavior) what the intellectual challenges are. . . . No one seems to know . . . what are the big questions in executive research."[75] In this study we have tried to isolate two, related intellectual challenges that future research must take up: to relate followers to leaders, and to compare presidents. The former, we contend, is a prerequisite to the latter. Cultural theory provides a way to relate followers to leaders so that it is possible (and fruitful) to compare presidents across time. In this way it will be possible to preserve and put to use the experiences of past presidents.

Notes

1. Daniel Walker Howe, *The Political Culture of the American Whigs* (Chicago: University of Chicago Press, 1979). Our interpretation of the Whigs also relies on John Ashworth, *'Agrarians' and 'Aristocrats': Party Political Ideology in the United States, 1837-1846* (Atlantic Highlands, N.J.: Humanities Press, 1983); and Ronald P. Formisano, *The Transformation of Political Culture: Massachusetts Parties, 1790s-1840s* (New York: Oxford University Press, 1983), esp. pp. 268-80, 461.
2. David Hackett Fischer, *The Revolution of American Conservatism: The Federalist Party in the Era of Jeffersonian Democracy* (New York: Harper & Row, 1965); James M. Banner, Jr., *To the Hartford Convention: The Federalists and the Origins of Party Politics in Massachusetts, 1789-1815* (New York: Knopf, 1970); Linda K. Kerber, *Federalists in Dissent: Imagery and Ideology in Jeffersonian America* (Ithaca: Cornell University Press, 1970).
3. Arthur M. Schlesinger, Jr., *The Age of Jackson* (Boston: Little, Brown, 1945); Richard Hofstadter, *The American Political Tradition* (New York: Vintage Books, 1973); Bray Hammond, *Banks and Politics in America from the Revolution to the Civil War* (Princeton: Princeton University Press, 1957). A similar synthesis to ours is reached in Ashworth, *Agrarians and Aristocrats*.
4. See Kenneth M. Stampp, *The Imperiled Union: Essays on the Background of the Civil War* (New York: Oxford University Press, 1980), p. 246.
5. See Henry Fairlie, "Thoughts on the Presidency," *Public Interest* (Fall 1967): 28-48.

6. Alexander L. George and Juliette L. George, *Woodrow Wilson and Colonel House: A Personality Study* (New York: Dover, 1964), p. 12; James David Barber, "Adult Identity and Presidential Style: The Rhetorical Emphasis," in *Philosophers and Kings: Studies in Leadership* (New York: G. Brazilles, 1970), ed. Dankwart A. Rustow, pp. 367-96, quotation on p. 392. The tenth article of impeachment against Johnson accused him of making "scandalous harangues."

7. Erik H. Erikson, *Dimensions of a New Identity* (New York: Norton, 1974), p. 13.

8. Alexander L. George, "Some Uses of Dynamic Psychology in Political Biography: Case Materials on Woodrow Wilson," in *A Source Book for the Study of Personality and Politics*, ed. Fred I. Greenstein and Michael Lerner (Chicago: Markham, 1971), p. 92.

9. See Fred I. Greenstein, "The Impact of Personality on Politics: An Attempt to Clear Away Underbrush," *American Political Science Review* (September 1967): 629-41.

10. Edward S. Corwin, *The President: Office and Powers, 1787-1957* (New York: New York University Press, 1957), p. 23.

11. James C. Curtis, *Andrew Jackson and the Search for Vindication* (Boston: Little, Brown, 1976), ch. 6 and passim. Jackson's personality is also analyzed in Michael Paul Rogin, *Fathers and Children: Andrew Jackson and the Subjugation of the American Indian* (New York: Alfred A. Knopf, 1975). Our view—that, in attacking the bank, Jackson was exercising political leadership rather than exorcising personal demons—is supported by Robert Remini's recently completed three-volume treatment of Jackson's life.

12. Herbert A. Simon, *Administrative Behavior* (New York: Free Press, 1976), p. xxviii.

13. Adams, quoted in James Hart, *The American Presidency in Action* (New York: Macmillan, 1948), p. 31.

14. Barber, "Adult Identity and Presidential Style"; George and George, *Wilson and Colonel House.*

15. James David Barber, *Presidential Character: Predicting Performance in the White House* (Englewood Cliffs, N.J.: Prentice-Hall, 1972). See also Erwin Hargrove, *Presidential Leadership: Personality and Political Style* (New York: Macmillan, 1966).

16. Clinton Rossiter, *The American Presidency* (New York: Harcourt, Brace & World, 1960); Corwin, *The President*; Wilfred E. Binkley, *President and Congress* (New York: Vintage Books, 1962).

17. Rossiter, *American Presidency*, pp. 89, 144.

18. Binkley, *President and Congress*, pp. 121-22.

19. Rossiter, *American Presidency*, p. 106.

20. Binkley, *President and Congress*, p. 131.

21. Corwin, *The President*, p. 20; Binkley, *President and Congress*, p. 132.

22. See, for example, Rossiter, *American Presidency*, ch. 1; Corwin, *The President*, chs. 3-7; and Louis W. Koenig, *The Chief Executive* (New York: Harcourt Brace Jovanovich, 1975), chs. 6-10.

23. Rossiter, *American Presidency*, p. 16.

24. Barbara Kellerman, *The Political Presidency: The Practice of Leadership from Kennedy through Reagan* (New York: Oxford University Press, 1984), p. 13.

25. Louis Brownlow, "What We Expect the President to Do," in *The Presidency*, ed. Aaron Wildavsky (Boston: Little, Brown, 1969), p. 35.

26. Bruce Buchanan, "Contrasting Visions of the Presidency: The Evaluative Priorities of Liberals, Moderates, and Conservatives" (Paper delivered at the 1984 An-

nual Meeting of the American Political Science Association, Washington, D.C.). The core findings of this paper have been published as chapter 3 in *The Citizen's Presidency* (Washington, D.C.: Congressional Quarterly Press, 1987).

27. This assumption underlies the discussion of contradictory expectations in George C. Edwards III, *The Public Presidency: The Pursuit of Popular Support* (New York: St. Martin's Press, 1983), pp. 195-98, and in Thomas E. Cronin, *The State of the Presidency* (Boston: Little, Brown, 1980), ch. 1.

28. Andrew S. McFarland, *Power and Leadership in Pluralist Systems* (Stanford: Stanford University Press, 1969), p. 202.

29. Richard E. Neustadt, *Presidential Power: The Politics of Leadership* (New York: Wiley, 1980), p. 10.

30. Neustadt characterizes Johnson and Nixon as "men who victimized themselves" (ibid., p. 184). Carter's experience in the White House, however, led Neustadt to look outside the president's personal qualities for more systemic causes of presidential defeat (ch. 11).

31. Donald B. Cole, *Martin Van Buren and the American Political System* (Princeton: Princeton University Press, 1984), p. 174.

32. In thinking about this problem we have benefited from Stephen Skowronek's "Notes on the Presidency in the Political Order," *Studies in American Political Development*, vol. 1, esp. pp. 290-91.

33. Fred I. Greenstein, *The Hidden-Hand Presidency: Eisenhower as Leader* (New York: Basic Books, 1982). On Harry Truman's difficulties in winning acceptance from the liberal wing of the party, see Alonzo L. Hamby, *Beyond the New Deal: Harry S. Truman and American Liberalism* (New York: Columbia University Press, 1973).

34. Thomas A. Bailey, *Presidential Greatness: The Image and the Man from George Washington to the Present* (New York: Appleton-Century, 1966), p. 36.

35. James David Barber, *The Pulse of Politics* (New York: Norton, 1980), especially pp. 3-4.

36. Erwin C. Hargrove and Michael Nelson, *Presidents, Politics, and Policy* (New York: Knopf, 1984), p. 68.

37. Ibid., p. 9.

38. Skowronek, "Notes on the Presidency," p. 294.

39. Ibid., pp. 296-97.

40. Stephen Skowronek, "Rethinking Presidential History," *Presidency Research* (Fall 1984): 23, emphasis added; Skowronek, "Notes on the Presidency," p. 300.

41. See, for instance, an attempt by David Resnick and Norman C. Thomas to apply Skowronek's framework on comparing Andrew Jackson and Ronald Reagan. "Reagan and Jackson: Parallels in Political Time" (Paper presented at the Annual Meeting of the Midwest Political Science Association, Chicago, April 9-11, 1987).

42. Fred I. Greenstein, "The Need for an Early Appraisal of the Reagan Presidency," in *The Reagan Presidency: An Early Assessment*, ed. Greenstein (Baltimore: Johns Hopkins University Press, 1983), p. 3. See also the preface to Fred I. Greenstein, Larry Berman, and Alvin Felzenberg, *Evolution of the Modern Presidency: A Bibliographical Survey* (Washington, D.C.: American Enterprise Institute, 1977), pp. i-xiv.

43. Skowronek, "Notes on the Presidency," p. 292.

44. But see Henry Jones Ford, *Rise and Growth of American Politics* (New York:

Macmillan, 1898). "The agency of the presidential office," wrote Ford, "has been such a master force in shaping public policy that to give a detailed account of it would be equivalent to writing the political history of the United States" (p. 278).

45. Louis Hartz, *The Liberal Tradition in America* (New York: Harcourt Brace Jovanovich, 1955). Like Hartz, Hofstadter stressed "the common climate of American opinion." "The range of vision embraced by the primary contestants in the major parties," argued Hofstadter, "has always been bounded by the horizons of property and enterprise. However much at odds on specific issues, the major political traditions have shared a belief in the rights of property, the philosophy of economic individualism, the value of competition; they have accepted the economic virtues of capitalist culture as necessary qualities of man" (*American Political Tradition*, pp. xxxvi-xxxvii).

46. Hartz, *Liberal Tradition*, pp. 4, 62.

47. J. David Greenstone, "Political Culture and American Political Development: Liberty, Union, and the Liberal Bipolarity," *Studies in American Political Development: An Annual*, 1:4.

48. Samuel P. Huntington, *American Politics: The Promise of Disharmony* (Cambridge: Harvard University Press, 1981).

49. See also J. David Greenstone, "The Transient and the Permanent in American Politics: Standards, Interests, and the Concept of 'Public,' " in *Public Values and Private Power in America*, ed. Greenstone (Chicago: University of Chicago Press, 1982), pp. 3-33.

50. Huntington, *Promise of Disharmony*, p. 12.

51. Ibid., pp. 4, 32, and passim.

52. This distinction is elaborated in Richard J. Ellis and Aaron Wildavsky, "A Cultural Analysis of the Role of Abolitionists in the Coming of the Civil War" (typescript, 83 pp.).

53. Huntington, *Promise of Disharmony*, pp. 96-97.

54. This distinction is made in Wilson Carey McWilliams, "On Equality as the Moral Foundation for Community," in *The Moral Foundations of the American Republic*, ed. Robert H. Horwitz (Charlottesville: University Press of Virginia, 1977), pp. 183-213, esp. 185-86.

55. Huntington, *Promise of Disharmony*, p. 41.

56. Ibid., p. 172.

57. "Unfurling the golden banner of Horatio Alger," writes Hartz, "American Whiggery marched into the Promised Land after the Civil War and did not really leave it until the crash of 1929" (*Liberal Tradition*, p. 203).

58. Huntington's category error is evident in the following passage: "The 1960s saw a recrudescence of individualism and moral passion in American politics, as intense as any in American history" (*Promise of Disharmony*, p. 23). Capitalists have been accused of many things, but subordinating profit to "moral passion" is not among them. The moral passion of the 1960s, we contend, stemmed from the upsurge of egalitarianism. See Mary Douglas and Aaron Wildavsky, *Risk and Culture* (Berkeley: University of California Press, 1982), esp. pp. 83-125.

59. Alternatively, advocates of hierarchy, concerned with support for authority, could go the social democratic route. Egalitarian support for authority could be won (radical egalitarians will say co-opted) in exchange for an extension of the welfare state. Given the weakness of hierarchy (and the strength of individualism) in the United States, however, it is uncertain whether this is a viable option for shoring

up authority. In European nations like Sweden and Germany, hierarchy was secure enough to make an alliance on its own terms, confident that co-optation of
egalitarians would not subvert authority.

60. Neustadt, *Presidential Power*, p. 6.
61. Arthur M. Schlesinger, Jr., "After the Imperial Presidency," in *The Cycles of American History* (Boston: Houghton Mifflin, 1986), p. 288.
62. See James MacGregor Burns, *Roosevelt: The Lion and the Fox* (New York: Harcourt, Brace & World, 1956), ch. 10.
63. See, for instance, Hugh Heclo, *Studying the Presidency* (New York: Report to the Ford Foundation, 1977); Norman C. Thomas, "Studying the Presidency: Where and How Do We Go From Here," *Presidential Studies Quarterly* (Fall 1977): 169-75; William C. Spracher, "Some Reflections on Improving the Study of the Presidency," *Presidential Studies Quarterly* (Winter 1979): 71-80; Joseph A. Pika, "Moving Beyond the Oval Office: Problems in Studying the Presidency," *Congress and the Presidency* (Winter 1981-82): 17-36; George C. Edwards III, "Quantitative Study of the Presidency," *Presidential Studies Quarterly* (Spring 1981): 146-50; Ryan J. Barrileaux, "Toward an Institutionalist Framework for Presidency Studies," *Presidential Studies Quarterly* (Spring 1982):154-58; David F. Prindle, "Toward a Comparative Science of the Presidency: A Pre-Theory", *Presidential Studies Quarterly* (Summer 1986): 467-80.
64. Pika, "Moving Beyond the Oval Office."
65. Edwards, *The Public Presidency*, p. 190.
66. Ibid.; Stephen Wayne, "Expectations of the President," in *The President and the Public*, ed. Doris A. Graber (Philadelphia: Institute for Study of Human Issues, 1982), pp. 17-38, at p. 19.
67. See Aaron Wildavsky, "The Three Cultures: Explaining Anomalies in the American Welfare State," *Public Interest* (Fall 1982): pp. 45-58.
68. Angus A. Campbell et al., *The American Voter* (New York: Wiley, 1960), esp. ch. 10; Philip E. Converse, "The Nature of Belief Systems in Mass Publics," in *Ideology and Discontent*, ed. David Apter (New York: Free Press, 1964), pp. 206-61. See also Richard A. Brody, "Public Evaluations and Expectations and the Future of the Presidency," in *Problems and Prospects of Presidential Leadership in the Nineteen-Eighties*, ed. James Sterling Young (Washington, D.C.: University Press of America, 1982), pp. 37-55.
69. By providing definitions of cultural propensities, the cultural approach should help lend precision to James MacGregor Burns's conception of transforming leadership. See Burns, *Leadership* (New York: Harper & Row, 1978).
70. See Aaron Wildavsky, "Frames of Reference Come from Cultures: A Predictive Theory," in *The Relevance of Culture*, ed. Morris Freilich (forthcoming).
71. Joseph White and Aaron Wildavsky, *The Deficit and the Public Interest: The Battles of the Budget From the Last Year of Carter Through the Reagan Administration* (Berkeley: University of California Press, 1989).
72. Aaron Wildavsky, "Ronald Reagan as a Political Strategist," in *Elections in America*, ed. Kay Schlozman (Boston: Allen & Unwin, 1987), pp. 221-38.
73. See Dean Keith Simonton, *Why Presidents Succeed: A Political Psychology of Leadership* (New Haven: Yale University Press, 1987).
74. James David Barber, "An Active-Positive Character," *Time*, January 3, 1977. On John Adams as an active-negative character, see Barber, *Presidential Character*, p. 14; and William D. Pederson, "Amnesty and Presidential Behavior: A 'Barberian' Test," *Presidential Studies Quarterly* (Fall 1977): 178.
75. Anthony King, "Executives," in *Handbook of Political Science*, ed. Fred I. Greenstein and Nelson Polsby (Reading, Mass.: Addison-Wesley, 1975), pp. 173-256; quotation on p. 174.

Index

Abolitionism, 187–97, 200. *See also* Egalitarianism
Adair, Douglass, 26
Adams, Abigail, 55
Adams, Henry, 82, 86, 158
Adams, John: appoints Vans Murray, 54–55; assumes authority inheres in position, 9, 12, 53, 55, 57, 216; cabinet of, 55; compared with Jimmy Carter, 57, 231; fails to understand cultural context, 9, 12, 53, 57–58, 211, 226; Federalist party split by, 54–57; greatness of, 54; as hierarch without a hierarchy, 9, 53–58; individualistic bias of Constitution underestimated by, 53–54; and pomp and ceremony, 44–45, 211; and XYZ affair, 55–56
Adams, John Quincy: compared to his father, 101, 109; "countercultural" behavior of, 212; cultural conflict denied by, 101–2; explanations for failure of, 102–3, 209–10, 211–12, 219; as hierarch without a hierarchy, 9, 101–4, 216; hierarchical propensities of, 100–1, 109, 110–11; insensitivity to cultural context, 99, 101, 103, 211; and patronage, 101–2, 211; successes of, prior to being president, 209–10
Alien and Sedition Laws, 45–46, 67
American Revolution, 11–12, 19–25, 29–31, 37–38, 43, 67, 222, 229
Ames, Fisher, 26, 48
Amlund, Curtis Arthur, 17
Ammon, Harry, 91, 95–96
Anti-authority coalition: defined, 5; American exceptionalism due to, 5, 72; American Revolution as product of, 19–20; and belief that equality of opportunity produces equality of condition, 20, 111; conflicts between egalitarianism and individualism within, 11, 94, 127–32, 160, 223; dependence

of, on common hierarchical enemy, 67, 93–94, 129, 223; difficulty of leading in, 10–11, 12, 67–68, 112; Old Republicans as extreme instance of, 76–78; War of 1812 undermines faith in, 80–82, 229. *See also* Cultural dilemmas, Jeffersonian Republican party, and Jacksonian Democratic party
Appleby, Joyce, 83–84
Arieli, Yehoshua, 198
Articles of Confederation, 9, 23–24, 31, 39, 42, 50, 221–22, 229
Ashworth, John, 82, 112, 116, 146, 160, 171–72, 232
Ashworth, M.W., 62

Bache, Benjamin, 49
Bailey, Thomas, 14, 54, 88, 151, 170, 174, 217
Bailyn, Bernard, 19–20
Baldwin, Abraham, 24
Baldwin, Luther, 45–46
Bancroft, George, 141, 145
Banks, Nathaniel, 198
Banner, James M., Jr., 58, 60, 206
Banning, Lance, 64, 67, 83, 84
Barber, James David, 40, 60, 212, 218, 233
Barbour, James, 97
Barnard, Daniel, 117
Barrileaux, Ryan J., 236
Bartlett, Irving, 192, 201, 202, 203
Bates, Edward, 184, 196, 203
Bauer, K. Jack, 170
Beard, Charles, 12, 29, 35
Beecher, Henry Ward, 194
Belohlavek, John M., 122
Bemis, Samuel Flagg, 121
Benson, Lee, 16
Benton, Thomas Hart, 128, 132, 139, 142, 144
Biddle, Nicholas, 127

237